Jocelyn Sharlet is Associate Professor of Comparative Literature at the University of California, Davis. She holds a PhD in Near Eastern Studies from Princeton University, and has published articles in journals such as the *Journal of Arabic Literature*, the *Journal of Persianate Studies*, the *Journal of Arabic and Islamic Studies* and *Middle Eastern Literatures*.

PATRONAGE AND POETRY IN THE ISLAMIC WORLD

Social Mobility and Status in the Medieval Middle East and Central Asia

JOCELYN SHARLET

I.B. TAURIS
LONDON · NEW YORK

Published in 2011 by I.B.Tauris & Co Ltd
6 Salem Road, London W2 4BU
175 Fifth Avenue, New York NY 10010
www.ibtauris.com

Distributed in the United States and Canada
Exclusively by Palgrave Macmillan
175 Fifth Avenue, New York NY 10010

Library of Middle East History 24

ISBN 978 1 84885 369 0

A full CIP record for this book is available from the British Library
A full CIP record for this book is available from the Library of Congress

Library of Congress catalog card: available

Printed and bound in the UK by CPI Antony Rowe, Chippenham and Eastbourne

Camera-ready copy edited and supplied by the author

To Ruth and Irving

CONTENTS

Acknowledgments ix

INTRODUCTION 1

1 THE PROBLEM WITH POETRY 7

2 POETS TAKING RISKS TO GET AHEAD 22
Intimacy and distance in unequal relationships 22
Coercive patrons and resistant poets 28
Breaking up 35

3 INTRODUCTION TO ABŪ TAMMĀM, AL-BUḤTURĪ, ᶜUNṢURĪ, FARRUKHĪ AND THEIR PATRONS 45
Abū Tammām and his patrons 46
Al-Buḥturī and his patrons 49
ᶜUnṣurī and his patrons 52
Farrukhī and his patrons 54

4 TOOLS FOR THINKING: MOTIFS AND SYNTAX 57
Speaking of power: motifs 58
Configurations of intimacy and distance: syntax 71

5 PRE-INDUSTRIAL LIGHT AND MAGIC: RHETORICAL DEVICES AND FIGURATIVE LANGUAGE 94
Constructing relationships: rhetorical devices 95
Imagining relationships: figurative language 109

6 GETTING TO KNOW YOU: CLOSE OBSERVATION AND EVALUATION 125
Seeing and being seen: close observation in praise 125
Thinking it over: evaluation in praise 139

7 DOING BUSINESS: COMMUNICATION AND INTERACTION 150
Talking it over: communication in patronage 150
Give and take: interaction in praise 169

8 THE COSMOPOLITAN PROFESSIONAL POET 187

9 THE SOCIALLY MOBILE PROFESSIONAL POET 204
Socio-economic identity 205
Religious identity 216
Ethnic identity 224

CONCLUSION 236

Notes 239
Bibliography 305
Index 319

ACKNOWLEDGMENTS

I am deeply indebted to my teachers at Princeton, especially Jerome Clinton, Andras Hamori, and Margaret Larkin, who enabled me to develop the research skills for this project. A number of colleagues in comparative literature and area studies, especially Margaret Larkin and Seth Schein, have provided invaluable moral support while I completed the second stage of this project. Elliott Colla offered collegial support and advice during my year in Providence, and Shawkat Toorawa did so during my year in Ithaca. My own patronage has come from a variety of sources, including Princeton University, a Foreign Languages and Area Studies scholarship, the Center for Arabic Study Abroad, the University of Michigan and the Eastern Consortium in Persian and Turkish, the Mellon Foundation, Fulbright, the American Research Center in Egypt, course release time arranged by colleagues in the Department of Comparative Literature at the University of California, Davis, research grants from UC Davis, and the Title VIA grant to the Middle East/South Asia Studies Program at UC Davis. My family Baki, Teo, Kayhan, Bob, Nancy, Irving, Evelyn, Ruth, Charles, Fiona, Jeff, Julia, Roxana, Emine, Ayhan, Gülgünler, and Gökhanlar helped me in different ways to complete my studies and finish this project. This book is dedicated to my mother's mother Ruth, because her interest in books was important for my family, and to my father's father Irving, because his hard work and careful planning to pay for education was important for us too. Friends and their families in Davis and Sacramento, especially Beth, Deatra, Elisabeth, Janice, Julie, Martina, Nina, Teena, and Victoria, have made this area a place to live, not just a place to work. I have also enjoyed the support of friends who live in other places at different stages of the work on this project, especially Asma, Elyse, Hanaa, Janet, Kamran, Kristin, Miriam, and Orit. Muhammad Ali, who worked with me in the

Cairo book market, and Jahangir Assarepour, who worked with me in the Tehran book market, helped me to build a library of my own, and the librarians at UC Davis, Cornell, Brown, and Princeton enabled me to secure the rest of the research materials for this book. All of this moral, collegial, and financial support allowed me to complete this project, while of course the shortcomings of the book are all mine.

Jocelyn Sharlet

INTRODUCTION

In the medieval Middle East and Central Asia individual loyalties, rather than more formal institutional ties, were the building blocks of social life. This social order of individual relationships was in many ways more resilient than that based on institutions in other regions, such as the Church, guilds, and aristocracy in Europe, caste in India, and the civil service in China.[1] The flexibility of this kind of social order helps to explain the cosmopolitan quality of the medieval Middle East and Central Asia. Medieval Arabic and Persian poetry and narratives about literary patronage offer insights into the flexibility of individual patronage relationships, and medieval criticism provides approaches to the use of elaborate rhetoric in poetry to explore these.[2] Such relationships involved working together across the distance in status between the patron and the poet. In poetry and narratives about patronage these relationships were put on display for an audience of participants in the patronage network so that they could compare and contrast their own experiences and aspirations with those of the poet and the patron.

The flexibility of patronage relationships goes hand-in-hand with uncertainty. Modern research on medieval Arabic and Persian literary patronage has often focused on poems that were unusually well known, well documented in narrative sources, for major patrons or related to particularly serious situations. This book takes a more general look at the genre of panegyric poetry and the stories, criticism and ethical writings that relate to it. The analysis deals with poetry by the Arabic poets al-Buḥturī and Abū Tammām of the third century Islamic Era/ninth century CE and the Persian poets ᶜUnṣurī and Farrukhī of the fifth/eleventh century, as well as a wide range of medieval Arabic and Persian stories about patronage. In narratives and poetry, uncertainty about patronage is particularly salient during crises in individual relationships.[3]

However, it is not restricted to such crises.[4] Instead, uncertainty is a widespread feature of poetry and narratives about patronage.[5] Participants in patronage may have enjoyed more flexibility than participants in more formal institutions in other times and places, but they often paid a price in the instability of individual relationships. Uncertainty about patronage relationships in medieval Arabic and Persian poetry and narrative literature is less a social problem or a demand for reform than an awareness of the integral role that uncertainty played in the flexible social order based on the contingency of individual relationships. The insecurity of protégés also related to the insecurity of their patrons.[6] Uncertainty is part of the normal functioning of this form of social order, not a dysfunction of it.

Poetry about patronage articulates its uncertainty and flexibility through the use of elaborate rhetoric. Such rhetoric could express complex and multifaceted perspectives, enabling poets to explore the possibilities of patronage. Poets combined motifs and configured them in syntax, constructed them using rhetorical devices, and imagined them in figurative language. This is not the complexity of language for its own sake, but a way to cope with the complexity of the social order of patronage.

Stories about literary patronage, like the poems that were exchanged, demonstrate the importance of flexibility and uncertainty. Writers presented, rewrote and organized stories to analyze past experiences and explore future possibilities. In addition to stories about literary patronage, medieval literary criticism and prose writing on ethics offer more general perspectives on its uncertainty and flexibility.

Poetry about literary patronage, exchanged for pay, was dedicated to a specific person on a specific occasion, and was comprised of conventional motifs.[7] While panegyric poetry included references to historical characters and events, these were in effect absorbed into the flow of discourse on patronage. The exemplary quality of panegyric poetry did not represent a failure to make a social connection with historical characters and events: rather, it allowed poets to integrate themselves, their own experiences, and the characters and events in their poetry, into a community of literary patronage. Although characters and events were absorbed into this discourse, they did not necessarily fit easily or comfortably; the tension between the poem and its referent was a crucial feature.[8] In the exemplary portrayal of patronage, the possibilities of success and failure are woven together in elaborate rhetoric, expressing the contingency of individual, unequal relationships characterized by intimacy as well as distance.[9]

In using elaborate rhetoric to explore the possibilities of patronage relationships, panegyric poets asserted an emerging professional identity which put them in an advantageous position. As with major world languages and crucial technologies today, skills in refined rhetoric could be acquired in the medieval Middle East and Central Asia.

Arabic and Persian poets who offered elaborate rhetoric in exchange for pay helped to shape for themselves a cosmopolitan, professional identity that was distinct from that with more limited and established dimensions, including socio-economic background, religious affiliation and ethnicity. Elaborate rhetoric was professional insofar as it involved conventions, training and evaluation – not only because money changed hands. Professional skills in refined rhetoric allowed panegyric poets to cope with, and take advantage of, the shifting quality of individual patronage relationships. This professional identity also enabled many poets to cross socio-economic, religious and ethnic boundaries. However, the cosmopolitan cultures that took shape – in Arabic in the Middle East, and in Persian in Central Asia – true to their imperial contexts, were hegemonic as well as diverse. Poets often paid a price in the obligation to assimilate or make accommodations to imperial culture.

Panegyric poetry combined an ideology of stable prosperity with the changing conditions of patronage relationships. Louis Althusser proposes that individuals are constituted through ideologies, and ideologies are contested sites of non-violent social control.[10] Participants in patronage experienced their individual and communal identity through this social order. Medieval Arabic and Persian poetry and narratives concerning patronage did not simply reflect or reproduce social order, they produced and transformed it. Terry Eagleton suggests that historical context appears within a text in the form of ideology, so that the text's referent is not the real, but rather 'the significations by which the real lives itself, which are a product of the partial abolition of the real' that takes place in ideology.[11] The discourse on patronage promotes an ideology of stability and prosperity while exploring the uncertainty and flexiblity of this kind of social order. Judith Butler views the constituting effect of regulatory power as 'reiterated and reiterable,' suggesting that the expression of a particular social order in a literary text occurs in conjunction with the changing quality of that order.[12] This narrative literature and poetry emphasize the reiterated and reiterable dimensions of a social order that is rooted in individual, unequal relationships.

The combination of the ideology of stable prosperity and changing conditions of patronage relationships demonstrated the contradiction at the heart of panegyric. Ernesto Laclau and Chantal Mouffe explain that a hegemonic relation, where particularity assumes the representation of universality that is incommensurable with it, leads to an unresolved tension between universality and particularity. In addition, the incommensurability between the universal and the particular in such a hegemonic relation means that the hegemonic universality is acquired in a temporary way and is reversible.[13] The ideology of stable prosperity was a crucial feature of the social order of patronage, and was presented in poetry as a hegemonic universality. However, this ideology is connected to uncertainty about the possibilities of success and failure in the practice of patronage. Elaborate rhetoric enabled poets to articulate the contradiction between the hegemonic universality of patronage and the changing conditions that included the possibilities of success and failure. Uncertainty was a feature of the flexibility of patronage, and this flexibility facilitated social mobility. As a result, the contingency of individual relationships is not only a risk that can be handled, but also a benefit that can be enjoyed.

Close reading of texts has sometimes been viewed as a way to avoid their social and political implications. However, Gayatri Chakravorty-Spivak has pointed out that close reading can also be a way into politics.[14] This need not mean linking writers or texts to a particular ideology. Literary culture that is closely and explicitly connected to political life can be understood as a celebration of political power or a mediation strategy that makes power acceptable, by portraying it as anguished and aware of its own limitations. The insights of close reading can help us to move beyond black-and-white alternatives, such as the celebration of power and resistance to it.[15]

Close reading is not only a way into politics: it is a way into social life. Teresa de Lauretis identified the gaze as a technology of gender.[16] Elaborate rhetoric in panegyric, with its complex approach to the themes of observation, evaluation, communication and interaction in relationships, is a technology of social position – of the relational subjectivity and identity of the poet, the patron, and audience.[17] Close reading offers insights into elaborate rhetoric as a technology of identity. This identity is both relational and subject to change.[18]

Panegyric poets, with their emerging professional identity, display social mobility based on refined rhetoric rather than political, military or religious authority. They work in a cultural sphere that takes shape in the valorization of refined rhetoric, and which continues to expand in the development – during the late third/ninth and fourth/tenth centuries – of short descriptive poetry in Arabic, which was often circulated in informal gatherings without the need for patrons.[19] Likewise, the mystical turn in different genres of Persian poetry entailed an expansion of this cultural sphere beyond formal literary patronage, beginning in the late fifth/eleventh century.[20] In both cases, poets who turned away from this formal patronage often continued to compose panegyric. Interestingly, it was the establishment of panegyric in Arabic and Persian which turned refined rhetoric into a way for poets to transform their experience of social life in these other genres. The professional skills and identity of panegyric poets paved the way for new methods of using refined rhetoric, among seekers of pleasure in short descriptive poetry and seekers of God in mystical poetry, in an expanding cultural sphere.

Through a close reading of poetry in conjunction with stories, criticism and ethical writing about literary patronage, this book explores refined rhetoric as an approach to the possibilities that patronage offered. Elaborate rhetoric in this poetry, and attitudes toward it in narratives and criticism, are neither conformist nor subversive. Instead, they convey the complications of using refined rhetoric as the basis for a professional, cosmopolitan identity and social mobility in the medieval Middle East and Central Asia.

Chapters 1 and 2 focus on the integral role of uncertainty in narratives and notices about patronage. Chapters 3 to 7 demonstrate the way elaborate rhetoric articulates the possibilities of success and failure. Finally, Chapters 8 and 9 examine the problems of cosmopolitan, professional identity based on refined rhetoric, and its importance as an alternative to more established categories of identity: socio-economic background, religious affiliation and ethnicity. The first chapter investigates the problem of exchanging poetry for pay.

1

THE PROBLEM WITH POETRY

The exchange of poetry for pay remained a significant feature of medieval Arabic and Persian literary culture for many centuries, but panegyric was a contested site of cultural production and social interaction. The use of elaborate rhetoric in panegyric poetry was met with both praise and blame.[1] The gift exchange of poetry for pay in the medieval Middle East and Central Asia was viewed as an embedded exchange. An *embedded* economy is an economy in which exchange generates and maintains relationships. A *disembedded* economy is one in which the monetary value of an object allows the relationship of exchange to end as soon as the exchange is completed.[2] Marcel Mauss points out that participating in embedded gift exchange is a way to express relationships, while declining to participate in gift exchange may be considered antagonistic.[3] Scott Cutler Shershow observes that Marcel Mauss sometimes emphasizes the distinction between pre-modern, embedded exchange and modern, disembedded exchange, while at other times he implies the difficulty of distinguishing between the two.[4] In medieval Arabic and Persian discourse on patronage there is a widespread concern that the exchange of poetry for pay may have more to do with material wealth and individual ambition than ethical evaluation and communal relationships. This discussion of attitudes toward panegyric investigates positive and negative attitudes toward the validity of poetry for pay.

Most medieval Arabic and Persian definitions of rhetoric stress its aesthetic more than its social impact, though some imply the use of rhetoric for a goal, including the Persian innovation of the figure of the apposite request. In addition, many encyclopedic compilations demonstrate the practice of using language to get what you want.[5] The reason that poetry for pay caused problems for many writers may be the contradiction between the aesthetic values and social uses of refined rhetoric. Elaborate rhetoric allowed poets to say two or more things at the same time: an interesting intellectual experience from an aesthetic point of view, but one that could lead to complications in the social use of rhetoric. In the praise poetry that circulated in the medieval Middle East and Central Asia poets used elaborate rhetoric to assert the success of their individual patronage relationships and the stability of the social order of patronage in general. At the same time they explored the intersection of intimacy and distance in the unequal relationships of patronage. Poets needed the complexity of elaborate rhetoric to capture the uncertainty and flexibility of patronage and give it a little suspense, but this rhetoric also made it more difficult to pin down the terms of a relationship. Elaborate rhetoric enabled poets to articulate the dynamic quality of patronage and the potential for their social mobility within it.

The diversity of attitudes toward poetry in general, and especially praise for pay, shows that the validity of panegyric was open to debate. The panegyric poet Abū Tammām describes poetry as the basis for making sense of ethical and social status – 'If not for poetry, seekers of greatness would not know where noble qualities come from.'[6] Similarly, the writer al-Rāghib al-Iṣbahānī cites a proverb that portrays the shared ethical evaluation of poetry as the meaning of life itself – 'Let one who is not moved to pleasure by praise or who does not react to blame with repulsion be reckoned dead.'[7] One who is not moved by praise and blame would be alienated from the social order that is shaped by the discourse on patronage in poetry.

Religious themes and poetry competed as forms of ethical discourse. In some cases writers emphasize cooperation and coexistence between religion and poetry. Ibn Abī al-Dunyā cites a saying of the Prophet Muḥammad in which the Prophet is asked if a man lowers the value of his good deed by taking pleasure in mention of it (in praise). The Prophet says 'Certainly not', and refers to Abraham in the Qur'an and the motif of a voice of truth (The Poets 26:84).[8] Al-Tawḥīdī cites a lengthy critique of poetry for pay by an opponent, and responds with a saying of the Prophet about how there is wisdom in poetry and magic in rhetoric.[9] The validity of praise derives from the risks that praise can dispel. Al-Rāghib al-Iṣbahānī's chapter on poetry opens with a combination of the Prophet's demand for invective to repel his adversaries, and his acceptance of praise. The famous transmitter of the Prophet's sayings, Zuhrī, is questioned after he gives money to a poet. He responds by saying that seeking good includes protection from evil. The Prophet's companion and early caliph Abū Bakr questions the Prophet about his use of both poetry and the Qur'an. The Prophet responds, 'sometimes this and sometimes that.'[10] In his biography of poets, al-Jumaḥī relates a narrative in which a man asks Ibn Sīrīn – an authority on religious matters – as he is about to pray, if he must take ablutions after reciting poetry. 'What are you worried about?', he seems to say: he turns to the side, recites a vile line of invective, and turns back to begin his prayer.[11]

In other cases writers situate negative portrayals of poetry in the ethical discourse of religion. The Arabic writer al-Ghuzūlī cites the well-known saying of the Prophet about throwing dirt in the faces of the praise poets, explaining that the sentiment applies to all exaggeration in poetry or in prose because of the confusion that it causes in the audience.[12] In his chapter on poetry, al-Rāghib cites the Prophet, who first says that giving to poets is a kind of filial piety, and then says of a poet who had praised him and then censured him, 'Cut off his tongue!'[13] In a chapter that deals with praise, he cites opposition to praise for pay, including the views of the Prophet, the early caliph ᶜUmar, and the Umayyad caliph Hishām b. ᶜAbd al-Malik, as well as the initial opposition to praise for pay by the governor al-Ḥajjāj until the Umayyad caliph ᶜAbd al-Malik ordered him to allow it.[14] In one brief narrative, a man praises God and the Prophet, and the Prophet pays him for the praise of God but not for praise of himself.[15]

Negative portrayals of poetry need not be religious. ᶜAbd al-Malik excludes poets of a tribal confederation that is affiliated with his political opponent, and al-Mahdī forbids the introductory description of love due to his severe jealousy.[16] The Persian writer Naṣīr al-Dīn Ṭūsī folds poetry into his ethical social order, but not all poetry fits in there: your children are what they read, so they should be introducted to poetry in the short meter of *rajaz* and then to the *qaṣida*, but avoid silly poetry about the themes of love and wine drinking, such as the poetry of Imrūᵓ al-Qays and Abū Nuwās.[17] One might conclude that if problematic poetry comes from five hundred years earlier and a different language, it is not that big a problem.

The combination of positive and negative portrayals of the same topic is an important technique of analysis in medieval Arabic and Persian literary culture. In many cases, the writer juxtaposes points of view and implicitly urges the audience to become engaged in the analysis and comparison of them. The importance of both positive and negative portrayals of poetry in literary culture demonstrates ambivalence about the status of poetry as a form of ethical discourse.

Professional identity based on the use of refined rhetoric and the social mobility that it facilitated for poets, and implied for patrons, was viewed with suspicion. One form that this suspicion took was the debate over praise as lies. In support of the view that lies are a crucial feature of the professional use of refined rhetoric, the Arabic writer al-Bayhaqī cites the grammarian and literary critic Khalīl b. Aḥmad, who says, 'Poets are princes of speech for whom it is permissible to break with logic and free meaning, and extend what is short and shorten what is extended.'[18] According to this perspective, the freedom to transform the world in language is a crucial feature of refined rhetoric. Other perspectives define the transformation of the world in refined rhetoric as a threat to the validity of poetry as a form of ethical discourse. Al-Tawḥīdī combines citations of Socrates about speechmaking and the Arabic writer Ibn al-Mudabbir about poetry. Both describe elaborate rhetoric as a way to lower great matters or men, and raise lowly matters or men.[19] Al-Tawḥīdī also cites the governor Ziyād b. Abīhi, who says that poetry is the lowest virtue of the good man and the best quality of the lowly man.[20] Similarly, al-Rāghib al-Iṣbahānī cites a source who says that poetry raises the moral virtue (*muruwwa*) of the lowly man and lowers the moral virtue of the virtuous man, and al-Bayhaqī cites a man who says that poetry makes the vice of the lowly man virtuous and lowers the virtue of the virtuous man.[21] Although al-Tawḥīdī defends poetry to an opponent who views it as inferior to prose because it is lies, and cites the saying of the Prophet about the wisdom to be had from poetry, he also says, 'As for the lords of praise and invective, those who make things vile or good, they have no other way to earn a living.'[22]

Some writers do not attack the validity of poetry in general, but do criticize the misuse of poetry as a form of ethical discourse. Al-Māwardī cites Persian, Greek, and Arab sources to argue that publicity of good deeds in praise is not appropriate unless the publicity is performed by people whose speech is transmitted and truthful.[23] He warns against praise that exceeds benefit and leads to incredulity.[24] Al-Rāghib al-Iṣbahānī cites the Prophet's statement to a praise poet, 'I am below what you say and above what is in your heart,' meaning that excessive praise not only fails to publicize virtue, but also displays the disloyalty of the one who offers it.[25] Al-Rāghib warns that inaccurate praise is actually invective.[26] Several writers cite the Umayyad caliph Muᶜāwiya's advice to ᶜAbd al-Raḥmān b. al-Ḥakam, 'You have dedicated yourself to poetry, so beware of love introductions lest you insult an honorable woman, beware of invective lest you compose it about a noble man or incite a vile man with it, and beware of praise for it wins disgrace, but rather take pride in the deeds of your tribe, and use proverbs with which you can embellish yourself and the refined manners of others, and if you must do praise, do it like al-Mālik al-Murādī when he offered praise in which he joined himself and his patron, "I undid my bundles in Banī Thuʾl, for the noble man is the noble man's place to undo his bundles."'[27] These views emphasize that poets need to focus on representing things as they are, not define the way they are viewed. However, since the way things are is in part a function of the way people encounter them in language, the advice is problematic.

One solution to the problem of the relationship between experience and language is to deny poetry the authority of ethical evaluation in community life. Isḥāq b. Sulaymān went in to see the caliph al-Manṣūr, whose gathering was full of members of the royal family. The caliph said, 'I heard you are a poet.' Isḥāq said 'Yes', and al-Manṣūr asked him to recite. Isḥāq recited a long poem including praise of al-Manṣūr. Al-Manṣūr responded, 'What are you doing with panegyric, my son, beware of praise and invective. You should just compose two or three verses out of pleasure, mentioning in it virtue and affection.'[28]

The criticism of poetry, and praise poetry in particular, can be quite explicit and even aggressive. According to these views, poetry doesn't just do a bad job of representing experience, it impacts experience by corrupting it. Al-Māwardī warns his reader to beware of accepting panegyric from flatterers, for hypocrisy is ingrained in their character.[29] He also describes flattery as a problem for refined manners in general, and a form of deceit that leads to impetuous ignorance (*jahl*) – a crucial dimension of vice in medieval Arabic culture.[30] Al-Bayhaqī asserts that there is no one worse than the poets and goes on to cite poetry on this topic, as if to say 'Look, even the poets think that poetry is vile!'[31] For Al-Jāḥiẓ, the Bedouin figure, who is cited widely as an authority in praise and in poetry in general, is the worst – a tyrannical beggar who flatters, and when he praises or composes invective, he lies.[32] Opponents of poetry for pay, such as those cited by ᶜAwfī , emphasize that it all misses the mark. It is all about praise or love and both are based on blatant lies. Most of the poets have disgraced their eloquence with acquisitiveness and bewildered virtue with vileness.[33] Similarly, Saᶜdī advises, 'Do not believe the tricks of enemies and do not be deceived by panegyrists ... the stupid man likes praise, since it makes the skinny one whose bones show seem fat.'[34] Though his narrative poetry includes praise of patrons, the mystical poet Sanāʾī depicts poetry as the music of the devil and cites the saying of the Prophet, 'Better your belly should fill with pus than with poetry, throw dirt in the faces of praise poets.'[35] Poetry not only fails to contribute to the community, it actually harms it.

Stories may depict poets as con artists rather than professionals. Ibn Abī Ṭāhir says of the successful panegyric poet al-Buḥturī, 'I've never seen anyone less loyal than al-Buḥturī: first he stands there reciting praise to Aḥmad b. al-Khaṣīb, then he uses him to intercede with al-Muntaṣir when al-Muntaṣir is angry at al-Buḥturī … then al-Mustaᶜīn fires Aḥmad b. al-Khaṣīb soon afterward, and al-Buḥturī writes poetry expressing approval of the firing and killing of Aḥmad.'[36] The caliph al-Hishām says to one poet, 'You praised that man in spite of your low opinion of him.' The poet answers, 'Yes, because in what the commander of the faithful asks of me, I am like the one who said: The price is enough that I told you the truth in friendship and enmity/ When you charge me with a task, your love is greater than mine.' Al-Hishām responds, 'That's what people think of you.'[37] The patron of the poet Ibn Mayyāda complains about the low quality of his praise in comparison with his praise of the corrupt caliph al-Walīd, and Ibn Mayyāda explains that a poet's praise is based on the amount of the gift, so how could he ever say that al-Walīd is corrupt after receiving 400 camels with equipment and servants to keep them? The patron is pleased with his loyalty, orders the same gift, and demands the same quality of praise.[38] One poet describes Khālid b. ᶜAbd Allāh al-Qaṣrī as courageous, and one of the people in the gathering pulls him aside and says, 'Khālid has never been to a single battle.' The poet says, 'Be quiet, endurance in generosity is greater than endurance in war.'[39] These views undermine the professional identity of poets.

The disagreement about the validity of poetry for pay is also a disagreement about the validity of refined rhetoric as a basis for professional identity and social mobility. In other words, criticism of poetry for pay is also criticism of the social mobility that it makes possible for poets. The anxiety about social mobility through poetry for pay is bound up with the separate, but related, issue of social mobility for patrons. Al-Jāḥiẓ criticizes the role of common people as patrons of poetry. In his work on rhetoric, he begins with a description of ancient poetry bound up with military deeds rather than material rewards, when the poet was superior to the speechmaker. Al-Jāḥiẓ writes, 'And when poetry and poets became abundant, and they took poetry as a source of income and went over to the common people, and hastened to the masses, the speechmaker came to be above the poet, and because of that was the first to say, "Poetry is the lowest nobility of the virtuous and the most virtuous nobility of the lowly."'[40] The Arabic writer al-Marzūqī links the shift toward poetry for pay, especially poetry for common people, with the decreasing status of poetry relative to prose.[41] Al-Tawḥīdī criticizes the role of ordinary people in composing praise and blame, since they presume to take on the elite status associated with voluntary, independent ethical evaluation, although their poetry is neither voluntary nor independent. He also criticizes ordinary people for attempting to perform the deeds that attract praise. He asserts that one must be rich to have friends, which means participating in the cultural elite about which the term 'friend' is used in al-Tawḥīdī's work, including his work on the topic of friendship.[42] As for the poor man, 'if he praises he wastes it, and if he blames he falls short, and if he does a good deed he messes it up, and if he endeavors in something it gets screwed up.'[43] The poet Dhū Rumma expresses contempt for Marwān b. Abī Ḥafṣa for taking money from patrons other than rulers.[44] Ambivalence about praise for pay may be expressed indirectly, by poets who simply avoid rulers. Sām Mīrzā mentions a poet who, though a poor oculist, never did praise for pay.[45] In a more common theme, ᶜAlīshīr mentions a poet who was a mystic and avoided rulers.[46] The trend toward incorporating people of lower status into literary patronage exacerbates the tension between material interests and the appearance of the professional, independent, and voluntary depiction of patrons in panegyric as a form of ethical discourse.

Ambivalence about praise for pay also appears in attitudes toward begging, which can be degrading for the beggar, while it maintains and increases the status of the person who gives to him. People can only display the virtue of being other-centered if they have the opportunity to meet the needs of others and choose to do so. Al-Jāḥiẓ observes that poets are the most avaricious of all, since it is their job to seek benefit.[47] Al-Tawḥīdī cites a proverb saying that when honor is better than benefit, poverty is better than begging: in other words, the only honorable way for outsiders to be honorable is to remain outside the loop, denying themselves the benefits of material gain.[48] A minister from the Barmakid family responds to a member of his gathering who calls his attention to some beggars who have arrived. He disapproves of calling the people beggars, and instead assigns them the considerably more honorable epithet of 'visitors'.[49] It is not surprising that this anecdote is attributed to a member of this family, which enjoyed a great deal of inward and upward mobility, until they became one of the most powerful political families in Islamic history, before they were perceived as a threat by the caliph al-Rashīd and imprisoned, killed, or cast out. The stigma that links poetry and begging appears later in Sām Mīrzā's reference to an administrator's son who is a poet with the pen name *sāyilī* or beggar, in a section on people who are identified primarily as poets. The poet's genres are not specified. The writer comments, 'I am just bewildered by his combination of his good name with this inappropriate pen name. Why must he compose poetry with such a pen name?'[50]

The problem of poetry for pay was also linked to the social, ethical, and literary issue of recycling or plagiarizing poetry. Recycling praise means that other poems, in addition to the patron himself, serve as models. As a result, recycling poetry for pay has an impact on the appearance of poetry as a voluntary, independent, and professional evaluation of the patron, and the role of poetry as a form of ethical discourse. Stories show that this phenomenon complicated the exchange of poetry for pay but did not undermine it. The caliph al-Hādī's favorite poem about another patron serves as the model for praise of al-Hādī himself.[51] One protégé presents a poem to Muᶜāwiya, who asks him, 'Whose poem?' The protégé says that it is his own, but the actual composer of the poem then enters and recites the same poem. The patron confronts the first protégé, who pardons himself by saying that he used the other protégé's poem because it expressed what he himself felt.[52] Another poet asks for a refund of his praise when he fails to secure a reward, as if to imply that the poem could be reused in a different patronage relationship.[53] One patron compares Abū Tammām's praise for him with his elegy for another patron, and says that he wishes that his praise resembled the other patron's elegy.[54] The poet Marwān b. Abī Ḥafṣa recited a praise poem for a group of people before delivering it to the patron, but the patron was killed before he could make contact with him. A member of the rehearsal audience approves of the poem and suggests that he buy it for reuse, and Marwān agrees, swearing that he will not attribute it to himself again or recite it. However, he then takes it home, changes a few verses, and uses it to start his career with an important patron.[55] In a well-known story, al-Buḥturī recites a poem and a man in the gathering claims the verses for himself. The man turns out to be none other than Abū Tammām, and after some tension the two men embrace each other.[56] The recycling of poetry in panegyric both contributes to and complicates the use of poetry in literary patronage. Stories about recycling poetry emphasize the function of poetry as a commodity. There is a contradiction between poetry as an ethical discourse and poetry as a commodity, but this contradiction was not a big problem.

Patronage relationships based on poetry require secure and open lines of communication. Praise that misses the mark, and other distortions, compromise the use of poetry in patronage. The most basic way for a poet to miss the mark is to fail to take his patron's likes and needs into consideration. The minister al-Fatḥ advises the poet al-Buḥturī, 'You don't need all that [elaborate style] in praise of the caliph: take it easy, he likes what he understands.'[57] When the poet Bashshār praises the caliph al-Mahdī with a poem that includes a well-wrought love introduction, it turns out that the caliph has forbidden such introductions because of his severe jealousy.[58] One prospective patron says to a poet, 'Haven't I told you not to use meanings like that?' The patron then proceeds to offer an example to follow.[59]

Praise that misses the mark can be comic. The poet al-Akhtal tells the caliph ᶜAbd al-Malik that he has praised him, and ᶜAbd al-Malik says, 'If you are comparing me to a snake or a lion, I have no need for your poetry.' He continues, 'If you said something like the sister of the Banū al-Shurayd, meaning the ancient poet al-Khansāᵓ, let's have it.'[60] The Khālidī brothers, who were poets, writers, and court librarians, praise the ruler Sayf al-Dawla, saying that he has a face that is a moon and a body that is a lion, and Sayf al-Dawla likes that and repeats it. When the poet al-Shayzamī enters and Sayf al-Dawla makes him listen to the verse, al-Shayzamī says 'Praise God, for they have made you one of the wonders of the sea'.[61] In a book of slips of the tongue, one poet recites verses on the occasion of an oath, but the verses imply that the oath is invalid.[62]Another who is drunk sees a patron of his fleeing from the army and utters a verse about fleeing, offending the patron.[63] The poet al-Farazdaq praises al-Ḥajjāj with a verse that implies that the latter has no strength, and then apologizes.[64] The fact that al-Farazdaq, one of the major poets of the Umayyad period, could make a mistake like this suggests that missing the mark in praise is not necessarily a shortcoming of the uninitiated. However, some slips clearly are. In a book on foolish people, a man praises the general Maᶜn b. Zāᵓida, saying, 'I came to you when no one else was left.' The patron says, 'That's not praise', and offers an example for the poet to follow.[65] Missing the mark in praise is a risk of using poetry in patronage.

Praise is governed by conventions that clarify the safe and effective range of topics in panegyric. Praise based on ancestors is inappropriate, since many people do not resemble their ancestors.[66] There is no virtue in opening a giving hand when the misers' hands are closed, but rather when the noble men's hands are closed.[67] One must also avoid the negative in a final line.[68] To avoid offending the patron, one should not mention his mother, and the name of a male slave or a woman can only be used in love poetry and the love introduction to panegyric if the poet knows that the patron has no relationship to someone of that name.[69]

In spite of these conventions a patron may be uncomfortable with an expression that falls within them, and this discomfort can complicate the use of poetry in patronage. The patron's discomfort is usually expressed as a superstitious aversion to a perceived implication of misfortune (*taṭayyur*). When one poet opens his praise with the line, 'Do not say "good tidings" but rather "two good tidings"...,' the patron objects to beginning the poem with the word not (*lā*), and suggests that these parts of the verse be reversed. The poet points out that the statement of faith, 'There is no God but God...' is the most noble of statements and also begins with the negative particle.[70] Specific words can bring on *taṭayyur*, either at the opening of the poem or within it.[71] The attribution of communication problems of this kind to major figures, such as the poets al-Mutanabbī, Jarīr, and al-Buḥturī, and the minister al-Ṣāhib b. ᶜAbbād, shows that these problems are not necessarily a shortcoming of the uninitiated.

The patron's discomfort with an expression that falls within the conventions of praise may be due to a perceived, but unintended, allusion to the protégé or patron. One poet recites verses about fate at the caliph's request, so that the caliph fears that the verses may refer to him, but the poet clarifies that he is using his own nickname. A patron named Sharaf al-Mulk becomes anxious about a verse that says honor (*sharaf*) has not tumbled down.[72] Similarly, the second-person pronoun can make patrons uncomfortable. The Umayyad poet Jarīr succeeds through intercession in arriving at the caliph ᶜAbd al-Malik, and offers him a poem beginning with a verse that includes 'Your heart,' only to suffer the objection, 'Rather, *your* heart, you idiot!'[73] Similarly, al-Buḥturī gets in trouble when he praises a patron with a verse about love that includes, 'You have grief over a night whose end was long,' and the patron responds, '*You* have grief and war!'[74] When one poet presents a verse saying 'if anyone were eternal, you would be', the patron says, it's true that death is in store for all of us, but kings hate to be reminded of the end of life, so don't say what we don't want to hear.[75] Simply reciting poetry about fate can bring on this kind of anxiety, since it pertains to everyone. One patron becomes anxious about this, and the poet attempts to patch up the situation only to have the patron get up and walk out.[76] The patron's aversion to a poet's verse, whether warranted or not, can be a serious barrier to the use of poetry in patronage.

The risk of missing the mark in praise includes the problem of praise that is perceived to be excessive or inadequate for the patron. Shams-i Qays describes excessive praise as a rhetorical flaw.[77] In his book for secretaries, al-Ṣūlī disapproves of excessive or inadequate expressions in supplication (*duʿāʾ*), using examples of poetry.[78] When al-ʿUtbī writes to his friend and overdoes the supplication, the friend responds (in poetry) 'Take it easy, and do not refer to me in a way that makes me look foolish in front of everyone'.[79] Al-Tawḥīdī explains that excess and falling short in praise or blame display the speaker's emotional point of view rather than a more objective and valid ethical evaluation. He provides the example that al-Jāḥiẓ blames Muḥammad b. Jahm al-Barmakī and praises Ibn Abī Duʾād and exaggerates, turning the former into a demon and the latter into an angel, because that's what happens when one blames in anger or praises out of one's own personal interests.[80] In effect, such statements persuade the community of nothing but the personal opinion of the speaker or writer, so that they cease to have any function as ethical discourse.

However, al-Tawḥīdī also points out that such mistakes do not imply that praise and blame are ineffective in general. As with other kinds of miscommunication in praise, editing can address the problem. When the poet Abū Tammām praises the caliph al-Muʿtaṣim, a member of the audience says the caliph is better than that, so Abū Tammām adds a few lines.[81] Excess and falling short in praise interfere with the appearance of professional, independent, and voluntary evaluation that is crucial for the validity of poetry.

The overlap or juxtaposition of praise and blame, like excess or inadequate praise, is an ethical and social as well as a rhetorical issue. Intentional ambiguity of praise and blame is a positive attribute of elaborate rhetoric, as Ibn al-Jawzī points out in his book about clever people, using an example by the highly skilled poet al-Mutanabbī.[82] Several literary critics valorize the technique of evoking motifs of praise and blame in a single expression of praise.[83] In one story on this topic, a Bedouin gives a garment to a tailor. The tailor says he will sew the garment so that the Bedouin won't know whether it's one type or another. The Bedouin responds by offering verses that, he says, could be understood as praise or blame, and the story is followed by a pre-Islamic verse that could work both ways.[84] In a manual of rhetoric for secretaries, the author cites a saying of the Prophet that can be understood as praise or blame.[85] With this technique, the speaker shows that uncertainty is not a failure to accomplish ethical evaluation, but a strategy for demonstrating the capacity of refined rhetoric to shape the way people see the world.

The overlap of praise and blame in a single expression is complemented by the widespread phenomenon of juxtaposing praise and blame of the same topic or person. Monographic compilations may consist of paired chapters of praise and blame of the same thing, and many encyclopedias include such paired chapters, such al-Rāghib al-Iṣbahānī's chapters on praise and blame of forbearance, and chapters on praise and blame of avarice.[86] Al-Thaᶜālibī's compilation on making beautiful what is ugly also displays a similar interest in using rhetoric to transform the way we see the world.[87] Ibn al-Rūmī distinguished himself with his permutations of praise, blame, and oppositions in individual poems and pairs of poems, and the poet Furāt b. Ḥayyān composed invective on the Prophet and then praised him.[88] The juxtaposition and overlap of praise and blame demonstrate the capacity of elaborate rhetoric to generate ethical discourse that is both complex and flexible.

The problems start when praise that is paid for is viewed as blame. Citing Aristotle's advice to Alexander, Al-Māwardī lauds the use of praise of, by, and for noble men: men who are not accused of lying and who know nothing of play, and who do not make praise into a market by which they seek profit, and who do not seek through praise the execution of favors like effeminates, jokers and playboys. Al-Māwardī deems praise by people who do not meet these criteria to be blame, and the one who praises them is blamed, for they praise the blameworthy if he pays and blame the praiseworthy if he does not pay. If the ruler pays such men, God is angry and both noble men and men of religion regret it.[89] On the other hand, praise for pay that is not paid for can also be viewed as blame. Al-Rāghib al-Iṣbahānī cites a verse to the effect that praise that goes without reward by its recipient is actually invective.[90]

While intentional ambiguity of praise and blame was valorized, unintentional conflations of praise and blame were not. It is easy to see why. Unintentional conflation of praise and blame throws ethical discourse in poetry into chaos. The use of expressions for either praise or blame derives less from the meanings of the expressions themselves than from their customary and conventional use.[91] The Arabic literary critic Ibn Sinān al-Khafājī observes that one must not use language that is identified with blame for praise or vice versa, and offers examples of praise with what sounds like blame, of which some expressions are acceptable and others are not. Aiming for praise and blaming, or vice versa, is among the most serious flaws in poetry.[92] Stories of major poets who unintentionally conflate praise and blame show that this problem is not only a shortcoming of the uninitiated. The major Umayyad poet al-Akhtal can make such mistakes, as in his misguided effort to praise one patron and his similarly misguided effort to blame another.[93] Likewise, Abū Tammām is not immune to such mistakes, and is accused of blaming a group when he tries to praise them.[94] When al-Buḥturī praises a caliph by saying that no aggression blocks his nobility, a member of the audience objects, 'Who would block the caliph's nobility? That's more like invective than praise'.[95] Confusion over praise and blame can be part of a more general critique of poetry for pay. The mystical poet Sanāʾī views confusion between praise and blame as an inherent flaw of all panegyric. He points out that poets mix up hierarchies and get involved with commoners. In their desperation to secure food to eat and clothes to wear, praise and blame are the same to them, and they are like party-crashers.[96] In their desperation, those who serve a man (instead of God) will call a miser Ḥātīm al-Ṭāʾī (the ancient Arab figure who exemplifies generosity) just to get a piece of bread.[97]

In addition to confusion over praise and blame or mistakes of excess or inadequate praise, other distortions of the exchange of poetry for pay can complicate literary patronage. Praise is supposed to be an independent, voluntary, professional evaluation of a patron. As a result, praise of oneself (not boasting, which is a separate genre, though the distinction is not entirely clear) is viewed with ambivalence. Al-Rāghib al-Iṣbahānī cites criticism of a man who praises himself.[98] In contrast, the poet Abān b. ᶜAbd al-Ḥamīd facilitates patronage through self-praise, using it to get in to see a minister.[99]

Distortions may be comic, as in the use of invective in the course of a patronage relationship. This is not the normal use of invective against an unsupportive patron, but a parody of it. One patron, at the insistence of a poet's envious competitors, tests the poet by demanding invective of the patron himself. The poet passes the test, but infuriates the patron, who demands that the poet never again utter the verses or be killed. However, the patron also gives the poet a gift.[100] When the caliph al-Rashīd demands and receives invective about himself from Abū Nuwās, he says, 'Had I not brought this on myself, I would cover the floor with your blood'.[101] The comic protégé Abū Dulāma is the perfect character for this kind of scene. He is instructed to offer invective of any one member in the caliph's gathering, and he comes up with invective of all of them, prompting laughter and a gift.[102] The parodic use of invective implies the uncertainties of patronage and serves as an occasion to laugh them off.

Composing invective on oneself is another parodic use of invective. One poet composes invective on himself as a parody of the disappointment of being rejected. He accosts a prospective patron and says:

'I have praised the caliph – want to hear?'
The prospective patron says, 'No.'
'I praised you – want to hear?'
'No.'
'I've composed invective about myself – want to hear?'
The patron says, 'Let's have it.'

The poet recites and becomes the patron's favorite poet.[103] This poet is rejected, but his parodic use of invective allows him to literally laugh it off, so that he ends up accepted. Another poet hires a Bedouin to compose invective on him. The Bedouin expresses his incredulity, refuses the payment, and composes the invective anyway.[104] This narrative turns the use of poetry for pay around in several directions so as to view it from comic angles. You hire people to praise you, not to blame you. Patrons sometimes refuse to make a payment, but poets do not refuse to take it. If there is no payment, there should be no poetry. The only reason that the Bedouin has to compose invective of this poet-turned-patron is his offer to pay him for invective. The point is that the only reason any poet has to compose praise of his patron is the patron's offer to pay him for praise. The figure of the Bedouin, like the poets Abū Nuwās and Abū Dulāma, is a perfect character to play a role with the poet in making this point, since he is both an arbiter of lofty, refined rhetoric and a figure whose earthy, physical, comic quality offers a counterpoint to the sophistic seriousness of rhetoric. Parody does not imply that there was nothing to worry about in patronage, but rather that poets could laugh it off, before getting back to work.

Protégés and patrons can distort the practice of literary patronage in a variety of other ways, both reinforcing and complicating patronage as a form of social order. One protégé approaches a patron with a losing proposition that is rejected. When he is asked why he went to the trouble, he says, 'I wanted him to forbid benefit to me and to others so that they would blame him.'[105] While the convention of inexpressibility can contribute to patronage, it can also complicate patronage relationships. One poet makes his way in to see a patron by emphasizing the inexpressibility of his qualities.[106] In contrast, when another poet emphasizes the inexpressibility of the caliph's qualities upon arriving in his gathering, the caliph says, 'Take it easy, we don't like to be praised just for being seen.'[107] Upon receiving praise from a poet, Hishām b. ᶜAbd al-Malik says it has been forbidden to praise a man to his face. The poet replies, 'I didn't praise you, I mentioned you. May God bless you.' Hishām says, 'That is better than praise,' and orders a gift.[108]

A comic yet significant distortion of patronage occurs in the form of the exemplary figures of the miser and the party-crasher. The miser and the party-crasher are figures that don't fit into the social order of patronage and don't even bother to try. They are absurd, and their behavior makes a mockery of that social order. The miser has the material capital to serve as a patron, and often has a detailed and eloquent explanation for his avarice, but does not put his wealth into circulation. The party-crasher often seems to have the cultural capital to produce refined rhetoric and work as a protégé, but instead just takes the hospitality of others without giving anything in return.[109] There is a tension between material interests and the appearance of professional, independent and voluntary ethical evaluation in the use of rhetoric in patronage. These figures turn this tension into a spectacle of ridiculous, unethical behavior. In a well-known notice that focuses on avarice while making fun of the sophistry of rhetoric in patronage, a patron merely thanks a poet, and does not pay him. The patron explains that the protégé 'made us happy with words and we made him happy with words.'[110] The figure of the miser is a comic rejection of the role of the patron, and the figure of the party-crasher is a comic rejection of the role of the protégé.

Ambivalence about the validity of praise for pay was a literary, ethical, and social phenomenon in the medieval Middle East and Central Asia. It was both constitutive and disruptive of patronage as a form of social order. Poets used the flexibility of refined rhetoric to negotiate patronage relationships, but this same flexibility could compromise the effectiveness of rhetoric. Skills in refined rhetoric lent poets a professional identity, but the ambivalence about poetry for pay could undermine this identity, and interfere with the social mobility that it facilitated. The problem of exchanging poetry for pay not only shapes commentary and stories that focus on poetry in particular: it also defines stories of poets that feature themes of intimacy and distance, coercion and resistance, and breaking up in patronage relationships. This broader range of commentary and stories is the focus of the following chapter, which shows that poets had to take risks to get ahead.

2

POETS TAKING RISKS TO GET AHEAD

Relationships between poets and patrons were fraught with risks. Starting, ending, changing or simply maintaining these relationships in a competitive environment entailed a range of complications for poets. Skills in refined rhetoric qualified poets to participate in patronage, but did not guarantee them secure and prosperous relationships with patrons. Poets had to take risks to get ahead, and these risks were an integral feature of the patronage network. Uncertainty in patronage appears in narratives and notices about intimacy and distance in unequal relationships, the coercion of patrons and the resistance of protégés, and the potential for relationships to fall apart.

The prose writing upon which this and other chapters are based has sometimes been viewed as compilations in which the author plays no role other than organizing and categorizing material. These prose writers were authors. They use citations, categories, and relations of juxtaposition and contrast to compare different points of view, and to make arguments about literary patronage.[1] The author's explicit commentary may be less prominent, but the implicit commentary is abundant.

Intimacy and distance in unequal relationships

Patronage relationships are about transcending boundaries of status while also clarifying who belongs in which category.[2] As poets and patrons negotiate these relationships, aspects of intimacy and distance intersect. The dynamics of unequal relationships help to articulate the identities of both partners against the backdrop of the patronage network.

Patronage resembles the ideological state apparatuses discussed by Louis Althusser, such as religious and educational institutions, in that social control takes place through ideology rather than violence, although patronage is not as formally structured as these institutions.[3] Unlike more violent approaches to social control, patronage takes shape through the voluntary participation of poets as subordinates. Hannah Arendt clarifies that the people at the top can only exercise power with violence, and when it seems they have managed to impose their will on the majority, it is actually the majority that has decided not to exercise their power of numbers.[4] In other words, they have chosen to participate in some kind of ideological apparatus instead of a violent rebellion. Similarly, Jacques Derrida discusses the authority of the law using the image of the doorkeeper, noting that a person has the physical freedom to enter, but does not, so we must conclude that the person has forbidden himself from entering.[5] The intimacy and distance of unequal relationships may be fraught with risks, but they are more secure than violent alternatives.

Descriptions emphasize the broader patronage network in which individual relationships develop, and the continuity between ideas about political and literary patronage. The Arabic writer Ibn Rashīq, in a work on poetics, explains that the protégé must remain aware of his position and display respect for his superiors as well as respect for the rights of his inferiors.[6] In a book of political advice, the Arabic writer al-Māwardī observes that while serving as a minister, 'you manage commoners and you are managed by kings, so that you are controlling and controlled, combining the power of one who is obeyed and the submission of one who obeys.'[7] Individual relationships are inflected by a range of other relationships with superiors and inferiors.

The effort to secure intimacy across boundaries of status is also about clarifying those boundaries. The Arabic writer al-Jāḥiẓ advises protégés visiting the ruler that they should not sit on cushions and should always leave a spot between themselves and the ruler in case a more important guest arrives.[8] The anonymous author of the Arabic book of political advice *Kitāb al-tāj* emphasizes the importance of distance between a ruler and his associates. If the ruler wears perfume, no one else can wear the same one, and if he wears yellow slippers, no one else can wear them. If only he could avoid sharing air and water with his associates and others, that would be ideal.[9]

Poetry used in patronage must reiterate categories of status so that the poet can transcend the boundary between himself and the patron. In one book of poetics the Persian writer Shams-i Qays emphasizes that in poetry a person must be described with the attributes appropriate to his station, ranging from rulers to common people; and in another, the Arabic writer Ibn Ṭabāṭabā urges protégés to avoid mixing rulers with commoners in description.[10]

The poet's way of addressing the patron and referring to himself is a matter of power, not just style. Shams-i Qays notes that the protégé must avoid using the vocative form of address with the patron's name:[11] he seems to think that such an address would be too intimate. On the other hand, the Persian writer and ruling elite Kaykāvūs b. Iskandar, in his book of political advice, urges poets to avoid overusing the terms 'slave' and 'servant' in reference to themselves in their poetry,[12] suggesting that overuse of these terms implies too much distance between the protégé and the patron.

Too great a distance between superiors and their subordinates can complicate social order. The Persian epic poet Firdawsī, the Persian writer of mystical narrative poetry Niẓāmī Ganjavī, and the book of political advice by the Persian writer Niẓām al-Mulk each emphasize the danger of a gap so large that it leaves the ruler oblivious to his subordinates' wrongdoing, using the exemplary story of the ancient Persian king Bahrām Gūr and his failure to supervise his minister, who becomes oppressive.[13]

Competition does not disrupt patronage, it defines it. In a book of political advice, the Arabic writer al-Thaᶜālibī discusses how a patron should define the position of a protégé relative to his competitors. A king should promote a minister, distinguish him from his peers in his clothing, mount, procession, seating, and titles, and should not listen to opponents and gossips, since the minister is inevitably envied. The king should tell the minister anything he hears that he dislikes or thinks to be a lie, so that the minister asks pardon if it is true, and provides proof to end doubt if it is a lie.[14] Just as individual relationships are inflected by each partner's other relationships with superiors and subordinates, they are also inflected by relationships with peers.

Intimacy between the protégé and the patron can be a feature of success in patronage, but not all intimacy is a path to success. In his book of political advice, Kaykāvūs b. Iskandar makes a distinction between intimacy that is initiated by the patron and intimacy that is initiated by the protégé through service. He advises, 'However much the king brings you close do not be deceived: flee proximity but do not flee service, for from proximity comes distance, and from service to the king comes proximity.'[15]

Intimacy can cut both ways. The Arabic writer al-Jahshiyārī points out that the most appropriate man to forgive is the one who is most capable of punishing.[16] He observes that the one who is praised is insulted one day, and the one who is insulted is praised another day.[17]

The boundaries of status across which patronage relationships take place are not stable. The ancient Persian king Ardashīr was the first to assign degrees to drinking companions, saying that nothing causes a movement in the cycle of power or destroys a kingdom faster than mobile degrees of status, in which the modest person is raised and the noble person is lowered. Another ancient Persian king, Bahrām, changed everything and mixed up the degrees according to his desires and taste in music until a third, Anūshirvān, restored the previous degrees of status. Finally, Yazīd b. ᶜAbd al-Malik, the early Islamic Arab caliph who is associated with the assassination of a group of the Prophet Muḥammad's relatives in a succession dispute, disrupted the entire hierarchy.[18] Boundaries of status are a framework within which patronage occurs, but this framework is subject to change.

Praise and blame can support and transform social hierarchy. In his book of political advice, the Arabic writer al-Māwardī emphasizes that the minister should assign praise and blame according to good and bad qualities, so that he causes desire and dread in the right measure, and his voice is the scale.[19] Although poets help to articulate status for members of the community through the use of praise and blame, their ability to do this is contested. In a mystical narrative poem, the Persian poet Sanāʾī explains that poets who aspire to define status in this way mix up hierarchy in their use of praise, praise commoners, and in their desperation to eke out a living, do not differentiate between those worthy of praise and blame.[20]

Promises illustrate the intersection of intimacy and distance in relationships across boundaries of status. The Arabic writer al-Ṣūlī records the observation that promises are the nets with which noble men catch fine men; without promises, the virtue of being true to one's word would cease to exist.[21] Other views address distance and delay as an integral feature of the promise. The Arabic writers al-Ḥuṣrī and Ibn ᶜAbd Rabbihi explain that a protégé must sleep on a promise or enjoy the temptation that it involves, like the smell of food cooking, to really enjoy the benefits of patronage.[22] Discussions of promises, such as the one by the Arabic writer al-Bayhaqī, often include a significant proportion of examples of broken promises.[23]

Some of the most extensive discussions of distance and intimacy in patronage relationships appear in the theme of reception: the practice of employing assistants who filter the guests of a powerful person.[24] Like promises, reception does not just occur in social hierarchy: it helps to define it. The Arabic writer al-Ghuzūlī explains that reception is a crucial aspect of social hierarchy, since the awe of rulers derives from reception. Al-Ghuzūlī describes the contradiction of reception, which is necessary to inspire awe and also serves as a barrier to the execution of virtuous acts of generosity. He offers the example of a protégé who is denied access to a potential patron and writes to him, saying 'If the noble man is guarded by reception, what is the virtue of the noble man over the blameworthy man?'[25]

The citation of a series of short selections of poetry, which are linked into a kind of narrative, is an important technique in medieval Arabic and Persian literary culture. This technique enables the writer to present a range of views on a topic and to encourage the audience to compare and contrast them. The range of poetry cited in al-Jāḥiẓ's essay on this topic shows that reception could be a major complication for patronage relationships.[26] In a story that combines failure with success, a man waits at a prospective patron's door without success and finally leaves, reciting verses about how his cousins will know about the patron when they go through the (empty) suitcases. This comment prompts the patron to fill the suitcases.[27]

For the patron, the risk of reception may be portrayed as more of a political than a moral problem. Al-Thaᶜālibī notes that reception makes the ruler dependent on his minister to know what is true and false or right and wrong.[28] The early caliph ᶜUmar wrote to his governor Muᶜāwiya, warning him 'Beware of concealment before the people: let the powerless come to speak to you, for if they are restrained for long, they depart from righteousness and their hearts become weak.'[29]

While the patron faces the threat of disorder due to reception, the protégé faces the threat of dishonor in the absence of some kind of barrier. One ruler says, 'If you seek a favor from me make a curtain between you and me, and if it's prohibited it doesn't reach you, and if it's a success it comes to you.'[30] Similarly ᶜAlī, the Prophet Muhammad's cousin and son-in-law and the fourth caliph, explains 'Whoever needs a favor from me, let him put it forth in a letter so that I can protect your reputation (lit. face) from (the disgrace of) asking.'[31] Rejection is damaging for the protégé and reception insulates him from the full force of this damage.

The man who works in reception may block or facilitate a prospective protégé's effort to forge a relationship with a powerful person. The prospective protégé's interaction with him can be a way of contesting the boundary that he represents. Prospective protégés may use poetry to get past the receptionist, as in a narrative mentioned by al-Jahshiyārī.[32] Protégés who are unable to get past reception may send poetry in to the patron from the outside, as in a narrative recorded by al-Ṣūlī.[33] One man working in reception blocked a poet from entering to see a patron because he found the poet's clothes ugly, though the poet manages to censure the receptionist.[34] In another story a Bedouin waits at a ruler's door and asks that he feed the hungry, so the receptionist says 'How many a hungry person there is among you (Bedouin)!' The Bedouin replies by mocking the receptionist, who is fat.[35] The extremely successful poet al-Buḥturī was blocked by a man at reception and asks what is going on. The man just laughed.[36] The men working in reception can also be helpful. One poet goes through a number of stages of intercession and reception, including a female slave, a ruler who passes away, a second ruler, and an intercessor who falls out of favor, culminating with a man working in reception who offers helpful advice that enables him to finally get an appointment.[37]

Other members of the community can facilitate a poet's effort to traverse the barriers of reception.[38] The poet Farrukhī traveled from his provincial home to the Ghaznavid court, apparently to earn more money to support his expensive new wife. He attempts to get past an administrator (*kadkhudā*), but the administrator at first does not believe Farrukhī wrote the poem he wishes to present to the ruler, and tests him by having him improvise a description of the ruler's current entertainment, then has him recite both poems before the ruler.[39] The poet Muᶜizzī, in spite of being introduced as a poet by his successful father, remains unfunded for a year until he is able to have recourse to intercession in order to get a foot in the door.[40] The great epic poet Firdawsī, a provincial landlord, is initially held in contempt by the leading poet at the Ghaznavid court, ᶜUnṣurī. After testing Firdawsī in poetry and the history of Persian rulers, ᶜUnṣurī apologizes for the slight and commissions him to write the epic of Persian kings for the current Ghaznavid ruler, Maḥmūd, beginning with praise of Maḥmūd. In this story, when Firdawsī returns with the masterpiece, he praises the minister Maymandī but ignores the palace favorite, the young man Ayāz. Ayāz is offended and convinces Maḥmūd, a stalwart advocate of Sunnī doctrine, that Firdawsī is a proto-Shi'ite, so that Firdawsī is not rewarded, at least not in his lifetime.[41] Just as individual patronage relationships are inflected by the protégé's relationships with other superiors, subordinates and peers, they are also shaped by his relationships with the people who help or hinder his effort to secure a relationship with a powerful person.

While reception is about separating the patron from the community, the patron himself can help the protégé to cross this threshold. One man waits at a prospective patron's door for a year and then leaves, offering three verses. The caliph brings him back and asks him, 'Are you too good to wait at my door? The man replies, 'No, but I have stayed for a long time, and I have a farm and debt (to get back to).'[42] The caliph inquires about the debt and offers him a job. Stories of reception are stories of social mobility for poets – or barriers to it.

Mystical narrative poetry offers a critical commentary on the dynamics of political patronage, although these poets often had much to gain from it. The Persian mystical poet Rūmī provides a story of a poet who seeks a gift from a king. The minister approves a large gift. When the poet returns a year later, a new minister suggests a small gift due to financial constraints. The poet reflects that both men are named Ḥasan (good), though the name is true for the first minister and false for the second, and Rūmī follows up with a story that implies a comparison between the bad minister and the minister of pharaoh.[43]

If mystics promoted a spiritual alternative to political patronage, merchants displayed a material one. Al-Jāḥiẓ, in one of his polemical and playful yet serious essays, praises merchants and blames the ruler's men. He contrasts merchants who live like kings, constantly approached by seekers of assistance, with the ruler's men, who are degraded and engage in flattery, living in terror of regime change, inquisitions, or purges. Al-Jāḥiẓ urges his reader to resist having mercy on these people, whose enemies treat them better than their own masters.[44]

Patronage relationships involve intimacy and distance across boundaries of social status. Poets often had to assert these boundaries in order to cross them. These boundaries illustrate the uncertainty and flexibility of patronage relationships, as well as their potential to facilitate social mobility.

Coercive patrons and resistant poets

The patron's coercion and the poet's resistance to it were built-in features of literary patronage. The poet's appeal to the patron relies on the limitation of the patron's power and a negotiation between superiors and subordinates.[45] Michel Foucault views discourse as 'both an instrument and an effect of power, but also a hindrance, a stumbling-block, a point of resistance and a starting point for an opposing strategy.'[46] The poet's representation of the patron is an assertion of authority that both contributes to, and competes with the patron's authority.[47]

Particularly salient instances of coercion intensified the uncertainties of patronage for the protégé and also compromised the flexibility of the patronage network. The poet's resistance to coercion entailed confronting the uncertainties of patronage head-on, or just moving on to bigger and better things.[48] The poet's resistance to the patron's coercion allowed him to reassert the flexibility of patronage, as well as its capacity to facilitate social mobility.

The appearance of an independent, voluntary, and professional use of refined rhetoric in panegyric contributed to the social significance of the genre. When patrons interfered with this aspect of the poet's work, that significance was compromised. When one caliph designated an heir, he ordered a poet to stand up and speak, listened to him, commended him, and then ordered him to take a seat.[49] The poet's composition is an implicit evaluation of the patron and his chosen heir: however, if made to appear involuntary, the social significance of that evaluation is changed. Another caliph says, 'Whoever can say the like of what the poet Manṣūr al-Namarī said of [the caliph] Rashīd, let him come in.'[50] This patron's attempt to define the content of poetry interferes with the appearance of it being voluntary.

The distinction between a professional portrayal that is paid for by the patron, and a more coercive commission in which the poet is not free to exercise his professional skills with the same latitude, is a subtle but important one. The powerful minister al-Ṣāḥib b. ᶜAbbād received a letter about an elephant in the Khurasani army, and ordered the poets in his presence to describe it with the same rhyme and meter as another poem by a famous pre-Islamic poet.[51] Similarly, al-Ṣāḥib b. ᶜAbbād tests the poet and writer Badīᶜ al-Zamān al-Hamadhānī by demanding poetry as well as a translation from Persian to Arabic, and Badiᶜ al-Zamān invites al-Ṣāḥib to pick the rhyme and meter of the Arabic translation.[52] Patrons may also interfere with the recitation itself.[53]

The patron's demands can put the protégé under pressure, further undermining the appearance of a poet's voluntary, independent, and professional work. The grammarian al-Mubarrad went in to the caliph al-Mutawakkil, who was drunk and said, have you ever seen a better-looking person than me? Since praise that is physical is not really praise, al-Mubarrad explains, 'I said no, by God, nor one who is more generous. Then I dared to offer him verses on his beauty and generosity. He said, "You've done well."'[54] When one patron pressures a poet by asking if he has anything new, the poet circumvents the pressure to improvise by saying, 'All praise is beneath you and all poetry about you is above me,' and cites verses by another poet.[55]

The pressure to improvise may be about a poet's work for the patron rather than the specific task of portraying him. Ḥammād the transmitter of poetry went in to see the caliph al-Walīd, who was behind a curtain, and al-Walīd gave him two words meaning 'then they were stirred up'. Ḥammād said, 'What?' Al-Walīd continued to pressure him until Ḥammād got it and recited the sought-after verses in which the two words occur.[56] In another story, a good-looking servant enters a gathering, and the narrator pressures al-Buḥturī to improvise verses about him. Al-Buḥturī responds, 'But I don't improvise,' and recites a few verses. When the narrator demands more, al-Buḥturī adds, 'That's enough until I can compose a *qaṣīda*.'[57] The patron's coercion complicates the professional status of the poet's work.

In many stories, word tames power: the right word need not be persuasion, but a context that allows for intimacy between unequals without actually dismantling the barriers of social hierarchy or undermining the patron's status.[58] As the minister and Arabic writer Ibn al-Muqaffaᶜ recounts in his Arabic version of the ancient Indian and then Persian work *Kalīla and Dimna*, the Indian minister Bidpai says to his followers, 'It is not possible for us to struggle against [the ruler] with anything but our voices, and even if we sought the support of others, it would not be feasible for us to oppose him.' Bidpai follows up with an open critique of the ruler in which he invokes ancient models: a common approach to guiding the behavior of rulers in an indirect way. 'O king, you have it all, and yet you did not do right by your obligations, and instead you were a tyrant. You should have followed your predecessors.'[59] However, the tragic results of Ibn al-Muqaffaᶜ's own career show that participants in patronage who do not go with the flow of authority place themselves in danger. Similarly, Kaykāvūs b. Iskandar advises, 'do not say anything that the king does not want to hear or oppose him, for anyone who opposes a king dies before his time.'[60] In a much less dramatic approach to the possibility of resistance in patronage, the same writer offers the advice that 'the poet must be aware of the patron's nature and know what he would like, and praise him with what he likes, since if you don't say what he likes he won't give you what you want.'[61] Skills in refined rhetoric in patronage are about telling people what they want to hear, or telling them what they do not want to hear in a tactful way. The importance of indirect expression for safe and successful patronage is a factor that shapes the use of refined rhetoric.

The poet's resistance may take the form of conflicts between the poet and the patron over the use of poetry in patronage. The Syrian ruler Sayf al-Dawla demands poetry from the highly skilled poet al-Mutanabbī, and then stops him and criticizes his poetry in the middle of the performance. Al-Mutanabbī argues against the critique and Sayf al-Dawla accepts his argument.[62] One patron criticizes the praise for bravery that he receives, and says that al-Aᶜshā's verse of praise, in which he says that his patron advances without a mail coat, is better. The poet responds, 'I described you as resolved and al-Aᶜshā described his patron as foolish.'[63] These conflicts over the use of poetry complicate the patronage relationship, but the poet's resistance to the patron also contributes to making this relationship successful.

The poet may express his resentment of the failure of patronage relationships. Khālid b. Ṣafwān submits a request to the caliph Hishām, who rejects the request, saying that beggars will proliferate and the treasury cannot withstand such a request. Khālid is asked, 'Why did you go to Basra to set yourself up for rejection by the caliph?' He responds, 'I liked the idea that he would prohibit others besides me and that those who blame him would increase.'[64] The poet Nuṣayb expresses his resistance to a failed relationship, and impresses his interlocutor so much that he receives a reward.

Maslama asks him, 'Did you praise so-and-so?'

Nuṣayb responds, 'Yes.'

'So what did he do for you?'

'He rejected me.'

'So didn't you compose invective against him?'

'I don't do invective.'

'Why not?'

'Because I am more entitled to compose invective against him if I consider him worthy of my praise (and I don't).'

Maslama is so pleased with Nuṣayb's description of this patron's rejection that he gives him a reward.[65]

In such responses, the poet goes public with the patron's poor treatment of him.

Comic forms of coercion on the part of patrons, and resistance on the part of poets, help to define the parameters of patronage. The brother of the Arabic poet ᶜUmar Ibn Abī Rabīᶜa forbade him from uttering poetry and gave him one thousand dinars not to do so. ᶜUmar took the money and went to stay with a relative outside of town, since he feared that he would be tempted to utter poetry in the city. One day he slips up and says some poetry, which gets back to his brother, who forgives him.[66] The wine poet and playboy Abū Nuwās went in to see the caliph al-Amīn and said, 'I have verses for you but I won't say them until you get off the throne and let me sit there.' The caliph agreed, warning Abū Nuwās of the consequences if the verses were not satisfactory, and fortunately the arrangement ended well.[67] In another story, the caliph al-Rashīd likes a proverb and wants poetry about it. He is told that Abū Nuwās would know, but it turns out that he is in prison. Al-Rashīd summons him in chains, and, as expected, he provides Bedouin-quality verses about the proverb. After promising not to drink and performing well in an improvisational quiz, Abū Nuwās is released.[68] One poet makes a mockery of praise by telling his patron, 'How noble you are except for three qualities.' He describes the patron, who responds with a reward as well as a rebuttal of the criticism.[69] The poet al-Buḥturī is pressured to drink out of turn, which would make him incapable of performing well in the gathering. Instead of confronting the caliph al-Mutawakkil directly, he appeals to the minister al-Fatḥ b. Khāqān for intercession.[70] The protégé Abū Dulāma was a comic character who was good at poetry and knew many good stories. He liked to go out and drink with his friends to escape the artificial atmosphere of the palace. The caliph al-Saffāḥ asked him why he didn't stick around, and Abū Dulāma said, 'All honor is here but I don't want to be bored.' Al-Saffāḥ objected, 'We don't bore you,' and had him locked in the palace and made to go to mosque with him. Finally, Abū Dulāma appealed for release in verse and the caliph let him go.[71] Playful coercion and resistance parody the real thing.

Resistance in patronage may have a spiritual connotation. The poet Abū al-ᶜAynāᵓ went in to the caliph al-Mutawakkil and performed well in a poetry quiz. The caliph asked him what he wanted (in terms of a reward), but he said that he preferred to take care of his needs with God. The caliph urged him to join the court gathering, but Abū al-ᶜAynāᵓ said, 'No that's not right for me'. The minister al-Fatḥ b. Khāqān remarked, 'This man knows himself.'[72] Abū al-ᶜAynāᵓ dispelled rumors about himself for al-Mutawakkil in a particularly tactful way, and was invited to join the caliph's gathering. He rejected the invitation, but received ten thousand dirhams anyway.[73] The caliph al-Rashīd tried to force the poet Abū al-ᶜAtāhiyya to recite love poetry after he had become an ascetic and renounced such poetry. The poet refused, so the caliph imprisoned him in a house, but allowed visitors and ordered that he be treated well.[74] A Persian story of a Greek scholar presents spirituality as a reason to resist patronage. The scholar becomes famous, chooses isolation, and moves to a cave. When the king is ill and his doctors can't do anything, the king sends his minister to bring the scholar back. The minister encounters the scholar wearing (or possibly eating) plants, and the scholar refuses to go back. The minister points out that if the scholar were to serve the king, he would not have to eat (or probably wear) plants. The scholar laughs and says that if the minister could eat (or wear) plants, he would not have to serve the king.[75]

Other cases of coercion and resistance are neither comic nor spiritual. Instead, they are simply expressions of the uncertainties of patronage and the friction that could occur in relationships. Poets may express resistance to unsatisfactory terms of patronage. The minister Yazīd b. al-Muhallabī asked the brother of the poet al-Farazdaq to bring al-Farazdaq to commemorate a conquest, and offered payment to the poet's family. Al-Farazdaq wants the payment for himself, and when he can't have it, he simply rejects the job.[76] The minister Jaᶜfar b. Yaḥyā al-Barmakī gave one poet thirty thousand dirhams, another twenty thousand, and just three thousand to the poet Ashjaᵓ. Ashjaᵓ objected to the arrangement in writing (in verse) and received twenty thousand more.[77] The poet Bashshār praised a patron and was made to wait for his payment, so that he stopped the patron on his way to mosque in order to secure the payment.[78] These stories demonstrate the uncertainties of patronage as well as the ability of the poet to negotiate with the patron.

Imprisonment is a particularly salient form of coercion in patronage. Yaḥyā b. Khālid al-Barmakī imprisoned the poet Abān b. ᶜAbd al-Ḥamīd in a house until he finished his versified *Kalīla and Dimna* for him.[79] Given the fate of the Barmakid ministers, stories about their coercive treatment of protégés imply that what goes around comes around. The poet Muḥammad b. al-Dawraqī approached a patron and had differences with him so that he was imprisoned until he managed to secure his release and compose invective on the patron.[80] One poet ended up in a group of prisoners of war and eventually entered the service of the ruler who had captured him, and another is imprisoned by his patron and writes an epigram to appeal for release.[81] The brief imprisonment of the poet Khāqānī and the long imprisonment of the poet Masᶜūd-i Saᶜd-i Salmān are well known.[82] Like the problem of reception, the more serious problem of imprisonment displays the boundaries between the patron and the protégé in a spatial way that is not just about how the protégé experiences rejection, but also about the public display of that rejection.

As a kind of counterculture, mystical texts appropriate tales of relationships with rulers as parables. In some cases, these stories portray resistance to rulers and patronage. A mystic dreams of Sultan Maḥmūd, and learns in his dream of the sultan's misery in the next life due to his earlier life as a ruler.[83] One king builds the perfect palace, only to have an ascetic perceive a flaw in its design.[84] In a story that compares the ruler Maḥmūd and a commoner who happens to have the same name, the commoner observes that he and the ruler are equal in death.[85] A righteous man dreams that a dervish is in Hell and a king is in Heaven: the paradox is explained by the fact that the king is in Heaven due to the wishes of dervishes, and the dervish is in Hell due to his proximity to the king.[86]

The tragic stories of Isfandyār and Siyāvash in the *Shāhnāmeh* (the Persian *Book of Kings)* explore the dynamics of coercion and resistance in unequal relationships by way of the relationship between a king and his son.[87] Like the indirect expression of fables in *Kalīla and Dimna*, the indirect expression of legend in epic allows the poet latitude in exploring the problem of unequal relationships. The use of images from the epic in Persian panegyric suggests that these stories offered a backdrop to poems about contemporary rulers.

In rare cases, patronage is linked to downright cruelty. The ruler al-Walīd requires one protégé to dance and recite poetry while wearing the lower half of a monkey skin. So it is not surprising that another story is recorded in which al-Walīd's protégé and companion leaves while the ruler is passed out drunk. Al-Walīd has his male slave go out and bring back the man's head. He regrets his deed so much that he picks up the head and composes an elegy for the murdered companion.[88] These stories have less to do with typical patterns of patronage than with the reputation of this caliph in literary culture, as well as displaying the potential for coercion.

The coercion of patrons demonstrates the uncertainties of patronage, and the resistance of poets illustrates the flexibility of this form of social order. The Umayyad caliph al-Muᶜāwiya asked the poet Aḥnaf al-Qays why he had nothing to say. The poet responded that if he were to tell the truth, he would fear the caliph, and if he were to lie, he would fear God, so silence is best.[89] This brief narrative, about characters from the seventh century in the Arab Umayyad Empire of Syria, appears in a Persian version of a tenth-century Arabic collection of stories from Iraq, by the Persian writer ᶜAwfī, who lived in the thirteenth century and traveled throughout Central Asia and as far as Delhi. Stories of coercion and resistance expressed and relieved some of the anxiety that surrounded literary patronage.

Breaking up

Patronage relationships sometimes fall apart, or come close to doing so.[90] At the same time, relationships that fall apart make way for new connections. Breakdowns and near-breakdowns in patronage are not outside the social order: they are a feature of that order. Mary Douglas discusses the relationship between social order and disorder in the phenomenon of abjection, which does not cut off the subject from what threatens it, but rather acknowledges that the subject is in perpetual danger.[91] Success may be the norm in the depiction of patronage, but threats of breakdown, which seem to be fairly common, also receive a good deal of attention. Actual breakdowns seem to be less common, but instances that are recorded sometimes receive a disproportionate amount of attention.

Images of nature imply the unstable conditions in which the breakdown of patronage relationships can occur. The Arabic writer Ibn Qutayba compares the ruler's power to rain, wind, summer, winter, night and day, each of which brings God's benefit and also causes damage.[92] An Indian source compares companionship with the sultan with a wild mountain that has both delicious fruit and dangerous wildcats.[93] The minister of the caliph al-Saffāḥ used to say, 'The one who sails on the sea exposes himself to danger, and the danger of one who enters the service of kings is greater.'[94] Similarly, al-Māwardī explains that there are three things with which there is no security – the ruler, the sea, and time: since the ruler is swayed by his passions so that he makes assumptions, and since he makes accusations when he is bored.[95] Al-Māwardī also compares the ruler's love and affection to the morning dew, and compares the ruler's companion to one who rides a lion: people fear him because of his mount, and he himself is even more fearful.[96]

Writers also offer more direct commentary on the potential for breakdown in patronage. ᶜAwfī links the use of poetry with conflict, as well as the possibility to move beyond it. He refers to Adam, in the wake of Cain's murder of Abel, as the first person to utter poetry.[97] The unstable personality of the patron leads to instability in patronage and the potential for breakdowns. Kaykāvūs b. Iskandar emphasizes that protégés should 'always fear the king's anger, for two things are never unimportant, the king's anger and the wise man's advice. Anyone who sees them as unimportant becomes unimportant.'[98] Ibn al-Muqaffaᶜ conveys the advice that one ought to let the ruler know that leadership is viewed as infidelity and the forgetting of affection – in other words, that power corrupts. Envy is a problem for the minister, and one should not alienate colleagues when one is in a position of power lest one need assistance from them in the future.[99] Similarly, the Arabic writer Ibn ᶜAbd al-Barr cites advice that one should not hasten to praise or blame someone, for perhaps he will make you happy today and harm you tomorrow.[100] One minister says that he has never seen anyone with contentment that is closer to disapproval, or who is quicker to shift from proximity to distance, than rulers.[101] Another minister says that in the ceremony in which he was granted the position of minister, he was like a camel ornamented for slaughter.[102] Likewise, in his book of poetics and its cultural context, Ibn Rashīq observes that kings are irritable, and are liable to find fault where there is none and to exclude one who does not deserve to be excluded.[103] These personality traits are not dysfunctions of patronage, but rather they are a default setting for it.

One solution to the dangers of patronage is to withdraw, or at least keep a safe distance. The Arabic writer Al-Ābī cites a notice asserting that the ruler's gathering is like the [steaming hot] bath – the one who is inside wants to get out, and the one who is outside wants to get in.[104] He also cites one person who is asked why he does not work for the ruler, who explains, 'Because I see him giving to one who has done no good, and killing another who has done nothing wrong. And I do not know which of the two I am, and I do not aspire to obtain a big enough amount for me to risk it.'[105] However, it can be difficult to resist the opportunities that patronage offers. One minister explains that he does not want the job except to benefit a friend and harm an enemy.[106]

Withdrawal from the danger of patronage may have spiritual connotations. The Persian writer Saᶜdī relates a story about a minister who is fired and joins a group of dervishes, insisting that for wise people, being out of a job is better than being at work. A group of wild animals invites him to join them and he refuses, saying that he would not be safe from their attack.[107] Rūmī offers a story that argues against the benefits of patronage. The narrator notes that the panegyrist has a trace of grief in him that gives the lie to his praise and shows it to be flattery. When his less materialistic companions ask about his absence, he says that he has been earning robes from the ruler, but the companions insist that his poor condition shows that it's not true. The poet objects, saying, 'I earned a great deal but gave it all away.' The companions mock him, saying, 'The money is gone, what is left?' They contrast the praise of patronage with the praise of God.[108] Stories about avoiding patronage imply a critique of this form of social order.

The link between refined rhetoric and material wealth entails the risk of problems in patronage. Ibn ᶜAbd al-Barr cites the Torah to explain this link, and to clarify the potential for difficulties. 'Thank the one who has bestowed benefit upon you, and bestow benefit upon the one who has thanked you, for there is no end to benefits when they are thanked, and there is no place for them when they are met with ingratitude, and thanks are an increase in benefits and security from the vicissitudes.'[109] Ibn ᶜAbd Rabbihi further explores the potential for problems in the link between refinement and wealth. A protégé approaches a prospective patron saying, 'I have come to ask a favor, and if you want, you can fulfill it and we will both be noble, or you can refuse it and we will both be degraded.'[110] Finally, al-Tawḥīdī highlights the tension surrounding the exchange of refined rhetoric for material wealth. One person gives a gift to another and receives nothing but blessings in return. The giver of the gift responds with blessings to indicate his satisfaction with the exchange, and the narrator laments the rarity of such good will, citing the advice of the philosopher al-Kindī to one of his disciples, 'Be like a chess player, keep your king and try to take the king of others.'[111]

Stories of downturns in patronage relationships demonstrate the role of risk. At the same time, the protégé in dire straits may provide the patron with the perfect opportunity to show people what he is made of. In Ibn al-Muqaffaᶜ's Arabic version of part of the Indian *Panchatantra*, the minister Bidpai is bound and imprisoned because he offended the ruler by giving him advice. The ruler has second thoughts and summons him in chains, and Bidpai assures him that he was only offering advice to help the ruler maintain his subjects and his power. The king asks for the advice again, and Bidpai provides his advice in the form of fables: as entertainment for all and strategic training for the elite.[112] Like the elaborate rhetoric of praise poetry, these fables offer an indirect and multifaceted message about intimacy and distance in patronage relationships.

Elaborate rhetoric can get a poet into difficult situations, but it can also get him out of such situations. The story of Kaᶜb b. Zuhayr, whose poem for the Prophet Muḥammad is linked to the Prophet's forgiveness of Kaᶜb for his opposition to the Muslim community, is an exemplary narrative of the connection between verses and forgiveness.[113] One caliph becomes angry at a secretary and treats him harshly, but the secretary recovers with an apt verse.[114] Another protégé gets on his patron's nerves and is thrown in prison, until he sends verses from prison and wins his release.[115] A protégé begins a relationship with the official al-Ḥasan b. Rajāᵓ, then censures him and even composes invective, so that he ends up fleeing to Oman. He offers a poem to pardon himself and returns.[116] When the caliph al-Amīn imprisons Abū Nuwās, he writes verses from prison and is released and rewarded.[117] Downturns are an integral feature of the dynamics of patronage, as are the verses that are used to recover from them.

Poets may use verses to avert impending crises with fickle patrons. Literary critics are interested not just in what makes the best poetry, but also in what the best poetry can accomplish. Shams-i Qays promotes his manual of rhetoric by pointing out that one must use fine speech to work one's way out of difficulties.[118] Similarly, Ibn Rashīq depicts the value of spontaneous verses when one's life is on the line, offering examples of poets who escaped with verse.[119] Poets' skills in elaborate rhetoric and refined manners allow them to articulate solutions to problems. The ruler Maḥmūd ordered his favorite, Ayāz, to cut his hair, and then regretted what he had done and became distraught, until the leading court poet ᶜUnṣurī offered verses that calmed him down.[120] Similarly, one young ruler becomes angry when a backgammon game does not go well for him, but the poet Azraqī offers verses that defuse the situation.[121] Azraqī is also summoned to help an unhappy ruler who suffers from impotence, after the usual cures do not work. While he does not solve this problem with poetry (he arranges for the ruler to spy on a male and female slave having sex), the choice of the poet to solve the problem suggests the special role that poets play in averting crises.[122] In another version, Azraqī provides the ruler with a picture book to prevent future problems.[123] A prisoner who is about to be executed uses verses in Persian and Arabic to save himself. The misreading of the poet's Arabic verse as a Qur'anic verse turns out to be to his advantage.[124]

Poets may combine the rhetorical strategies of verse with intercession. The poet Abū Tammām chooses to boast of his own tribal affiliation rather than that of his patron. When a poem does not suffice to repair the relationship, Abū Tammām offers poetry to secure the assistance of an intercessor.[125] Some companions of the ruler Sayf al-Dawla become jealous of his favorite male slave and kill him. The ruler is furious, and the poet Abū Firās, also a member of the ruler's family, repairs the relationships of the group with the ruler through his poetry and intercession.[126] Poetry and intercessors as a form of mediation allow powerful people to move on without losing face.

In addition to poetry and intercession, a protégé in a downturn can use other kinds of refined rhetoric to appeal to a patron. The ancient Persian king Nūshirvān hears an accusation about his minister Buzurjmihr and throws him in prison. The king insists on knowing what he says while he is there. Buzurjmihr says nothing for months. Nūshirvān sends a group of the minister's friends to him, who tell him that he looks great in spite of his situation, and ask him how he manages that. Buzurjmihr explains twelve ethical and religious principles that he follows. When the men convey this report to Nūshirvān, he releases Buzurjmihr and takes better care of him.[127] A caliph finds the writer Sahl b. Hārūn annoying one day. In order to recover his prestige in the gathering, Sahl waits until the caliph has been talking for a while, and then steps forward and addresses the gathering, saying 'How can you listen to such eloquence without taking pleasure and describing it!' The caliph approves of the comment and ceases to be annoyed.[128] Another caliph becomes angry and excludes a protégé from his presence. The protégé enters discreetly with a group of plaintiffs who are admitted to plead their cases, says his piece, and restores his relationship with the caliph.[129] The comic protégé Abū Dulāma recites a poem that makes the audience cry, and the caliph al-Manṣūr becomes angry, warning that if he recites it again, he will cut his tongue out. Abū Dulāma describes his relationship with the caliph Abū al-ᶜAbbās and the exemplary story of Joseph and his brothers, and al-Manṣūr forgives and rewards him.[130] As well as talking their way into relationships, poets can often talk their way out of relationship problems.

In more elaborate narratives about relationship problems and solutions, the permutations of plot, like the elaborate rhetoric of poetry, juxtapose and compare the possibilities of patronage. The poet ᶜAlī b. Jahm gossips about the other drinking companions in the caliph's gathering. They manage to convince the caliph that ᶜAlī is fooling around with the servants and gossiping about the caliph himself. The caliph has him exiled to Khurasan and imprisoned, where he is crucified naked for a day. ᶜAlī writes to the caliph and secures his release by way of the local governor.[131] In another version, ᶜAlī has been linked to the Shi'ites, Christians, and the theology of the Muᶜtazila, leading his adversaries to conspire against him until he ends up crucified naked in Khurasan and is taken down only after he recites verses.[132] The poet al-Kumayt is imprisoned by a patron, and is visited so frequently by his mother that the guards do not notice when he escapes wearing her clothes. He finalizes his release by offering verses.[133] The caliph al-Walīd's favorite poet, Ṭurayḥ, falls out of favor when envious competitors conspire with the poetry transmitter Ḥammād and the caliph's eunuch to attribute blame of the caliph to Ṭurayḥ. The poet must then contrive to repair the relationship with praise.[134]

While many escapes by way of verse imply that the speaker has composed or improvised the verses, an apt quotation can also do the trick. In one story, the narrator goes in to see the minister al-Faḍl b. Rabīᶜ after the caliph al-Rashīd learned that al-Faḍl has just released a very important prisoner. When al-Rashīd asks why he released him, al-Faḍl explains that the prisoner asked him with an appeal to al-Faḍl's proximity to the Prophet, as well as a promise to be more obedient. Al-Rashīd goes off to think for an hour, and then tells al-Faḍl to track down the former prisoner and bring him in. The narrator enters the story and cites verses, using them to praise al-Faḍl for his resolve and righteousness. Al-Faḍl has the narrator find out the amount that the poet had received for the verses for their first use, and then offers him that price for his apt citation.[135]

In more elaborate narratives, the significance of poetry in the solution to a problem may be overshadowed by other events and characters. One narrator follows the flight of the Abbasid Ibrāhīm b. al-Mahdī from the caliph al-Maᵓmūn as he encounters or seeks refuge with a cupper, a soldier and his wife, and the wife's female protégé. Ibrāhīm secures his safety and restores his relationship with al-Maᵓmūn, and recites verses contributing to the resolution. However, the story focuses on the observation of the people he meets along the way, who either shelter him or give him up for money.[136] In these stories, patronage relationships take place in broader networks of interaction.

Minor complications and hurt feelings can interfere with patronage, and demonstrate the role of uncertainty in these relationships.[137] The poet Ibn al-Rūmī praises a secretary who in turn gives the praise to his servant, saying, 'Praise someone else, I don't want it.'[138] The early Islamic poet al-Farazdaq recites poetry to the people of a mosque. The poet Jarīr hears about this and goes to the same mosque to recite, but one of the elders sends him away, saying the mosque is not the place for poetry. Jarīr objects, pointing out that they had just allowed al-Farazdaq to recite poetry, and leaves angrily, offering three verses in opposition.[139] The caliph al-Maᵓmūn becomes angry at ᶜAlī b. Jabla because of his verses about the general Abū Dulaf in which he says that other people borrow their noble qualities from Abū Dulaf. When al-Maᵓmūn finally apprehends ᶜAlī, he explains that he meant other less important people, and al-Maᵓmūn forgives him.[140]

Payment problems are ubiquitous in the narrative literature on patronage. One poet seeks a refund of his poetry when he receives no reward, and another questions a patron who has disappointed him.[141] One poet praises al-Mahdī when the latter is still young and receives twenty thousand dirhams as a reward. When the caliph learns about the reward he deems it too large and has sixteen thousand taken back. After the caliph dies, the poet seeks the lost money in court: the judge finds the case hilarious and returns the money with interest.[142]

Invective can be the best solution. One patron not only doesn't pay, he also says, 'I don't give the husband of Ḥasanawiyya the whore a reward for his praise,' prompting the poet's invective in response.[143] One poet receives two coins, instead of the two thousand dinars that he expected, from a miserly member of the Abbasid family, and responds with invective. When the miser complains to the caliph about the invective, the caliph learns what happened, chastises his relative, pays the poet thirty thousand dirhams and makes him a drinking companion, while also telling the poet not to mention the exchange in his poetry.[144] Another poet, who typically charges four thousand dirhams for his work, appeals to a secretary and is refused, so that he responds with two verses in protest.[145]

Middlemen can complicate the exchange of poetry for pay. One poet has a document to collect his reward of 400 camels from the caliph al-Walīd, but is unable to obtain the reward until he appeals to al-Walīd a second time and al-Walīd pressures the agent who is supposed to provide the camels.[146] When the poet Abān al-Lāḥiqī is in charge of distributing payments to poets for the Barmakids, he shortchanges Abū Nuwās and includes a message to rub it in, until Abū Nuwās responds to a boast poem by al-Lāḥiqī with an invective and al-Lāḥiqī pays up, begging him not to circulate the invective, which Abū Nuwās circulates anyway.[147]

Relationship problems are an integral feature of patronage, and may even involve some physical coercion, but the total breakdown of relationships is an entirely different matter. Patronage is an alternative to violence. When the interaction between unequals gives way to violence, it's no longer patronage. However, patronage works well in spite of all of the complications that can arise, and violence is rare. One poet angers an Umayyad elite by praising one of his competitors. The Umayyad elite stakes him out and attacks him when he leaves a friend's house drunk, and gives him eighty lashes.[148] The poet ᶜAmr b. ᶜAbd al-Raḥmān, because of his invective against the Muhallab administrative family, is pushed into the Tigris and survives only because some sailors rescue him.[149] The ancient Arabic poets al-Mutalammis and Ṭarafa are drinking companions of the King of Hira. When they compose invective on him, the king writes to a governor and implies that he has ordered payment for them, while the letters actually order their execution.[150]

The anger of powerful people, which is featured in stories about poets mainly to illustrate the power of rhetoric to defuse dangerous situations, can in rare cases lead to actual violence. The poet Sudayf made the caliph Abū al-ᶜAbbās so angry that he turned to his men from Khurasan and ordered them in Persian to beat the poet.[151] Likewise, envious people are usually featured in these stories to illustrate the perils of patronage that must be avoided, but in rare cases they can engage in violence. One king confiscates money from his minister Bū Tammām, but the minister escapes with other funds and settles down in a remote place. When the king summons him, he returns to the king's administration and succeeds, but warns the king that he is an outsider, so the king must not listen to his critics. The king agrees, but is nonetheless taken in by the plot of four envious ministers. The ministers draw Bū Tammām into a risky marriage proposal on behalf of the king, and then manage to turn the king against Bū Tammām so that he has him killed. The king cannot sleep after the event, and while wandering around the palace he overhears the four ministers dividing up the money that they gained through the plot. The king punishes the ministers but still feels guilty about Bū Tammām.[152]

It is noteworthy that this king, like the caliph al-Walīd who kills his close companion in the story cited earlier in this chapter, regrets his actions. In addition, this story features justice for the envious ministers who deceived the king. In both, the ruler departs from the social order of patronage, but looks back in grief with nostalgia for the lost relationship. The king's moral and emotional distress appears in his insomnia, and the caliph's distress takes the form of poetry.

The degeneration of the social order of patronage into violence may be used by writers to interpret history. Al-Iṣfahānī records a story explaining why the early Abbasid caliph al-Saffāḥ killed the members of the former dynasty, the Umayyads. In the story, al-Saffāḥ confronts them with praise of himself and says, 'Did anyone ever praise you with such a poem?' The members of the former dynasty cite praise of themselves, saying 'No one will ever praise you as this poet praised us'. Al-Saffāḥ becomes enraged and has them arrested and killed.[153] This story is used to make sense of the Abbasid revolution.

Writers can also use patronage stories that end with violence to emphasize multiple perspectives on relationships. Al-Jahshiyārī and al-Iṣfahānī include several of the stories about the poet Bashshār in their collections. In one version, Bashshār composes invective of a minister's brother and the minister responds by claiming that Bashshār composed invective of the caliph al-Mahdī. Al-Mahdī tells the minister to bring him in, and fearing that he would praise al-Mahdī and be forgiven of the accusation, the minister has Bashshār killed on the road. In another version, ongoing tension between the caliph al-Mahdī and Bashshār culminates with the latter's drunken call to prayer, so that the caliph has him beaten until he dies.[154] When patronage relationships, as historical events involving historical characters, enter into the circulation of narratives, they become part of a discursive interaction among competing interpretations.

The literary critic Ibn Rashīq emphasizes that the point of patronage is not to present a view that is so independent, professional, and voluntary that it places the poet in danger: professional identity means that it's just a job. He observes that the most foolish of poets is the one who risks his life, saying 'Rather he is the one who seeks benefit, so why should he lose his capital (*raʾs mālihi*), especially when his capital is his head (*raʾsuhu*)?' He concludes, 'If necessary, it is better for a man to take sides with the people in power.'[155]

While poets must strive to avoid relationships that lead out of the social order of patronage and into violence, their relationships often involve them as accomplices in their patrons' violent deeds. Al-Buḥturī is infamous for composing poetry in the wake of the assassination of the caliph al-Mutawakkil that was planned by his son al-Mustaᶜīn and his Turkish generals. He switches allegiance from the assassinated ruler to his successor.[156] In addition, al-Buḥturī praises Ibn al-Khaṣīb, using him as an intercessor, and then celebrates his firing and execution.[157] Poets were summoned to celebrate the killing of the minister Yazīd b. Al-Muhallab, and al-Buḥturī celebrated the caliph al-Mustaᶜīn's killing of the general Utamish and his secretary.[158] The fact that al-Buḥturī is sometimes implicitly or explicitly censured for his shifts of allegiance in the context of violence shows that this behavior was viewed as problematic. However, the fact that he is also very successful demonstrates that this behavior is an expression of the protégé's professional identity and a feature of the social mobility based on that identity.

The random juxtaposition of violence and patronage implies anxiety about their proximity. They are supposed to be alternatives, so it's disturbing when they happen in the same place at the same time. One poet relates, 'We went in to see the caliph al-Rashīd, these other poets and I, and al-Rashīd had just cut off the heads of a group of people.'[159] Similarly, another poet completes his recitation of a praise poem just as a Kharijite prisoner of war is brought in. The patron says to his male slave, 'Give this guy a hundred gold coins and cut off that guy's head.' The poet jumps up and says, 'Give me a break!' The patron immediately understands his consternation and laughs.[160] Patronage for insiders and violence against outsiders were complementary, and sometimes overlapping, features of social life.

The resolution of a patronage crisis may be as simple as the patron pining for the absent protégé, especially if he happens to be a particularly good companion in gatherings. Envious competitors convince the caliph al-Amīn that the poet Abū Nuwās is up to no good. He is sent away and kills time by drinking at a bar. Al-Amīn misses him and brings him back after a few verbal exchanges in which the relationship is restored.[161] In a more serious confrontation, the caliph al-Rashīd becomes angry at the musician Ibrāhīm al-Mawṣilī and has him bound and imprisoned. In a gathering the caliph says 'Is there a flaw in our gathering?' His companion says 'Yes, the absence of Ibrāhīm'. Ibrāhīm is brought in chains and unbound, and ordered to sing.[162] These resolutions show that distance in patronage relationships can work both ways. Distance is a barrier to the relationship, but absence makes the heart grow fonder. The uncertainties and complications of patronage relationships are a disruptive yet integral feature of this kind of social order. Social order is not the absence of disorder, but the management of it.

Chapters 3 to 7 investigate the use of refined rhetoric to express the uncertainty and flexibility of patronage relationships in panegyric poetry. This investigation is based on poetry by two Arabic poets of the Abbasid Empire based in Iraq, Abū Tammām and al-Buḥturī, and two Persian poets of the Ghaznavid Empire based in what is now Afghanistan, ᶜUnṣurī and Farrukhī. These poets are introduced in the next chapter.

3

INTRODUCTION TO ABŪ TAMMĀM, AL-BUḤTURĪ, ᶜUNṢURĪ, FARRUKHĪ AND THEIR PATRONS

Poems are not just exchanged *in* patronage relationships: they provide a commentary *on* them. Narratives and poetry illustrate the importance of refined rhetoric for poets who needed to negotiate uncertainty, to enable them to take advantage of the flexibility of patronage as a form of social order and use it to get ahead. Panegyric poems were presented to specific patrons at specific times, but their commentary on patronage is mostly exemplary. This exemplary quality allows poets and patrons to display their affiliation with the broader community that participated in the circulation of poetry for pay. In this exemplary discourse on patronage, poets do not so much fail to be 'original' as succeed in exploring the values of a community defined by professional identity based on acquired skills in refined rhetoric.

The four poets discussed in this chapter have a number of characteristics in common that justify a comparative study. The two Arabic poets Abū Tammām and al-Buḥturī were pioneers in the 'modern' style of Arabic poetry that came to prevail in the third century Islamic Era/ninth century CE in the Abbasid Empire of the Middle East, based in Iraq. The two Persian poets ᶜUnṣurī and Farrukhī were leaders in a new phase of Persian cultural production during the Islamic period, limited in the first centuries of Islamic rule by the widespread use of Arabic as a literary language for Persian speakers. Literary culture in Persian expanded considerably in the fifth/eleventh century under the Ghaznavid Empire of Central Asia, based in what is now Afghanistan. Arabic literary culture in the Abbasid Middle East was heavily populated with and influenced by writers, poets, and patrons of Persian descent; Persian literary culture in Ghaznavid Central Asia was, in turn, heavily influenced by literary and religious cultural production in Arabic.

All four poets are best known for the *qaṣīda* – a metered, monorhyme poem that ranges from about fifteen to over one hundred verses. The medieval Arabic and Persian *qaṣīda* is descended from early Islamic editions of pre-Islamic Arabic poetry, and also displays affinities with cultural production in Persian, Greek, Latin, and other languages that flourished in the ancient Middle East and Central Asia. This genre was a significant feature of Arabic and Persian culture, as well as Ottoman Turkish, Urdu, Punjabi, Swahili, Malay and other literatures of pre-modern Muslim communities.[1] The poems discussed in Chapters 4 to 7 are panegyric *qaṣīda*s dedicated to political elites. They begin with a love introduction, or *nasīb*, and continue with a longer praise section. Most panegyrics by the poets discussed here consist of these two main sections; panegyrics form the majority of each poet's *qaṣīda*s; and *qaṣīda*s form the majority of each poet's work. This pattern of poetic production appears in the collections of many, though by no means all, medieval Arabic and Persian poets.

The biographies of Abū Tammām, al-Buḥturī, ᶜUnṣurī, Farrukhī, and their patrons have been retold many times from very thorough research. The purpose of this chapter is not to retell them, but to survey their experiences of uncertainty and flexibility in patronage; professional identity based on refined rhetoric; and the social mobility that it facilitates. The poets are discussed in chronological order, beginning with a summary biography, followed by selected stories about each poet and his patrons.

Abū Tammām and his patrons

Abū Tammām, Ḥabīb b. Aws b. al-Ḥārith was born around 190/806 in the village of Jāsim near Damascus.[2] His father, Thādhūs, may have been a Christian, and he had a wine (or possibly perfume) shop in the city. Abū Tammām may have invented his affiliation with Ṭayyiʾ and seems to have changed his father's name, within his own name, from Thādhūs – a non-Arab and possibly Christian name – to Aws, an Arab name. His affiliation with Ṭayyiʾ eventually became accepted: being Christian would not have precluded the possibility.

Ḥabīb was apprenticed to a weaver in Damascus and then worked as a water carrier in the Great Mosque in Cairo. While doing these day jobs he seems to have learnt history, poetry, philosophy, Islamic law and the sayings of the Prophet. His first patrons were ᶜAyyāsh b. Lahīᶜa, a tax collector in Egypt, and, beginning around 214/829, Abū al-Mughīth b. Ibrāhīm al-Rāfiqī, a governor of Homs in Syria.

When the caliph Maʾmūn (r. 196–218/812–33) returned from war against the Greeks, Abū Tammām, dressed in Bedouin attire, offered him a panegyric, but the caliph did not like the idea of Bedouin reciting poetry in the urban style. Abū Tammām then sought patronage among provincial generals and rulers in northern Syria, Iraq and Armenia, and may have met al-Buḥturī in Homs during this time. Abū Tammām gained access to the caliph al-Muᶜtaṣim (r. 218–27/833–42) and after working in Baghdad and Khurasan may have joined him and his general Afshīn in the conquest of Amorium. While trapped in a snowstorm on the way from Khurasan to Iraq he used a friend's library to compile his large anthological selection. After al-Muᶜtaṣim completed the conquest of Amorium, the Muᶜtazilī judge Aḥmad b. Abī Duʾād may have been the one who sent Abū Tammām in to al-Muᶜtaṣim in Samarra, where he recited his famous poem on this conquest. After al-Muᶜtaṣim, Abū Tammām praised the caliph al-Wāthiq.

Once he started working for caliphs, Abū Tammām did not stop praising other types of patrons. He worked for the governor Mālik b. Ṭawq of al-Jazīra and the judge Ibn Abī Duʾād. He praised the general Afshīn and later congratulated the caliph on the execution of Afshīn. He had a close relationship with the secretary Ḥasan b. Wahb, who secured him an income as postmaster of Mosul at the end of his life.

In addition to his large anthological selection, the *Ḥamāsa* – a selection of mostly pre-Islamic poetry organized by genre – he compiled a shorter anthology, *al-Waḥshiyyāt*, and other selections that are mentioned in literary books of the time. His *dīwān* is among those collections of poetry that led to the most commentaries, including those by al-Ṣūlī (fourth century), al-Marzūqī (fifth century) and al-Tibrīzī (sixth century). *Al-Ḥamāsa* is also the subject of a number of commentaries, including the ones by al-Marzūqī and al-Tibrīzī. Abū Tammām died around 231/845 in Mosul.

The careers of Abū Tammām and his patrons illustrate the uncertainties of patronage. His first two recorded patronage relationships – with ᶜAyyāsh b. Lahīᶜa the Egyptian tax collector and Abū al-Mughīth al-Rāfiqī the Syrian governor – ended in disappointment, to which Abū

Tammām responded with invective.[3] His initial failure to connect with the caliph al-Maʾmūn also illustrates the element of risk in patronage. The story concerning al-Maʾmūn is not about a straightforward failure to connect. Instead, it is an indication of the problems that surrounded Abū Tammām, as a poet who was a pioneer of the 'modern' style. Later on, he also experienced conflicts with the judge Ibn Abī Duʾād over cultural issues. He praised the southern Arab confederation, which included the tribe to which Abū Tammām asserted an affiliation, over the northern confederation, to which Ibn Abī Duʾād's own tribal affiliation was linked.[4] The fact that Abū Tammām first praised the general Afshīn and later congratulated the caliph on Afshīn's execution demonstrates once again the shifting alliances of patronage.

The careers of Abū Tammām's patrons also illustrate the uncertainties of patronage relationships in politics. Ibn Abī Duʾād participated in executions of high-ranking insiders, the general Afshīn and Aḥmad b. Naṣr al-Khuzāʿī, and was a leader of the inquisition that took place 218–34/833–49, in which he oversaw the persecution of the leading jurist Aḥmad b. Ḥanbal. He participated in an alliance of administrators and Turkish military elites that selected the caliph al-Mutawakkil, only to become one of the people from this alliance whom al-Mutawakkil purged in 240/854.[5] Abū Tammām's patron and friend al-Ḥasan b. Wahb had a successful career until the caliph al-Wāthiq imprisoned a group of court secretaries and confiscated their money.[6] Ibn al-Zayyāt served as minister under several caliphs until the caliph al-Mutawakkil killed him in 233/847.[7] The minister Sulaymān b. Wahb was also purged by al-Wāthiq in 269/882.[8] The careers of these patrons show the uncertainty of literary patronage to be part of a broader pattern of instability.

In addition to instability in the politics of office, Abū Tammām's patrons faced challenges from subordinates and external adversaries. When Abū al-Mughīth al-Rāfiqī was governor of Homs, the people of the city overthrew him and the tax collector. The caliph al-Mutawakkil appointed a new governor who was also overthrown, so that the caliph ordered that three leading members of the community be whipped and, if they died, crucified.[9] Abū Dulaf al-ʿIjlī fought the Tahirid dynasty, and he and Isḥāq b. Ibrāhīm b. Muṣʿab are described as fighting the Khurrami heretic Bābak.[10] Al-Ḥasan b. Sahl fought Alid and popular revolts, and the caliph al-Wāthiq confronted rebellions in Palestine, Jordan, Syria and Arabia.[11] The politics of office defined patronage; violence disrupted it.

Patronage was a cosmopolitan context in which people from a range of backgrounds and affiliations could interact through the shared experience of refined rhetoric in poetry exchanged for pay. Abū Tammām had worked in several trades in addition to his profession as a poet. He first worked as a weaver and later as a water carrier at a mosque, where he was able to acquire the knowledge in a variety of fields that he needed to succeed as a poet. His patrons worked in a range of professions, including caliphs, provincial governors, tax collectors, ministers, secretaries, generals, and judges. They came from a variety of religious, ethnic and tribal backgrounds, and from a range of places, including Aleppo, Homs, Egypt, Khurasan and northern Iran, and al-Rahba in the Jazira. Abū Tammām himself was probably from a Christian background, as was his friend and patron al-Ḥasan b. Wahb, and Abū Dulaf was known to be affiliated with proto-Shi'ism.[12] The caliph al-Maᵓmūn contributed to the cosmopolitan nature of patronage by advocating the integration of Persian and Greek learning into intellectual discourse in the Abbasid Empire.[13] Although he attempted to impose his theological views on participants in religious discourse, often in violent ways, literary patronage appears to have carried on alongside this inquisition without direct interference.

Abū Tammām's innovations in the 'modern' style exemplified the use of refined rhetoric to express a multifaceted perspective on patronage, and to forge a cosmopolitan professional identity that could lead to social mobility. As the story of his initial attempt to connect with the caliph al-Maᵓmūn while dressed in Bedouin clothing suggests, Abū Tammām used refined rhetoric to articulate a common ground between Arab identity, which he had assumed through his assertion of a tribal affiliation, and a more cosmopolitan and professional identity, in which anyone who could master Arabic could participate. His archaic vocabulary and elaborate rhetoric, as well as his anthologies, were not an assertion of Arab identity, but about using acquired skills in refined rhetoric in Arabic.

Al-Buḥturī and his patrons

Al-Walīd b. ᶜUbayd b. Yaḥyā b. ᶜUbayd b. Buḥtur b. ᶜAtūd b. Ṭayyiᵓ was born in Manbij in Syria in 206/821 to an elite family. At around the age of 15 he went to Aleppo, where he met ᶜAlwa, the daughter of a professional singer. ᶜAlwa's mother wanted a rich man for her and chose a friend of al-Buḥturī's, who built her an enormous house. Al-Buḥturī never lost touch with Manbij and acquired property there, and started out by praising his own tribe. Al-Buḥturī may have presented his work to Abū Tammām, the leading poet of the time, in Homs. Abū Tammām was impressed and connected al-Buḥturī with patrons in Maᶜarrat al-Nuᶜmān. Al-Buḥturī returned to Manbij and then Aleppo, and may have encountered Abū Tammām for the first time at the residence of the general Abū Saᶜīd al-Thaghrī in a comic story of misrecognition. This entertaining story probably arose later than the more straightforward version.[14] Abū Saᶜīd al-Thaghrī, his first major patron, was of the same tribal affiliation as al-Buḥturī.[15]

Al-Buḥturī joined Abū Tammām as a protégé of the governor Mālik b. Ṭawq of al-Jazīra and then followed him to Baghdad, where he continued his education as a poet and member of the cultural elite. Al-Buḥturī tried to gain access to the caliph through the minister Ibn Zayyāt, but Ibn Zayyāt had offended al-Mutawakkil before his rule, so that when he took over after the death of al-Wāthiq, al-Mutawakkil had him killed. Al-Buḥturī had recourse to a family of his tribal affiliation, the Banū Ḥumayd, and left Baghdad for a while to praise al-Thaghrī again at Mosul. Al-Buḥturī did not grieve at the death of Abū Tammām in 231/845.

Upon his return to Baghdad, al-Buḥturī used Ibn al-Munajjim to get to al-Fatḥ b. Khāqān, whom he used to get to al-Mutawakkil in 233/847. He did not restrict himself to the caliph, but also continued to praise ministers, secretaries and generals. Al-Buḥturī was at the party in which al-Mutawakkil was assassinated. He quickly left town for the pilgrimage and then used the minister Ibn al-Khaṣīb to get to the new caliph, al-Muntaṣir. Later, when the subsequent caliph al-Mustaᶜīn purged Ibn al-Khaṣīb, al-Buḥturī supported al-Mustaᶜīn's effort in this regard. After praising al-Mustaᶜīn, who was removed by the Turkish military elite and replaced with al-Muᶜtazz, al-Buḥturī composed invective on him. When he received no reward for a poem for al-Muᶜtazz, he returned to Manbij. He praised the following three caliphs, though he only offered one poem to the third. He sought patronage from the provincial ruler Khumārawayh b. [Aḥmad b.] Ṭūlūn, and died in his hometown of Manbij around 284/897.

Toward the end of his life, he was accused of heresy due to some verses of elegy for friends. Though he supported Shi'ite ideas, he always went with the flow and subscribed to the ideology in power. Like Abū Tammām, he compiled an anthology called *al-Ḥamāsa* for al-Fatḥ b. Khāqān, but his selection is divided into small topics rather than broad thematic genres. He also compiled a book of poetic motifs that is lost.[16]

As one of the most successful classical Arabic panegyric poets, al-Buḥturī did not encounter a great deal of friction in his dealings with patrons. However, his repeated efforts to connect with the caliph al-Mutawakkil – first with a minister who fell out of favor and was killed, then with a family from his own tribe, and later in a second initiative with a series of two intercessors – show that even he was not insulated from the uncertainties of patronage. Similarly, al-Buḥturī headed home when he failed to secure an award from the caliph al-Muᶜtazz. As in Abū Tammām's praise of Afshīn followed by his support for his execution, al-Buḥturī is infamous for using Ibn al-Khaṣīb as an intercessor and later supporting the caliph's decision to purge him, as well as for his praise of the caliph al-Mustaᶜīn and his invective of him after he was removed from power by the military. Al-Buḥturī's use of intercession, including Abū Tammām, Ibn Zayyāt, Ibn al-Munajjim, al-Fatḥ b. Khāqān, and Ibn al-Khaṣīb, illustrates the complexity of shifting alliances in patronage. It is not a coincidence that Abū Tammām and al-Buḥturī were opportunistic in these alliances, and were also very successful. Nobody is surprised today when top lawyers represent one group or another, and by the same token, people were not surprised, though they were sometimes critical, when top poets praised one patron or another.

As with Abū Tammām, the careers of al-Buḥturī's patrons demonstrate the uncertainty of patronage in politics. Al-Mutawakkil and al-Fatḥ b. Khāqān were assassinated together in a coup.[17] Abū Nūḥ ᶜĪsā b. Ibrāhīm was arrested in 255/868 at the end of the caliph al-Muᶜtazz's reign, in an effort to confiscate money for military salaries, and later whipped to death at the beginning of al-Muhtadī's reign.[18] Although he held important positions and fought the rebel Fāris al-ᶜAbdī in 275/888, Aḥmad b. Muḥammad al-Ṭāʾī was imprisoned by al-Muwaffaq.[19] The minister al-Qāsim b. ᶜUbayd Allāh imprisoned Ibn Bisṭām in his house over a personal conflict.[20] Ismāᶜīl b. Bulbul was removed from office, plundered of his wealth, tortured and locked in shackles until he died and was buried in them, simply because a new caliph took office with whom he did not have a good relationship.[21]

Like Abū Tammām's patrons, those of al-Buḥturī had violent relationships with provincial groups. Khumārawayh b. Aḥmad and the central government in Baghdad clashed repeatedly over control of Egypt and Syria.[22] Isḥāq b. Kundāj fought on behalf of the central government against the Zanj, the Kurds, Kharijites, and a Taghlibī tribal leader until he was defeated by Khumārawayh.[23] The weak position of the caliph al-Muᶜtazz, who was enthroned by the military, and who killed two of his brothers, allowed rebellions to take root in the form of political autonomy in Egypt and southern Iran, the Kharijite movement in northern Iraq, the Alid movements in Arabia and northern Iran, and the Zanj slave revolt and religious movement in southern Iraq.[24] Literary patronage sometimes flourished because of these conflicts and sometimes in spite of them. Patronage was an alternative to violence, but was also intimately connected to it. The fact that it flourished at all is testimony to its role as a flexible form of social order that provided an alternative to violence.

Although he used members of his own tribe to get ahead at several points –including Abū Tammām, who asserted an affiliation to that tribe – al-Buḥturī's patrons display the diversity of his circle of patronage. They include al-Fatḥ b. Khāqān, who was of Central Asian Turkish descent, Ibn Nawbakht and Ibn al-Fayyāḍ of Persian descent, Muḥammad b. Badr of Arab and Persian descent, al-Khiḍr b. Aḥmad from the tribe of Rabīᶜa, Isḥāq b. Kundāj from Khazar, Muḥammad b. ᶜAbd Allāh b. Ṭāhir from Khurasan, Abū Saᶜīd al-Thaghrī from Marv, and the Turkish slave soldier Wāṣif al-Kabīr. His use of intercessors from his own tribe to expand his diverse circle of patronage displays an intersection of local and cosmopolitan identity in the use of refined rhetoric. Likewise, al-Buḥturī's lifelong bonds with his tribe and his hometown offer a counterpoint to his success in the imperial capital.

ᶜUnṣurī and his patrons

Very little is known about the life of Abū al-Qāsim Ḥasan b. Aḥmad ᶜUnṣurī before he became a poet. His relatively short collection of poetry, which may be a selection, is almost entirely dedicated to the Ghaznavid sultan Maḥmūd, his brothers Naṣr and Yaᶜqūb, and his minister Maymandī. It includes just one poem to Maḥmūd's son Masᶜūd, which may mean that ᶜUnṣurī died soon after Masᶜūd became sultan, probably before 431/1049 – a date of death that has been recorded for him. ᶜAwfī says that, in addition to panegyric, ᶜUnṣurī dedicated narrative poems to Maḥmūd and lists three titles, including one that survives – *Vāmiq va ᶜAdhrā*. Bayrūnī says that he translated the same three texts into Arabic, so it may be that these were the sources for ᶜUnṣurī's Persian versions, or vice versa.[25]

ᶜUnṣurī's career was narrower in scope than the work of the Arabic poets discussed here, but it also displays some of the same basic features of patronage. Like al-Buḥturī, ᶜUnṣurī was a particularly successful poet who did not encounter too many problems in patronage relationships. However, one legend conveys the risks of working closely with the sultan Maḥmūd. Maḥmūd ordered his favorite, Ayāz, to cut his hair. When he was sober and regretted his command, Mahmud became distraught until ᶜUnṣurī offered verses that calmed him down.[26] The story becomes a central episode in depictions of the poet.[27]

ᶜUnṣurī's patrons also experienced the uncertainties of political patronage. Yūsuf b. Sabuktegīn, the brother of the sultan Mahmud, at first supported the rule of Maḥmūd's son Muḥammad and then changed sides to support Maḥmūd's son Masᶜūd. When he took over, Masᶜūd sent Yūsuf on a distant mission so that he could consolidate his power without competition. When Yūsuf returned, Masᶜūd imprisoned him.[28]

In the Ghaznavid Empire violence was both a basis for and a threat to the power of ᶜUnṣurī's patrons. In addition to his well-known conquests in South Asia, Maḥmūd b. Sabuktegīn had to deal with competitors in the Buyid dynasty in northern Iran and the Saffarid dynasty in southern Iran.[29] Abū al-Muẓaffar Naṣr b. Sabuktegīn, another brother of Maḥmūd, became governor of the restive region of southern Iran after the Ghaznavids defeated the Saffarids there.[30]

The narrower range of patrons praised by ᶜUnṣurī does not reflect the same cultural diversity as those of the Arabic poets described in this chapter. However, the Turkish and Persian backgrounds of ᶜUnṣurī's patrons meant that they played crucial roles in the interdependence of the Turkish military and political elites and of the political and cultural elites from a Persian background. The circulation of literary patronage complemented the military, political and cultural interests that these two very different groups had in common. Sabuktegīn, the father of Maḥmūd, began his military career as a slave who was captured, trained, and sold by a Turkish tribe to a Turkish leader in the Samanid dynasty.[31] However, the dynasty that his family established greatly expanded the patronage of Persian cultural production. The image-making process by and around poets like ᶜUnṣurī helped to link Turkish military rulers to Persian cultural values and facilitated the social mobility that occurred in the integration of Turkish and Persian elites. This integration involved new connections between the Middle East and Central Asia: connections between Islam and other religions, and between imperial and tribal traditions.

The complications of integrating Persian and Turkish interests, with ᶜUnṣurī's role as a kind of power-broker of cultural production, are demonstrated by stories of the writing of Firdawsī's version of the Persian epic in the Ghaznavid court. In one story, Firdawsī, a provincial landlord, is initially held in contempt by ᶜUnṣurī, the leading poet at the Ghaznavid court. After testing Firdawsī in poetry and the history of Persian rulers, ᶜUnṣurī apologizes for the slight and commissions him to write the epic of Persian kings for the current Ghaznavid ruler, Maḥmūd, beginning with praise of Maḥmūd himself. In this story, when

Firdawsī returns with the masterpiece, he praises the minister Maymandī but ignores the palace favorite, Ayāz. Ayāz is offended and convinces Maḥmūd that Firdawsī is a proto-Shi'ite, so that Firdawsī is not rewarded until after his death.[32] Together, the two poets demonstrate the vagaries of fame and the relationship between literature and politics. Firdawsī was marginalized by the court in his own time but went on to be the more famous poet of the two; ᶜUnṣurī was central in the court and then faded into relative obscurity. The story offers a commentary on the comparison and contrast between epic, with its legendary status, and panegyric, with its gesture toward legend that remains bound to historical characters.[33] In one narrative, ᶜUnṣurī integrates Firdawsī into the panegyric scene by sitting him down for a test next to two other junior court poets, Farrukhī and ᶜAsjadī.[34] While he is integrated into the panegyric context this way, ᶜUnṣurī concludes from the test that Firdawsī is particularly well versed in the epic theme of ancient Persian kings. It seems strange for the expert in panegyric to evaluate the expert in epic on themes more closely related to the latter. The circulation of the narrative calls attention to the conjunction and disjunction of the two genres.

While Persians had played a central role in the elaboration of cultural production by and for Muslims in Arabic, in ᶜUnṣurī's time cultural production in Persian was just beginning to recover from centuries of marginalization. In addition to his role in integrating Persian and Turkish interests, ᶜUnṣurī played a role in articulating the interaction of Muslim and Persian culture in the Persian language. In this way, ᶜUnṣurī's poetry contributed to the political goals of his Turkish patrons, who aspired to consolidate orthodox Sunni Islam. While ᶜUnṣurī's poetry was about connecting Turkish rulers to Persian culture and weaving together Muslim and Persian culture in the Persian language, Ghaznavid wealth was based largely on conquests in South Asia. ᶜUnṣurī recorded these violent conquests in an idealized and stylized way in his poetry. His work combined cross-cultural cooperation with cross-cultural conflict.

Farrukhī and his patrons

Most of what is known about Abū al-Ḥasan b. Jūlūgh Farrukhī Sīstānī Sijzī comes from the essay in Niẓāmī's *Chahār Maqāla,* while a range of other sources offer details about his patrons.[35] Farrukhī was the son of a *ghulām*, probably a slave soldier, of the ruler of Sīstān, Khalaf-i Bānū, who was affiliated with the Saffarid dynasty. Farrukhī worked for a landowner and was probably his slave. He didn't earn enough to support his wife, who was also affiliated with the landowner. As a result, he left the estate and Sīstān and sought patronage from the ruler of Chaganian, Abū al-Muẓaffar Fakhr al-Dawla Aḥmad b. Muḥammad. His provincial appearance when he encountered ᶜAmīd-i Asᶜad, a member of Abū al-Muẓaffar's court, almost undermined his effort to secure patronage there. In spite of this inauspicious beginning, Farrukhī managed to impress the ruler and his court with a poem about travel from Sīstān to Chaganian, in which he referred to the overlap of the festivals of Eid and Nowruz, thereby invoking Muslim and Persian cultural contexts in his appeal for patronage. He further managed to impress the ruler with a poem about the branding grounds where the ruler was at work when Farrukhī arrived, since he needed to compose a poem on demand to prove himself. After working for this ruler, he moved on to the Ghaznavid sultan Maḥmūd (d. 421/1030), to whom most of his poems are dedicated. Farrukhī often accompanied Maḥmūd on hunting, military and other journeys and he visited Qanuj, Sumnat, Rayy, Kashmir and Gurgan during this time. His collection of poetry also included poems for Maḥmūd's two sons and successors, Muḥammad and Masᶜūd. His work shows that he sometimes experienced conflicts with his patrons. Farrukhī died sometime after 422/1031, probably around 429/1037. A manuscript of a narrative poem refers to Farrukhī, and to Maḥmūd as the patron, but a different name has been written over Maḥmūd's name and the manuscript includes a prologue dedicated to this other patron.[36]

The complications of Farrukhī's initial efforts to secure patronage from Abū al-Muẓaffar Fakhr al-Dawla demonstrate the uncertainty of patronage. Like the story about the initial rebuff of Firdawsī by ᶜUnṣurī, the arrival of Farrukhī at the Chaganian court illustrates the barriers between provincial communities and the court. In these stories, Firdawsī and Farrukhī overcome these barriers to make connections with the court.

Farrukhī's patrons confronted their own risks in political patronage. The minister Aḥmad b. Ḥasan Maymandī and the sultan Maḥmūd were nursed by the same woman and studied together as children, but this early connection did not prevent him from being deposed, having his wealth confiscated, and being imprisoned in a remote location. However, he was able to resume work at the end of his life.[37] Abū Bakr Ḥaṣīrī had problems dealing with the minister Maymandī.[38] ᶜAbd Allāh b. Aḥmad b. Lakhsan, who worked for Yūsuf b. Sabuktegīn, ran into problems after Yūsuf was imprisoned by Masᶜūd b. Maḥmūd b. Sabuktegīn. His wealth was confiscated, but he eventually made a comeback.[39] Masᶜūd, who managed to override his father's designation of his younger brother as the next ruler of the Ghaznavid Empire, had trouble maintaining control of the empire's eastern and western parts, which ranged from Iran to India. After he was defeated in the west in 431/1040, he tried to establish himself in the east but was killed by his troops.[40]

Farrukhī worked for a wider range of patrons than ᶜUnṣurī, including military and political elites of Turkish background and political and cultural elites whose background was Persian. Like ᶜUnṣurī, the circulation of his poetry contributed to the integration of the interests of these two groups and to the intersection of Muslim and Persian values in the expanding Persian cultural production of the Islamic period. Farrukhī's poetry not only negotiated cultural cooperation among Turkish and Persian elites, and between Persian and Muslim values expressed in the Persian language; it also played a significant role in the ideological articulation of the ongoing conflict between the Ghaznavid Empire and South Asia.

The stories of these four poets and their patrons illustrate the importance of refined rhetoric as a way for disparate groups to connect and work together. The instability and flexibility of patronage as a form of social order were two sides of the same coin. These stories show that the cosmopolitan integration of disparate groups in patronage was intertwined with risks for insiders and violent conflict with outsiders. The following chapter explores the way these four poets use motifs and syntax to express the uncertainty and flexibility of patronage relationships.

4

TOOLS FOR THINKING
MOTIFS AND SYNTAX

Medieval Arabic and Persian praise poets spoke of power in the vocabulary of panegyric, and configured the intimacy and distance of patronage relationships in the syntactic structures of their poetry. Patronage as a form of social order was constantly shifting as relationships formed, evolved, and ended, within a network of other relationships with peers who were allies or competitors, and other patrons and protégés. In the vocabulary and syntax of praise, poets exploited the contradiction between the hegemonic universality of moral order and the constantly changing conditions of patronage.

Segmented composition was a way for poets to investigate the texture of experience in a variety of genres.[1] This conveyed the complexity of emotional experience in the love introduction to panegyric and the shorter genre of wine poetry.[2] It drew the audience into a dynamic experience of nature in the garden introduction to panegyric, and contributed to the articulation of spiritual experience in mystical poetry.[3] The verbal expression in the discrete segments of descriptive poetry emphasizes the role of the audience in analysis and interpretation.[4] In addition to the love introduction to panegyric and the genres of short wine, mystical, and descriptive poetry, segmented composition is an important feature of the entire panegyric poem.

Panegyric poetry is recorded in the following ways: in collected works of individual poets, mostly in longer poems; in literary criticism, almost always in short segments; and in other kinds of prosimetrical works, often but not always in short segments. Each of these reuses of panegyric poetry, which was first presented to a patron orally or in writing, is an important part of literary culture in the medieval Middle East and Central Asia. In stories about poets as well as literary criticism about their work, panegyric poems were broken up by their authors and audiences, and by writers and critics.[5] Motifs and rhetorical devices, which were comprised of a verse or short sequence of verses, were probably more important than whole poems for social success.[6] This segmented composition, and the medieval Arabic and Persian critical focus on the individual verse, do not preclude the study of whole poems, but they do suggest that it is not necessarily the only way to approach this genre.[7]

In panegyric poetry, segmented composition contributed to poets' articulation of the uncertainty of patronage. The segmented quality of composition in panegyric poetry shaped the use of vocabulary and syntax, rhetorical devices and figurative language, and thematic approaches to patronage connections. One medieval Arabic critic emphasizes that description should deal with the various situations and conditions of what is described and include a variety of meanings.[8] Panegyric poets used the segmentation within the verse to introduce a topic and then comment on it, modify it, contrast it with something else, or focus on an aspect of it.[9]

Structural and ideological closure, in analyses that focus on the unity of the poem, are intertwined. An emphasis on closure can lead to the neglect of competing versions of experience in the text. Though they may be subordinate or implied, these alternative versions of experience are relevant to the text and its articulation of social life.[10] In the vocabulary and syntax of praise, poets used the segmented quality of refined rhetoric to explore the contradiction between the ideology of prosperity and the practical experience of uncertainty in patronage.

Speaking of power: motifs

Poets used the vocabulary of motifs in medieval Arabic and Persian poetry to situate the individual patron in the social order of patronage. This conventional vocabulary does not fail to be individualized: it succeeds in being communal. While each poem is deployed in a specific situation for a specific person, the commentary on patronage in panegyric poetry is more general. This genre focuses on an idealized portrayal of political power. No one – neither the poets, the audience, nor the patrons themselves – believed what was said about a patron in a literal way, because the genre was not about accurately depicting the social and historical reality of his experience.[11] Conventional expression offers an indirect commentary on social life more than a direct message about people and events. Theodor Adorno explains that the lyric work strives for the realm of the general, and that this general quality is essentially social in nature.[12] However, the general or exemplary quality of poetry is always bound up with the particular. Panegyric poets use the vocabulary of praise to make sense of the contradiction between the ideology and practice of patronage, and between intimacy and distance in the patronage relationship. The conventional motifs of desire, time, space, nature, religion, virtue, legend and violence are essential building blocks of praise in the work of Abū Tammām, al-Buḥturī, ᶜUnṣurī, and Farrukhī.

Desire is both a motif and a defining feature of medieval Arabic and Persian panegyric poetry. Many of these poets, including the four whose work is analyzed here, open most of their panegyric poems with an introductory section about love. There are important differences between the love introduction in Arabic and Persian, but in both languages it revolves around desire that remains unfulfilled, or fulfilled only in a transient way. In Arabic, this section evokes ancient poetry;[13] the poet-lover desires a woman who has left, or is about to leave with her tribe in a nomadic pattern of pastoral life in the desert. In Persian, the love introduction takes place in the court; the poet-lover desires a beautiful young person, whose gender is often unspecified and sometimes identified as male.[14] He is a slave, so he is available in theory, but in practice the game of love makes him inaccessible, or accessible only for transient pleasure. The motifs of desire that fill the opening section of the panegyric poem are a crucial feature of the contradiction between intimacy and distance in patronage relationships, and the possibilities of success and failure.

The portrayal of a beloved person is a sign of her absence and of her presence, and is tantamount to asserting a bond with her.[15] Lack of fulfillment and dissatisfaction do not simply cause desire: these experiences are inherent in it.[16] The focus of the love introduction is the one who desires, not the one who is desired, and the description of love alludes to abstract ideas about companionship, separation, consolation, and loss.[17] These ideas about love help to articulate the patronage relationship. The description of the beloved as inaccessible implies that the patron is inaccessible as well.[18] The description of the beloved, a sign of her absence and her presence, implies that in the dynamics of intimacy and distance in patronage, the patron is both present and absent for the protégé. The combination of a love introduction and a praise section in panegyric poetry is a literary expression of a broader phenomenon: the game of love as a way to hone skills in refined manners for professional relationships with patrons, protégés, and other colleagues.[19] The love introduction is a mise-en-abyme of panegyric; a way for the poem to turn back on itself and appear as a reflection that brings out the meaning of the poem.[20]

The role of the love introduction in the panegyric poem links the discourse on literary and political patronage to the broader discourse on love in love poetry, and in the narratives that complement this poetry. The theme of love in panegyric is generally not distinguished from an independent love poem.[21] The beloved's overwhelming effect on a lover does not necessarily translate into the power of the beloved. Power is not just the ability to have an effect on someone: it is the capacity to control that ability, to use it if and when a person wants to, and to achieve a desired effect.[22] In love poetry, the poet fragments the depiction of the beloved as a way of asserting control over him or her.[23] In the segmented rhetoric of the love introduction and the praise section, beloved and patron alike are emphatically present in a series of carefully wrought motifs, and implicitly absent.

In the desert imagery and motifs of the Arabic love introduction, and the garden imagery and motifs of the Persian love introduction, the natural world is an important dimension of the beloved's absent presence for the lover, and the significance of this absent presence for the patronage relationship. The representation of the beloved (female or male) as a kind of mediation between nature and culture is a persistent and important cultural construct.[24] Their representation as intermediaries between nature and culture makes them both absent and present from the point of view of patriarchal culture.[25] Images and motifs of nature in the depiction of desire link the patron to the transient fertility and seasonal changes that define the desert in Arabic poetry and the garden in Persian poetry.

Roland Barthes proposes that in descriptions of the absent beloved, the always present 'I' not only portrays the beloved, but 'is constituted only by confrontation with an always absent you.'[26] Freud's discussion of the child whose mother leaves him revolves around the child repeating the experience in play as a way of taking an active role and attempting to achieve mastery. In contrast, Lacan focuses on the fact that the object in the game represents not the mother, but a little piece of the child that 'detaches itself from him while still remaining his', and with which the child 'leaps the frontiers of his domain.'[27] The love introduction to panegyric and the motifs of desire that define it are about the poet-lover as a protégé in the social order of patronage.

Desire revolves around a beloved who is typically inaccessible, or is accessible only in a limited way, in a transient sensual or sensory experience. At the same time, the lover enjoys the beloved's presence, either in a brief experience of this kind, or in contact that is imagined, dreamed, or recollected. This intersection of the absence and presence of the beloved contributes to the combination of intimacy and distance in patronage. This beloved, probably a boy, is present for the lover, but only in a transient, sensual or sensory way:

> I have a companion, a youth with a silver body and ruby lips; wherever you see one of them, I am a seeker[28]
> What are those curls in chains that give off the fragrance of ambergris, but are not ambergris?[29]

In recollections, as in dreams and other imagined contact, the poet-lover reinforces the inaccessibility of the beloved while conjuring her presence:

> I recollected in her the branch of the *bān* tree when she appeared to strut along in beauty.
> She resembles it in shaking and bending, and she imitates it in stature and straightness[30]

The absorption of this beloved into the natural sphere complements her absence from the lover. At the same time, the animated nature imagery with which she is conjured also represents her presence for him.

Desire, in love and patronage, defines the distance between people as a chasm as well as a bridge. The poet-lover may experience his desire *for* the beloved as a kind of joyful connection *with* him or her:

> I fastened my heart upon you and in you I dispensed with the world, and my heart wanted nothing in the world but to see you[31]
> Happiness has taken shelter in my heart because of love for him, the soul of one who has a beloved like him is happy[32]

The alternation between separation and connection shapes the identity of the poet-lover, as well as the identity of the beloved and the patron:

> Ask her, how did you lose contact [and how were] the bonds of our affection cut?[33]

These identities take shape in a relational way. Compared to the praise section in panegyric, the love introduction is more explicit about the uncertainties of relationships. This poet capitalizes on that contrast to speak of his delightful praise, while also linking it to the frustrated desire of love:

> Praise of him was so sweet and pleasant that it surpassed the description of the abodes and love
> If the pillar of the *nasīb*, Kuthayyir, came upon its meanings, he would think that they were a *nasīb*[34]

The poet playfully calls attention to the role of desire in the love introduction as a feature of the commentary on patronage in panegyric. The game of love is just a game, and it is also an insight into the more serious business of patronage.

Motifs of space demonstrate the distance in relationships. In the Arabic love introduction to panegyric, which is often set in the desert, the poet-lover uses vast expanses of space to express longing in the love relationship. The poet-lover explores the dynamics of intimacy and distance in patronage through motifs expressing the distance between the lover and the beloved:

> He lent an ear to separation, deluded, and there is no avoiding the fact that distance left a remainder of derangement in his heart[35]

Distance and the animated figure of separation assert the absence of the relationship, while the derangement in the lover's heart illustrates the continuing presence of the beloved for him. In the following verse, distance emphasizes the absence of the relationship, as do the legal motifs of prohibited contact and permitted abandonment:

> She made it clear in Syria that she views contact with me as prohibited and abandonment of me as permitted[36]

At the same time, the motif of contact expresses the deferred presence of the beloved for the lover. The traces of this beloved's abode show that she and her people have moved on:

> I think that the tears upon my cheeks will remain traces of my crying in the traces[37]

However, the correspondence between the traces of tears and the traces of the abode displays the persistence of the lover's attachment to the beloved. In the Arabic introduction, place names may be 'fully imaginary locations which are nothing and nowhere … felt as "the abodes of the hearts" … of al-Mutanabbī, never seen by the poet, having no contours.'[38] Similarly, the Persian love introduction to panegyric sometimes refers to Central Asian locations that are made exotic because they are known for luxury products and beautiful people. The intersection between the absence and presence of the relationship for the lover informs the intersection of success and risk in patronage.

The patron's authority over vast areas demonstrates his power as well as potential challenges to that power:

> The governor of Basra seeks the land tax in your name, the preacher in Baghdad gives sermons in your name
> If the order to empty Iraq comes to you from the sultan, it makes the necks of those who are disobedient pliable like tendons
> The letter describing your conquest comes from Syria, and another from Egypt; Halvan is one of your resting places and Aleppo is another[39]

This description of Ghaznavid power over the western provinces begins with an assertion of existing economic and religious authority in Iraq, and continues with the possibility of resistance there, as well as a plan to deal with it. It concludes with references to two conquests. The area is not so much under control, but part of an ongoing effort to achieve control.

Natural fertility evokes success in patronage. Nature images also relate to seasonal change, conveying the changing conditions of relationships in patronage. Nature description in this poetry is not about a natural sphere that is beyond human experience. Human culture in this poetry is defined by the natural world and also threatened by it, insofar as it becomes a way to express the instability of patronage.[40] The power of nature, both essential to human life and a source of destruction, alludes to the uncertainties of patronage as a form of social order.[41]

In the overlap between nature and human culture in panegyric poetry, fertility asserts success in patronage while the transience of fertility also refers to the contingency and uncertainty of patronage relationships:

> When a stranger descends with them, they nourish him with verdant meadows in which the herbage has sprouted up yet remains untouched[42]

Rainfall and the sea in the following verses refer to successful patronage. At the same time, the temporary abundance of rainfall implies the instability of patronage, as does the danger and unpredictability of the sea:

> Qualities like downpours from which gifts pour forth like abundant wells [that collect water from] the torrents that follow the rain[43]
> You have a heart like the sea and a hand like a cloud; from the former you scatter pearls and from the latter you rain gold[44]

Lightning may come from rain clouds or rainless clouds, a commentary on the possibilities of success and failure in patronage:

> I keep watch on lightning in rainless clouds of theirs, and does anyone notify us of lightning in a cloud that does not rain?[45]

Like images of the natural sphere on earth, images of the cosmos assert success in patronage relationships, while the changing and cyclical qualities of the cosmos also imply instability:

> They have noble men who, when their overwhelming brilliance lights up, are thought to be rivals of the stars[46]
> When he appears and the greatness of kingship covers him, you deem him to be the moon whose fullness has completed its beauty[47]

The brilliance of the moon and stars implies the patron's role in a successful relationship. However, this brilliance is only visible on clear nights, so that these images also imply uncertainty. The motif of time allows the poet-lover to explore intimacy and distance in the love relationship and in patronage:

> And it [the abode] showed you well-being, and did it ever, when life was fresh and time was a youth
> Years of contact whose extent the recollection of distance makes forgotten, so that it is as if they were days
> Then days of abandonment commenced, that followed up with lovesickness, grief, and it was as if they were years
> Then these [years] and their people came to an end, and it was as if those years and their people were dreams[48]

Time as a youth evokes the pleasure of the relationship as well as the fact that it is caught up in the flow of time. The years of pleasure turned into days, and the days of separation turned into years, conjure the presence of the relationship while asserting its absence.

The patron may be a refuge from the vicissitudes of time. However, the motif of time also suggests that the patron, like everyone else, is caught up in the flow of time, so that his participation in a successful patronage relationship is subject to change: 'When we are in a vicissitude of time that is rough, his moral qualities are smooth.'[49] The motif of the turn in power displays the patron's political authority, and it also shows that this authority is caught up in the flow of time:

> The Omnipotent has made his turn in power solid in eternal permanence as long as his customs form the structure of kingship[50]
> O master of the sultan's turn in power, supplicate for him in every prayer, for he is worthy of supplication
> Be enemies with the enemies of his turn in power, since his turn in power is your turn in power[51]

When the turn in power appears in conjunction with the natural cycle, natural fertility implies the patron's prosperity:

> The new year in the new garden is a new turn in power and happiness; each new, they become foundations for the new turn in power[52]

Changing natural conditions imply the temporary quality of prosperity.

Religious motifs demonstrate that, according to panegyric poets, the patron's legitimacy comes from God:[53] poets make the patron into one of God's favorite people. They also use motifs of religion to imply the contrast between divine power and the worldly power of the patron:

> O you whose ways are those of Muḥammad and whose name is Muḥammad, everything that derives from Muḥammad derives from the religion of the Lord[54]
> Around the world there is no *minbar* other than the king's throne for the sermon of kingship[55]

These combinations of religious authority and the patron's worldly power reinforce the reliance of the patron on the poet to construct the patron's special relationship with religion in rhetoric. The following example clarifies that the poet links divine power and the patron's power in rhetoric, while the two kinds of power are quite distinct in experience:

> You think that his hand on the day of generosity is the spring of Kawthar, and it is not Kawthar[56]

In the following verse, the poet emphasizes that while the patron is one of God's favourites, he is still just another one of His people:

> O commander of the faithful, you are the most contented of God's servants with Him[57]

In this poetry, God is the best source for the qualities of the patron: 'God gave the king an internal quality greater than which he has no external quality.'[58] However, everything that God bestows on people is always on loan, contingent upon their performance. As a result, when the poet explains that God gave the patron his qualities, he also implies that his possession of them is contingent upon good behavior and therefore subject to change.

The permanent quality of the divine order of things shores up the practice of patronage, but it can also be at odds with the temporal quality of this practice. The following example turns God's contingent benefits for the patron into a kind of three-way financial transaction:

> God recompensed a hand that, in filling [others] with prosperity, sought the destruction of money when money was sleeping[59]

The patron's special relationship to God in this verse is contingent upon his deeds in the social order of patronage. This makes the special relationship something that is reiterated and reiterable. The following verse links the people, the patron and religion. However, it does so in the context of the turn of power, which is caught up in the flow of time and subject to change:

> In his security is everyone's security, and in his endurance is the endurance of the turn in power of Islam[60]

Religious motifs are a crucial feature of hegemonic universality as a dimension of successful patronage, but they also demonstrate the incommensurability of the temporal practice of patronage and any assertion of universality. In theory, religion and patronage are interdependent, but in practice they don't fit together very well.

Religion mediates between patronage, as a form of social order, and violence. Violence is an alternative, for situations in which patronage is not a realistic option, and a threat to the peace of that social order. In these descriptions, poets use religion to assert the patron's status as a successful participant in patronage. They also use the military and religious threat to demonstrate the risks to that status:

> He was like the calf by which the people of the Time of Impetuous Ignorance were deceived, and you were Moses who guided the people who were ignorant[61]
> The eye of religion was soothed at Qurran when the eyes of polytheism were swollen and cut out at al-Ashtarayn[62]
> So that religion on every horizon is laughing and joyful, and unbelief in every land is frightened and timid[63]
> When you saw religion's heart beating rapidly, when unbelief was strutting and insolent[64]

In each of these verses, the patron's religious status is rhetorically intertwined with the military and religious threat. In religious motifs, the specific crises of violence are complemented by the more widespread uncertainties of patronage:

> God sufficed for you in that which you fear, and He covered you with the shade of His benefit[65]

God is there for the patron, but His presence in this poem is about highlighting the risks of patronage.

Virtue is a dimension of religious discourse, but it also transcends religious boundaries. As a poetic motif, virtue is descended from pre-Islamic Arabic and Persian culture. The identification of the patron with abstract virtues helps to define his success in patronage. In addition, the identification of the patron with such virtues, like the description of the patron in religious motifs, implies the incommensurability between the unchanging quality of abstract virtues and the changeable quality of the patron's behavior. The medieval Arabic critic Qudāma b. Jaᶜfar, based on his study of the philosopher al-Fārābī, thinks that virtue and vice are not innate, although there could be a natural predisposition to virtue and vice. However, one cannot be praised for a natural predisposition, but only for repeated actions.[66] In the following examples, patrons are identified with timeless virtues due to their good deeds. The fact that their deeds take place over time also implies that their identification with virtues is subject to change:

> When he opened his hand, you called it generous and rightly so; the reputation for generosity of the river, cloud, and sea is slandered[67]
> O you who possess the first and last of the most noble deeds, and by the generosity of whose hands the example is set[68]

The virtues may be timeless, but the identification of the patron with them is not.

The patron is normally a good person in this poetry, and rhetorical intersections between his virtue and the vice of others reinforce that point. In addition, the contrast between the virtue of the patron and the vice of others refers to risk in the social order of patronage:

> Upon him is a sign of greatness by which he was distinguished from those good-for-nothings who are heedless of greatness[69]
> Wherever there is unhelpfulness, it becomes victory with his justice; wherever there is victory, it becomes unhelpfulness without his resolve…
> O lord of lords of kingship and leadership, leadership and kingship are loss without your management[70]

The vice of others is not outside of the dynamics of patronage as a form of social order; it is an integral yet disruptive feature of this order:

> The soul of the miser protected the soul of the generous man from the fates and their calamities[71]

Identity in patronage is relational, and just as the patron becomes a patron through his interaction with a protégé, a virtuous person becomes a virtuous person in contrast with, and in conjunction with, good-for-nothings.

Sometimes the identification of the patron's deeds with timeless virtues is inverted, with the poet using the deeds to define the virtues instead of using the virtues to define the deeds. These hyperbolic descriptions reinforce the attribution of the virtue to the patron based on his deeds. A central feature, and problem, of panegyric poetry is the incommensurability of hegemonic universalities, such as timeless virtues, and temporal practice, such as deeds. In these hyperbolic descriptions of timeless virtues defined by deeds instead of vice versa, it is as if the poet acknowledges the difficulty of getting from the particular to the universal, and takes a new angle by going from the universal to the particular. While this tactic does not solve the problem, it offers a new perspective on it:

> Eternity relies upon the impressions that he leaves [of deeds or words]; generosity leans upon his hands [lit. fingers][72]
> The apex of glory for Iyād, wherever it rises, is with him, and it has from him structure and supports[73]

This angle on the problem of universalities and temporal deeds reflects the use of panegyric for social mobility, as the following example shows:

> In refined manners, a student of relationships; when you look more carefully, you are the cause of your own virtues
> Both the lord of generosity and the lord of speech, both the lord of the sword and the lord of individual merit...
> There is no king like you among kings of the world; O king, the noble descent of kingship originates with you[74]

In the social order of patronage, a person who is a cause of his own virtues is, in a sense, a self-made man.

The goal of the panegyric is to transform the particular deeds of the patron into a hegemonic universality of legendary proportions.[75] Poets describe their patrons in conjunction with legendary figures, linking their deeds here and now with the vastly greater significance of legend. This kind of description amplifies the patron's deeds while also contrasting their performance with their legendary counterparts:

> If Sulaymān bound the wind beneath his saddle when he set out on a journey
> The commander has also bound the head of the blowing wind in his stirrup when he travels[76]
> And if he declares what he knows [in] a meeting on a day of distinguishing between the true and the false, you see the like of Luqmān the wise[77]

As in the identification of the patron with the eternal validity of religion or timeless virtues, the identification of the patron with a legendary figure is a gesture toward universality that is bound up with a look back at the more humble reality of the particular. Likewise, as with the use of particular deeds to define timeless virtues, the hyperbolic assertion that the patron surpasses the legendary figure can reinforce the patron's power. Unlike Bahman, Kaykhusraw, and Isfandyār learning from Rustam, this patron does not need to study with Rustam, or with anybody else, to know everything:

> When Bahman became the student of Rustam for a time, until his qualities became flawless and his deeds choice
> Just as Rustam-i Dastān taught culture and refined manners to Kaykhusraw and Isfandyār the hero
> You too have known from intellect every aspect of culture, without humbling yourself as a student and without any effort[78]

Like the description of the patron as someone who causes his own virtues, describing him as someone who knows everything without studying with Rustam is a way of saying that he is self-made.

Motifs of violence are akin to motifs of nature. Just as the combination of fertility and change in nature motifs implies success and instability in patronage, the combination of victory and danger in the description of violence alludes to the prospect of success and the risk of failure. Violence is an alternative to the often unpleasant but essentially peaceful social order of patronage. While the experience of violence is not part of patronage, motifs of violence in the panegyric poems that were exchanged for pay are a part of patronage discourse. Hannah Arendt explains that violence is not easily contained in human plans made in advance, or in analyses after the fact:

> Moreover, while the results of men's actions are beyond the actors' control, violence harbors within itself an additional element of arbitrariness; nowhere does Fortuna, good or ill luck, play a more fateful role in human affairs than on the battlefield, and this intrusion of the utterly unexpected does not disappear when people call it a 'random event' and find it scientifically suspect; nor can it be eliminated by simulations, scenarios, game theories, and the like. There is no certainty in these matters, not even an ultimate certainty of mutual destruction under certain calculated circumstances.[79]

The soldiers in these examples are the patron's own soldiers:

> Lions of death lurking in concealment, with no thickets but swords and spears[80]
> They entered into the fray without turning aside or being put to flight, and they greeted death without men leaning insecurely on their mounts or unarmed men[81]

These descriptions demonstrate the patron's power over his adversaries, imply the dangers that led him to deploy his army, and allude to the risks of employing these men, especially in the context of keeping the army happy in the history of the medieval Middle East and Central Asia (and other medieval societies). Within this context, the description of the men as 'lions' in the first example reinforces their fighting prowess while alluding to the challenge of keeping them under control. Likewise, the deferred possibility of cowardice in the second example reinforces the description of bravery, and also implies the challenge of keeping the army motivated.

Motifs of violence sometimes portray the close connection between the two very different experiences of violence and the social order of patronage:

> He increases cheerfulness when he is in the gathering; he adorns the army when he is on the battlefield[82]

This verse shows that violence and patronage are complementary. It is this complementary quality that explains the following verse:

> When his sword became ruler over skulls, his forgiveness became a ruler over the sword[83]

Just as patronage can give way to violence, violent conflict can give way to the peaceful social order of patronage – at least in poetry. The conventional vocabulary of panegyric poetry, including motifs of desire, time, space, nature, religion, virtue, legend and violence, implies the possibility of success and the risk of failure in patronage relationships.

Configurations of intimacy and distance: syntax

Formal features of syntax are not an escape from social experience, but an important way into it. Medieval Arabic and Persian panegyric poets used the configuration of the vocabulary of praise in syntax to compare and contrast the possibilities of patronage. For the medieval Arabic literary critic and theologian al-Jurjānī, what matters in discourse is not what is predicated, but the act of predication and the configuration of elements into a form. This form, which is bounded by the conscious intention of the speaker, includes both the intellectual experience and the linguistic expression of it, and this critic seems to suggest that thought and expression are two sides of the same process.[84] Like the vocabulary of praise, the configuration of praise in syntax offers insights into the possibilities of success and failure, intimacy and distance in patronage relationships. This discussion of the syntax of praise looks at how Abū Tammām, al-Buḥturī, ᶜUnṣurī, and Farrukhī articulate motifs of praise using questions, negation, conditionals, and proverbs; the vocative, exclamations, and the nominative; and verbs in the indicative, imperative, and optative moods.

Questions offer an open-ended approach to the possibilities of patronage. In many cases, questions in panegyric are rhetorical questions, in which the obvious answer derives from the conventions of praise poetry. Paul de Man points out that rhetorical questions work in two ways, since the literal meaning demands a clarification that is defined as unneeded in the rhetorical meaning. For de Man, this type of tension means that the rules of syntax are combined with the creative possibilities of figurative language.[85] The literal meaning of a rhetorical question can conjure the possibilities of the presence and absence of fulfillment in love, even while the figurative meaning conveys the lover's frustrated desire: 'Is youth approaching me, its days returning for me at the end of my days?'[86] The literal meaning of this question implies that the pleasures of youth may or may not be in store for the aging poet-lover, while the rhetorical meaning clarifies that the pleasures of youth are over. At the same time, the literal meaning of the question is figurative: it is as if youth may or may not return. The rhetorical meaning is literal: youth never comes back once it's gone. In the context of panegyric, this interplay of pleasure that is deferred, oscillating between past and future, permanent and temporary deferral, expresses the uncertainty of patronage relationships.

> What spell have you cast on me that I gave you my heart? Why did I give my heart to the wind in vain for the sake of your spell?[87]

The literal meaning of these questions asserts that the experience of unrequited desire is mysterious and even incoherent, but the rhetorical meaning implies that it is the convention of being unable to resist the beloved that leads to this predicament. This rhetorical meaning also has a literal dimension in the rules of the game of love: the literal meaning has a figurative dimension, in the poet-lover pretending that he doesn't know what's going on. In the context of patronage, the poet asks 'Why do I get myself into these difficult situations?', and also asserts, 'Because it's the best way for me to get ahead'.

The rhetorical questions of praise articulate success in patronage, for patron and poet alike, as well as problems that can impact the relationship:

> He keeps the hearts of the people and the wealth of the commander,
> where is such an effective person to be found on the horizon?[88]

The rhetorical meaning, that of course there is no one like the patron, insists on his unmatched superiority. The literal meaning implies that the poet and others are always on the lookout for other options.

> So when will I water my ambition by meeting you? My speech and
> use of language awaken others[89]

In this verse, the rhetorical meaning ('I will get through to you pretty soon given my track record') is weak. The literal meaning ('When will it work out?') carries more weight.

> After tribes have made their mark on my page, and I knew the land
> inside out with insightful knowledge,
> Does the miser hope to deceive or trick me so that I will offer praise
> to him for free?[90]

The rhetorical meaning ('No way!') opens out onto the literal meaning ('Is it possible for me to be deceived?'). In this question, the rhetorical meaning is also literal, since the social order of patronage includes checks and balances that prevent poets from giving their valuable commodity to people who will not pay. However, the deferred possibility of the literal meaning, 'Could I be deceived?', impinges on the rhetorical meaning, 'No way!'. These questions insist on the success of the exchange and suggest the multiple possible outcomes of appeals for patronage.

Poets also use questions to absorb the danger of violence into the social order of patronage:

> They sought to escape, and how can a group that is wanted by God and the ruler escape?[91]

The poet says 'Of course they can't escape – or could they?'.

> How is it that they did not accept [surrender and] security, when there was life for the like of them in [surrender and] security?[92]

In this verse, the poet expresses amazement at the foolish resistance of the patron's opponents, as well as consternation about their decision not to make a move from conflict to the social order of patronage. Questions can also address future conflict:

> With his ambition and turn in power and wisdom, who would oppose him and rise up against him?[93]

No one would ever dream of it, but perhaps someone will, and it's just a question of who and when.

Negated statements express the success of patronage by presenting and denying other possibilities. Emile Benveniste follows up on Freud's observation about negation, explaining that it is a way of first asserting or accepting a proposition in order to negate it.[94] Negation can link the poet-lover's hope and his hopelessness in the prospects for fulfillment: 'Do not, you two, think that Hind is the only one who is deceitful by nature; every young girl is Hind'[95] The poet-lover's interlocutors dare to hope for a faithful beloved and the poet dashes their hopes. Although the poet-lover's view is the dominant one, the negated view is entertained as well.

Poets can use negation to present two ways of thinking about patronage and deny one of them. These patrons manage their relationships effectively, and the use of negation reinforces that fact. The description also refers to potential problems that can arise:

> He is not foolish when he gives rewards; he does not rush when he metes out punishment[96]
>
> My hope in you is not weak, and my supposition of its success is not false[97]
>
> He does not mix betrayal with fidelity, nor does he sell the familiarity of companions for boredom[98]

In the following examples, the poet intensifies the patron's positive impact by juxtaposing it to a view of the world without him. These descriptions portray the chaos of violence that is the alternative to patronage, an external threat that constitutes the boundaries of social order:

> The world without you is the devil's plunder; the wolf tears apart the lamb when there is no shepherd[99]
> If not for his benefit and if not for the sword of his vengeance, the mill of religion and this world would revolve around people's bereavement of their most cherished loved ones[100]

As with the use of questions in praise, in negation the poet can insist that the patron really stands out, while also presenting the deferred possibility of competition:

> O you for whom sovereignty never seeks a substitute, O you who, among sovereigns, is the one who is [most] appropriate for kingship[101]
> I, who have become known to worship him, do not bend my back to worship everyone[102]

Poets use negation to make sense of what the patron, the patronage relationship and the social order of patronage are not. They also express their awareness of the risks involved in patronage.

Conditional sentences allow poets to impose the sequential logic of the conditional on the sometimes unpredictable experience of patronage. Counterfactual conditionals in the love introduction may focus on the poet-lover's frustrated desire as well as the fulfillment that might have been:

> O ᶜAlwā, if you wanted to, you would change rejection into contact for us, and your hard heart would soften for one who is lovesick[103]

The poet-lover's hopelessness about the situation is intensified by thinking of the happiness that might have been. In the following verse, the poet-lover hopes for a chance to confront time itself, which he holds responsible for the departure of the beloved ones with their tribe:

> If time returned an answer, or held back its long censure I would censure it for two effaced traces at Amra, of Zaynab and Rabāb[104]

The poet-lover's counterfactual conditional statements emphasize the importance of hope for success even in the most inauspicious situations. At the same time, the counterpoint between the love introduction and the praise section implies the importance of the poet knowing when to walk away. The poet in effect walks away, from his poet-lover persona and the beloved, to his poet persona and the patron. If the patron acts like a beloved, the poet can walk away from him too.

Like the use of negation to juxtapose the patron with the world without him, counterfactual conditionals can contrast the patron's success with a world of chaos:

> If not for his resolve, the turn in power would not proceed, and if not for his determination, the kingdom would not be stable[105]
> If not for the commander of the faithful and his beneficence, the saffron dye on the collars of garments would be blood[106]

The alternatives of violence and disorder are a crucial feature of the articulation of patronage. However uncertain and unstable this social order may be, it compares favorably with the alternatives.

Similarly, in factual conditionals, the poet can form a logical sequence from disorderly conditions to the social order of patronage embodied in the patron:

> When the favors of God fled like wild animals, you were allowed, in spite of time, to enjoy them as if they were domesticated[107]
> When the tribe is incapable of bearing what is right, he stands firmly for it with a strong voice, not in a subdued way[108]

The patron's identity and the social order of patronage take shape within the context of these disorderly conditions. Poets can also use factual conditionals to impose logic on the threat that violence represents:

> If his adversary makes his body of iron in combat, the soft wind becomes a file as it passes over his body[109]

In the logic of the conditional statement, violence is no longer an unpredictable threat. It all makes sense when it is repackaged in panegyric. The less immediate but more ominous threat of just thinking about disobedience can also be dismantled as it is incorporated into panegyric:

> If someone thinks of anything but obeying him in his heart, the hair upon his body becomes like an informer[110]

The threat is displayed yet subordinated to the logic of the conditional.

Finally, in the following example, the poet uses the conditional to explore the conditions of representation in panegyric:

> When thoughts revolve around you, they perceive that your noble qualities are not encompassed by thought[111]

On the one hand, in praise, the poet takes control of the representation of the patron in the patronage network. On the other hand, in this representation, the poet assigns a hegemonic universality to the patron by way of his specific thoughts and the verbal expressions that result from them. This universality and the specifics of thought (and speech) don't fit together neatly. In the conditional statement, the poet shows that the representation of the patron in panegyric is a continuous effort to fit these things together that does not work.

Proverbs, or *gnomai*, are universal and independent of time and specific experience. However, they also provide a context for references to the patron.[112] Proverbs are laws of experience that fit into the universal aspirations of panegyric poetry. They do not fit well because they contain, or are juxtaposed with, different points of view. Proverbs make frustrated desire the rule of the game of love, but they can also evoke the deferred possibility of pleasure:

> The deceitfulness of the promise from her unbinds my determination, and the sweetest of women's promises are the deceitful ones[113]
> The censurers despaired of curing my intoxication; the intoxication of vehement passion is the most deadly intoxication[114]

The laws of love are contradictory, and this perspective on relationships shapes the experience of patronage.

In less explicit ways, the laws of patronage are contradictory as well. This patron has achieved success because of his good fortune, but he also has to work hard to achieve it:

> One upon whom the *homā* casts an auspicious shadow arrives through hard work at nobility and command[115]

On the one hand, he is a self-made man; on the other hand, his success is contingent upon his good fortune. In the following proverb, appearances can be a good thing, but action is what matters:

> The beauty of an embellished sword is in its silver [when it is] worn, and its cut is in its blade[116]

The juxtaposition of appearances and deeds implies the use of close observation to sort out appearances and realities in political life, and the complexities of analyzing and predicting the course of relationships.[117]

Proverbs, as laws of experience, make experience predictable but that can be of limited usefulness. This proverb portrays danger – probably meaning the violence that is an alternative to patronage or the risks within the social order of patronage itself – and an approach to dealing with it:

> They say that the one who seeks danger without resolve ends up in the midst of danger because of his wish[118]

The patron can avoid the worst of the storm by deploying the virtue of resolve, but not the storm itself. In the following proverb, what is predictable about experience, and patronage in particular, is its unpredictability:

> Indeed annihilation comes to the blameworthy with full stomachs and to the noble who are hungry[119]

The same is true in the following pair of proverbs:

> All of the qualities of the one who does not surrender to the vicissitudes become vicissitudes for him
> And the sword called fate could miss, and the triumphant man could return disappointed[120]

The first proverb explains that qualities are like vicissitudes for people who do not surrender to the vicissitudes; the second proverb shows that it doesn't matter what you do. The awareness that it doesn't matter what you do means surrendering to the vicissitudes: so the second proverb actually explains the first. These proverbs are laws that reveal the lawlessness of experience, whether the social order of patronage or the alternative of violence.

When proverbs fill half a verse and specific experience related to them fills the other half, poets call attention to the disjunction between hegemonic universality and particular experience in this genre. As in genitive metaphors (such as the hand of fate), this kind of verse makes the abstract proverb concrete in experience, and transposes concrete experience into an abstract law in the proverb. This general statement is paired with a comment that solicits the participation of the audience:

> The heart of the lover is that which is never without love, O pity a heart that goes after love[121]

This law turns the temporal experience of love into endless desire that the poet-lover carries inside of him, regardless of specific circumstances. If the general statement transposes specific experience into a law, the exclamation of pity turns the law about the lover's inner state into a shared emotional experience. Endless desire is unfulfilled but becomes an end in itself, like the ongoing effort to maintain and begin relationships in patronage.

General statements combined with specific experience can be a way to view the patron's power from ideal and practical angles at the same time. This specific experience of God granting power to the patron is linked to an abstract law of experience:

> God gave [the caliphate] to you [all], knowing you [all], and God gives to whomever he wants and prohibits[122]

This law of experience clarifies that the patron's power is contingent upon God's wishes, and that God can just as easily take it away if He sees fit. Similarly, the following verse combines a general statement that people in power get what they want with the specific experience of God granting the patron a turn in power:

> Everyone whose turn in power is youthful arrives at every object of desire; God has given him a turn in power that is victorious and youthful[123]

Repetition of the word 'youthful', associated with fertility and prosperity, complements the link between the general and the specific. While everyone in power gets what they want, the patron's power is contingent upon God, and is identified as a turn in power.

A proverbial statement can be a coping strategy for a difficult specific experience. The fact that people envy him demonstrates this patron's success, but envious people are also a risky feature of patronage:

> And how many a person is envious of you, and in a little envy there is a bounty for the one who envies[124]

The proverbial statement absorbs the risk of envy into an assertion of the benefit that envy brings to the envied person's reputation. Abstract, general statements allow poets to acknowledge and work through the risks and uncertainties of patronage.

The vocative emphasizes the relationship of the speaker to the interlocutor. Emile Benveniste explains that it is in and through language that the subject is constituted, and in particular, in the dialogue of 'I' and 'you'.[125] The vocative simultaneously intensifies the presence of the speaker and the interlocutor and asserts their distance from each other. The vocative enables poets to affirm the identity of the poet-lover and the identity of the beloved in a relational way, while also acknowledging the distance between them:

> O traces of [the abode of] Hind, you are a poor compensation for Hind; did you exchange the black-eyed [lit. black-and-white-eyed] women for onagers and ostriches?[126]

The vocative address of the traces elaborates on the multi-dimensional quality of this motif. The vocative makes the traces emphatically present for and distant from the speaker, just as this motif, as 'compensation' for the beloved, conjures her presence and displays her absence. At the same time, she is also 'exchanged' for the wild onagers and ostriches that now populate the abandoned abode. The beautiful young people in heaven also have black-and-white eyes, a further layer of the poet-lover's articulation of the sensual presence and inaccessibility of his beloved. Onagers are an old image for a poet's camel, also referring to an assertion of life in its escape from a hunter and its appearance with female onagers. Ostriches are yet another old image for a poet's camel that connotes life and fertility, often hastening back to look after their eggs. The traces left behind by the tribe, and the wild onagers and ostriches – whose family life echoes community life in counterpoint to individual, romantic desire, while also complementing desire through references to fertility – lend the beloved a flickering presence for the poet-lover. The vocative address of the traces frames and complements the complexity of these layers of imagery.

The vocative can have a similar framing effect in the very different context of the Persian love introduction. The tiny mouth of the beloved is one of his or her alluring features. The paronomasia on the tiny mouth of the beloved, and the heart of the lover that is constricted by longing, displays the intersection of sensory pleasure and emotional distance in the relationship:

> Do not make my heart constrict [give pain to my heart] so much all the time, O idol with a tiny mouth, O beautiful and cherished countenance[127]

The vocative address of the beloved as an idol and a beautiful face contributes to their presence and distance. The idol is both a sign of the beloved's presence and his absence. It alludes to the often violent Muslim hegemony in other religious communities of Central and South Asia, as well as cultural exchange with these communities and their pre-Islamic heritage in the region. The image of the idol for the beloved, who was often a slave, evokes the capture of members of these communities as well as their impact on the Muslim and Persian culture of the Ghaznavid Empire. The idol image effaces and alludes to the divine referents of idols. The idol image for the beloved, with its many layers, is set in counterpoint to the much more straightforward motif of the beautiful face. While the idol image is a trajectory toward the Ghaznavid imagination of distant places, pre-Islamic time, other religions, conquered peoples, and aspirations for conquest, the face is simply a face. Like an idol, the face is cherished or valuable. Emotional experience takes off into cultural conflict and exchange in the idol image, and returns to the body of the beloved in the motif of the face. The use of the vocative address for the idol and the face, two radically different ways of thinking about the beloved, joins these two expressions of desire and highlights the contrast between them.

The vocative affirms the identity of the poet and the patron in a relational way, while displaying the distance between them, and offers this relation in language as a commentary on the possibilities of intimacy and distance in patronage in general. The poet may express this relational identity in the vocative with an awareness of the complications that can arise in the interaction. In this verse, the reference to kingship that never seeks a substitute for the patron shores up the link established by the vocative and alludes to the risk of competition:

O you for whom sovereignty never seeks a substitute, O you who are [best] suited among kings for kingship[128]

In the following vocative relation between poet and patron, the threat is the wayward people who are not integrated into patronage:

O king who selects knowledge and is pure of religion, the people of [wayward] desire are held in contempt because of your religion[129]

The trajectory of desire that is implied by the vocative establishes the identity of poet and patron in a relational way, while they both look aside to consider the people who have opted out of the social order of patronage. The following poet–patron relation established by the vocative alludes to the image of rain for the benefit of patronage:

O Abū Muslim, turn east and look up at the flashing lightning
Soaring, it presents itself across the night like the presentation of morning[130]

However, the poet uses the vocative to define their relationship with a shared view of lightning, not rain. Lightning may come from rain clouds or rainless clouds, suggesting the possibilities of success and failure in patronage. The poet–patron relation in the vocative can be a way for the poet to shore up the patronage relationship against the onslaught of competition:

O Mūsā b. Ibrāhīm, [here is] the appeal of one who drinks [only] once in five days
whose thirst is that of blame, not [thirst due to lack of access to] drinking water
One who is hardened against the censure of the vicissitudes when they strike,
though he is not hardened against the censure of companions[131]

The image of an arduous desert journey for the poet's difficulties complements the affirmation of the presence of the poet and patron for each other and also displays the distance between them. The vocative relation is an intimate alternative to the alienation that is expressed with the image of the desert journey.

Exclamations turn up the volume of whatever the poet is saying, and increase the intensity of assertions of success in patronage as well as the potential for failure. Exclamations reinforce the poet-lover's frustrated desire, and also serve as an affirmation of the poet-lover's relationship to the beloved:

> How many a night did I stay awake over you, and [how many a] pain of love for you do I conceal[132]

This poet-lover has been sleepless, not once or even many times, but so many times that he can't begin to count them. In his exclamations over how bad it can get, the poet-lover shows how much his love matters.

Exclamations increase the volume of praise and the risks that it involves. The exclamations addressed to this patron link the increased volume of praise to the seasonal change and transient fertility of spring, and the cyclical motion of the heavens:

> Bravo, you are a king from whose wisdom the new spring season derives all of this brilliance[133]
> Felicitations for Yamīn al-Dawlat, the one with lofty stars and a record of great deeds[134]

The following exclamation emphasizes the uncountable benefits of the patron, as well as the uncountable times that the poet has managed to avoid behaving badly toward him:

> How many a benefaction like abundant rainfall have you given me, finding in me no ingratitude and no failure to acknowledge your favors[135]

The risk of bad behavior is realized in the following verse, but on the part of the patron, not the poet:

> Excellent you are, a noble man, even if you almost constricted my affairs and obliterated my reputation[136]

In this case, the clear contrast between the exclamation and the bad behavior shows the flexibility of patronage relationships.

Exclamations can be a way to expand on and reinforce the risks that the patron faces. This exclamation turns specific problems into an uncountable series of confrontations with time:

> How many a calamity rained forth upon him that was then cleared away, and both God and you are praised for clearing it away
> And how many a time was he a morsel for the vicissitudes, so that they all became toothless and unable to chew his flesh[137]

Violence, though outside of the social order of patronage, defines the identity of the patron in the following verse:

> What a mill of kindled battle you are, when spears flow with the last of the blood of necks[138]

Similarly, these patrons derive their status in praise from the exclamation about the uncountable men they have destroyed:

> What great men the Banū ᶜAbd al-ᶜAzīz are, for how many a great man among enemies, who holds his head high in arrogance, have they destroyed[139]

Exclamations about violence outside of patronage turn up the volume of the social order as well as the challenges to it. In exclamations that involve repeated actions, the poet can express constant prosperity as well as persistent risks.

Nominative expressions, especially when they occur at the head of a line, reinforce the presence of the patron and the prospect of success in patronage. The emphatic presence of the beloved is often at odds with the oscillation between presence and absence that the description implies:

> A sun that shone before the sun, when she appeared while traveling in their departing group, in covered camel saddles strapped to the burdens on the mounts[140]

As a sun that outshines the sun, the beloved is overwhelmingly and emphatically present for the lover. At the same time, the sun is visible only by day, so that the nominative expression combines her presence and her absence on the day of departure. The beloved women in the following verse are emphatically present in the nominative expression of the image at the head of the line, but they have been absorbed into the natural sphere, so that they are also absent for the poet-lover:

> Antelopes that refused that sadness should leave any endurance for me, and [my] eye is a spring with rushing water of yearning[141]

The presence of the beloved in the nominative expression is set in counterpoint to imagery that implies her absence in the following verse:

> A visitor in dreams who flees one who is awake, and her contact approaches with sleep[142]

She is present for the lover, but only as a visitor; available to him, but only in dreams. The nominative expression of the beloved as an idol in the following verses is set in counterpoint to the significance of the image:

> An idol because of which the house is like spring, and it is not surprising, since houses are made into spring because of idols...
> An idol because of whom my eye became a house of idols due to abundant images of his face, even if the images do not show[143]

The image of the beloved as an idol makes him simultaneously present and absent for the poet-lover.

Poets reinforce the presence of the patron with nominative expressions, but may also link them to motifs that imply risk and instability in patronage:

> A brother of resolve, the determination of whose resolve did not bring forth any improvisation of a random, defective perspective[144]

The emphatic presence of the 'brother of resolve' is set in counterpoint to the deferred risk of ineffective decision-making. The poet reinforces the following patron's presence with nominative expressions. In addition, the poet sets these expressions in counterpoint to his wonder at finding a young man with a good reputation or a patient king:

> He is one with a good name, and a youth with a good name is amazing; he is patient and forbearing, and still more amazing is a king who is patient and forbearing.[145]

The poet is more explicit about the contrast between the nominative expression and the risky behavior of the patron in the following verse:

> A forbearing one, and zealous anger is a disposition in him, and what fire does not have sparks?[146]

The nominative expression at the head of the line is a way to set up the patron and then examine his behavior from a variety of angles, some of which imply the uncertainties of patronage.

Verbs in panegyric poetry are about observing the patron in action. The poet-lover may use past tense verbs to assert the relationship. However, past actions are not necessarily predictive of the future. This poet-lover had trouble with his companion and solved his problems, and has become involved in a new phase of the relationship, in which the outcome is uncertain:

> I reconciled with my companion after a long battle on the condition that he would no longer be coy with me
> He regretted what he had done and asked pardon for it all, and I accepted his pardon and placed my heart in his hands once again[147]

The poet-lover in the following verse uses two sentences to present the counterpoint between the relationship in the past and separation in the present:

> An intimate friend, cut loose from a relationship, pretended to forget the past, and a friend who is bored carried away his affection[148]

The past tense verb expresses certainty about past actions in relationships, and it also opens out onto the changes of the present and the future. In praise it can combine the patron's accomplishments with the risks that he has faced:

> And you pursued a course of good deeds, comprised of benefit, a course that cured [us] of our blameworthy time[149]

Negative experiences in the past contribute to uncertainty about the patron's willingness or ability to follow up on the good deeds that are described using the past tense:

> He looked down from above with his benefits, and who could surpass him? He gave extensively of his gifts, and who could vie with him?[150]

Hopefully no one can, but the references to competition both insist on the patron's superiority and imply the risk of competition. Past military victories reinforce the patron's power and display the threats to which it may be exposed:

> On the day of Manuel, when he had touched right guidance with his claws, or intended to do so
> You defended Islam from that which, if it struck it, would have caused it to remain a shrunken figure afterward[151]

The use of the past tense verb offers past experiences as models against which to measure the patron's deeds in the present and the future.

Present tense verbs display the relationship in progress. This beloved appears to be interested in the poet-lover, but she is not:

> She lends you an eye that is moist [as if due to illness = lovesickness] but beneath its utmost effort [in seeming affected by emotion] is a heart that is healthy [= free of lovesickness][152]

The present tense verb, 'lends an eye', is a gesture that appears to come from the beloved's affection but in fact conceals her indifference. Instead, the eye that she lends to you is one that causes you to fall in love with her, not an outward sign of her interest in you. Present tense verbs display general conditions of patronage:

> He increases cheerfulness when he is in the gathering, and adorns the army on the day of battle[153]

The patron always does things this way, but the present tense verb also implies the potential for change. This potential is complemented by the diversity of the patron's activities.

Future tense verbs are about plans that are difficult to complete:

> I will turn my heart away from you, or follow passion to you if my heart rebels or refuses[154]

The description of two options for the future of this relationship complements the contingency that is implicit in the future tense verb in panegyric poetry. Future tense verbs can only offer a promise of patronage. These poets assert success, but only as one among many possibilities: 'I will persevere until I encounter your contentment, whether far or near.'[155] The possibility that the patron's contentment may be far or near complements the contingency of the future tense verb.

> I will exert my resolve and the mounts, for I see that forgiveness is not granted except through exertion[156]

The motifs of the journey and seeking forgiveness reinforce the open-ended quality of assertions that involve a future tense verb.

The imperative provides an authoritative counterpoint to the contingency of the demands that the poet-lover makes on the beloved, or that the poet makes on the patron in panegyric. The imperative conjures the beloved's presence for the lover and also displays the limitations on his ability to maintain and control that presence. This poet-lover implores his beloved to make love, not war:

> O my boy! Set aside war, bring kisses; what good is all of this war and roughness?[157]

For this poet, violence would be better than the distress that the beloved causes in the game of love:

> Break my back, do not make waves in your hair; strike my heart with the sword, do not strike with the sword of your glance[158]

It doesn't really matter what these poet-lovers want, since the convention of the game of love is that they are not in control, so that their use of the imperative becomes a parody of the real thing.

One convention in the Arabic love introduction, of demanding that companions stop at the traces of the beloved's abode, is another way for the poet-lover to make a spectacle of his desire:

> Stop, you two, let us give the abodes [tears] from eyes that have had copious sips of passion[159]

This command focuses on the absence of the beloved, while it also evokes the presence of the relationship for the poet-lover:

> It is a characteristic of the traces of the abode that they do not answer, and the right thing for the eye to do is to flow

So ask them, and make your crying the answer; you find that your passion is the one that asks and answers[160]

The imperative is a way to interact with other people, but for this poet-lover, the demand to ask the abode gives way to his own tears. The demand to ask and the answer are within him, a figure of his alienation as well as his persistent attachment to the beloved.

The imperative implies the speaker's authority over his interlocutor. The poet has the authority of professional skills in refined rhetoric, but the patron has the authority that comes with wealth and social status. In this sense, the poet's use of the imperative addressed to the patron is both literal and figurative. The imperative calls attention to the fact that there are multiple possible outcomes of the command:

Why did the king of the east give the inkwell to you? Look carefully into this statement and inspect it well[161]

The juxtaposition of the command to a question and the need for close inspection imply the uncertainties that surround the patron's status. The multiple possible outcomes of the imperative impinge on the poet's authority even when there is no emphasis on uncertainty in patronage:

You possess well-being – I am allied with you, so make an effort on my behalf; I am speaking to you, so listen[162]
Be extensive and broad in giving benefit, for my extensive and broad praise of you has prevailed[163]

The poet's professional role gives him the authority to make these demands, but the outcome is up to the patron. The poet may make other demands related to the patronage network, as in the following verse:

Pardon Usāmā for their crime, and forgive them for it, bestowing the gift of what belongs to the One Who Bestows Gifts[164]

In this verse, the poet shores up his demand with recourse to religious authority, but the actual authority remains with the patron.

The poet may use the imperative to solicit the participation of the audience in his publicity on behalf of the patron:

Ask about him and learn of amazing things, even if hearing a

> narrative from an uninterrupted chain of transmission is inferior to seeing it with your own eyes[165]

This command to participate in publicity is undermined by the poet's admission that hearsay is inferior to eyewitness reports. The poet in the following verse solicits audience participation in publicity in a more aggressive and confrontational way, which also complicates their role in the relationship:

> Do not lie about his virtue and fidelity, for in these qualities he is none other than Samawʾal [the pre-Islamic poet known for his fidelity][166]

The imperative is an assertion of authority, but in these appeals to the audience, the poet compromises the authority of the shared publicity that he leads on behalf of the patron.

The poet can have recourse to formulaic imperative verbs, in which the authority associated with the formula complements his limited authority in the use of the imperative. The poet in this verse amplifies his relationship with the concatenation of hope, proximity, connection and doing business together:

> Take it [the poem] as an affinity to you from one who hopes, who is in proximity to you, joined with you, and doing business with you[167]

In the following verse, the poet draws on the authority of his professional identity, since a 'strange' poem is one that is well-wrought and unique:

> Take it [the poem] as one that is a stranger in the land, companionable with every unusual intellect when it becomes strange[168]

These commands assert the poet's authority while implying the multiple possible outcomes of his order. This poet emphasizes the network of relationships with superiors and subordinates: 'Serve him, and be served and live happily, I have seen things like this for fifty years.'[169] In the following verse, the job offer is more like a threat:

> Take up service of him if you wish for [valid] boasting; if you do not take up service of him, he will take your boasting from you[170]

Regardless of the exact phrasing of these formulas, the imperative is a way in which panegyric poetry opens out onto the future possibilities of patronage.

The largest single use of the imperative in this poetry occurs in the Persian conclusion. In this way, the poet makes a point of opening the poem out onto the future of the relationship and the patron's career. The poet's command for the patron's happy future often includes plans for his adversaries as well:

> Live happily and be fulfilled, and encounter triumph over desire and the heart's passion, and over the deceitful adversary[171]
> Take the world and show enmity toward the evil wishers, be king and enjoy benefit and the kingship[172]

The use of the imperative in the Persian conclusion to demand eternal life and power for the patron offers a particularly salient example of the contradiction between universality and lived experience, since in lived experience, everyone dies eventually:

> Live forever with the same customs and habits, and cast down the house of the Qarmatians one wall after another[173]
> Possess the world and be its lord forever, happy and with your heart's desire fulfilled, your enemies grieving[174]

Like the use of the imperative to command eternal life, the imperative in the Persian conclusion may be used to order pleasant experiences for the patron:

> Live happily as the leader according to the customs and ways of the generous, in eternal happiness, with musk-fragrant red wine[175]

These pleasant experiences also echo the motifs of the love introduction, and other introductory themes that are significant in Persian such as the garden, wine and seasonal holiday festivities. The command for the patron's pleasure is about success for him. In addition, the transient quality of sensory and sensual pleasures, especially against the backdrop of the introduction to panegyric, implies uncertainty about the future for the patron.

The optative verb expresses a wish that opens out onto the future of the relationship and the patron's career, and is a key aspect of the conclusion to the Persian panegyric. Here again, wishes for eternal life and youth demonstrate the contradiction between universal aspirations and practical experience. These conclusions integrate the patron into the delights and instability of seasonal change:

> So long as the seasons of the world change because of the revolution of the cosmos, sometimes Tammūz and sometimes of Tīr [both summer months], sometimes winter and sometimes spring
> May the king's head [i.e. hair] be green [i.e. black], his soul in place and his body strong; may his sword be sharp and his command effective, and his heart joyful[176]
> Forever, as long as they make the house and pavilion warm and delightful when the air grows cold and the garden depressing ...
> May the cosmos be at your command in fulfilling your every desire; may God be your assistant with every inclination[177]

Poets combine wishes for eternal life and power with motifs of the changing seasons, the cycle of night and day, and the passing years. The imperative of stability and the experience of change are interrelated. Good wishes or supplication for the patron may incorporate a wide variety of motifs, from the pleasure and comfort of the human body to God and fortune:

> Forever, as long as marble resembles beloveds' bodies; forever, as long as coral resembles the lips of beauties
> Forever, so long as the vine leaves in autumn resemble the cheeks of lovers
> May you live according to your desires and attain your wishes, and be thankful for a long life and youthful fortune[178]
> May the king of the world and his glory and turn in power endure, his body sound and God the just his keeper
> May his Eid be joyful and his fast accepted; may the year, month, night, and day be joyful for him[179]

These conclusions combine the immediacy of bodily well-being with the forces of divine will and fortune that shape human experience. While moral behavior is connected to God's approval, fortune is random. The contradiction between the universal and specific experience in panegyric poses the question of how the two relate to one another. The genre of panegyric insists on the relevance of moral order to connect specific experience with universal values, and also acknowledges the relevance of unpredictability. This combination of moral order and unpredictability can make patronage uncertain, but it is also a feature of the flexibility of this form of social order.

Vocabulary, and the features of syntax in which this vocabulary is configured, are a way into the dynamics of patronage. The portrayal of the possibilities of success and failure did not involve a rejection of moral order, but a combination of moral order and unpredictability. This combination helped to articulate the relationship between the social order of patronage and the importance of uncertainty and flexibility within it.[180] The following chapter investigates how poets used the vocabulary of patronage and features of syntax to elaborate on praise for pay in rhetorical devices and figurative language.

5

PRE-INDUSTRIAL LIGHT AND MAGIC

RHETORICAL DEVICES AND FIGURATIVE LANGUAGE

Elaborate rhetoric is a way of encoding meaning, and interpretation is a way of decoding it.[1] At the same time, a poet's use of elaborate rhetoric to encode meaning incorporates his interpretation of his topic.[2] Panegyric poets encoded commentary on the dynamics of patronage for the audience, including the patron, to decode. As a result, the commentary on patronage in panegyric poetry entailed a shared intellectual experience. This experience of elaborate rhetoric was intertwined with the diversity of past experiences, present predicaments, and future aspirations of the poet and his audience. The indirect expression of rhetorical devices and figurative language allowed poets to discuss the ideology of stable prosperity as well as the multifaceted experience of patronage in practice.

Rhetorical devices and figurative language in elaborate rhetoric go hand-in-hand with segmented composition.[3] The poet worked the individual verse like a gem, and this technique of composition allowed him, and his audience, to compare and contrast different perspectives.[4] In the context of panegyric poetry, the analytical focus on motif, syntax, rhetorical device and figurative expression, and the comparison and contrast of different perspectives, was about exploring the dynamics of patronage.[5]

In rhetorical devices and figurative expressions, the poet and audience do not just examine what has already happened.[6] Through the construction of experience in rhetorical devices and the imagination of experience in figurative language, poets and their audience delved into the past and the present as a way to think about the future.[7]

Poets used elaborate rhetoric, and especially rhetorical devices and figurative language, to enhance the value of poetry in the give and take of patronage. Rhetorical devices and figurative language helped poets to promote the value of their discourse about patronage and enhance their professional status.

> If … the poet wants the reader to be able to grasp the discourse itself, beyond the mediation of meaning, then this mediation must be 'disturbed' by elements that, through deviation from the norm, set up a cognitive tension between proposition and implication. Only then will the transparency of purely communicative discourse become blurred, as a glass becomes visible when it mists over. For discourse to attain valued status as an autonomous system, it must have its own opaque depth and specific density… At the same time, however, it must remain an expression of extraliterary humane values …[8]

The professional status of poets derived from their ability to make sense of the contradiction between the ideology of stable prosperity and the practical possibilities of success and failure in patronage.

Constructing relationships: rhetorical devices

Rhetorical devices in panegyric poetry enable poets to join uncertainty in the practice of patronage with the ideology of stable prosperity. Paul de Man distinguishes between the multiple possibilities implied in rhetoric and contradiction, pointing out that 'The text does not simultaneously affirm and deny identity but it denies affirmation. This is not the same as to assert and deny identity at the same time.'[9] Rhetorical devices are not something that poets apply to ideas about the uncertainties and ideology of patronage. Instead, these ideas take shape in rhetorical devices.[10] The constructed quality of these devices implies the possibility of alternative constructions of rhetoric, and, by extension, the possibility of alternative experiences of patronage. As a result, the constructed quality of rhetorical devices displays flexibility and facilitates social mobility. Repetition, parallel, paronomasia, antithesis and paradox juxtapose a pair or series of meanings and generate contrasts and comparisons through the interplay of sameness and difference.

Repetition emphasizes the relationship between the terms or phrases that are repeated, and between their broader contexts. Gilles Deleuze suggests that in repetition, where things are distinguished in number, space, and time while their concept remains the same, 'In the same movement, therefore, the identity of the concept in representation includes difference and is extended to repetition.'[11] As a result, repetition, which is about sameness, is also about difference. In addition, repetition that is combined with contrast emphasizes that contrast.[12] Since some instances of repetition are not obvious in translation, each repetition discussed is underlined in the translations used here. Repetition reinforces the simultaneous link and separation that define desire:

> We <u>traveled</u>, while you were <u>remaining</u>, and perhaps the <u>one who stays</u> was an attachment for the <u>traveler</u>[13]

The first clause sets up the separation betwee-n the lover and beloved using the antithesis between the traveler and the one who stays behind, while the second clause uses the same antithetical terms to consider the possibility of a link between them. The repetition of the terms clarifies that we are offered two very different perspectives on the same situation. Separation is just physical separation in the first perspective, or it is modified by emotional connections in the second. The poet-lover in the following verse compares and contrasts the possibility and impossibility of recovery from love:

> Do you suppose that I will <u>find the path</u> to consolation? Death, in that case, would have <u>found a path</u> to me[14]

The repeated phrases about finding a path reinforce the bifurcation of the trajectory of desire in this verse. The poet-lover in the following verse attempts to shore up his case with the beloved by invoking the age-old rules of the game of love. Repetition links the general rule to the specific experience, while it also contributes to the contrast between them:

> Why do you become distressed when I <u>play at love</u>, <u>playing at love</u> with beauties is an ancient custom[15]

The orderly rules of the game are contrasted with the beloved's resistance to them.

Repetition allows poets to join motifs of success and failure. The poet in these verses compares access and lack of access to wealth:

> The residence and place where the lord stays is another of his bene-fits; I have been far from that benefit for two or three years
> So long as the generous man consumes and gives silver coins; so long as the miserly man seeks and loves silver coins[16]

The patron's residence is the source of benefit, but the poet has been distant from the patron and his benefit. The generous man will always spend and share, while the miser will always hoard his wealth. Similarly, repetition highlights the contrast between the patron and other prospective patrons in these verses, and also links them as two possibilities in patronage:

> If these leaders fall short, he has aimed for glory and honor that did not fall short[17]
> His gifts are constant for his visitors; do not suppose that anyone other than him gives gifts continuously[18]

The patron in the following verse enjoys the turn in power of lions, but repetition emphasizes the contrast and comparison between this turn in power with the turn in power of servants:

> When the kingdom became rightly directed and its sides quivered [like a fine sword] in the turn in power of lions, not the turn in power of servants[19]

This comparison asserts social hierarchy while referring to its inversion.

Repetition may contrast and compare points of view that focus exclusively on success in patronage, in which the possibility of failure is implied. In this verse, repetition articulates a distinction between hope that is opened out onto a life, and the limitation of hope by the extent of a life:

> Hopes are opened up in appointed life spans; appointed life spans have become equivalent to hopes[20]

Both sentences situate hope in a lifetime, but the first does so in a way that emphasizes the starting point of hope, while the second reinforces the limitation on hope at the end. It is good that God assists the patron in the next verse, but the fact that God assists everyone who worships Him means that the patron's competitors have a fair chance too:

> King of the east, whom God assists everywhere; God assists everyone who worships God[21]

Repetition emphasizes that the patron's power, and the power of anyone else, is contingent on his worship of God. The forces of nature are on the patron's side in the following verse, and repetition reinforces the alliance:

> The new year in the new garden is a new turn in power and happiness; both new, they become foundations for the new turn in power[22]

However, repetition of the word 'new', to link the patron with the new season and the new year, also calls attention to the flow of time and natural change, implying the transience of the patron's power.

Poets use repetition to demonstrate the troubled relationship between the social order of patronage and violence. In this verse, repetition focuses attention on the distinction between the patron and his adversaries, as well as the risk that their conflict entails:

> The eye of religion was soothed at Qurran when the eyes of polytheism were swollen and cut out at al-Ashtarayn[23]

The repeated word, the eye, reinforces the identity of each community. The use of repetition intensifies the conflict and the connection between the allies and the adversaries in the following verse:

> In him good for the ally is increased, in him evil for the opponent is increased[24]

Rhetorical devices can impose a discursive version of order on the troubled relationship between the social order of patronage and violence, as well as the unpredictability within patronage. However, the imposition of discursive order also demonstrates that other rhetorical constructions of relationships are possible.

Parallel expressions consist of patterns of words and syntax, and they generate contrasts and comparisons between segments of verses. These comparisons contribute to a multifaceted portrayal of patronage. Many verses include a parallel expression between the two half-verses or a syntactic break that divides the two half-verses, and these features produce a pattern of anticipation and resolution of ideas as well as language, including complementary words, images or sounds.[25] Segmented description focuses on the process of description rather than the person or thing described.[26] It fragments what is described, so that it is both emphatically present for the speaker and his audience, and concealed in an anti-narrative series of attributes.

Parallel expressions in description fragment and objectify the beloved so that s/he is devoid of any subjective presence as a person. In this way, parallel expressions reinforce the distance between the poet-lover as a person and the beloved as a person turned into a series of parts. At the same time, the series of parts intensifies the beloved's sensory and sensual presence for the poet-lover:

> And one whose sides tremble, who inclines, with soft fingers [of one with a leisurely life] and languid eyes[27]

She is reduced to a series of parts, but each part conjures her identity as it relates to the lover's desire. Her body moves gracefully, her soft fingers are a sign of a life of leisure with time to be beautiful and have affairs, and the description of her eyes is about attraction. The beloved in the following verse is broken down into parts that are described in exclusively visual and static images, but the trajectories of the images lend him a dynamic presence:

> The cavity behind his ear is moonlight [in the night of his hair] and his new beard is a hyacinth, his face is sunshine and his stature is a cypress by a stream[28]

The poet and his audience would not have thought this description sounded like an absurd combination because the description is supposed to be enjoyed in segments. The pleasure of the description in segments derives from the beloved dissected into his best features, with each image leading off in a different direction: two images about shape (a hyacinth and a cypress) and two about light (sunshine and moonlight). The combination of sunshine and moonlight distills the passage of time, in the cycle of night and day, into a visual experience of this person, so that his physical beauty is both caught up in the flow of time and described as if it transcends it.

The closure of parallel expression in language is an argument that sums up the patron and the social order of patronage. In parallel series, the patron just gets better and better, so that he is all the more present for the poet and the audience. However, in the process, he becomes more and more abstracted, so that he is distanced from them. The description of this patron is bifurcated, as he looks up to glory but humbly attends to his obligations:

> Raising his eyes to glory, a peer of refined manners that are neglected,
> cleaving to generosity like a cloth placed beneath the saddle[29]

In the following verse, the first three adjectives (successful, victorious, supported) are Persian words derived from Arabic, while the final expression, which deals with an ancient Persian concept, is not, perhaps for a crescendo effect:

> You are a successful king and a victorious sovereign, you are a commander whose wise views are supported, and a ruler with fortunate royal splendor [*farr*][30]

Other people may possess his other qualities, but only people who are supposed to rule have royal splendor. The patron in the following verse is the most abstracted and distanced of all:

> He is noble, free, and cheerful; he is youthful, calm, and serious[31]

The focus in all of these verses, especially this one, is on the poet's craft, not the patron. This focus implies that the poet is the one who constructs the identity of the patron in a series of attributes. If the poet has constructed his identity in language, then it can be reconstructed in language, and attributes can be mixed and matched as needed.

Paronomasia organizes and imposes order on the things and people that it is used to describe.[32] It also complicates the relationship between signifier and signified, since the use of the same or similar names for different things makes this relationship seem random.[33] Because this device imposes order on experience, but only in language, it implies an argument for the possibility of using language to reorder and reorganize experience. Likewise, it complicates the relationship between signified and signifier by evoking, though not actually causing, confusion about it. As a result, it complicates the use of elaborate rhetoric as a source of information about the patron in the dynamics of patronage. The terms in which paronomasia occurs are underlined in the translations. Some examples of paronomasia in Arabic and Persian appear to be instances of repetition in English translation, although the words in their original languages are from different morphological patterns.

Paronomasia both reinforces and offers a counterpoint to the poet-lover's frustrated desire:

> The lover craves an encounter with the beloved; in this world there is nothing that is more difficult to accomplish [34]

Their encounter in language offers a counterpoint to separation, since it conjures the relationship. At the same time the encounter, which is only in language, reinforces the poet-lover's frustrated desire. A little sleep will bring the comfort of the beloved's presence in dreams to the poet-lover in the following verse:

> I demand sleep so that scant sleep will bring back an apparition whose deceit is sweet for me[35]

The paronomasia on scant sleep and deceit rejects the comfort of the apparition's presence by emphasizing that it's nothing but a dream. On the other hand, this deceit is sweet, so the illusion suffices for the poet-lover. The poet-lover in the following verse conjures his relationship, or perhaps a shadow of it, in his addiction to the traces, a link to the beloved that is reinforced by paronomasia:

> I see that you have increased my addiction to the traces, and the burden of passion that I bear openly and concealed[36]

While the paronomasia conjures a shadow of the relationship, it also emphasizes the poet-lover's loss. The poet-lover in the following verse portrays not his own feelings, but the feelings that he yearns for from the beloved tribe. Paronomasia conjures a link between the imagined feelings of the tribe and the pasture that they have left behind:

> O pasture, if only they were affectionate toward a lovesick son of worries who surrenders to the pain of separation[37]

At the same time, the use of paronomasia for feelings that are only imagined and not felt, and a pasture that is abandoned and not occupied by the animals of the tribe, reinforces separation.

When it involves the name of a person, paronomasia is particularly problematic in its portrayal of relationships in a salient yet illusory way:

> Will Suᶜdā return my sleep to me, and exchange [my] unlucky stars for fortunate ones?[38]

Paronomasia argues for a link between the beloved's name and good fortune and displays the illusory basis for the argument. The argument takes place in the context of the lover's sleeplessness and misfortune, and is presented as a question, reinforcing the illusory status of the claim.

Paronomasia both parts and joins the love introduction and the praise section of panegyric:[39]

> Who will keep me from his [the beloved's] injustice, except perhaps service of the just king[40]

Paronomasia argues for a contrast between the beloved and the king, but the link between them in the rhetorical device implies that they are intertwined.

The combination of paronomasia with antithesis complicates the use of paronomasia to impose order on things. Paronomasia in the description of this poet's ambitions and worries reinforces his success in patronage, while it also calls attention to the deferred possibility of failure:

> You made the breeze of hope blow for me so that my ambitions advanced with it until they plundered my worries[41]

This rhetorical device argues that ambitions and worries are distinct yet related in the dynamics of patronage.

Paronomasia may organize the participants in patronage into a hierarchy. In this verse, the patron is in the middle position between God and his subordinates:

> They came to trust in the mercy of one who trusts in God whose omen is auspicious for them[42]

The construction of a hierarchy in language also calls into question its validity in experience, and implies that alternative constructions are possible. The protégé is in the middle position between his subordinates and his patron in this verse:

> The one who hopes for him is hoped for, since wealth is anticipated from what he gives, and the one who is protected by him is sought out for protection[43]

This paronomasia argues that the protégé returns the patron's favors through his own help to subordinates. This fulfillment of obligations in rhetoric also implies the possibility of other arrangements.

Paronomasia displays the contradiction between the universality and specific experience of patronage. The universality of the age of generosity in this verse is linked by paronomasia to the lifespan of the patron, at least in rhetoric:

> May you live long, sound of body, O commander of the faithful, for the age of beneficence and generosity [exists] insofar as you are granted long life[44]

This emphasizes the patron's importance, while also demonstrating that the universal is limited by specific experience. Similarly, the patron in the following verse must enjoy his power and not pass away:

> You possess the world and greatness and the turn in power, experience these three and do not pass away[45]

Paronomasia displays the contradiction between the universal quality of power and the lived experience of it, in which he will eventually pass away.

Paronomasia on proper names provides a particularly salient identification of an attribute with a patron, as well as a reference to the construction of identity in language:

> The beauty of the Jaᶜfarī palace has been completed, and it would not have been completed except by the caliph Jaᶜfar[46]
> In the east is prosperity for Mūsā and Mufliḥ, and in the west triumph is hoped for Abū Naṣr[47]

Similarly, paronomasia can stake a claim for links between people:

> The prince Muḥammad, wise and just king, Abū Aḥmad son of Maḥmūd, who purchases wisdom[48]

The constructed quality of the link joins the father Maḥmūd with the son Muḥammad, who was embroiled in succession disputes, and implies that this rhetorical argument can be configured in other ways.

Antithesis helps poets to contrast and compare the different possibilities of relationships. Poets use antithesis to impose order on things. Especially in the love introduction but also in praise, this technique implies that 'separate things can be thought of as conjoined ... which in the end fosters a doubt about the true conjunction of separate things.'[49] The patron works both ways, incorporating kindness and gentleness as well as coercion and anger, so that he seems to bring one thing into existence while destroying another.[50] Antithesis is at odds with the hegemonic universality of the patron's power:

> The patron's attributes are often cast in oppositional pairs ... The contrasting individual virtues engender a wider paradox between the patron's unity in his striving and his diversity in excellent attributes. Dualism and paradox leave the character of the *mamdūḥ* [patron] ambivalent, abstract and beyond the scope of definition and predictability – despite the generally familiar topoi of excellence.[51]

Antithesis captures the nuances of relationships while making them harder to pin down. It emphasizes the beloved's sensual presence for the poet-lover, while fragmenting the depiction of the beloved so that s/he is distanced from the lover:

> Darkness is a slave to your new beard, light is a servant to your face[52]
> And she bends with the softness of the eastern breeze, and a figure that is sometimes feminine and sometimes masculine straightens her[53]

Like the more random fragmentation of the person in parallel expressions that are not antithetical, in the use of antithesis the poet-lover objectifies the beloved and makes her/him dissimulate. Antithesis in the love introduction may be a rhetorical intersection between the assertion of the relationship and the limits placed upon it:

> When the gazelles of your companionship had not been exchanged for the gazelles of your absence, as one who departs for one who stays[54]

Companionship and absence, along with the one who departs and the one who stays, are linked and opposed in this verse. In the contradiction between the conjunction and the disjunction in the two pairs of terms, the poet attempts to impose order, but order remains elusive.

Antithesis may arrange the social order of patronage in language. It is fortunate that this patron is generous rather than stingy like others:

> They are paltry and you are a sea; they are darkness and you are dawn[55]

This contrast also portrays the deferred possibility of failure in patronage.

The antithetical qualities of the patron and his subordinates are why they are a good match:

> The desired thing is dear to us and seeking is contemptible; seeking is cherished by him and the desired thing has become contemptible[56]

In the following verse the patron doesn't care about money, even though everyone else does; it is as if there were something wrong with him, but that is exactly what is right about him:

> According to you, silver coins are contemptible, and cherished for the people; how is it that you hold what the people cherish in contempt?[57]

These antithetical qualities of the patron and his protégés make them a perfect match, and they also emphasize the distance between them.

Antithesis illustrates the transformation of the needy protégé through patronage. The patron in the following verse is committed to helping the underdog get ahead:

> Concerned with hastening the slow one when he leans back [lit., wrapped in his robe so that he leans back upon it], and ardent in advancing the one who is urged on gently, who lags behind[58]

The implication of helping the underdog is expressed in the following verse, where the poor catch up with the rich:

> Your benefits encompassed all creation, and poor and rich alike met in wealth[59]

Finally, the more problematic implication of the person coming from behind is his impact on the person who is ahead of him:

> Gifts that enabled the poor man to acquire wealth over and over, and assisted the impoverished man against the wealthy man[60]

These transformations convey the importance of patronage for social mobility. The upward mobility for the poor is articulated in downward mobility for the rich, as poor and rich meet in wealth, and the patron assists the poor man against the rich man: the flexibility of patronage works both ways.

Poets use antithesis to articulate the complications of relationships. In this verse, antithesis links haste and delay, so that hope turns into wealth, and the first meeting becomes the day to collect a postponed reward:

> Hope in you for the one who desires wealth is the hastened portion of wealth, and the first day of meeting you is the postponed portion[61]

The combination of haste and delay is used to collapse the process of the relationship into instant success: the link between them is also a rhetorical intersection of success and the risk of failure in delay. Antithetical statements about the patron are a familiar feature of this genre:

> There is no breeze in paradise like his kindness, there is no fire in hell like his rage[62]
> One who has been cast into a deep well by your rage might then say to your kindness, bring me up from this well[63]

The conventional combination of rage and compassion demonstrates the role of risk as an integral yet disruptive feature in the social order of patronage. The multifaceted quality of the patron contributes to its uncertainty and flexibility.

The social order of patronage and violence are distinct and opposed, yet bound up with one another. Antithesis imposes order on this troubled relation by sorting patronage and violence, allies and adversaries, into clear categories:

> When you saw religion's heart beating rapidly, when unbelief was strutting and insolent[64]

The use of antithesis to impose order on things is a way to absorb the complexity of experience within patronage, and the dangers of violence outside of it, into the elaborate rhetoric of panegyric. The imposition of order in language implies the potential to change that order .

Paradox displays an ambivalent attitude toward the things, ideas and people that are described.[65] This rhetorical device 'creates obstacles that the reader has to acknowledge and negotiate,' so that the audience becomes engaged in interpretation.[66] Paradox displays the complexity of relationships and their construction in the elaborate rhetoric of panegyric poetry. These qualities imply the possibility, if not the necessity of reconstructing relationships in language – a crucial dimension of the flexibility of patronage.

Paradox emphasizes the poet-lover's contradictory experience of the beloved, who is there but not there for him. In these verses, contradiction is not just a feature of the beloved – the poet-lover's relationship with the beloved is nothing but contradiction:

> Obedience from me and commands from him, he is both contact and prohibition; he is both pain and cure, he is both thief and judge[67]
> My pain is that face, and my cure comes from the sight of it; have you seen pain that, when you look into it, becomes a cure? ...
> His abandonment is sweet like contact due to hope for contact; his contact becomes bitter like abandonment due to dread of his abandonment[68]

The description of these relationships involves emotions and interaction, and both are fraught with contradictions:

> Separation made every person with a youthful passion laugh and cry that day, and made him happy and unhappy
> So that we made farewell that day a greeting, and we made separation that day a meeting[69]

While the paradox of love is obvious, its significance in the panegyric poem and the social context of patronage is not. The contradictory quality of love offers a commentary on the contradiction of intimacy and distance in the unequal relationships of patronage. Contradiction is not a flaw of patronage, but a built-in feature with which protégés and patrons alike had to contend.

Paradox enables poets to analyze the contradiction of intimacy and distance in unequal patronage relationships. In this verse, the patron is so loyal that when he is not there, it is as if he were there:

> And you are present and not present with him together, and you are absent and not absent from him[70]

This assertion of proximity also implies the deferred possibility that distance plays in the relationship. The flaws of the non-patrons in the following verse lead to a paradoxical description of their unavailability:

> Proximity to them is distance from the soul, and loneliness, with the like of them, is companionship[71]

The paradoxical description of these flaws offers a counterpoint to the description of the patron, and also implies the deferred possibility of failure in patronage.

Poets may use paradox to articulate the contradiction between the hegemonic universality of patronage and the practical experience of it. This poet places his patron in a grand scheme that includes his defeated enemies. However, he points out, the patron has no enemies:

> You are iron, by analogy, and your enemy is a mountain; many a mountain has been cast down by iron …
> I say enemy in my poetry, but I know of no enemy of yours in the world[72]

Similarly, the poet in the following verse situates his patron in a grand scheme of philosophical concepts, with a caveat:

> What is mankind, mankind is an accident; aside from his pure heart, it has no essence
> His form is the substance of nobility, even if nobility is not expressed in form[73]

Poets always have to deal with the problem of the mismatch between the ideology of stable prosperity in patronage and practical experience, but these paradoxical descriptions make this mismatch particularly salient.

The use of poetry in patronage was both effective and problematic, and this poet sums up his problem with the paradoxical reaction of his audience:

> My variegated discourse makes a group happy and garners their disapproval; that discourse about them endures and my speech is prolific
> The repeated attacks of time have left nothing but contentions in speech that satisfy the listeners and anger them[74]

Panegyric poetry is a site of contention for this poet.

The constructed quality of rhetorical devices implied that reconstruction was always possible, and the shifting alliances of patronage made it necessary. The devices discussed in this section – repetition, parallel, paronomasia, antithesis and paradox – show that rhetorical devices expressed the complications of patronage relationships. Poets used these devices to combine the ideology of stable prosperity with the practical uncertainties of patronage.

Imagining relationships: figurative language

Poetry 'happens' in the simultaneous presence of two different realities whose competition with one another produces a more complex reality.[75] The simultaneous operation of mimetic description and its figurative implications can create a 'multi-layered imagery.'[76] In panegyric poetry, images present arguments about the patron's life-giving and death-dealing powers.[77] Patrons expected poets to project them above and beyond the practical interaction of patronage, 'into a universe of hyperbole, paradox, oxymoron, feigned wonder and other imaginary modes of portrayal.'[78]

The combination of an image and its referent generates a multifaceted and comparative perspective on these two components of a figurative expression. First, the figurative expression brings together an image and a referent based on a primary comparison, but the context of each one remains a marginal yet relevant feature of the figurative expression. Second, figurative expressions imply a comparison in figurative language as a link that also involves distinctions between the image and the referent. Third, figurative expressions both reveal and conceal their referents in images. Finally, the constructed quality of figurative language demonstrates the possibility of alternative ways to imagine patronage. Poets used these comparative and creative dimensions of figurative expression to explore the mismatch between the ideology of stable prosperity and the practical uncertainties of patronage. This discussion of figurative language begins with simile and metaphor and analyzes compound images, images in series, negation in images, imaginary etiology, conditional images, images of becoming, images built on images, hyperbole, incongruent images, paradoxical images, expressions of wonder, genitive images and animation in figurative language.

Similes conjure the presence of the beloved for the poet-lover and imply the limits on love:

> O promise of yours that, like your tresses, is not straight, where are those fine promises that you made?[79]

The referent of the broken promise illustrates the limitations on love, while the image of the beloved's curly or wavy hair implies his or her sensual presence for the lover.

The contexts of images and their referents, though marginal, both enrich and complicate the image-making process. The image of a star for this patron's spear conveys his military power:

> Like a bright star, your spear travels a path in the revolving heavens[80]

The context of the image also includes the cyclical motion of the cosmos and implies the importance of change in patronage. Likewise, the nature images for the power and wisdom of the patron in the following verses portray his prosperity:

> However ruined Khurāsān is today, however few are the people remaining there
> Another year of the lord's turn in power and benefit becomes like a garden full of roses in the month of Ādhār
> The lord's wise perspective and point of view are like rain and spring; when he joins these two, the rose in the rose garden laughs[81]

In addition, these seasonal images, in conjunction with the recent changes in the region, imply the change and instability in the area under the patron's control. The patron in the following verse is like Alexander, but as in the motif of legendary figures, this kind of comparison links and contrasts the legendary figure with the patron:

> You combine every aspect of nobility and bravery, traversing the world like Alexander[82]

Alexander the Great is a hard act to follow, but the patron is identified with him in conjunction with the hegemonic universality of patronage. The distinctions between Alexander and the patron, like the implications of cyclical change and instability in the similes about nature and the cosmos, fall within the realm of the lived experience of patronage.

Metaphors challenge us to see things in new ways, and to be aware of change, because 'Metaphor fixes identity as a temporary point of view or judgment; it defines the self as engaged with reality, in a posture of critique or affirmation.'[83] Metaphors are a rebellion against the system of naming in which signifiers are assigned to particular things, although the image is a disruption of the system of naming that language itself permits, so that metaphor is a disruption from within.[84] Although the referent is not explicitly mentioned, the metaphor is a comparison of the image and the referent, not an assertion of exact equivalence between them.

In metaphor, this beloved's sensual presence becomes vivid while his subjective presence is concealed:

> He has countless open pouches of musk beneath his tresses; he has a hundred thousand tulips crushed beneath the pouches of musk[85]

The beloved takes shape for the lover in images, and is also obscured within these images.

The conventional image of a lion for the patron offers a vivid portrayal of the patron's military and political power:

> Until he [the adversary] fell into the claws of a lion whose growl filled hearts with terror[86]

This image also evokes the danger associated with the patron's power – a danger that is directed toward adversaries yet present for allies as well.

Compound images, in which a single referent is split into two or more images, offer a multifaceted and vivid portrayal of the referent. The pairing or stringing of metaphors (one analogue and one topic each with two elements; one topic and two analogues; two analogues and two topics) was an important feature of mannerist poetry in the medieval Middle East and Central Asia, and it was used because it could produce special effects.[87] These special effects were just one dimension of the pre-industrial light and magic of elaborate rhetoric and especially figurative expression.

One special effect is a sense of motion that reinforces the presence of what is described. This beloved is not going anywhere, but his hair is both curly and wavy, and the use of two different images for it implies motion:

> Because of many curls and waves, sometimes the beloved's hair becomes like a polo stick and sometimes like a ring[88]

The implication of motion animates him, but the focus on a single feature that is disassembled in two separate images also suppresses his subjective presence for the poet-lover.

In this compound image, the patron is described using two aspects of the same image, and the relation between the two aspects generates motion. The result is an exploration of the intimacy and distance of patronage relationships.

> Like the moon he was exceedingly high, his light extremely close for a group of travelers[89]

This image directly addresses the mismatch between the ideology and practical experience of patronage. The poet identifies the patron with the image of the moon – the universal dimension of patronage. The aspect of light that is close for travelers evokes practical experience. The light refers to success in patronage, while the fact that the people are travelers also implies future interaction that remains to be seen.

Images in series concatenate two or more referents in a complex of images.

In compound images, the referent is disassembled at the level of the image. In images in series, the referent is first disassembled at the level of the referent and then transformed into images. These images can make what is described more vivid, but they also fragment it:

> Sometimes he makes a shadow of hyacinth over the tulip; sometimes he puts a mail coat of ambergris upon the moon[90]

These images are about the beloved and about the image-making process. His new beard and long hair conceal his face from below and above, so that it is as if he becomes less available for the poet-lover. At the same time, the new beard and the long hair are themselves made sensual in images. The images in series in the following verse offer insights into the relationship:

> From afar my tears became like carnelian because of the carnelian of his mouth; listen to his speech and pass over that carnelian [with a kiss][91]

This verse uses images in series to generate an imaginary concord between lover and beloved while the referents of the images clarify the limitations on love. Images of carnelian for the lover's tears (often depicted as tears of blood in the Persian love introduction) and for the beloved's mouth create a figurative intersection between the beloved's sensual presence and the limitations on love. The image for the beloved's mouth is complemented by the motif of speech, which contributes to his subjective and sensual presence. The images of carnelian join the lover and beloved as if they were in contact in the relationship, a figurative contact that is reinforced by the motif of the kiss. The complex of images in the following verse creates a figurative scene of hospitality that joins the poet-lover, his tears, and the abandoned abode:

> Flowing tears are the food that I offer to their abodes even though my morning after their departure became pitch black[92]

Images of a host, a guest and hospitality refer to the connections with the lover, and imply the persistence of the attachment. The referents of the lover, his tears, and the abode display loss.

Images in series may join referents that are harmonious with one another. This patron is emphatically present in the images of a lofty tree and a brilliant star. His intangible qualities therefore become visible:

> Because of [valid] pride and happiness, he became a lofty pine tree and a brilliant star[93]

The poet also disassembles him and distances him from the give and take of interaction in patronage. In the following verse, two images for two aspects of the patron's military prowess turn him into a fantastic adversary of the natural world:

> Toppling the mountain of iron with his spear, plundering the cold wind with his attack[94]

This series of images makes his military activity more vivid, and conceals it in fantastic images of the natural world.

Alternatively, images in series may enable poets to juxtapose opposing referents. These patrons are compared to robes of time, and the negative circumstances that follow their demise are compared to time's coarse wool garments:

> They were the [fine] robes of time and they split, and it was as if time donned [coarse] garments of wool[95]

The juxtaposition of the two referents of the patrons and the negative circumstances is enhanced by the corresponding images of the robes of time and the coarse garments. These images in series impose order on the uncertainties of patronage.

Images in series may offer a commentary on the relation between the social order of patronage and violence. This image series absorbs the theme of violence into the figurative language of panegyric:

> In battle, they exchange drinks from the cup of death and it is conjoined with the cup of wine [in heaven, or in kissing captured women][96]

The referents of dying in battle, capturing women, and going to heaven are joined by the image of the cup, of death or of wine. The soldier either drinks the cup of death and gets to drink the cup of wine in heaven, or lives and gets to drink the cup of wine in celebration. As a result of these images in series, death, the pleasures of this world, and the pleasures of the next world are intertwined. Death no longer seems so bad. The pleasures of this world become more significant in their relation to battle; the cup of wine in heaven, and the pleasures of the next world – which ought to be particularly intense for people who die in battle – are increased. The poet absorbs the violence of battle into panegyric and makes it mean more. However, there is no patronage *in* the battle. Instead, violence is like a day job for participants in the loftier pursuits of patronage.

Negated images complicate the image-making process and its commentary on patronage. Negation in an image implies that the claim has been made or can be made, though it is denied.[97] In this image of the beloved, the exception complicates the comparison:

> She is the sun except that a sun reveals itself to its observer and she is in her clothes[98]

Concealment in the image complements the capacity of images to both reveal and conceal. Just as the image reveals and conceals the beloved, the beloved as the sun is revealed, but with her clothes on, she is concealed. On both of these levels, revealing and concealing is not just about elaborate rhetoric, it is about imagining the availability and unavailability of the beloved to the poet-lover.

This poet denies that he has misplaced the pearls of his fine rhetoric, or pierced them in the wrong place, but he does raise the possibility that it could happen:

> Pearls of poetry not misplaced by the one who strings them, and the one who pierces them did not err by deviating from the center[99]

The possibility that is denied with negation is deferred, but remains a feature of the image. The theme of stringing pearls, and the deferred risk of making a mistake, comment on the image-making process and elaborate rhetoric in general. The product is valuable, but it is difficult to get it just right.

In the following sequence of verses, the poet-lover conjures the beloved's sensual presence in images, while the beloved negates his description. This beloved's backtalk interferes with the image-making process. In the ultimate form of animation of an image, this referent throws out images that are used to describe him and replaces them with new ones:

> That sugar sweet mouth said to me discreetly, O poet, look deeply into speech
> You have compared me to a pine tree in stature, and identified my face with a star
> How does a star resemble my beautiful face? How does a pine tree resemble my lofty stature?
> Since when does a star have a hyacinth decorating it? Since when does a pine tree have a crown of tulips?
> From now on when you want to describe me, choose something that is more beautiful than me
> He said this and then went away, and as he went, he said softly under his breath,
> Is there a star with roses scattered on its face like me? Is there a pine tree with a moon on top of it like me?
> I became confused by what he said, and I sought another name for him

I called him a fairy, for that silken body had a fairy face
Once again he made war with me, saying you are putting me down, you oppressor
You are right that I am a fairy in beauty – fairies are my servants and agents –
[But] since when does a fairy play the lute, sing, throw lassoes, ride horses, and tie on the sash [for battle]?[100]

The beloved's resistance emphasizes his subjective presence for the lover. However, this resistance to and rejection of the poet-lover's description implies the limitations on love. In his challenge to the poet-lover and his image-making process, the beloved offers a commentary on that process. 'You called me a star', he says, 'but since when does a star have a hyacinth upon it?' He has simply added an image in series. However, the poet-lover then hears him murmuring, 'Is there a star with roses scattered upon its face like me?' In other words, just to add an image in series is not enough. Bewilderment with beauty is part of the image-making process, and prompts the speaker to imagine the beloved in new images. This poet-lover's confusion leads him to imagine the unusual beloved in new images. This time, the beloved admits that the poet-lover is right, for the beloved is a fairy, and also employs fairies in his service. Here, the beloved's objection to the image is not about choosing a better image next time: instead, he objects that his active life is too complex to be distilled in an image. There is no image series or compound image that can encompass all of his talents. The animation of images falls short of the animation of subjectivity in the referent.

Images with imaginary etiology explain the relationship between the referent and the image with fantastic logic. Fantastic logic provides an explicitly constructed conjunction between referent and image, emphasizing the possibility of alternative constructions. It offers an argument on behalf of the image, while expressing uncertainty about its validity. The military might of these patrons becomes a cosmic event through images with fantastic etiology:

Fate and destiny are in iron and silver, for your dagger and ring are of iron and silver[101]
Because of fear of your army's attack, the stars of the heavens have become rings of mail coats and the sun a shield[102]

These patrons are not doing anything at the moment. Panegyric poetry can absorb violence into patronage by acting it out in language as a complement to or substitute for the real thing.

Conditional images, in which a condition defines the connection between the referent and the image, present an argument for the image and also express uncertainty about it. It is good that this patron's star will rise with all other stars, but it is not actually certain that his star will rise:

> If his star rises one year, that year, all stars in the world rise[103]

He is a cosmic event, but a conditional one. The poet in the following sequence of verses reinforces his status as a protégé and a poet with a series of images. The conditional works both ways – it makes the image uncertain, and also intensifies it.

> This [description] goes back to an earlier obligation [that I have] to you; if it were a child, it would be a servant
> And a heart that burns with advice and passion; if it were time, it would be summer
> And speech from the heart about you whose splendor endures; if it were a frontier, it would be a place of fear[104]

The obligation is not only a child, it is a child who is a servant, but only if it is a child in the first place. The result is that each of these conditional images is either more intense than a simple image, or non-existent. If the double image happens, the poet is an extra-special protégé, whose speech is not only a frontier, but a scary one. If it doesn't happen, he is less than average – a protégé whose speech remains obscure due to the absence of an image.

Images of becoming are images in which the image-making process is laid bare. They emphasize the focus of all elaborate rhetoric, and of rhetorical devices and figurative language in particular, on constructions in language that can be reconstructed. They are a significant feature of medieval Persian panegyric poetry. They offer a counterpoint to the hegemonic universality of patronage by foregrounding the fact that patronage is always in process. Images of becoming highlight the transformative capacity of figurative language and its implications for the changing conditions of patronage.

Images of becoming animate the presence of the beloved for the poet-lover, and also make this presence transient:

> That beloved's hair tied chain mail in a thousand ways; rings of musk became broken upon one another
> Just as the wind, whenever it blew upon that hair, became one who opens knots, scatters musk and counts rings[105]

Persian poems in which the rhyme word is a form of the verb 'to become' offer extensive use of images of becoming, but the use of this type of image is not limited to poems with this rhyme word.[106]

Images of becoming emphasize the transformation of patronage relationships. This patron transforms his protégé's senses of hearing and sight:

> Hearing the king's speech and seeing his ways makes hearing an idol temple and sight a treasure house[107]

This transformation displays a successful connection between the patron and the protégé. It also calls attention to the changing conditions of patronage.

The patron's capacity to transform can make the criteria by which he is evaluated what they are:

> O source of all goodness and measure of happiness, goodness became good through you and happiness became joyful[108]
> Justice became famous because of you and virtue illuminated, kingship became pleasant because of you and religion advanced[109]

The patron's fashioning of the criteria of evaluation reinforces his power, and also calls into question the use of these criteria as a source of knowledge about him.

The patron's transformative capacity in patronage is complemented by his transformative capacity in the sphere of violence. This image of becoming emphasizes the adversary's danger and also neutralizes it by turning it into a force of self-destruction:

> Out of fear of his pen, his upside-down enemies' hair becomes snake teeth upside-down upon their bodies[110]

The neutralization of the threat in language is one way in which the danger of violence is appropriated by the discourse on patronage. The enemy in the following verse is so successfully absorbed into this discourse that he gradually stops being an enemy:

> The enemy who speaks, because of that sword that sears the world,
> in time comes to speak more wisely[111]

It is worth noting that the taming of the enemy is evident in his speech, so that he comes to participate in the use of discourse as an alternative to violence. This transformation displays the porous boundary between patronage and violence. This boundary is a site of danger for the social order of patronage as well as a way for it to expand.

Images built upon other images emphasize the creative and transformative dimensions of figurative language and imply the changing conditions of patronage. This image, from a conclusion, builds an image of love upon an image of nature:

> The Nawrūz cloud sheds tears, and from the tears of its eyes, the
> rose and the rosebush laugh in the meadow like a beloved[112]

Natural fertility refers to prosperity in patronage, while the transience of fertility implies changing conditions. The tears of the cloud, which resembles a lover, and the laughter of the rose, which resembles a beloved, combine to portray a love relationship. However, the figurative lover's sadness and the figurative beloved's laughter demonstrate the limitations on the relationship. The position of these images in the conclusion reinforces the relevance of nature and love images to the commentary on patronage. The referent of the cloud/lover image is the protégé, and the referent of the rose/beloved image is the patron. The image upon an image suggests that the protégé's desire, imagined as tears, generates the patron's prosperity, imagined as the laughing (i.e. blooming) rose. The two-step process of images built upon images turns these steps into a sequence of events as if in a narrative. The poet does not just define the way things are perceived, he defines the way they happen and implies that they could happen differently.

Hyperbolic images turn up the volume of the portrayal of patronage. A range of meaning can be implied in a single hyperbolic expression or passage:

> Read hyperbolically, [the passage] poses the unanswerable question 'Where (on this scale of possible readings) can one situate meaning?' Viewed ironically, it confronts the reader with the more radical question of whether to opt for any of the positions on offer … or none of them?[113]

The impossibility of hyperbolic images emphasizes the constructed quality of figurative language and its role in the flexibility of patronage. Hyperbole also projects the referent beyond the determinate meaning of the image, resulting in an indeterminate description of the referent. This patron is so good at maintaining order that he turns the hierarchy of nature upside down:

> In your security, the lion does not strike the gazelle; with your command, the gazelle pulls out the lion's claws[114]

Exactly how good is he at maintaining order? We can't know for sure, because he is described in an indeterminate way. The patrons in the following verses surpass various natural phenonena:

> And in his generosity with the sea – if the sea sought [to match] an hour of it, it would not complete it –[115]
> More pure than light and more burning than fire, more giving than a cloud and more necessary than moisture[116]

As a result, these patrons are both extra vivid and obscured, since they are concealed in indeterminate images.

Incongruent images project the referent beyond the scope of the image by virtue of the incongruence between the referent and the image. Like hyperbolic images, incongruent images turn up the volume of the description and also make it indeterminate. In the description of violence, incongruent images are a way for poets to appropriate violence in the elaborate rhetoric of patronage. The horror of this scene is made vivid with the image of pleasure:

> How many a prisoner who has been spared or killed has garments stained with blood like perfume[117]

The horror is also made indeterminate. The incongruent image in the following verse infuses violence with the moral order of religion and refined pleasure:

> Your fine days with the Greeks are red with morning and evening drinks
> Marked days, as if with their bloodshed they were the day of the sacrifice and the three days that follow it[118]

Violence is appropriated and inserted into the discourse of patronage, in the images of pleasure and sacrifice. Pleasure and sacrifice make violence more vivid, but they also conceal it with the incongruent image. The vivid quality of incongruent images reinforces the description of the patron, but it also distances him from the audience by situating the referents of his description beyond the scope of their images.

Paradoxical images express ambivalence about that which is described, and express 'mysteries which transcend everyday logic and sense.'[119] This beloved takes up residence in abandonment (at least the poet-lover knows where she is):

> If you take up abandonment as an abode and you take the purest of aversion as a portion[120]

The referent of abandonment conveys separation, while the image of the abode suggests a determinate location for her and the potential to make contact.

Similarly, the patron in the following verse is both there and not there for the poet:

> You see his prestige reaching everywhere, so that you would say the king has become present[121]

The paradox in the image contributes to the patron's power, since it is as if he is there when he is not. However, when he is not present, he is also distant from the poet and his people. These images convey the complexity of patronage relationships, in which it is sometimes hard for people to know where they stand.

Expressions of wonder intensify images and their role in portraying relationships. Expressions of wonder open up distance between the observer and what he observes. In this way, they link the observer to what he observes and also separate him from it:

> The blooming rose grinds musk – this is amazing, and that which the narcissus works by magic is more amazing[122]

This expression of wonder intensifies the beloved's sensual presence and also distances him from the poet-lover.

Genitive images fuse an abstract concept with a concrete image. Genitive images emphasize the contradiction between universality and practical experience that informs panegyric.[123] These genitive images make their abstract or intangible referents concrete in figurative scenes. They also obscure those referents by funnelling their broad meaning into a concrete image. However, the broad meaning cannot fit the concrete image:

> Ruin took the traces and with the hand of the days before yesterday,
> cast them upon the surfaces of the desert[124]
> We pour [tears] over [the experience of] drawing close and near,
> and a cup bearer gives us drinks of yearning[125]
> Antelopes of the tribe were drawn off by an intention that left you
> bleeding away the wine of separation[126]

These metaphors do not miss the mark – their narrow, concrete images are not meant to encompass their broad and abstract referents. Instead, these images are meant to be partial signs of the broad referents: traces of them that demonstrate the capacity of figurative language to evoke experience, and the limitations on the capacity of language to spell it out. In particular, they are experiences over which we have little or no control, such as overwhelming emotion, loss, and the passage of time. The love relationship, as a figure of the patronage relationship, is articulated in traces and obscured by the limitations on language.

The importance of figurative language in these images is that the abstract referents cannot be exactly known, but they can be imagined; and if they are imagined, they can be re-imagined. This patron got the wind of purity under control, but it had been out of control:

> He made the wind of purity blow in gentle southern breezes, and it
> had been pounding winds that blow between other winds[127]

Similarly, the patron in the following verse possesses the treasure of glory, but must be careful not to spend it:

> And you will not see anything like the treasure of glory as earnings
> whose earner carefully preserves them from being spent[128]

Here again, a deferred risk complements the assertion of the patron's power.

The sphere of violence, which is beyond the scope of patronage, can be approached through figurative language. In this verse, the abstract concept of death becomes material in the image of the market:

> And he contained the market [of Darwaliyya in Anatolia] and left in it a market of death that rose high over every other market[129]

Like an incongruent or hyperbolic figurative expression, this genitive metaphor with its figurative scene projects the referent beyond the scope of determinate meaning. However, while hyperbolic expressions do this by projecting the referent above and beyond the image, and incongruent images do it by projecting the referent off its beaten track, genitive images do it by cramming the referent into an image that is too small, so that much of the referent ends up unspecified.

Animated images are the inverse of genitive images. Genitive images squeeze broad referents into narrow referents. Animated images insert inanimate referents into animate images, or inarticulate referents into articulate images. While in a genitive image one might encounter wine of separation, in an animated image wine might experience nostalgia for the grape vine. Genitive images shrink their referents, as major phenomena become lifeless and objectified; animated images expand them, as motionless or speechless things start to move or speak, and even take on a kind of figurative subjectivity. Genitive images make do with the allusive quality of figurative language, when more precise expression is not possible, as if to acknowledge the limited capacity of language to capture experience. Animated images exaggerate the capacity of language to articulate experience. In this verse, the vicissitudes are animated and the animate quality of the gazelles is amplified as they meet and avert the gaze of the vicissitudes:

> When the vicissitudes cast a glance at you, your gazelles turned back their gaze averted[130]

The gazelles are a sign of the beloved's absence and an echo of her presence.

Religion and Islam become characters in the following verse. Each one takes on figurative subjectivity:

> Religion called out in supplication and Islam sought help from you for victory with the appeal of a drowning man[131]

This figurative subjectivity contributes to the assertion of the patron's success. In addition, figurative or amplified subjectivity, with its implication of re-imagining subjectivity, implies the possibility of re-imagining patronage.

Imagining patronage in figurative language entails the possibility of re-imagining it, just as constructing patronage in rhetorical devices entails the possibility of re-constructing it. Motifs, syntax, rhetorical devices and figurative language combine to form the themes in which patronage is articulated. The following two chapters investigate some of these themes of connection, including connections that are expressed in terms of observation, evaluation, communication and interaction, beginning in the next chapter with the close observation and evaluation of the patron.

6

GETTING TO KNOW YOU
CLOSE OBSERVATION AND EVALUATION

Medieval Arabic and Persian panegyric poetry both performs and describes relationships in patronage.[1] The fact that these relationships are performed means that they can be refashioned in other ways, and this instability opens out onto the uncertainty and flexibility of patronage as a form of social order. Such relationships revolve around how people see and think about the patron and the social order of patronage. Elaborate rhetoric grows out of skills in close observation, or how one sees the world, and evaluation, or how one thinks about it. In panegyric poetry, these two skills become themes of close observation and evaluation. Poets use these themes to investigate the shifting terms of intimacy and distance in patronage. They compare and contrast perspectives on how participants in patronage should see and think about the patron and the social order of patronage.

Seeing and being seen: close observation in praise

Motifs of observation give information not only about what is observed, but also about the observer, and the relationship between him and what he observes.[2] Ways of seeing not only convey or imply social roles, they help to define them. The gaze is a technology of social position.[3] In the shifting terms of intimacy and distance in patronage, the theme of observation does not pin down the patron in a particular role. Instead, it offers a multifaceted perspective on the patron and the social order of patronage. This discussion of the theme of observation examines motifs of visual contact and concealment.

The gaze is not necessarily the primary site of power in the dynamics of close observation. While the gaze is often associated with control in modern cultural production and criticism of it, medieval readers had other ideas about observation:

> The subject one looked at was thought to be as important as the act of looking itself, and the act of looking always a dynamic interchange between viewer and viewed ... The human gaze does not merely fall upon inert creation; rather, all subjects are objects, all objects are subjects. To look is to participate in a web of connections.[4]

In medieval Arabic and Persian panegyric poetry, observation is one way in which the connections of patronage are explored. The medieval Arab scientist al-Hazen emphasizes the impact of that which is seen upon the viewer. However, this does not make the observer passive. On the contrary, for al-Hazen, in the impact of what is observed upon the observer, the act of observation is an intellectual as well as a sensory act:

> The forms sent out to the visual faculty every time the eye glances at the object, though unconfused and organized, are but the raw material from which the 'true form' will be built up, insofar as it is attainable, by the faculty of judgment.[5]

Close observation in medieval Arabic and Persian panegyric poetry was bound up with evaluation and the function of panegyric as a kind of ethical discourse: to see is to think. One who visually perceives something without thinking it through has really seen nothing at all.

Like al-Jurjānī's assumption that fine rhetoric and intellectual activity are two sides of the same coin, al-Hazen's theory of vision makes the boundaries of the self porous. The observer does not just visually perceive the world around him and other people. In observation, he both thinks through what he sees and is impacted by it. As a result, he experiences continuity with the world and other people, and this experience helps to explain patronage as a form of social order.

Observation is about thinking through and being impacted by the world and other people, and experiencing continuity with those people, but observation did not guarantee continuity. While vision is a privileged source of knowledge, it is also the delusive basis of appearance.[6] Poets use motifs of observation not only to assert connections in patronage, but also to investigate the uncertainties of those connections.

Motifs of visual contact present connections between people as well as some of the complications that these connections may entail. The depiction of the beloved's eyes implies visual interaction between the poet-lover who observes the beloved and the beloved themselves. The portrayal of the beloved's eyes, like the description of her other attributes, contributes to her sensual presence for the poet-lover. More importantly, the depiction of her eyes lends her a figurative subjectivity within the poet-lover's description of her. Her figurative subjectivity makes her emphatically present for the poet-lover. However, it also alludes to her explicit or implicit resistance to the poet-lover's advances. It is delightful for him for the beloved to be somebody, but being somebody also means that she need not be somebody just for him. This beloved's eyes make her emphatically present in a sensual way, and lend her a figurative subjectivity that contributes to and complicates that presence for the poet-lover:

> And love guided many a warrior of passion to those who are loved,
> with large eyes, kept close and raised with care[7]

The description of the beloved's eyes in the implied animal image makes her oscillate between the wild and human culture, and between absence and presence for the poet-lover.

The eyes of the beloved in the following verse are not only depicted, they also see. Both the appearance of her eyes and the way she glances refer to the intersection of intimacy and distance in relationship:

> With one with diseased eyelids that are not [really] diseased, and
> glances that occasion doubt that do not [really] occasion doubt[8]

Antithetical repetition of the word 'diseased' at the beginning and end of the first half-verse, and of doubt at the beginning and end of the second, allows the poet-lover to impose an order on experience while clarifying that the order is illusory. The eyes that appear moist with sickness refer to their languid and alluring quality for the poet-beloved. The languid eyes of the beloved appear emotionally affected, but her glances dispel that impression. The glances lead to a suspicion of erotic desire and emotional turmoil, but the beloved is indifferent to the poet-lover. The illusions demonstrate the role of vision as a reliable source of knowledge and a misleading source of delusion.

The beloved in the previous verse glanced around, but it was not clear what she was looking at. When a beloved looks at the poet-lover, she is often disappointed by what she sees. He keeps getting older, but she stays the same age. This poet-lover avoids the gaze of young girls for just this reason:

> I take precautions against the young girls seeing forelocks of mine
> showing the first of white hair[9]

Her figurative subjectivity for the poet-lover is reinforced by the fact that she looks at him, but it is not to his advantage. Paronomasia, underlined here, dismantles the lover's efforts, since it joins his precautions against the girls seeing his gray hair to the fact that it shows. The poet-lover in the following verse uses a rhetorical question to argue that he is in fact eligible for love:

> Or did she not see my two forelocks from the weave of youth, and
> did she not see the dye of God, and it is my dye?[10]

The poet-lover makes his argument with his question, 'Did she not see my eligibility?' Indeed she did not. However, the deferred literal meaning of the question holds out hope for a connection in the relationship. The doubling of the question reinforces that she did not notice the poet-lover, and also makes for two attempts to hope that she could.

The beloved in the following verse takes a good, hard look at the poet-lover, but her look is inscribed in the disappearance of the beloved herself behind an animal image:

> She [an oryx of the sand, i.e. a woman] grazed her gaze upon a head
> that had concealed itself when its shoots had dried [i.e. white hair],
> the first to sprout[11]

The oryx image that draws the beloved away from the poet-lover, as she is absorbed into nature, also brings her toward him because it involves grazing her gaze upon the shoots of his hair. In this verse, the poet-lover is absorbed into nature along with the beloved and becomes her landscape. What she sees is shoots that have dried as if dying, white hair. The shoots are also the first to sprout: an ironic echo of fertility as a figure of youth. Her gaze uncovers this contradiction of life and death, concealing and revealing it.

The beloved girls in the following verses not only see the poet-lover's gray hair, they react to it with grief. Their grief demonstrates the love that once was, and enhances the beloved's figurative subjectivity for the poet-lover:

> She displayed distress that she saw me with black and white strands of hair, and what was pleasing became a source of wonder[12]

Her grief mimics that of the poet-lover in his unfulfilled desire, and contrasts with it. Her grief responds to the fact that people change for the worse, while his unfulfilled desire holds out hope for a better future. The paronomasia on pleasure and wonder both links and distinguishes the beloved's pleasure and aversion. In the following verse, the beloved girls' figurative subjectivity is enhanced by the fact that they both see, and experience emotion about what they see:

> The fact that they saw my scalp dyed dyed their cheeks down to the pearls of necklaces with blood[13]

The corresponding color imagery, of white hair tinted reddish with henna and pearls reddened by tears of blood, conveys the intersection of intimacy and distance. This link in figurative language reinforces the distance between them, but shows that this distance can be re-imagined in language. Paronomasia on the word 'dyed' creates a counterpoint between the dye that conceals the lover's true age and the tears of blood that reveal the beloved's true feelings. This counterpoint also turns on the distinction between the lover dying his hair because of his desire that resists change, and the beloved crying because she submits to change and lets go.

Like the beloved's observation of the poet-lover, the poet-lover's observation of the beloved is about evaluation and being impacted by what he sees. This beloved is concealed but she still makes a sensation:

> She pulled a veil over her face and stood there with a figure that cannot be hidden[14]

Paradox in observation demonstrates that the beloved is there and not there when she is wanted. The poet-lover in the following verse makes his observation of the beloved turn into a figurative transformation of his eyes:

> From seeing and touching the face and hair of the companion, I have musk in my hands and a tulip garden in my eyes[15]

It is as if the beloved that he observes takes up residence in his eyes, in the sense that tulips are a conventional image for the beloved's rosy face. The poet-lover not only experiences the beloved's sensual presence: he absorbs it. Parallel syntax and morphology reinforce the total body experience that includes looking and touching. However, the finality of this closure in language also conveys the transient, sensual quality of the relationship. The imagery in the following verse combines the transience of the relationship with a reference to separation:

> You see that black hair above that face like a moon; every time I see her sun, I am in distress[16]

The impact and interpretation involved in seeing the beloved combine pleasure and distress. The cosmic imagery complements the intersection of intimacy and distance. As a moon and a sun she transcends time, appears alluring, and becomes emphatically present. However, this contradictory portrayal also makes the beloved seem distant. Similarly, the visual impact of the beloved in the following verse implies the poet-lover's evaluation that joins pleasure and distress:

> A dye of a cheek whose roses or pomegranate flowers almost bloody the eyes with redness[17]

The rosy cheeks – which become emphatically present and also dissimulate in two different images – and their impact, reinforce the presence of the beloved. The impact itself, of eyes bloodied with redness, also illustrates unfulfilled desire.

The implicit exchange of looks, when the beloved's look is depicted within the context of the lover's visual description of her, becomes explicit when the lover and beloved are portrayed looking at each other. The eyes of the beloved in the next verses appear to be moist with sickness but they are moist with tears. In her figurative subjectivity, she is emphatically present because she not only sees, she also feels; and she not only feels, but she also feels sad about the departure over which she has no control, which is not the same thing as crying over the lover's gray hair and rejecting him:

> She looked, and I turned my gaze to the most beautiful contrast of black upon white [= eyes] that I have seen
> On a day when she turned away with a diseased gaze and eyelids, and her tears were not of disease[18]

The beloved's eyes in the first verse are alluring but sightless: just a beautiful feature for the poet-lover to enjoy. The pleasure is his alone, and her eyes are objectified. In the second verse, she gazes and takes on a figurative subjectivity, but does not gaze at the poet-lover: she has turned away. As a result, her tears are about desire that is inscribed in separation. The two (different, in the original) words 'I turned' and 'she turned' join the poet-lover and the beloved and display the contrast between them: he turns toward her, and she turns away from him.

Observation may entail the impact of the patron upon the poet who observes him, as well as the poet's evaluation of him. This impact contributes to the connection between them, while it may also complicate this connection. This poet has a sensory experience of the patron that leaves his senses transformed, like the transformation of a poet-lover who looks at his beloved:

> Listening to the speech of the king and seeing his ways makes hearing an idol temple and sight a treasure house[19]

These images imply bewilderment and amazement, which also complicate the connection established through observation. Parallel syntax imposes an order on experience that offers a counterpoint to its bewildering quality. The ability of the observer in the following verse to speak and to see – in other words, to express his subjectivity – is compromised by the impact of the patron:

> Because of his custom of nobility and the [valid] boasting of his praise, the speaker and the one who sees become mute and blind[20]

This hyperbolic image emphasizes the connection between the patron and his observers, and parallel syntax organizes this connection. The hyperbole also undermines the ability of the audience to observe, evaluate and express ideas about the patron. Instead of blinding his audience, the patron in the following verse serves as a guiding light for those who could not see:

> He set up the lamp of righteousness so that he who had not been able to see at all could be guided by it and see it[21]

The antithesis juxtaposes the possibilities of complete and incomplete visual experience. The patron's success is defined by the deferred risk of those who at first did not see. The poet in the following verse contrasts his observations about his hope for the patron and for others:

> I saw my hope in you alone as an ambition, but in other people, it is [merely] a craving[22]

The effective and ineffective versions of hope contrast the possibilities of success and failure in patronage. Though these other people are inferior, the comparison shows that the poet is always on the lookout for other options besides the patron. Poets configure motifs of observation in the following verses so as to compare and contrast these possibilities. The poet asserts success with a rhetorical question in the following verse:

> How could you be seen without a jewel of a noble deed when the vicissitudes of fate are seen in your money every day?[23]

The rhetorical meaning of this question is: no, of course you could not be seen without a jewel of a noble deed. The literal meaning alludes to the possibility that the patron could be seen without a noble deed to his name if he doesn't prove himself. A conditional sentence in the following verse enables the poet to confirm patronage and refer to uncertainty:

> If we saw certainty as an ineffective plan, we would not have sought intercession with repeated appeals[24]

The repeated appeals also imply the contingent quality of intercession and complement the use of the conditional to combine the possibilities of success and failure. This patron's associate is not observed as one who neglects his obligations, and negation introduces the possibility that neglect could occur:

> We did not see Ḥusayn neglect what is right ever since you participated in management with him[25]

Negation in the following verse reinforces the poet's insistence on a connection expressed through observation of the patron at work.

> Do you not see [that] thanks came from the ones [poems] that he ties up to keep, and that praise that pastures where it pleases is brought in by him?[26]

Negation also alludes to the possibility of not seeing things that way.

The patron's observation of the poet may entail an impact and evaluation. This poet just gets better and better in the eyes of the patron. He does not actually look at the poet, but the reaction implies that he does:

> You are made good in his two eyes when you are visiting, and you increase in goodness every time you come seeking[27]

The positive impact, and further improvement of it, each assert the connection between the poet and the patron. In addition, the repeated visits convey the contingent and flexible dimension of patronage connections, which remain in process.

When the poet and patron look at each other, the poet reinforces the connection made through observation. The patron has real subjectivity in the world, but in the poem, the poet lends him figurative subjectivity. In the motif of exchanging looks, the poet defines this figurative subjectivity as receptive to the relationship. This poet makes the first move by deeming the patron suitable for his praise, so that a patron's positive evaluation of the poet would reflect back on the patron. Likewise, a patron's negative evaluation of the poet would reflect back on the patron:

> What do you see in one who saw you to be suitable for his praise, and whose destinations came to be in your hands?[28]

The rhetorical meaning of the question locks the patron into a connection expressed in terms of observation, while the literal meaning implies the uncertainity of this connection. The poet reinforces his act of locking the patron into a connection with the motif of the poet's destiny in the patron's hands. In the reflection of the patron's evaluation of the poet back on himself, the patron's own destiny becomes contingent on the connection.

In the following verse the patron engages in a visual interaction – not with the poet, but with his poem. Both the patron's own face and the face of the poet's praise are figures of the patron's generosity:

> When I saw [that] you had nourished my affection with your countenance and deemed the face of my praise beautiful [and/or good][29]

While the face of the patron and the face of the praise are sources of knowledge about the patron that reflect one another, they can also be illusory appearances. Outer appearance may reveal or conceal the inner qualities and deeds of the patron.

Concealment is the opposite of visual contact, since it is about barriers to visual contact between the observer and what he observes. Concealment can also articulate the presence of what is observed, while motifs of concealment state or imply the possibility of revealing what is concealed. This poet-lover explores desire in motifs and images of concealment that turn on the counterpoint between sensual beauty and violence:

> Do not cover your bright face under the helmet, since your bright face under mail will get rust on it
> Why on earth do you put the mail of the helmet over your face when your rose colored face is beneath chain mail the color of mixed perfume?[30]

Covering the face with a helmet refers to the separation of the poet-lover and the beloved when the beloved goes off to war, while the face concealed in dark hair is also part of the beloved's sensual presence for the poet-lover. In the motif of the helmet and the image of chain mail for the beloved's dark hair, separation and sensual presence become intertwined. The description of the chain mail as the color of mixed perfume reinforces the sensual presence of the beloved in counterpoint to the motif of the helmet. In this way, the beloved is concealed while the sensual beauty of his hair is put on display. In the following verse, concealment is abstract, but it conveys sensual presence as well as separation:

> And young girls, as if the heedless qualities of youth had draped them in fine robes[31]

The beloved girls are emphatically present in the image of robes of heedless qualities of youth. The heedless qualities are part of their charm, and they are also the reason why they will not be faithful to the poet-lover.

Cosmic imagery implies a cycle of revealing and concealing that defines the visual experience of the heavens. This poet-lover makes his beloved both present and absent with a motif of concealment:

> So I enjoyed a sun whose light appears when it is concealed so that it is as if it were not concealed[32]

The description evokes the cycles of night and day and changing weather that conceal and reveal the sun to the observer. The juxtaposition of the factual statement about the concealed beloved, and the figurative statement about the beloved not concealed, displays the possibilities of the relationship. In the following verse, the radiance of the beloved has the capacity to change the way the observer sees the cosmos:

> And the sun was turned back to us in spite of the night, with a sun from among them that appeared from the side of the covered camel saddle [between curtains]
> Whose light cleared the dye of darkness and because of whose splendor the variegated robe of the sky folded up[33]

While her presence is like a cosmic event for the observer, it is also a look from between curtains as she departs.

The poet-lover may use the conditional to join and compare the possibilities of visual contact and concealment. This beloved does not smile, but the poet-lover conjures her smile, and all that it would mean to him, in a conditional sentence:

> If she had smiled, we would have turned a gaze to hailstones, and to chamomile flowers watered by wine and honey[34]

The conditional becomes a way to turn his fantasy of the beloved's presence into a logical progression. Lightning did not illuminate the beloved in the following verse:

> And the lightning would have been beloved for me if it had illuminated a dark-eyed [lit. black and white eyes] gazelle at Bityas[35]

The poet-lover makes the presence that isn't into a presence that not only exists, but also follows logically from the conditional sentence.

Negation may compare and contrast seeing and not seeing. This poet-lover uses negation to articulate the dual function of the traces of the abode as a sign of both the beloved's presence and of her absence:

> They said, are you crying over traces? And I said to them, the traces that remain lead the passion of the one who has missed [the sight of] the real thing[36]

The juxtaposition of the traces to the real thing reinforces their dual function. The double negation in the description of observation in the following verse contributes to the oscillation between the presence and absence of the beloved for the poet-lover:

> When we had not lost her elegant appearance and a pasture populated with the oryxes of pleasures [37]

The oscillation between presence and absence offers a commentary on the dynamics of patronage relationships.

Observation is about clarification, but hyperbole in observation makes what is observed indeterminate. This patron becomes amazing through hyperbole, but he also becomes indeterminate and distant:

> There are no images or designs in the *Artang* like the thousand [and] one refinements in his character[38]

The ekphrastic image of this non-Muslim scripture further estranges the patron by projecting him beyond the scripture, which is itself already beyond the immediate Persian and Muslim cultural sphere.

Clothing both reveals and conceals the one who wears it. This patron is displayed in the robe of his power, and also concealed in it:

> The righteousness between the warp and weft of the robe of his turn in power has scattered his virtue in the countries and abodes[39]

The temporary quality of power is reinforced by the phrase 'turn in power', and the image of clothing complements this temporary quality, since clothing can be put on and taken off. Just as patrons sometimes drape poets in robes of honor, poets drape patrons in clothes of praise:

> Here are the clothes of praise, so [wear them and let them] trail behind you, and here is the mount of praise, so ride it[40]

The image of clothing conveys the constructed quality of the patron in praise. The fact that clothes can be put on or taken off also shows that praise is a temporary honor, and contingent upon behavior.

Just as the beloved is there and not there when one wants her, the patron is there and not there when one needs him. This patron is highly effective and very powerful, so that his absence is equated with his presence:

> And when he disappears to deal with enemies, his absence and his presence are equivalent[41]

However, this contradictory portrayal of the patron also complicates his availability in the patronage relationship. The contradiction in observation of the patron that leads to blindness reinforces the patron's amazing qualities:

> Because of his custom of nobility and the [valid] boasting of his praise, the speaker and the one who sees become mute and blind[42]

It also complicates the use of observation in patronage to establish connections. Similarly, the poet's desire in the following verse is so fulfilled by the patron that it resembles a blinded eye:

> The eyes of my heart were constant craving; you blinded craving with abundant gifts[43]

The image demonstrates the successful relationship and also cuts off the figurative visual contact as an expression of it.

The hyperbolic image in the following verse both reinforces the patron's presence for the poet and obscures him by making that presence indeterminate:

> The eyes of the lover do not incline toward seeing the beloved as you do to listen to the voice uttering a request[44]

This image inverts the convention of the seeker desiring the patron just as the lover desires the beloved. The inversion is one step in a hyperbole that takes another step when the referent of the patron's desire for the seeker is projected beyond the image of the lover's desire for the beloved. The image asserts intimacy in the relationship, but its indeterminate quality estranges the patron and makes him distant from the observer.

The barriers between the patron and his subordinates define his power and also make him distant. This patron resembles a woman concealed in women's quarters:

> Of necessity the faces of the elites are all turned toward him; you would say that they are doormen and that the lord's door is the women's quarters[45]

Reception is a barrier to visual contact and interaction with the patron, and a source of his status. The poet in the following verse clarifies that reception is not a sign of the patron's weakness:

> If the sight of him is sometimes prohibited, the thicket of every lion with bone-crushing strength is dense
> Or if you are met with respectable reception before him one day, veils have been draped before you
> And the brilliance of morning gives off the light of the sun when the first visible part of the sun is [still] concealed behind the horizon[46]

The cordial barrier of reception and the image of the sun's radiance from behind the horizon each display the patron's presence for the poet. The conditional sentence demonstrates that the barrier is not permanent, but is part of the ongoing negotiation of the patron's status relative to his subordinates. In the following verse, the parallel between concealment and doing evil to a relation implies that the two are equivalent:

> You did not cast evil upon a relation, nor did you address your tribe from behind a veil[47]

The negative statements both present and reject the possibility of doing these things.

The poet, like the patron, may disrupt the visual contact that expresses the connection between them. This poet complains about his grief over turning away from the patron but does it anyway:

> My turning of my gaze from his face is a period of time, and my hour of separation from him is an age[48]

The amplification of separation into an age reinforces the protégé's commitment to the patron, while it also illustrates the distance between them.

Motifs of concealment can demonstrate the patron's superiority in battle as well as the danger that violent conflict poses to him and to the social order of patronage. This image of concealment demonstrates the patron's contribution to security:

> If not for Abū Saᶜīd's fighting, the chest of the frontier would still be without a garment to cover it[49]

The enemy in the following verse got away; the poet reworks his flight into a fantasy of what he would have seen of destruction had he remained:

> If you did not flee, you would have occupied a position in which your eyes would see how the cauldron of war boils over
> Where you would have listened to howls when they rise up and seen the dust of death when it is stirred up[50]

The enemy's observation of destruction doesn't happen, reinforcing the fact that he got away and could come back.

Observation in panegyric poetry depicts patronage connections in various stages of completion, reflecting the dynamic quality of these relationships. The act of observation conveys information about the one who observes and what he observes. Visual contact and concealment in the poem contribute to the individual yet fundamentally relational identity of the poet, the patron, and other participants in patronage.

Thinking it over: evaluation in praise

Observation and evaluation are distinct yet overlapping dimensions of patronage. Just as motifs of observation convey information about the one who observes and what he observes, motifs of evaluation convey information about the one who evaluates and what he evaluates. Like the act of observation in the use of the gaze, the act of evaluation is a technology of social position. In poetry, elaborate rhetoric is a way to perform close observation and detailed and in-depth evaluation. The theme of evaluation contributes to the ideology of stable prosperity in patronage and also explores the possibilities of success and failure in relationships. Henri Lefebvre proposes a complex relationship between knowledge and power:

> The connection between knowledge (*savoir*) and power is thus made manifest, although this in no way interdicts a critical and subversive form of knowledge (*connaissance*); on the contrary, it points up the antagonism between a knowledge which serves power and a form of knowing which refuses to acknowledge power.[51]

Patronage connections expressed in terms of evaluation convey the contradiction between intimacy and distance in unequal relationships. This discussion of the theme of evaluation examines motifs of thought and awareness that entail the evaluation of relationships, including memory and forgetting, sleep and dreams, wonder, bewilderment, secrecy, deceit, knowledge and wisdom.

Memory and forgetting are an indirect approach to evaluating the dimensions of intimacy and distance in relationships. This poet-lover insists on the presence of the beloved in memory, and acknowledges the inability of mankind to cling to experiences of the past:

> Do not forget those times, for you were called man because you forget[52]

The poet-lover does not just acknowledge the forgetfulness of mankind: he deploys paronomasia, on the words 'forget' and 'man', to argue that the forgetfulness of mankind is inherent and inevitable. Paronomasia also shows that this inevitable and inherent quality of forgetfulness is a construction in language that can be reconstructed, not a fact of experience. The motif of being *called* a man, not just *being* a man, complements the contingent quality of paronomasia.

Demanding that someone not forget something is not the same as insisting that they remember it. This poet weaves his own non-forgetfulness together with that of the patron, so that they are connected in a tenuous way:

> Do not forget the one who did not forget your praise, and hopes beneath the darkness assert that you remember him[53]

The patron's recollection of the poet displays their relationship, but it is based on the somewhat fragile foundation of hopes beneath the darkness. The animated image of the hopes reinforces the assertion, while also calling attention to the fact that it is imagined in figurative language.

Sleep is an alternative form of awareness. The poet-lover's knowledge of this beloved is complicated by his uncertainty about the beloved's state of awareness:

> That dark eye is not sleeping or awake; that dark hair is not drunk or alert
> One is awake by nature and appears to be sleeping; one is sober by nature and acts intoxicated[54]

The uncertainty, expressed in images, shows that the beloved is not always what he seems to be. The dream of the beloved provides a dramatic experience of her presence and serves as a sign of her absence for the poet-lover in the following verse:

> How many an encounter did she show you close up, contact with the apparition coming by night and its visit[55]

The exclamation of amazement amplifies the dream into repeated dreams. The flickering presence of the beloved, who appears in dreams only to disappear by day, offers a commentary on patronage relationships. In the following verse, the poet-lover makes the intersection of intimacy and distance in the experience of the apparition more explicit:

> She did not approach with the apparition except to grow distant, and she did not make contact in sleep except to abandon [me][56]

The exception clauses allow the poet-lover to juxtapose the beloved's presence and absence. The poet-lover in the following verse expresses the tenuous link to the beloved with a question:

> A visitor in sleep, I ask, shall I arrive by night in her dream, or visit her?[57]

The poet inverts the conventional motif of the beloved visiting the poet-lover in his dream. The poet's proposed visit complements the beloved's visit and reinforces the relationship. However, this inversion also reinforces the experience of the relationship as a dream. The uncertainty of the relationship that takes place in dreams, and the question about it, are set in counterpoint to the closure implied by the paronomasia on the words 'visitor' and 'visit' at the beginning and end of the line. This rhetorical construction of closure calls attention to the tenuous quality of the relationship.

Wonder and amazement in motifs of evaluation amplify the presence of the person or thing that is evaluated. However, they also amplify the distance between the one who evaluates and the one who is evaluated. The amazing qualities of this beloved make him present for the poet-lover, and they also distance him from him:

> Of all the letters in the alphabet I am enamored by [the tiny loop of] *mīm* and [the upright line of] *alif* since your figure and mouth resemble *alif* and *mīm*[58]

For the poet-lover in the following verse, the days of love were the strangers among days because they were both unique and amazing:

> We will exceed the bounds in renewing your time with tears and you [days] were nothing but strangers among the days[59]

The days of love become more prominent for the poet-lover because of their strangeness, but this also makes them more distant and difficult to repeat.

Wonder intensifies connections with the patron that are expressed through evaluation. The description of the patron's unique superiority in the following verses emphasizes his estrangement from the community:

> Great deeds made him strange to most people so that he became concealed from those closest to him
> May he live long so that if he died in Marv [his hometown] while living there, he would die a stranger[60]

If he is concealed from those closest to him and a stranger in his own hometown, his unique superiority must also distance him from the patronage network. When the patron is made distant from the protégé and the patronage network, he is more difficult to observe and evaluate, and therefore more challenging to work with in patronage relationships. The patron does not have a monopoly on the distancing effect of unique superiority – the poet also valorizes himself and his work in this way, in the following verse:

> We sent you unique poetry after it had taken its time [grazing] in the pasture of amazing meanings[61]

This highly valued poetry contributes to the poet's effort to secure patronage. In addition, amazing poetry challenges the audience and complicates the effort to secure patronage. The strangely superior patron and strangely superior verse make a perfect match in the following:

> His moral qualities were strange [i.e superior] and a poet used strange terms about him, and one who uses strange terms did well with one who is strange[62]

This verse combines the potential for complications of the strangely superior patron and the strangely superior verse.

Bewilderment and confusion in the evaluation of the patron and patronage make the distance implied by wonder more pronounced. The poet-lover's evaluation of this beloved oscillates between empirical certainty and the indeterminacy generated by hyperbolic expression:

> I have always said that there is no one in the world as beautiful as my companion, and this statement is impossible
> What I claim is impossible, and it is not, since I have never set eyes on his equal[63]

The beloved's sensual presence is reinforced, while he is also obscured in the indeterminate description of hyperbole.

Bewilderment intensifies and makes problematic the connection with the patron that is expressed in terms of evaluation. If one can't figure this patron out, one can't very well evaluate him:

> God is great, there has come the greatest one whose nature men's imaginings have tried to plumb, only to end in confusion[64]

The hyperbolic negation of knowledge about the patron projects him beyond the range of evaluation. Even the elites in charge of evaluation can't figure out this patron:

> Those elites who know how to make calculations cannot calculate your refinement and virtue[65]

The point of evaluation is to draw conclusions based on determinate knowledge, but hyperbole generates only indeterminate information about the person or thing that is evaluated.

The indeterminate quality of information about the patron in hyperbole may be reinforced by confusion. No one can distinguish this patron's palace from the Ka'ba:

> Due to the abundant circumambulation of seekers around your palace day and night, no one knows your palace, O king, from the sanctuary[66]

The community confuses these patrons' orders for great deeds with the Qur'an:

> Orders for great deeds are recited [so often] among them that a tribe thought that they were chapters of the Qur'an[67]

The figurative confusion helps to clarify the fact that nobody really believed what was said in panegyric. Nobody listened to a verse like this and wondered if what it said was real. The poet projects the patron beyond the range of determinate knowledge, while also inviting the audience to compare his work to religious values.

The patron's generosity in the following verse overwhelms the poet to the point where he doesn't know where to begin in thanking him:

> I owe you thanks for many things, O king; because of this abundance of obligations, I do not know where to begin[68]

Negation both reinforces and complicates the knowledge upon which evaluation of the patron is based. The poet does not know where to begin, but has already said so in a poem, and so has already begun.

Secrecy may enhance or hinder relationships, and storing up secrets that are on display demonstrates the constitution of individual identity in a communal way.[69] This beloved is all the more sensually present for the beloved because of the image of secrets for kisses:

> Sometimes with conversation my body bound a contract with his; sometimes with kisses my mouth spoke secrets with his[70]

However, the poet-lover's figurative knowledge of these secrets is in kisses, so that his knowledge of the beloved is limited to a transient, sensual experience. The patron's secrecy valorizes what he knows, but makes it more difficult for the poet to evaluate him:

> One with deep secrets; that which [his] consciousness concealed was not accessible in the search of the one who examines it closely[71]

Secrecy implies the desirability of what the patron conceals, and intensifies the poet's connection to him, but also makes it harder to evaluate him. The inability of the patron's adversaries to keep their secrets from him, in the following verse, demonstrates the patron's superiority:

> His turn in power is the reporter of intelligence on the hearts of evil-wishers; it listens to everything they say and extracts secrets[72]

This interaction also illustrates the problem of adversaries keeping secrets from the patron in the first place.

Deceit undermines the possibility of using evaluation to make connections in relationships:

> Plain ignorance [is] the man with gray hair who came to be deceived by the naïve gazelle foal[73]

Paronomasia defines the contradiction between the beloved's naïve appearance and the poet-lover being deceived by her. The promise in the following verse displays the relationship and dismantles it in deceit, only to reconstitute it in the paradox of promises of deception:

> What Su^{c}dā promised was deception, and the sweetest of her promises is deception[74]

The paradox combines the connection with the beloved and its unraveling. Deception complicates the evaluation of the patron. For the poet in the following verse, good news has arrived, but only if it is true:

> The one who bears good news articulated news because of which we rejoiced if he is telling the truth to us[75]

The conditional sentence emphasizes the contingency of the good news, and the repetition of the word for 'bearer of good tidings' in the original highlights the contrast between the assertion of good news and the caveat. The poet in the following verse presents the threat of deception in praise only to reject it:

> He is the downpour, in whose praise, if I were excessive in description on purpose in order to lie, I would not be a liar[76]

The nominal sentence at the opening of the line reinforces the patron's presence, while the risk of lying compromises it. The conditional and negation each enable the poet to present and dismiss the risk of lying in praise. The patron in the following verses must use deceit to do his job:

> It is fortunate that his direction destroys a thousand tricks and spells and a thousand strategies and plots

> The plotting magicians do not know any way to put their strategies and plots to work on him[77]

The patron maintains his power by circumventing the plots of adversaries, while the circulation of such tricks – thousands of them – demonstrates the challenge that he faces. The most successful patron will combine skills in decoding the deceit of others, while encoding his own information in discreet and clever ways, as in the following verses:

> He subdued deceit in them; indeed, among the greatest aspects of cleverness is to not be called clever
> Their subterfuge is eloquent for him, and if they addressed his subterfuge, they would see it as the [foreign] language of a prisoner of war who is sold as a slave[78]

It is good for this patron that he has mastered these skills, while the fact that he needs them illustrates the risks he faces.

Knowledge secures connections in patronage, but may be compromised by uncertainty. The poet-lover in the following well-known verse negates the most basic knowledge, the knowledge of identity that persists in time. The beloved and her abodes are not themselves:

> You are not you and the abodes are not abodes; love has departed and affairs have changed[79]

By conjuring them, the poet-lover makes them present. Since they are not themselves, they are also absent for him in a radical way, because they have ceased to be themselves. The poet in the following verse asserts the significance of his departure from the beloved as a way to secure intimacy in the patronage relationship:

> Did you (f.) not know that resolve upon night travel is the brother and friend of success in catastrophes?[80]

The rhetorical meaning of the question reinforces the knowledge about resolve – it is saying 'You must know this'. The literal meaning of the question implies that the knowledge remains uncertain. Why would the beloved care? Knowledge about the significance of resolve is manifest, but the look back toward love dissolves it in uncertainty.

Knowledge connects the poet and the audience to the patron. This poet uses negation to present and reject the possibility of considering other options:

> And my consciousness is not shared in remembering you, and my way to your gift is not forked[81]

These patrons are known to be superior through antithesis, while the deferred possibility of inferiority alludes to other possibilities of patronage:

> Only because of the king of the east, the authority of whose virtue [reigns] over every king, do I know that virtue is light over darkness[82]
> Behold, certainty has displayed its page, and the distinction between fine bow quality wood of boasting and inferior wood has appeared[83]

Antithesis in these verses highlights the relational dimension of evaluation in patronage.

The patron has an obligation to seek certain knowledge to do his job. In the following request for pardon on behalf of a tribe, the poet provides him with the opportunity for an investigation:

> And if you investigate them you find in them noble souls and a paucity of manners[84]

The antithetical combination of nobility and lack of refinement, which is augmented with parallel syntax, facilitates the request for pardon by acknowledging the tribe's wrongdoing while distancing them from it. The patron in the following verse can be counted on to clarify obscure reports, and the poet urges the audience to take advantage of his acumen:

> Reports that are obscure and problematic are clarified by him; if you do not know go and ask him about what is obscure and problematic[85]

The circulation of obscure reports also interferes with the patron's use of knowledge to do his job.

In theory, wisdom is the most reliable source of information, but in practice poets may place it in contexts that imply ambivalence about it. This patron shares credit for wisdom with his own patron, the caliph:

> A caliph whose wise perspectives are shooting stars is guided to you, led by the light of wise perspectives[86]

The corresponding imagery of shooting stars and light reinforces this cooperation.

Shared credit demonstrates that the patron can work effectively with other people, and it also implies the potential for competition and differences of opinion. The patron in the following verse relies on his associate:

> He does not swerve from success and hitting the mark in wisdom while Ḥusayn is his minister[87]

He gains wisdom by working well with his associate, but this approach also makes the patron vulnerable because of his dependence on him. The ruler seeks wisdom from the patron in the following verse, demonstrating the patron's success in the patronage network:

> In every deed the commander seeks instruction from him even if he is not supposed to seek instruction from anyone[88]

The caveat that the ruler is not supposed to seek instruction from anyone also implies ambivalence about the patron's privilege as a source of information for him.

The authority of the patron's perspective is bound up with his power. This patron's wise perspective is as good as his turn in power, and together they generate stable virtue:

> In him, since the turn in power and his wise perspective are connected so that he has stable justice and virtue[89]

The poet imposes the order of parallel syntax to imply the ideological closure of the connection between power and wisdom on the one hand, and justice and virtue on the other. This construction in language alludes to the possibility of re-construction. It is as if the patron's wisdom will run out when his turn is done.

Motifs of wisdom enable the poet to co-opt the threat of violence and absorb it into the social order of patronage. This poet appropriates violent imagery and transforms it into the humility of lowered eyes and the careful reflection of thought:

> One who bares a sword of wisdom from his resolve for [use against] time, a sword whose polish is lowering of the eyes and thought
> With a sharp blade because of which, when he draws it in the face of a catastrophe, the daughters [i.e. vicissitudes] of time come to him to seek pardon[90]

With lowered eyes and thought, not violence, the patron confronts the challenges that time brings. The patron's gravity is contagious in the following verse, so that he transforms the enemy with his wise example instead of violence:

> His gravity brings forth gravity in the nature of the one who is without gravity; his stability brings forth stability in the wise perspective of the one who lacks stability[91]

His confrontation with these impetuous and unstable people also implies the risks that violence poses to the social order of patronage. The patron in the following verse uses violent means to achieve peaceful ends in the social order of patronage:

> The speech of the enemy, due to that world-burning sword, in time becomes more knowledgeable[92]

The porous boundary between the social order and violence beyond it can be an opportunity for the patron as well as a threat to the social order.

Connections expressed in terms of evaluation take shape in motifs of memory and forgetting, sleep and dreams, wonder and bewilderment, secrecy and deceit, and knowledge and wisdom. Close observation and evaluation define the portrayal of patronage relationships in panegyric poetry. These themes articulate connections as well as complications in patronage. The following chapter explores connections that take place in action, in terms of communication and interaction between the poet and the patron before the poet's audience.

7

DOING BUSINESS
COMMUNICATION AND INTERACTION

In the medieval Middle East and Central Asia, patronage connections expressed in terms of observation and evaluation occurred in conjunction with the more concrete activities of communication and interaction. Communication in this context refers to communication by, for and about the patron and the social order of patronage; interaction refers to how the poet seeks and deals with the patron's deeds of generosity. Observation and evaluation allow participants in patronage to judge the relationships of the past, cope with the ones in the present and consider relationships in the future. In connections expressed in terms of communication and interaction, participants in patronage do not just gather information and analyze it: they do business. Patronage as a form of social order enabled people of different status to do business together, by talking it over and engaging in the give and take of exchange. The first section of this chapter examines connections expressed in terms of communication, and the second focuses on connections expressed in terms of interaction.

Talking it over: communication in patronage

Connections that are expressed in terms of verbal communication forge and maintain the relationships of patronage. Discourse determines and is determined by social exchange.[1] Communication not only constitutes social order, it also constitutes social change:

> Our very notions of hierarchy … are constituted by types of speech and patterns of linguistic exchange. Second (a related point), the

> social order, in any period or culture, is not something which is fixed and immutable. It is a kind of dynamic equilibrium: speakers are constantly enforcing or undermining their perception of the status quo.[2]

Communication does not just describe the patronage relationship: it is an integral feature of it:

> On the level of direct interaction, the dedication and other discrete acts of speech perform and describe the panegyric relationship in which they are embedded. They administer exact stipulations and explicitly connect the rights and benefits of one partner with the duties and benefits of the other through reciprocity or cooperation.[3]

While communication is an integral feature of patronage relationships, patronage connections expressed in terms of communication also complicate or disrupt those relationships. J. Hillis Miller observes that citation or repetition of discrete acts of speech is necessary for a felicitous speech act, since repetition provides a context for making sense of a discrete act of speech, such as 'I do' in a marriage ceremony. In addition, repetition and citation are capable of violating a speech act.[4] Austin's concept of 'infelicity', in which a speech act fails to function properly, is an integral yet disruptive feature of the use of verbal communication. The theme of verbal communication articulates the contradiction of intimacy and distance in the unequal relationships of patronage. This section discusses connections that are made in the theme of communication, including the motifs of claims, requests, greetings, promises, barriers to communication, writing, the transmission of legend, the patron's speech, and the poet's use of poetry.

Claims are appeals, and they are open to multiple possible responses. This poet-lover uses an oath to stake a claim for his relationship:

> I swore to her that I am sound except for the illness over her that has cleaved to my heart[5]

The oath implies the connection between the poet-lover and the beloved. At the same time, his oath that all is well except for his lovesickness clarifies that all is not well.

Claims, like the vocative form of address that sometimes accompanies them, reinforce the poet's relationship to the patron. They are also open-ended, since a variety of responses are possible:

> O Haytham, O Ibn ᶜAbd Allāh, [here is] a claim of one who proclaims advice or commends it[6]

The claim of the following poet emphasizes the difficulties that lead to the claim and factors that can complicate it:

> O Aḥmad b. Abī Duʾād, [here is] an appeal that has been submitted by way of [following up on] my thanks to you, and it [would be] refractory [outside of this established connection]
> When I drew you forth against the vicissitudes, I was sufficiently protected from them, and the sword does not suffice for you until it has been drawn[7]

The claim reinforces the relationship, and the relationship also takes place in the context of threats to the poet's well-being. He rejects the possibility of a similar connection through communication with other patrons, but also refers to it, as if to show that he has other options.

The patron's claims reinforce the relationship, but may appear weak in comparison with action. This poet contrasts his patron's meaning to claims, and his deeds to speech:

> He who displays more meaning than claims and he who has more deeds than speech[8]

The poet focuses on action while entertaining the possibility of mere talk. In the following verse, the poet contrasts the claims within patronage discourse with the action of violence beyond this form of social order:

> Rulers are all claims, proof is his sword; that which has proof is better than claims[9]

The social order of patronage is not good enough for him, but that is where patronage relationships, rooted in poets' claims about rulers, take place. The poet in the following verse emphasizes the contingent quality of claims by juxtaposing the ruler's proofs to mere claims:

> Indeed, Abū ᶜĪsā has superior proofs of virtue that were not falsely ascribed or [merely] a claim[10]

Unlike claims, which take place in language, proofs link language to deeds. However, the deferred possibility of false proofs shows that proofs can be as unreliable as claims.

When the explicit verbal act of describing the patron frames the description itself, it functions like a claim. This poet speaks on behalf of the community of participants in patronage:

> They call you again this year the king who increases day by day,
> since you increase each day like blossoms in spring[11]

The explicit verbal act of description reinforces the patron's status. It also calls attention to the constructed and therefore changeable quality of the description and the patron's status. Like the spring flowers in the image, his current position will change. The patron in the following verse benefits from images of the permanent delights of paradise:

> Here is the one whom they call *ṭūbā* [the tree in paradise from which the inhabitants can take branches for houses and delicious fruit to eat]; here is the one whom they call Kawthar [the river in paradise into which all of the streams flow][12]

However, his status is in and of this world, not the next, and a contrast between eternal life in paradise and our time in this world is implied. Calling the patron the tree of paradise and a river in paradise emphasizes not what he is, but what he will have to do if he hopes to live up to these images. Modeling behavior for him in imagery demonstrates that his status in patronage is always under construction.

Calls to action resemble claims about the patron. In calling him to action, the poet argues that he is the man for the job at hand. However, calls to action refer to action in the future. This poet calls on the patron to pitch in by referring to situations in which he has not done so:

> Wherever his hand has not opened, there is no prophet of the call to generosity[13]

The poet in the following verse attempts to lock in the patron between his noble family and a call to action – the response to the summons remains to be seen:

> O son of the noble man and woman, no one but you is called for what you are called for[14]

Requests display a connection with the patron in terms of communication, and they also convey the open-ended quality of patronage connections. This poet draws on the love introduction to convey his request:

> God knows that I say this before you; my body becomes thin out of shame, O commander[15]

The echo of the love introduction implies the uncertainty that is involved in the request. The poet in the following verse augments his request with reference to the patron's previous work in patronage relationships:

> It is not excessive that I should follow up supplication with its like, and that I should demand a gift from the giver of gifts[16]

The focus on the reiteration of the relationship also portrays the changeable and contingent circumstances of patronage. The poet in the following verse uses paradox to confront and reject the degrading aspect of making requests:

> And one who longs for something who travels by night to you is not one who longs for something, and one who requests something who pursues the caliph is not one who requests something[17]

The seeker is figuratively not a seeker because the request honors rather than degrades the one who makes it. Likewise, the seeker in the following verse uses a conditional sentence to confront and reject the immoral aspect of the focus on worldly gain in patronage:

> Pleasures that arouse the heart, whose seeker, were it not for their connection to God's good defense, would be tempted by the devil[18]

The requests from allies in the following verse are paired with the fate of enemies:

> Silver comes to seekers and gold to visitors from you, thrones to friends and gallows to enemies from you[19]

The parallel between what the allies seek and what the enemies get demonstrates the interdependence of the social order of patronage and violence beyond it.

Greetings make a connection expressed in terms of communication, and also illustrate the potential for uncertainty in that connection. This poet-lover conjures his beloved in a farewell that is made into a greeting, emphasizing the intersection of her presence and her absence for him:

> And we made farewell on that day into a greeting, and we made separation on that day into a meeting[20]

The motif of separation that is made into a meeting elaborates on the farewell that is made into a greeting. These rearticulations of experience in language argue for the use of language to fashion experience, and imply that it can change the way we view the world. Similarly, the poet-lover in the following verse offers greetings to the traces, as if to conjure the relationship, and also demonstrates his inability to do so:

> Traces that he approached and to which he uttered greetings – how many a time did [such] an encounter untie the knot of his patience[21]

Like the traces, the apparition of the beloved is a sign of her enduring presence for the poet-lover and a sign of her absence. In these verses, the problematic connection with the beloved by way of the apparition is articulated in part with greetings:

> The apparition of Ẓamyāʾ traveled in the middle of the night, so welcome, and greetings to the night journey of the apparition of Ẓamyāʾ from another night journey[22]
> She sends greetings, and the direction of her apparition and her sending it, from her distance, are amazing[23]

Whether the poet-lover or the apparition offers greetings, this tenuous connection made through communication unravels as the night passes and the apparition disappears.

Like the apparition, the patron is both near and far because patronage relationships combine intimacy and distance between people of unequal status. This poet demands salutations as a connection with the patron, but he is on his way out of the relationship:

> O Abū Muslim, give salutations twice over, and go forth by evening, safe and sound, for I am going forth by morning

> I will give thanks for your benefits, whose dense shade covers me, and would I forget the springtime of my homeland?[24]

He explains that he will not forget, but does so with a rhetorical question whose literal meaning implies the possibility of forgetting.

Promises make connections in patronage, and open the relationship up to future possibilities of success and failure. This poet's ambition links him to the patron's promise, but both are deferred in the passage of time:

> And I have an ambition that is, as the ages pass, pregnant with the days of your promise, like your pledge[25]

The poet in the following verse equates the promise with haste, and the gift with delay, and reinforces the equation with paronomasia on the words 'haste' and 'delay', as well as repetition of the word 'substitute':

> If there is in haste a substitute for delay, there is in his promise a substitute for his gift[26]

The superiority of the promise to the gift itself is set in counterpoint to the default of preferring the real thing. The poet in the following verse clarifies the uncertainty of the promise by presenting and rejecting the possibility of broken promises:

> And he was not one who promises a false promise, or a speaker who speaks without fulfillment [of what he says][27]

While the poet attempts to perform speech acts in refined rhetoric, he explains that speech and acts are not the same. Speech is just a prelude to future acts, so that communication opens out onto the possibilities of future experience. The context of religious discourse links the promise and the threat, as the poet does in the following verse, with paronomasia on two verbs:

> A group who, if they promise or threaten, flood with truth the flows of what they say with what they do[28]

However, this wordly promise and threat pales in comparison to the more significant one that relates to the next world. The link between the promise and the threat implies the boundaries between insiders and outsiders. It alerts the outsiders to the benefits of promises, and warns insiders of the risks of threats.

Barriers to effective communication can both reinforce and impinge on the use of communication to forge meaningful connections in patronage relationships. This poet-lover believes the beloved's lies, which undermines their relationship, but that is how he demonstrates that the relationship means something to him:

> [The beloved] lies to me, and I believe her out of affection, and an aspect of being in love is believing lies[29]

Instead of surmounting the barrier to communication, the poet-lover makes the connection to the relationship run right through it. The most severe problem that the poet-lover faces in the following verse is a complete breakdown of communication:

> There was no speech between you and me, and if there was once, you closed the door of speech[30]

The conditional sentence joins the lack of communication in the relationship with the deferred possibility of communication in the past. The repetition of the word 'speech' at the beginning and the end of the line displays the conjunction and disjunction between the lack of communication and the possibility of it.

Disruptive communication may interfere with the relationship. This patron fends off the interference of censurers, whose role echoes the conventional motif of censure as a disruption of the relationship between the poet-lover and the beloved:

> When the winds of your generosity blow, the speech of the censurers becomes dust that appears in rays of sun that fall in a room[31]

Their speech dissolves into dust motes visible only in sunlight indoors, but the reference to censure implies the risks that threaten patronage. Fortunately for the poet in the following verse, his patron does not listen to gossip about him:

> A forgiving ear whose narrow opening does not open to anything that is lowly, and fingers that have not been locked shut[32]

The parallel between not listening to gossip and not closing the hand that gives gifts implies that the circulation of gossip can be tantamount to the failure of patronage. While the patron refuses to listen to gossip, the circulation of it implies the potential for disruptive communication.

Writing can entail patronage connections at a distance. In the following sequence of verses, the poet requests a letter to confirm the relationship. This appeal asserts a connection and also implies the multiple possible responses to the appeal:

> So clear away the dust from my eyes with lines that clear away from my mind the anxieties of one who is worn out
> Black ones that make faces white with those selected clever stories and proverbs from you
> And hasten your graceful fingers between them until they make the rounds all the way around them
> They have not ceased to be nursed by eloquence all, raised and cared for by good deeds and benefit
> In the valley of an inexpensive sheet of paper whose contents have been filled with valuable pearls of speech
> Indeed I consider you to be an unattainable place the like of which does not exist among caves and mountains
> And I see your letter in its sound perfection dispensing with the letters of others, in pleasures and money[33]

The poet evokes intimacy through writing with images of the body of the writer, the relationship between the writer and his writing, and the impact of the letter on its reader. Lines of writing will clear away dust from the poet's eyes and black writing will make faces glow bright. The writer's fingers will make the rounds as he crafts his piece. The writer's good qualities have raised the lines of writing as if they were his children, and his eloquence has nursed them. In all of these ways, the distance associated with written communication gives way to intimacy between the writer and the reader. By valorizing the patron's writing, the poet valorizes his own craft as a persuasive case to demand the letter. While distance gives way to intimacy, the poet concludes the segment by referring to the distance between himself and the patron, and by presenting and rejecting the possibility of considering other patrons.

In the following sequence of verses, the possession of the inkwell displays the patron's relationship to the ruler, his father, in the context of succession disputes:

> One by one each one becomes apparent; the inkwell bears testimony to this tale
> Is it with the status and prestige of Faraydūn; is it with the position and good reputation of Alexander?
> Why does the king of the east give the inkwell to you? Consider this report carefully and look into it well
> The purpose of the inkwell is that there is a pen in it; the pen is equivalent to the sword if not better …
> There is a purpose in the inkwell and likewise in that long line of nobility (i.e. ink) that you received from your father there is a purpose
> He did not give you nobility because of ability; the ruler's mystery in that matter is concealed
> What in the world is more cherished than nobility? He sent you nobility with an inkwell with gold[34]

Paronomasia on the words 'ink' and 'nobility'reinforces the conjunction between the inkwell and the relationship. The link between the inkwell and the relationship circumvents the distance associated with writing in favor of an assertion of intimacy. Instead, the inkwell itself bears testimony to that assertion. Here again, the valorization of written communication as a dimension of relationships reinforces the poet's use of refined rhetoric as a way of performing them. The inconclusive investigation of the significance of receiving the inkwell reinforces the relationship with the ruler. It also implies ambivalence about it. Legendary kings are invoked to bear witness to the ruler's decision, but they do not do so, since they are invoked in a question. The patron's much less certain circumstances contrast with the legendary status of these two kings. The focus on the ruler giving the inkwell to the patron, as a symbol of the relationship and of the patron's status, also implies the possibility of the ruler taking it away and giving it to someone else.

Patronage, as we have seen, is an alternative to violence, but the frequent images of violence in the description of writing imply that communication can be just as antagonistic and adversarial as battle:

> When [the pen] bears the five fine [fingers] and the copious streams of thought are emptied upon it
> The tips of spears obey it and are demolished due to its secrets like numerous troops taking down tents

When it seeks abundance from the clever intellect and its upper parts approach the paper, and they are lower parts[35]

The conventional competition between pen and sword, which is carried out in the venue of the men of the pen because the men of the sword have other business to attend to, insists on the role of communication and patronage as valid alternatives to violence. This competition, which is evoked by violent imagery for writing, is an argument for the correspondence of speech and acts, but this correspondence appears in figurative language. The poet imagines speech in this way, but it can be re-imagined in other ways. He imagines the correspondence between speech and acts, writing and violence, as an inversion, in the description of the upper parts that are really lower parts, as the writer wields his pen. Correspondence leads to cooperation in the following verses. The repetition of the words 'pen' and 'sword' contributes to the articulation of cooperation:

For kings the pen and sword are the greatest army; the fierce male lion fears the pen and sword
The foundation of kingship is made strong by the sword and the pen; through these two things, kingship has splendor and dignity[36]

This cooperation calls attention to the interdependence of the social order of patronage and violence. Speech is promoted to the status of acts as the men of the pen become a figurative part of the army. However, the promotion is imagined in language.

The transmission of information about the patron may echo the transmission of legend. Legend reinforces the patron's power, but reading about the patron now is not the same as the time-tested authority of legend:

Everyone reads nothing but reports from the *Maḥmūdnāma*, just as they read the story of the *Shāhnāma*[37]

While other legendary kings share a book, Maḥmūd gets his own. This makes him special, and also leaves him excluded from legend. Legendary deeds are completed, but his remain incomplete. This patron has attracted the interest of those who transmit the sayings and deeds of the Prophet Muhammad:

> The reports of your battles with enemies and the stories about you have excited [the interest of] the transmitters of reports, O king of the market[38]

While Prophetic sayings circulated widely and were a central feature of the literary marketplace, they were viewed as an ethical discourse, not a commodity for sale. The reports about the ruler resemble Prophetic sayings, but they make the ruler king of the market.

The portrayal of the patron's speech displays the use of verbal communication to express relationships and the uncertainties of patronage:

> Refined manners are a necessary part of him just like the mind is a necessary part [of a person]; he utters words in sequence like pearls strung in sequence[39]

Parallel syntax in the depiction of this patron's speech demonstrates the correspondence between speech and inner life: his refined manners lead inward in the image of the mind. At the same time, his refined rhetoric leads outward in the concrete image of pearls in sequence. However, the response of the community to his speech remains to be seen.

The patron's speech enables him to connect with the community of participants in patronage, if they pay attention. The poet in the following verse demands that they do so, but the response to the command is uncertain:

> Listen to his speech if you seek pearls, for beneath each of his utterances is an armful of pearls[40]

In the following verse, they are paying attention; they also reinforce the patron's speech by circulating it:

> Those who are clever, alert, and possess foresight repeat [or speak of] your discourse[41]

The role of these clever people in circulating the patron's speech also suggests the potential for competition with the patron. The patron's speech may remain secret. The depiction of his speech in the following verse makes secrecy a source of cohesion for the community:

> His pen has secluded meetings without whose secrets these gathering places of kingship would not fill up[42]

Though it is a source of cohesion, secrecy also distances the patron from the community.

There is always the risk that people just won't pay attention. The poet in the following verse links this risk to the benefit of the patron's speech:

> The lord of the world has a purpose in this speech [about great deeds], so beware and do not hold this speech in contempt[43]

Negation and the imperative allow the poet to present and marginalize this risk. If people pay too much attention to him, other risks threaten the patron's status:

> When he is going to speak [of his] knowledge, it is necessary to burn wild rue to keep the evil eye [lit., the grief of evil ones' eyes] far from that great man[44]

The eloquence of the patron in this verse makes him vulnerable to the evil eye. There is also the risk that the patron won't tell the truth. This patron did his job, but everyone thought that he might not fulfill his commitments:

> He fulfilled [his obligations] and they [had] supposed that he was fate, about which they had heard that it tells the truth and lies[45]

The poet presents and rejects uncertainty about the patron's speech as a reliable prediction of his deeds.

The following verse offers a comparison between the patron's speech as a way to forge connections with allies, and a way to punish adversaries:

> I shall describe the two reeds of the king's pen with two explicated meanings:
> One is harm for ignorance without benefit, one is benefit for knowledge without harm[46]

The combination of antithesis and parallel reinforces the conjunction and disjunction between benefit and harm. These outcomes of the patron's discourse integrate the social order of patronage with violence beyond it.

The following verse links benefit and harm with complementary nature images, and distinguishes between them with antithesis:

> His pen's venom is that of deadly snakes, and the honey of the harvest that is gathered by the hands of the honey collectors[47]

This combination of related imagery and antithesis demonstrates the conjunction and disjunction between benefit and harm, and juxtaposes patronage to the alternative of violence.

The motif of poetry, or the poet's speech, provides a metapoetic commentary on the possibilities of connections expressed through communication.[48] Communication is not just about relationships, it is bound up with the experience of them. The more the poet desires the relationship with the patron, the more he has to say about it, as this poet-lover illustrates:

> And I complained abundantly of my love for her, and indeed the sign of the affliction of love is that we complain abundantly[49]

His complaint allows him to articulate a connection to the beloved, while the intertwined affliction of desire and complaint of love demonstrate the distance in the relationship.

In the motif of poetry, communication is bound up with experience, but they don't fit together well. This poet shows that the patron's qualities remain out of circulation until they are packaged in poetry:

> [Poems] whose verses return, when they are sent, the freely grazing parts of glory of the tribe as they [the poems] graze freely[50]

Freely grazing poetry means unique and valuable verse, while freely grazing glory remains an untapped potential for the patron's advancement. The correspondence of imagery is set in counterpoint to the different significance of the related images.

The motif of poetry in the transition between the love introduction and the praise section identifies problematic desire in love with praise:

> I speak of my heart's condition – no, it is not good to say a lot about the heart's sadness in praise of the commander[51]

This poet brings up his anxiety about love only to set it aside as he moves on to praising the patron. However, by bringing up his anxiety, he links it to the expression of praise. In the following verse, the poet who has given up his heart questions the possibility of moving on to praise:

> What are you saying, without a heart how can I utter praise of the just king in this condition?[52]

He does move on, swept along by the conventions of the poem, but his hesitation demonstrates the intersection between unfulfilled desire and praise. The question format reinforces this hesitation. The parallel syntax of the 'I-said-he-said' dialogue format in the following verse maintains the link between the poet and the beloved, even as the poet moves on to praise the patron:

> I said, from praise of him I am distraught; he [the companion] said, that is what the wisest men do[53]

In his figurative subjectivity, the beloved complements praise by expressing approval of it, and also interferes in it by speaking up as the poet moves on. The poet's distress as he is overwhelmed by the patron, in the context of the dialogue, echoes the distress of desire in love. This distress reinforces the patron's status and complicates the use of poetry to forge a connection with him.

The poet's movement from love to praise echoes the ancient theme of the journey to the patron, an expression of the intimacy and distance of patronage relationships. This poet is on his way to the patron, but he imagines applying the praise of his qualities to the whole world:

> [Mounts traveling] to the axis of the world whose excellent qualities, if I were to praise the people of the world with his superiority, would suffice for them[54]

This use of praise reinforces the patron's status and also imagines him blending into the crowd. The journey to the patron becomes a possible journey from one patron to another in the following verses:

> Gold coins that are paid for verses [that are] as if the one who selects them had been just and fair in their division,
> That facilitate the provisions of our journey when we travel and smooth out the camel saddle and resting place when we stay put[55]

Travel alludes to the importance of mobility in the flexible social order of patronage: the antithesis between traveling and staying put displays its possibilities.

As a way to forge connections with the patron, poetry remains open to future possibilities of success and failure in patronage. This poet is off to a good start:

> And all of your generosity is good, but the best of generosity is the good beginning[56]

While the general statement implies stable prosperity in patronage, the 'good beginning' emphasizes the reiterated and contingent quality of the relationship. The good beginning is a rhetorical term used in the criticism of poetry. The use of a term for poetry to describe the patron's generosity reinforces the complementary dimension of patronage. In the following verse, the poet intertwines his future needs and praise of the patron, and reinforces the connection with parallel syntax:

> So long as a number of cravings and yearnings have not been fulfilled by his generosity, a number of documents and notebooks have not been filled with his praise[57]

The reference to unfulfilled desire and unwritten praise implies uncertainty about the future of the relationship. The poet in the following verse emphasizes this open-ended quality of praise by asking when the connection with the patron will take place:

> When will I water my ambition by meeting you, when my speech and my language awaken others?[58]

The reference to success with other patrons serves as an argument for future success with this one, as well as a way to alert the patron that the poet has other options.

In some cases, questions regarding poetry relate to the inexpressible qualities and deeds of the patron. These hyperbolic questions reinforce the patron's status while making it indeterminate, and distancing him from the community. According to one view, in the related motifs of inexpressibility and wonder, the poet 'reminds the audience subtly but forcefully that it is not seeing what is described.'[59] Another way of thinking about this problem is that the poet, in displaying the indeterminate aspect of inexpressible qualities and deeds, leaves it up to the audience to imagine them. This patron's qualities may not fit neatly into speech, but they could be imagined:

> How can anyone say what you have done, how can speech attain [the expression of] your deeds?[60]

The poet in the following verse alludes to the importance of mobility, both physical and social, in patronage:

> How shall we praise Ibn Yūsuf, no, how did his glory travel by night so that it overcame praise?[61]

Both the patron's qualities and the poet's poem are on the move. In the following verse, the poet reinforces the hyperbolic question by doubling it in parallel syntax:

> What do I know to do and what do I know to say of thanks; how can the ground thank the clouds that pour down rain?[62]

Hyperbolic questions like these, which reject the link between the poem and the patron's experience, do business in poetry while undermining the possibility of doing so.

Motifs of poetry that incorporate antithesis also leave the interpretation of the description open: the poet presents antithesis so that the audience can consider the patron, poetry and the social order of patronage from different angles. This patron's generosity demands two separate descriptions – one that emphasizes its destruction of avarice and one that focuses on its promotion of virtue:

> Do two descriptions of his hand, for besides him, there is none who obliterates avarice or nourishes generosity[63]

The contrast illustrates the intersection of virtue and vice in the ethical discourse of praise, and the possibilities of success and failure in patronage. In the following verse, the poet intertwines the pleasures of praise with the difficulties that the patron must overcome in order to warrant it:

> And praise is honeysuckle whose gatherer is not seen harvesting it except from water with an infusion of colocynth[64]

These images illustrate the simultaneous conjunction and disjunction between the experiences of danger and prosperity.

The intersection of praise and blame, as a motif of praise, reinforces the use of communication to make connections in patronage. It also inscribes the possibility of failure in patronage relationships as an integral yet disruptive feature of praise:

> Shall I drape the garment of indecent speech upon the one whose good deeds to me, if I were to compose invective against him, would compose invective in response for him?
> A noble one, when I praise him, the people are with me; when I blame him, I blame him alone[65]

This poet praises his patron and considers the ramifications of blaming him. The image of draping a garment of inappropriate speech on the patron echoes the conventional image of draping praise on a patron, just as a patron will sometimes drape a robe of honor on a poet. This multidirectional image distinguishes and links praise and blame: likewise, the animated image of good deeds, which should inspire praise, responding to invective in kind. The poet also amplifies his relationship by noting that praise links him to the community while blame would alienate him. The motifs distinguish praise and blame, while the parallel syntax imposes a single order upon them. The poet in the following verse incorporates into his praise of the patron those people who just don't get it:

> Their faces turn gloomy [lit. black] when I descend with them for praise or gain
> May those among them who do not know the difference between my praise and my invective go as your sacrifice[66]

Praise only works as an ethical discourse if it is recognized as such. This reference to confusion about praise and blame offers a counterpoint to the patron's recognition of the ethical discourse, and also refers to the risk of a breakdown in communication in patronage.

Praise poetry may work in a self-effacing manner that problematizes the use of poetry to forge and maintain connections. Blame is an abject alternative to praise, meaning an alternative that constitutes, clings to and threatens the use of praise in patronage:

> He was loftier than the school of praise, so that praise of him was practically invective[67]

This poet projects the patron beyond the range of praise, so that praise resembles blame. The hyperbolic expression reinforces the connection made with praise, and makes the patron distant from the poet and the capacity of language to represent him. The poet also alludes to the fact that praise is, in effect, blame if the patron does not pay for it. Lies are another abject alternative to truth in praise – an alternative that constitutes, clings to and threatens the use of truth:

> I told a lie, but it was not out of lack of ability, for I did not have the display of his virtue in sight
> As he is, I did not know how to praise him completely, so there was no other way for me but to lie
> Whoever says that there are people in the inhabited areas of the world who resemble the king of the east in virtue tells a lie[68]

This poet exploits the threat of lies to project the patron beyond the capacity of truth in praise. The patron ends up beyond the range of truth because the poet remains distant from him. The poet juxtaposes the figurative lies in the hyperbolic expression with a literal motif of lies. In the motif of lies he considers and rejects the possibility of people claiming that there is someone like the patron. The juxtaposition clarifies the distinction between figurative and literal lies. However, the figurative lies allude to the deferred possibility of literal lies about the patron. The literal lies told by other people call attention to this deferred possibility.

The motif of poetry is a metapoetic commentary on the use of the poem as well as a mise-en-abyme – an internal reflection of the significance of the poem. Whether thought of as an overarching commentary or an internal reflection, the motif of poetry calls attention to the use of communication to experience relationships in all of their possibilities, uncertainties and flexibility:

> Take my voice to you, for the possession of voices is equivalent to the possession of slaves in judgment[69]

The poem represents an initiative in patronage more than an established connection.

Connections made through verbal communication play an important role in articulating patronage. Motifs of communication, especially but not only the motif of poetry, provide an internal reflection of, and a meta-poetic commentary on, the function of the poem in patronage. The motifs of claims, requests, greetings, promises, barriers to communication, writing, the transmission of legend, the patron's speech and the poet's use of poetry forge and complicate patronage connections.

Give and take: interaction in praise

Medieval Arabic and Persian panegyric poetry is material as well as moral.[70] No matter how persuasive it may be, panegyric poetry remains an argument for generosity that is distinct from acts of generosity. Refined rhetoric enables poets to insist on acts of generosity while acknowledging the difference between the request for a gift and the real thing.

Generosity connects people to their community and avarice alienates them from it.[71] Poets use indirect expression in refined rhetoric to explain to patrons: not that you are with us or against us, but that you are with us or you are all alone. Connections articulated through the theme of interaction are not just about the moral implications of material wealth and deeds: they are also a way in which the identity of the patron, the poet and other participants in patronage takes shape. This discussion of interaction examines motifs of love, service and bonds; the future, hope and ambition; the exchange of poetry for pay and material wealth; failure to connect, competition and violence; and nature, time and space.

Motifs of love, service, and bonds offer a complex perspective on patronage. Interaction in the love relationship offers a preview of interaction in patronage, and the unfulfilled desire or transient sensual experience of the love relationship helps to make the audience aware of the uncertainty of patronage. For this poet-lover, desire for the beloved does not just allow for the possibility of unfulfillment: unfulfillment defines the experience of desire:

> Do not give the reins to love, O heart, if you do not want pain, for every person who has become a lover is equal in living with the heart's pain[72]

The poet-lover warns his heart not to take the risk of being in love while he describes himself as being in love. If the poet-lover can take a risk in relationships when the odds are against him or he doesn't even have a chance, then the participants in patronage should be able to cope with the risks of relationships as well. The motif of the pledge in the following verse refers more directly to the dynamics of patronage and the motif of the promise in particular:

> How many a pledge [to meet] did they do away with and misrepresent, so that the first part of it is delay and the last is reversal?[73]

When the poet considers the possibilities of success and failure in praise, the uncertainty of love lingers in the background.

The poet-lover may succeed in enjoying the sensual presence of the beloved, and this enjoyment calls attention to the transience of sensual experience. This beloved's sensual presence is bound up with her unavailability to the poet-lover:

> And a neck that is tender when it bends, as if she came to you in [the two parts of] her night as a gazelle foal on its own [away from its mother]
> As if every necklace of beauty and grace were upon her neck, even if she is without a necklace by evening and into the late morning [because she gets plenty of beauty sleep and doesn't spend all her time doing housework and childcare]
> And [with] a diseased [i.e. languid] glance between the curtains and a slender figure to embrace and a cool smile
> With coal black curls and plump hips, with [a face that is] a moon of good fortune and gifts that are paltry[74]

She is sensually present as a frightened gazelle foal and also fades into the landscape. Her beauty recedes from view when she disappears for long hours of rest only to re-emerge refreshed, but this sign of her elite status distances her from the poet-lover. Her eyes imply the possibility of exchanging looks and make her appear emotionally affected by the poet-lover. Her waist is a place to embrace, and her mouth is about smiles and cool kisses, so that her sensual presence is in every way not just before the poet-lover's eyes, but for the purpose of loving him. However, this sensual presence appears from behind the curtains that conceal the beloved from the poet-lover. The pace of description, with its allusion to love, picks up in the final line of this sequence, from three features to four, and with a tighter arrangement of parallel syntax and morphology. However, the fourth feature in this sequence – her paltry gifts – interferes with the poet's reverie of desire. Similarly, in the following sequence of verses, suffering and yearning in the past imply distance, while the resounding presence of the beloved for the lover has transformed the relationship for one night:

> Now it is better for I was with him last night, for I had been very concerned without his face
> Now it is better because I slept with him last night, for I had insomnia over grief for him …
> Last night was a very good night; I purchased that night with my soul
> I embraced my idol, and I cleared out the treasure of his kisses
> I stroked his hair; the palace became a perfumer's tray because of its fragrance
> Sometimes I turned night to day with that face, sometimes I piled up roses with those rosy cheeks[75]

The images, especially the image of the idol, display his sensual presence for the poet-lover and also serve as signs of his absence. The repetition, in anaphora, of 'Now it is better' emphasizes the shift from grief to delight, and also emphasizes the changeability of relationships and the transience of sensual experience. The past tense in the description of the night of pleasure makes pleasure concrete, and also limits it to the single night that is described. The poet-lover turned night to day with the beloved's bright face, implying that his beauty transcends time. This image also alludes to the focus on the single night. It is obvious but important that the theme of love, which appears in much of this poetry, appears at the beginning of the poem, rather than in the middle or at the end. This allows for a narrative-like development from love to politics, but the poet-lover does not just grow up: love remains a background for the rest of the poem.

Motifs of service in Persian panegyric poetry enable the poet to solicit the participation of the community of participants in patronage in his relationship with the patron. An assertion of intimacy in the relationship, service also calls attention to the distance between the protégé and the patron in the social hierarchy. This poet compares the benefit of serving the patron with the risk of not doing so:

> Serve him if you wish to boast [with validity]; if you do not take up service of him, he will take your boasting[76]

Repetition of the word boasting joins and contrasts the benefit with the risk. The poet in the following verse uses parallel syntax and morphology to link the ruler's turn in power with the service of his protégés:

> All seek a [good] reputation from his turn in power, all are leaders [due to being] in service to him[77]

The temporary quality of the turn in power also implies the temporary quality of the protégé's status. While the protégés become leaders through serving him in this verse, in the next verse, rulers become like slaves in the patron's service:

> Rulers are all enamored of serving him, binding the sash in service like male slaves
> Since all are seeking the security of peace, kings think about nothing but serving him[78]

This upward and downward mobility in service demonstrates the potential for mobility in patronage. The poet implies that service can transform adversarial relationships into patronage relationships, as the social order of patronage expands at the expense of violence.

Poets define the bonds of patronage in panegyric poetry and take the uncertainty of these bonds into consideration. This poet's bonds are strong, not weak, but the reference to the deferred possibility of weak bonds implies uncertainty:

> A link of pure refined manners between us, strong of bonds, not weak[79]

The patron in the following verse promotes his protégés to the status of his most cherished person:

> O you for whom the dearest person is the guest, just as the most cherished person for you is the visitor[80]

The figurative promotion implies the intimacy of a strong and enduring relationship, while the literal status of the protégé as a guest and visitor demonstrates the distance between the patron and protégé, and implies the short term of their work together. Parallel syntax reinforces these figurative promotions and calls attention to the fact that they are constructed in language and subject to reconstruction.

Motifs of interaction between the poet and the patron may emphasize the possibilities of patronage with a focus on the future, hope and ambition. This poet describes the opportunities that lie in store for the seeker with this patron:

> A bright one whose hands are the opportunity for every seeker, and his gift is a pious endowment in the path of praise[81]

The religious motif of the pious endowment emphasizes the good prospects with the patron. It also refers to the future and the multiple possibilities of patronage. In the following verse, the poet attempts to link a good deed in the past with one in the future:

> And if you seconded it, it is not disliked for you to follow one good deed with another[82]

The conditional sentence emphasizes the contingent quality of the link between the past deed and the future. The position of the following verse in the conclusion of the poem reinforces its orientation toward the future of the patron's career; the imperative verb commands a prosperous future, while that future remains to be seen:

> Be happy and live well, give generously and consume in happiness[83]

The poet's hope opens out onto the future of the patronage relationship. Hope allows the protégé to imagine intimacy in the patronage relationship while demonstrating that it is deferred in the future:

> The name of kingship has found greatness in him, the hope of noble men has become strong in him[84]

The parallel syntax between the statement about kingship in general and the statement about hope illustrates the central role of patronage in the patron's power. The poet in the following verse contrasts the distractions and complications that he has avoided with his focus on the patron:

> I gathered in him the union of all hope, and I did not incline to scattering dispersion [of efforts in patronage] and factions[85]

The antithesis between the union of hope and dispersion in factions conveys the intersection of risk and hope. The image of imprisonment and release enables this poet to imagine a better future:

> There is no redemption for a man whose hope has been captured by fate except hope in you and your gifts[86]

Repetition of the word 'hope' links and contrasts captive hope and hope that is redeemed. Paronomasia on the words 'hope' and 'gifts' also reinforces the movement from failure toward success.

Ambition, like hope, defers success in the future. This poet uses the motif of ambition to express the conjunction and disjunction between loss in love and the prospect for gain in patronage:

> Let my ambition turn away from uselessness and let my standing at the abode be brief[87]

The repeated and parallel use of the energetic verb form intensifies the movement from the love relationship to praise. The position of the following verse at the end of the poem makes it a transition from praise to the future of the patronage relationship:

> And among wonders is a poet whose ambitions leave him sitting down, or who loses with a generous man[88]

The verse articulates the uncertainty of patronage, while the motif of wonder distances the possibility of failure.

Motifs of the exchange of poetry for pay and motifs of material wealth provide a metapoetic commentary on the use of the poem. The poet often constructs arguments in refined rhetoric for the exchange of poetry for pay. These arguments assert successful patronage, and their constructed quality shows that the exchange can be reconstructed and reimagined in different ways. This poet links his poem to the reward with the corresponding images of a bright countenance:

> I greeted his bright face with the beauty of bright praise and he greeted my bright face with generosity[89]

In the following verses, the poet acknowledges that the poem and the reward are not equivalent in material value, but insists that they are equivalent in the commitment that they represent:

> I ordered an alliance between my poetry and his generosity, equivalent in commitment to the alliance if not in wealth
> Rare exquisite ones of noble verse that he responds to in kind with rare gifts and exquisite things
> When the embroidery of poetry was plentiful for him, we received unusual embroidered silk, long pieces that flow and flutter[90]

The corresponding images link the poem and the reward, but they are offset by the acknowledgment of the incommensurability between them. The following verses define the intimacy of the relationship in terms of the link between the poem and the reward:

> And I was not one who was in desperate need of his own property nor was Ḥafṣ in desperate need of my praise …
> And the gifts that he had to offer did not pass me by, and the fine poetry that I had to offer did not pass him by[91]

The correspondence between poem and reward is expressed in parallel statements that convey the stand-offish quality of poet and patron alike. While the poem did not pass by the patron and the reward did not pass by the poet, it would not have mattered if they did, because neither of them is really interested in doing business.

The incommensurability of the patron's deeds and the poem about them complicates the connections that are forged in motifs of exchanging the poem for pay. These poets just cannot keep up with the patron:

> If I live for a hundred years and say thanks to him, I still would not say one part out of a hundred thousand of thanks due for his deeds[92]
> And how many a *ṣāmitī* [after the grandfather of the patron] hand have you with me, for which my thanks are scant and about which description falls short[93]

The poets amplify their status with hyperbolic expressions, and also make their patrons so distant that their qualities become indeterminate.

Material wealth is a display of the patron's generosity, and it also implies the constantly changing quality of patronage, since material wealth is consumed. This poet juxtaposes old and new wealth, calling attention to the fact that wealth is caught up in the flow of time:

> I shall thank Abū ᶜAlī, for from the gifts of his hands are my old and new wealth[94]

The poet in the following verse calls attention to the dissipation of wealth with an image of consuming musk incense:

> The desired thing, by analogy, is like musk; his generosity is the fire and his hand the censer[95]

The material wealth to be gained in patronage may be delightful, but it is also transient.

In the following verse, the contrast between the patron who holds money in contempt and the community that values it emphasizes the movement of wealth in patronage:

> Silver coins are held in contempt by you and dear to the people; how can you hold in contempt what is dear to the people of the world?[96]

Money changing hands is money consumed, and money in circulation relates directly to the uncertainty, flexibility and social mobility that occur in patronage.

Motifs of material wealth may focus on financial problems, as in the following verses:

> How many a time did a hand that uses wealth up when it leaves it behind raise my condition to his …
> Come and let us join the two sides of our condition in equivalence and just division
> And the condition is not equivalent [between us] if there is no return from the stronger to the weaker[97]

The argument for equivalence demands intimacy, while the contrast between the stronger and the weaker party displays distance in the relationship. These verses also imply that, within patronage, there is the potential for social mobility. The repetition of the word 'condition' links past experience, an appeal for the future and the timeless quality of the conditional. The imperative opens out onto the future of the relationship, while the conditional sentence warns of the possibility of failure. The following request appears as a rhetorical question that alludes to the uncertainty of the exchange:

> And a thousand among thousands is not a great deal of your gifts given, so how can I fear to miss out on a thousand from you?[98]

Compared to this rhetorical question alluding to possible complications, the problem in the following verses appears more serious:

> And I endeavor to keep your affection for the sake of that which it brings, and I am content with you [with] less than what suffices
> And I ask of you half for collection now, and I might refuse [such an arrangement] and not permit half from others[99]

The poet tries to arrange a payment plan to address the unsatisfactory exchange.

Similarly, late payments disrupt the relationship in the following verses:

> No delay tread in the ease of your munificence, nor did reversal creep in your promises
> Except a noble deed in which you preceded [others], of which half was sound and half was incomplete
> Is it my imagination or is every two thousand that was not taken at the beginning of the promise [just] one thousand?[100]

Promises, and the presentation and rejection of the possibility of delay, assert intimacy in the relationship. The exception of the late payment displays the distance between the poet and the patron. Repetition of the word 'half' emphasizes the contrast between the money that was received and the money that was not received. The question, the reference to the poet's imagination, and the motif of two thousand turning into one thousand, each demonstrate the uncertainty of the exchange. Similarly, the following sequence of verses, in which patronage is sought in conjunction with a tax break, explores the problems of exchange:

> O Abū al-Faḍl, great deeds have burdened you with their weight, and the miser is unencumbered by them …
> The land tax testified when you took it over that you are the most forbearing person entrusted with its collection
> So that there is no resistance by the one who pays in its collection, and no force in the conduct of the one who collects

> The path of the golden mean: roughness is not violence that exceeds all bounds and gentleness is not weakness
> Both your refusal and your kindness render the people uncorrupted
> ...
> For hardship and ease have alternated since time immemorial and each is dust in the wind[101]

Antitheses – between roughness and gentleness, refusal and kindness, hardship and ease – each convey the possibilities of success and failure. Negation allows the poet to present and deny the potential for resistance on the part of the taxpayers and force on the part of the patron. Likewise, the contrast between the patron burdened with responsibility and the unencumbered miser refers to the possibilities of patronage. Both hardship and ease become dust in the wind, emphasizing the transience of conditions.

Motifs that focus on the possibility of failure, competition, and violence make the risks of patronage explicit. The general statement about patronage in the following verse presents and rejects the risk of the patron making connections with the wrong people:

> No ignoble man's hand reaches the branch of that auspicious tree[102]

Risks may be presented and deferred in the past, as in the following verse:

> With [the patron's] pure religion and good benefit, no Muslim has encountered from him any trouble in his heart[103]

The poets in the following verses display and dispel the anxieties that surround the exchange of poetry for pay:

> And I came to be such that the disgrace of seeking did not strike me, and the terror of rejection was not kindled in my mind[104]
> You acted in a noble way and did not sully your gifts to me with reproach, nor did you leave your promise unfulfilled[105]

The deferred risks of failure are an integral yet disruptive feature of patronage as a form of social order. The following verse includes a rhetorical question to link and distinguish the possibilities of success and failure for the patron:

> How can what you sought pass you by when your two aspects are that you give a great deal and are praised?[106]

The rhetorical meaning is, 'You will of course get what you want'. The literal meaning would be 'Is it possible that you might not get what you want?' The poet in the following verse uses a conditional sentence to compare and contrast the life and death of the patron with the life and death of generosity:

> For generosity is alive as long as you live and if you die, its watering places would dry up and generosity will die[107]

The conditional possibility of the patron's death alludes to the inevitability of this event, and seems as if it might have been perceived as tactless.

Competition constitutes and complicates the social order of patronage. This poet escapes other relationships for the patron, demonstrating the possibility of failure, as well as the possibility of escaping again:

> In him, I dispensed with others, and my emaciated mounts were turned away from Su^cayd the unlucky toward Sa^cd the fortunate[108]

In contrast, the poet in the following verse compares his commitment to the patron with the other jobs that he will not take:

> So long as I am in his service I will not move from the work of congratulating him to other kinds of work [109]

Other options may not be as attractive, but their existence shapes the patronage relationship and demonstrates the flexibility of patronage as a form of social order.

While competition defines the social order of patronage, competition that entails violence lies beyond it. It is for this reason that violence can be appropriated as such a forceful source of imagery. In the description of love, violent imagery demonstrates the intensity of desire as well as its destructive nature. The bodies of beloved young people may resemble fine swords. The waists of the girls in the following verses resemble slender branches, in a description that evokes, with the help of paronomasia, the image of swords – but it is love itself that draws the fine swords here:

> Every girl of delicate build, who wraps her sash around a slender branch
> Who trembles due to the extreme thinness of her waist, and that which love sent from them is like fine, slender [swords][110]

The girls appear delicate and helpless, but the poet-lover's desire makes them dangerous because it is unfulfilled. The Persian description of love sometimes expresses the intersection of military and court life in the figure of a beloved young person:

> O my boy, set aside war and bring kisses, what good is all this war and roughness?[111]

War refers to the figurative inaccessibility of the beloved, and the contrast between war and kisses displays the possibilities of the relationship. The vocative amplifies the beloved's presence as well as his figurative distance, and the imperative asserts the poet-lover's authority, while the response remains to be seen. The poet-lover's rhetorical question illustrates the uncertainty of the relationship. It says 'This war makes no sense': its literal meaning says (as if in response) 'Or does it?'.

Violence may be a figurative expression of conflict within patronage. This patron's benefit has the capacity to revive and destroy those who envy him within the patronage network:

> Benefits that revive the envious one with their abundance when he is moistened by their favors, though they are death for him[112]

The patron's gifts can turn the envious one into an ally. Alternatively, benefit spells death for him because he is consumed by envy and because his reputation suffers in comparison to the patron. Violent imagery can articulate the impact of the patron's generosity, as in the following verse:

> You have revived the frontier of generosity with gifts from you because of which the frontier of every corruption died[113]

Corresponding battle imagery joins and contrasts the patron's generosity and corruption.

The social order of patronage may be distinct from violence, but cannot be detached from it. The poets in these two verses deploy parallel syntax, morphology and antithesis to weave patronage together with violence:

> On the day of the gathering, a speech from you and a hundred bags of money; on the day of battle, a male slave from you and a hundred troops[114]

The patron's speech implies his authority in patronage as well as violence, and wealth changing hands characterizes social order as well as military initiatives. The motif of the male slave on the day of battle leads into the motif of the army and also echoes the role of the beloved in panegyric poetry. The poet in the following verse uses Arabic in the phrases in quotation marks, as if to use the dynamic of patronage and violence to integrate Islamic, Persianate, and Turkic culture:

> As punishment and reward it is written in two bright lines upon his sword, 'do not feel safe', and upon his treasure, 'do not be wary'[115]

This verse resembles the following Arabic verse in which the patron wages jihad against wealth that is not like jihad, because one spends money on one's allies instead of killing one's enemies:

> You waged jihad in the name of generosity on wealth for its soul, and the holy war of money is not like jihad [since you give away money instead of taking life][116]

The possibility of killing people in this Arabic verse is merely figurative, and the negation of the image calls attention to the distance between the referent of spending money and the image of killing people. In contrast, the antithetical pair of images in the Persian verse joins the two alternatives of spending money and killing people in two inscriptions, so that they both appear in conjunction with a metonymic image of violence. While the Arabic verse points back at the referent of spending money through negation of the violent image, the Persian verse inscribes the parallel presence of patronage and violence upon the treasure and the sword. The Arabic verse appropriates violence as an image for patronage, while the Persian verse joins patronage and violence, but in the panegyric poem: the integration of patronage and violence is in effect absorbed into the discourse on patronage.

Motifs of nature, time and space shape the theme of interaction in patronage. Nature imagery in the description of love contributes to the sensual presence of the beloved and also implies that they are drawn away from the human sphere of the relationship into the natural cycles of the surroundings – usually a desert in Arabic or a garden in Persian:

> Love was crazed in her on the evening when she turned aside with the eyes of an antelope and the neck of a newborn gazelle foal[117]

Similarly, nature imagery in the following verses links the fertility of nature with the prosperity of patronage, and also identifies the patronage relationship with the cyclical change in nature:

> His blessed hand is a tree whose flower is benefit, and prestige is its fruit[118]

Corresponding images join material benefit and social status, but these natural images imply the changeability of both aspects of the patron. This verse refers to and rejects the conventional role of lightning and thunder as an expression of uncertainty in patronage:

> And if his gifts were a rainfall, its clouds would rain without lightning or thunder[119]

However, the image of rainfall is a temporary experience of the fertility of nature. The conditional image calls attention to the imagined status of the description and the possibility of re-imagining it. Fortunately, the patron can also be counted on to step in when nature fails:

> With the one who is the most reliable of them in terms of lightning when the lightning doesn't keep its promise, and the most truthful of them in terms of thunder when the thunder lies[120]

The good prospects with the patron are joined and contrasted with the failure of nature to provide. In the following verse, the conditional sentence parts and links the patron's reliability and the unreliability of nature:

> Moral qualities from whose noble deeds benefits follow in succession when rainfall is scanty in its clouds[121]

The explicit reference to the unreliability of nature calls attention to its implied unpredictability in motifs that equate the patron's generosity with natural fertility.

Motifs of time in this poetry often imply distance in relationships. The deferral of love in time allows the poet to conjure the beloved and experience her absence at the same time:

Traces from whose branches I harvested love, where I trailed pleasures as if trailing a silk garment with decorated borders[122]

This poet imagines the pleasure of love in conjunction with the traces, which are a sign of the beloved's past presence and her absence. The deferral of patronage in time complicates the patronage relationship. This poet emphasizes the improvement in his situation:

I was far from the door of the commander's palace for three months;
I did not sleep or eat during those three months
Now that I have arrived again at this triumphant king, now that I have laid eyes upon this blessed door
I have become strong with hope, and rich with energy; my heart has become tranquil and my grief has come to an end[123]

His grief and insomnia echo the suffering of a poet-lover, and his refusal to eat, though this motif does not appear explicitly in the description of love, evokes the convention of the poet-lover's emaciation. The fast pace of the four parallel sentences in the final verse of the sequence, each of which includes the verb 'become' in the Persian, offers a rhetorical expression of the poet's new lease on life. The four uses of the verb 'become' also reinforce the instability of patronage relationships, and the fact that they are always work in progress. In the following verse, the turn in power defines the instability of relationships in time:

There is no one in this turn in power and there is no one in this age who has not brought a need to him and has not obtained a mount's burden [of wealth][124]

Likewise, the following verses make time itself the source of instability, not just a temporal context in which it takes place:

How is it that the vicissitudes were unjust toward me as if they were ignorant of the fact that your generosity was lying in wait for them?[125]

The poet's expression of wonder at time's obliviousness to the patron asserts the patron's power and also implies the power of the vicissitudes, which are heedless because they can be. The poet in the following verse opens and concludes his statement with the word 'ally' to insist on the closure in his relationship:

> And my sworn ally against time is one who is generous and noble,
> a sworn ally of noble deeds[126]

The poet and his patron confront time, but the confrontation also evokes the risk that time represents.

Poets use motifs of space to think about distance in relationships. For this poet-lover, abandonment combines the absence of the relationship with its painful presence in his heart:

> How can I experience contact with that heart-stealing idol, the fire
> of whose abandonment has burnt my heart in my body?[127]

Spatial distance in patronage may echo the journey section, which often occupied a place in the ancient Arabic praise or boasting poem between the love section and the praise section, and which continued to inform praise in medieval Arabic, and to a lesser extent in medieval Persian panegyric. This poet's genitive image articulates hope in terms of space:

> And the tracts of hopes extend over a distance if your benefit is not
> my provisions while crossing them[128]

In genitive images the poet crams a less determinate idea into a more narrow, concrete and determinate image, making the idea more accessible and demonstrating the impossibility of fitting it all into the image. This oscillation between the indeterminate and the determinate in the genitive image is particularly relevant here, since space that can be managed with the patron's provisions echoes the convention of endless, inscrutable and dangerous open space in the desert. In other words, the poet moves from the indeterminate experience of hope to the determinate image of space, and back out to the convention of an indeterminate expanse of space. The poet in the following verse sums up his relationship in terms of travel:

> He is <u>the caliph</u> and if I travel with his gifts <u>behind me</u>, indeed it is
> a flaw <u>to leave him behind</u>[129]

Paronomasia, which is underlined in the above verse, joins the title of the patron, his gifts behind the poet in the past, and leaving the patron behind. This device imposes an order of closure that is at odds with the poet's ambivalence about leaving. The conditional introduces, yet limits, the prospect of distance in the relationship, implying contingency. The position of this verse at the end of the poem demonstrates the intersection between the theme of interaction in the poem and interaction in experience.

Distance in space as a dimension of patronage relationships also appears in the description of status. This poet combines the proximity implied by the patron's generosity with images of distance for his status:

> [And one who is] near in generosity whose gifts come from on high,
> and his position is inaccessible, its high points bare rock[130]

The concatenation of segments starts low and ends high, and shifts from the more concrete description of proximity in the patron's (giving of) gifts to the more figurative description of high points of bare rock. The shift from the concrete and material motif of gifts to the figurative and abstract motif of status takes place in terms of space. An inaccessible place is also a good place to be in battle. The spatial articulation of the relationship absorbs this conventional description of violence into the peaceful order of patronage.

The rulers in the following verse are just trying to get a foot in the door, and this spatial articulation of outside and inside demonstrates the potential for social mobility that patronage offered:

> For kings, standing at the door of his residence is better than reclining and reposing upon a throne of gold[131]

For these kings, being an outsider with the patron is better than being an insider in their own communities, so that social mobility in the patron's network is about dismantling other networks to build his own. This description shows that social mobility is a destructive as well as a creative feature of political life. The poet in the following verse enjoys a warm welcome, but expresses it in terms of the barriers that separate him from the patron:

> And his doors opened for me with permission, and his curtains rose for me to approach him[132]

Crossing the threshold reinforces intimacy and demonstrates the distance that defines unequal relationships.

Being outside and inside in patronage relationships may also define motifs of the outer and inner qualities of the patron himself. These poets get past the surface of the patron, but the division of his identity into outer and inner qualities demonstrates the distance that must be traversed to connect with him:

> A noble disposition, and an outer appearance of cheerfulness,
> behind which generosity was revealed[133]

The generosity that must be revealed from behind the outer appearance also alludes to the possibility of it being concealed from the community. The following verse makes explicit this link between concealing and revealing:

> [Mounts heading] to one radiant of moral qualities whose past and
> present possessions, and what he conceals or reveals of the matter,
> are [designated] for generosity[134]

The expression of concealing and revealing in present tense verbs implies the changeable conditions of access to the patron's generosity. The protégé must not only get to the patron, he must get inside his head if he is to connect and interact with him.

Connections expressed in terms of interaction demonstrate the uncertainty and flexibility of patronage relationships, as well as their potential to facilitate mobility for poets. The themes of communication and interaction complement the less direct encounter between the poet, the patron and participants in patronage that takes place in the themes of observation and evaluation. Poets' skills in refined rhetoric enabled them to make connections in poetry and to get ahead using a professional identity based on refined rhetoric. The final two chapters explore the attitudes of medieval Arabic and Persian writers toward social mobility based on professional identity, and their views on this as an alternative to socio-economic, religious and ethnic identity. The next chapter focuses on ideas about professional identity based on refined rhetoric.

8

THE COSMOPOLITAN PROFESSIONAL POET

Professional, cosmopolitan identity that is based on the use of refined rhetoric in Arabic or Persian panegyric poetry offered an alternative to the categories of socio-economic, religious and ethnic identity. In the expanding and mobile Hellenistic world, kinship gave way to friendship as a way of networking, and social forums such as symposia and gymnasia enabled displaced Greeks to enjoy a sense of community.[1] In a similar way, patronage in the medieval Middle East and Central Asia revolved around professional affiliations rather than kin groups.[2] Poets deployed this professional identity to cope with uncertainty and take advantage of flexibility in patronage and to experience social mobility. This discussion of the poet as a cosmopolitan professional examines the debates surrounding standards of professional evaluation, disciplinary boundaries and interdisciplinary work, and the critical articulation of poetry as a technology of identity.

While refined rhetoric in poetry was the basis for a professional identity, or an affiliation with a cultural elite identity in the case of people who did poetry on the side, kin groups remained relevant for many professional poets. Poets such as al-Buḥturī and al-Ṣanawbarī got started in part because of family connections and wealth, and Ibn al-Muᶜtazz and Abū Firās came from ruling families. Kushājim was descended from officials in the Abbasid Empire and Muᶜizzī was the son of a professional poet.[3] Amateur poets appear in biographical dictionaries in Arabic and Persian. In Persian, entries usually focus on a single poet, but a number of them mention the poet's close male relatives – sometimes by way of background and sometimes referring to another entry in the encyclopedia – and some poets appear in family groups.[4]

Individuals were the professionals, but what mattered was the deployment of professional identity at a community level. In this individual and group expression of professional identity, refined rhetoric was complemented by refined manners. Refined manners and rhetoric were a related set of practices that shaped social life in the medieval Middle East and Central Asia. In these practices, the individual demonstrated his membership of a group, and this group inevitably stimulated individualism.[5] Individuals increased their status through these social practices. Hannah Arendt explains, however, that power is always the property of a group that acts together, not of an individual.[6] The widespread genre of biographical dictionaries in the medieval Middle East and Central Asia enabled biographers to define new fields of expertise through the presentation of the work of individuals.[7]

Refined manners and rhetoric help to explain the cosmopolitan, imperial cultures of the Middle East and Central Asia, in which people from diverse backgrounds competed and worked with one another. In Arabic, non-Arabs – and Persians in particular – were prominent in the professional development and deployment of refined rhetoric. However, elaborate rhetoric in medieval Arabic poetry may also be understood as the natural result of poets of Arab, Persian and other backgrounds living in multicultural, multilingual urban centers.[8] The ministers who cultivated refined rhetoric in Arabic, and in poetry in particular, as patrons and amateur poets, promoted an Arabicate culture infused with Persian and Greek influences, but with its own distinct character: although some ministers from a Persian background were involved in the Persian pride movement, they continued to support the central role of Arabicate culture in society.[9] While Persians and other non-Arabs were not the source of elaborate rhetoric in Arabic, these groups contributed to change in Arabicate culture. The success of the poet Bashshār, who was from a Persian background, exemplifies a major shift in the role of non-Arabs as the individual comes to have value in society regardless of his ethnic or geographical origins. In general, the Persian pride movement in Baghdad contributed to a change in the concept of virtue, and the use of praise poetry to express it, from an emphasis on noble lineage to an emphasis on a person's actions.[10]

The use of refined manners and rhetoric occurs in conjunction with new ways of doing work with language. Medieval Arabic and Persian literary culture were characterized by new ways of managing knowledge through professional expertise based on scholarly practice.[11] In medieval Arabic culture, the expanding use of reading and writing in the third century Islamic Era/ninth century CE, alongside the more established and widespread use of listening and speaking in literary culture, contributed to an expansion of cultural production, since written literary exchange complements and enhances the circulation of literature through oral communication.[12] The fourth-/tenth-century Arabic poet al-Ṣanawbarī would go to booksellers, whose shops were like intellectual clubs.[13] This written and oral culture probably contributed to the increasingly elaborate use of rhetoric in medieval Arabic poetry, and to elaborate rhetoric in the Persian literature of the Islamic period as it emerged in the fourth/tenth century and expanded in the fifth/eleventh century. The written and oral dimension of medieval Arabic culture may have been an important way for people marginalized by their socio-economic, religious, geographical, or ethnic origins to make their way into professional networks. It enabled aspiring intellectuals to prepare for and follow up on gatherings with written material such as anthologies, literary criticism and compilations.

Elaborate rhetoric in poetry was a craft that displayed the power of the poet.[14] Fine rhetoric enabled poets to express ethical evaluation in part because fine speech itself defined status.[15] However, this craft involved communal exchange as well as individual accomplishment. Motif collections that focus on plagiarism or intertextuality, an important feature of Arabic rhetoric, were about the way individual poets amplify, contract or otherwise develop existing motifs.[16] Short lyrics written in response to other short lyrics – a particularly important feature of medieval Persian literary culture –functioned in a similar way.[17] In addition to the power of the poet, elaborate rhetoric could play a role in the power of the patron, since elaborate rhetoric allowed poets to shape the perception of the patrons about whom they composed poetry.[18]

Professional gatherings were both a form of entertainment and a way to accumulate cultural capital and, for poets, a source of material capital. Ministers and secretaries were expected to 'shine in high society, to seduce the caliph and elites of the empire with their refinement.'[19] Secretaries needed poetry for their education and their work, and a literary education was an asset for social climbing, since familiarity with Arabic poetry was a way of demonstrating participation in the cultural elite.[20] Ministers and rulers alike needed skills in refined rhetoric to maintain their status.[21] As medieval English poets competed for patronage with people from other professions, they came to emphasize less accessible forms of literature.[22]

A similar development occurs in Arabic and Persian, in part because people from other professions also composed poetry.

The protagonist of the *maqāmas* by al-Ḥarīrī – short comic narratives in rhymed prose – was probably a parody of the secretarial class whose precarious position in the patronage network leads them to engage in rhetorical sophistry to win the support of their patrons and earn a living.[23] They may also parody poets, especially since rhymed prose is a kind of midway point between poetry and prose. While the masters of refined rhetoric marketed their wares to patrons with higher status, the eloquent speaker in the *maqāmas* markets his sermons to a more random crowd. The stories are comic because this downward angle contrasts with the upward angle of more serious refined rhetoric. They are also comic because of the distance between more serious religious discourse and the *maqāma*. More serious religious discourse is language that links man to the divine, with the Qur'an as the main example of rhymed prose in particular. The shyster's sermons are language that is just words that link the speaker to some easy money, at the expense of the community.

Refined rhetoric enabled poets to manipulate motifs to provide a multifaceted and comparative perspective on what is described. In the description of patrons in poetry, refined rhetoric allowed poets to explore the multiple possibilities and permutations of patronage relationships. Medieval Arabic and Persian attitudes toward this professional identity based on refined rhetoric reveal an interest in its middle position between common people and rulers, and its relevance to social mobility. Al-Tawḥīdī cites advice to be like a secretary, since they have the refinement of kings and the modesty of commoners.[24] Writers may compare this middle position of professional identity based on refined rhetoric to other sources of status. This implies that this form of identity developed in competition with other dimensions of identity. Al-Jāḥiẓ cites a poet who says, 'I was granted a mind and I was not granted nobility, and what is nobility but a lot of money? If I want to move up, nothing is holding me back but the need to do a lot of work.'[25] Similarly, al-Tawḥīdī cites the famous early letter writer ᶜAbd al-Ḥamīd, who says that lineage is not praised or blamed, but is like the height of a tall man or the shortness of a short one, or beauty in the handsome or ugliness in the ugly.[26] In his book on clever people, whose cleverness is largely defined by refined rhetoric, Ibn al-Jawzī includes a chapter on how common people overcome elites with their wit.[27] Niẓāmī ᶜArūẓī's story of the minister al-Iskāfī relates how al-Iskāfī's message about a conquest so amazes the ruler that he is more impressed with the message than the conquest, and Niẓāmī observes that his career really took off (*kār-i u bālā gereft*).[28] Refined rhetoric enabled people to participate in a community through professional identity and to use this identity to discipline themselves. It is an acquired skill, as al-Māwardī emphasizes. He explains the importance of training in refined manners to avoid the hazards of desires and inclinations, pointing out that refined manners are acquired by experience and customs, not by reason or inherent nature.[29]

Skills in refined manners and rhetoric enabled participants in patronage to move upwards socially, while defective skills led to downward mobility. In the introduction to his book of meanings for poetry, al-ᶜAskarī explains that he compiled this material to fulfill the needs of the man of refined manners, who needs it in gatherings, where he raises his status by being quick to contribute and lowers it by being slow. He offers the example of a man who wants to get into the gathering of the minister Ibn al-ᶜAmīd, and finally succeeds after intercession with friends, only to fail to answer the question, 'What is the best that is said in the description of poetry?' The man leaves and is never seen again.[30] Al-Marzubān, in his book on virtue, points out that many a highborn man has been undone by a pretence of refined manners, while many a modest man has been lifted by the real thing.[31]

The performance of poets in refined rhetoric was complemented by the performance of patrons in their deeds, in accordance with the discipline of refined manners. Al-Tawḥīdī records the observation that praise and blame, reward and punishment, derive from deeds; deeds derive from command and prohibition, which are evident in the perfection and discipline of the mind, and supported by the revelation.[32] Poets argued for the stable prosperity of the patron and the patronage relationship, while clarifying that this prosperity, and the publicity of it, were subject to uncertainty because they were contingent upon the ongoing performance of the patron.

Refined rhetoric must be delivered with refined manners to be effective. Ibn Rashīq, in his chapter on the manners of poets, asserts that the poet must be good-looking, with good morals and clean clothes so that commoners will hold him in esteem, and he can enter elite gatherings without being laughed at.[33] Similarly, Kaykāvūs b. Iskandar advises, 'If you seek a patron and try to sell praise, do not be glum and sloppily dressed, always be cheerful and smiling …'[34] While professional identity in refined rhetoric is about judging people based on their acquired skills, poets had to package their skills in an attractive way.

Packaging skills involved refinement, but the fact that many undesirable or nasty people appear in biographical dictionaries shows that the poetry is what mattered. Producing poetry counted for something, even if it was bad.[35] Personality problems sometimes played a role in poets' biographies, as in the case of one accused of plagiarism and another who composed some nasty invective, leading people to explain that he had a bad side, though the author was surprised.[36] Elegant people said that one poet used to give his poetry to everyone to win fame, apparently in a tactless way, but the elegant people just laughed it off.[37] Some poets were just foolish and luckless, dolts, or not on the ball.[38] Others were arrogant with a bad personality, and ᶜAlīshīr remarks about one, 'To be fair he was a good Muslim, I've said enough'.[39] He expresses hope for some good-for-nothings, but also refers to one who tried Sufism without a guide, and failed, and another who performed the pilgrimage but remained vile.[40] Mental illness sometimes caused disruptive behavior, including one poet who thought he was the ruler, stockpiled weapons and wrote a *shāhnāma* (book of kings) about being king.[41] Sām Mīrzā criticizes a particularly destructive ruler, and also includes one who was famous for killing people, though he is not criticized for this talent.[42] Similarly, ᶜAlīshīr includes a poet who was particularly oppressive.[43] One poet is reputed to have eaten people during a drought.[44] Even tyrants and alleged cannibals were welcome in the cultural sphere delineated by refined rhetoric. The multifaceted understanding of identity allowed the community to focus on refined rhetoric in spite of other flaws and failures.

While not all poets accompanied their work with fine behavior, many Persian poets packaged their work in pen names.[45] The pen name contributed to professional identity based on refined rhetoric, since it set the poet off from the ethnic, geographical, kin, socio-economic and religious aspects of identity. Pen names were not just any names – they were beautiful names that identified the poet with refinement and the capacity to experience emotion and pleasure in a nuanced, intense and shared way, complementing the use of refined rhetoric in poetry.[46] The relationship between the poet's identity and his pen name was complex. One poet had a pen name, then went off to experience a spiritual awakening and changed his pen name. Perhaps to fund his spiritual aspirations, he composed panegyric for the ruler.[47] The same author hopes that one poet will mend his ways just as he changed his pen name.[48] The panegyric poet Anvarī started out with another pen name and began to use this one when he did well.[49] Just as a pen name was part of entering into an affiliation with the cultural elite, in a professional identity based on refined rhetoric a new pen name related to an improvement or an aspiration to improve.

The professional identity of poets grew out of shared standards or conventions of evaluation in literary criticism. Al-Jumaḥī was the first to articulate the professional role of the critic, and he seems to elaborate this new professional identity in opposition to the use of poetry by writers whose expertise is more diffused among different fields of knowledge, though he mentions only Ibn Isḥāq, the author of a biography of the Prophet, and the *saḥafiyyīn*, or people whose knowledge comes from notebooks.[50] The critic Qudāma b. Jaᶜfar added objectivity to the requirements for a critic.[51] These conventions situated indidivual accomplishments in a communal setting. Professional standards offered an alternative to the evaluation of people based on their religious, ethnic or socio-economic background and connections.

Shared conventions of evaluation could facilitate tolerance and professional competition. Ibn al-Muqaffaᵓ notes that it is incumbent on the intelligent person to love the view with which he does not agree, even if he is certain that it is wrong.[52] Similarly, al-Ṣūlī observes that one tells the truth about enemies not to advance them, but rather to preserve oneself and indicate one's virtues and knowledge.[53] Ibn Qutayba's famous comments about how he compiled his biographical dictionary – in which he says that he has not based his selection on other people's selections, prioritized the ancients or denigrated the moderns – emphasize objective, professional standards in criticism. This view seems to imply the potential for social mobility in a cosmopolitan and diverse context, since Ibn Qutayba also notes in another famous comment that God did not restrict knowledge of poetry and eloquence to one age or to one people rather than another: these abilities are equally distributed across the ages and among peoples.[54]

The use of professional standards in criticism contributed to a shared intellectual discourse, since these standards were a way to make a persuasive argument about texts. Al-Jumaḥī's famous passage comparing poetry to things that experts can judge, such as gems, coins and slaves, can be understood in the context of professional standards that enable persuasive arguments about poetry.[55] Al-Jumaḥī records the story of a man who says to Khalaf al-Aḥmar, 'I don't care what others think if I like poetry'. Khalaf replies, 'What if you like a silver coin and the money changer says it's no good?'[56] In his commentary on Abū Tammām's anthology, al-Marzūqī offers a series of specific standards for poetry criticism.[57] For Qudāma b. Jaᶜfar, the praiseworthy and blameworthy qualities of poetry must inhere in the poetry itself, not in the attributes of the poet.[58] Ibn Sinān al-Khafājī objects to critics who will only evaluate poetry after knowing the name of the poet, and includes the story of a student who fools the critic al-Aṣmaᶜī by telling him that two recently composed verses were the work of an ancient Bedouin poet. At first, al-Aṣmaᶜī praises the verses, but when he learns that they are not of ancient provenance, he rejects them completely.[59] Al-Āmidī implies clear preferences in his comparative study of Abū Tammām and al-Buḥturī, but he asserts that he avoids simply passing judgment, acknowledges diverse points of view, uses a method of comparing the work of the two poets through the comparison of poems with the same meter and rhyme, and the comparison of specific motifs.[60] The poet Abū Tammām approves of poetry by Ibn ᶜUyayna, although it is in a very different style, displaying Abū Tammām's adherence to professional standards.[61] As one critic explains, it's not about who wrote a poem or when, since old poetry was new once and new poetry will become old later.[62]

Perhaps the most direct way in which professional standards in criticism relate to literary production is through the step-by-step directions for composing good poetry that are found in many of these books, such as those by Ibn Ṭabāṭabā and Shams-i Qays.[63] These directions call attention to an important feature of professional identity and its disciplinary function. This identity may have allowed poets to enjoy social mobility that would otherwise be impossible based on other categories of identity, but it also required them to submit to a discipline of conventions and standards. The communal identity based on refined rhetoric and manners offered an alternative to some kinds of limitations in social life, and imposed others.

Professional standards in poetry were important but not hegemonic. In spite of the commitment to shared conventions and objective standards in literary criticism, other priorities sometimes prevailed. The professional valorization of objectivity could collide with another phenomenon related to social mobility – cut-throat competition. In contrast with Abū Tammām, al-Buḥturī is reported to have only liked poetry that was similar to his own in the use of meanings, diction and a 'natural' style.[64] Al-Ḥātimī says that he composed his book on *sariqa* (plagiarism or intertextuality) by al-Mutanabbī because the poet was remiss in his service of the minister al-Muhallabī in spite of the minister's abundant generosity, so that the minister asked al-Hātimī to compose a work on the flaws in al-Mutanabbī's poetry and run him out of Iraq.[65] Before proceeding to the supposedly technical and professional evaluation of the poetry, al-Ḥātimī makes several points that are definitely not about professional evaluation. He notes that al-Mutanabbī left his earlier patron Sayf al-Dawla as an enemy, and is arrogant, stubborn, bossy and overly ambitious.[66]

Writers sometimes cobble together a more objective view from a variety of perspectives that do not in themselves reflect professional standards. Al-Jumaḥī cites an observation that the learned men of Basra used to favor Imruʾ al-Qays, those of Kufa favored al-Aᶜshā, and those of the Hijaz and the desert preferred Zuhayr.[67] Al-Marzūqī notes the advantages of different qualities of poetry and points out that different critics may prefer different qualities.[68] These comments demonstrate that critics incorporated and appropriated less professional evaluation into their own more objective approach.

Like stories about unprofessional evaluation of poetry, comic stories about poetry demonstrate the limits of serious discipline in refined rhetoric. While acquiring the professional skills needed to participate in patronage was a serious business, putting them into practice was not. The refined manners that define this professional identity were as much about playfulness as they were about discipline. Al-Tawḥīdī cites a Bedouin who is asked, 'Where is seriousness with respect to refined manners?' He answers, 'The one heads east and the other heads west'.[69] The ancient Persian king Bahrām Gūr advises his companions, 'When you see me taking pleasure in music and leaving the door of seriousness for the door of jest, then ask for your favors'.[70] These two figures of authority at opposite ends of the social hierarchy, the provincial Bedouin and the ancient Persian king, each clarify that good manners need not mean serious manners.

The patron's amusement may puncuate exchanges of poetry for pay. When the poet Aᶜshā Rabīᶜa goes in to ᶜAbd al-Malik and finds him sitting with his sons, he recites about ᶜAbd al-Malik's father and ᶜAbd al-Malik, and the latter laughs and orders a gift.[71] A man gives one patron a covered dish with two birds and two verses on a piece of paper inside. When the patron opens the dish the birds fly away and the verses remain, making the patron laugh and offer a gift.[72] (It was a lovely gift to set before the king.) The patron's laughter reinforces the intimacy across social boundaries that poets achieve through patronage.

Comic poets also play an integral, if marginal, role in the discourse on patronage. Al-Thaᶜālibī describes Ibn al-Ḥajjāj as a poet with an inclination to be funny and share clever stories and jokes, and who also praised rulers, ministers, and other leaders. Each of his poems includes humor and obscenity, yet he is accepted by all and his poetry is more widely circulated than proverbs.[73] The comic poet Abū Dulāma appears in numerous stories of literary patronage in which the recitation of poetry overlaps with comedy.[74] When summoned by the caliph al-Mahdī to a gathering, Abū Dulāma is asked to compose invective on one person in the gathering. As he looks from one person to the next they each indicate with a wink that he shouldn't choose them as his target. He hesitates and then comes up with verses of invective on all present, so that al-Mahdī laughs and everyone gives him something.[75] Playfulness appears in ᶜAwfī's notices about several poets known for comedy, especially Sūzānī. Comedy sometimes fades into invective, and can also be set in counterpoint to piety.[76] Likewise, some less well-known poets are remembered primarily for their comic verse, in a few cases so obscene that it gets censored by the author or (medieval) translator.[77] The presence of comic poets in encyclopedias helps to delineate the parameters of other more serious work.

Poetry played a central role in refined rhetoric, but this includes a wider range of literary culture. The critics Ibn al-Athīr and Ibn Sinān al-Khafājī demonstrate the breadth of the field of rhetoric. It includes letters, poetry, the Qur'an, the sayings of the Prophet, law, entertaining stories and history.[78] These are not just options, but skills that professionals needed to combine to get ahead in patronage. In his book of political advice, Kaykāvūs b. Iskandar explains that the drinking companion must know Arabic and Persian for administrative communication, so that he can perform these functions if an administrator is not available, and those who are not poets must know Arabic and Persian poetry – good and bad verse – so that if a verse is needed there is no need to summon a poet. In addition, the drinking companion must know medicine and astronomy so that he can carry the conversation on such topics in the absence of a specialist, how to play an instrument in case a musician is not on hand, and funny stories, soothing phrases, backgammon, chess, the Qur'an (this follows backgammon and chess), stories of the Prophet, exegesis, jurisprudence, and the legends of kings.[79] Rāvandī's advice about refinement serves as a conclusion of his history, so that he emphasizes the integral relationship between refinement, including skills for drinking companions, and the serious business of political and military history.[80] Al-Ṣūlī announces that he can explicate obscure allusions in poetry because of his superior knowledge of anecdotes, emphasizing the breadth of professional expertise in the circulation of poetry.[81] The poet Abū al-Aswad al-Duʾlī also worked as a transmitter of sayings of the Prophet and a grammarian.[82] This overlap between numerous related disciplines of refined rhetoric helped poets to play a significant role in social life and gain access to social mobility.

The use of rhetorical skills in poetry served as a path of social mobility in part because writers situated these skills in a legitimating context. Ibn al-Athīr observes that his colleague al-Ṣābiʾ is wrong about the distinction between the two fields of poetry and prose, for both are about clarity and share the same themes.[83] His interest in transferring ideas between poetry and prose, and in the use of sayings of the Prophet, verses of the Qur'an, proverbs and anecdotes, implies the intersection between poetry and the broader field of cultural production and ethical discourse.[84] Ibn al-Muᶜtazz uses the rhetorical parallels between 'modern' poetry and the Qur'an, sayings of the Prophet and his companions, Bedouin proverbs and ancient poetry as a way to situate contemporary poetic style in a broader legitimating context.[85] Al-Jāḥiẓ complains about poetry scholars whose knowledge is too narrow, explaining that al-Aṣmaᶜī can only do strange diction, al-Akhfash can only do grammar, and Abū ᶜUbayda only transmits certain notices related to famous battles or genealogy. In contrast, he finds the necessary diversity of knowledge among administrators such as al-Ḥasan b. Wahb and al-Zayyāt.[86] The development of poetry as a professional discipline took place in conjunction with the broader development of refined rhetoric.

Professionals in other fields composed poetry and vice versa. In his biographical dictionary of poets, Ibn Qutayba says, 'I'm not including everybody who has composed and uttered poetry in passing, for there's hardly anyone with an ounce of refinement who has not.'[87] While writers of prose composed poetry on the side, some professional poets also wrote in prose. In the medieval Middle East and Central Asia prose did not just include citations of poetry: the concept of prose encompassed prosimetrical and poetry-less prose alike.[88] Al-ᶜAttābī is described as a poet who was also a writer.[89] The poets Ibn al-Muᶜtazz, the Khālidī brothers, al-Sarī al-Raffāʾ, al-Ṣanawbarī and Kushājim were best known for genres of short poetry, but they also wrote in longer genres such as panegyric. In addition, they composed prosimetrical works. Many Persian lyric poets such as Khāqānī, Sanāʾī, Amīr Khusraw and ᶜIrāqī composed panegyric as well as narrative poetry with a mystical emphasis, and sometimes combined the two.[90] Encyclopedias of Persian poets do not always specify the poet's genre, and this may not be obvious from quotations, but many notices refer to a range of lyrical and narrative genres. Vaṭvāṭ, perhaps best known for his book of rhetoric, was an esteemed writer who also composed panegyric.[91] Prosimetrical works and narrative poetry were less common among earlier poets and those known primarily for panegyric, but Abū Tammām and al-Buḥturī wrote anthologies and ᶜUnṣurī wrote narrative poetry.

Critics combine poetry and prose in their work. The critics al-Marzūqī and Rādūyānī discuss prose and poetry, and poets and prose writers together, and Vaṭvāṭ includes examples from proverbs, anecdotes and *maqāmas* (series of short narratives in rhymed prose) as well as poetry in his book of rhetoric.[92] Both al-Marzūqī and Shams-i Qays also make a point of distinguishing between the work of the poet and the work of the critic.[93] The professional use of refined rhetoric required interdisciplinary work as well as borders between disciplines.

Alongside the articulation of professional standards for poets, writers and poets alike complain of unprofessional approaches to evaluating poetry. Al-Ṣūlī complains that some people say they know everything, never admitting they don't know; and that there is a whole class of people who read poetry as dilettantes to memorize a few strange words and learn a few rules of grammar, going to gatherings but neither adding to them nor benefiting from them. When a genuinely learned person forgets a detail, such people think that they know more than he does, not realizing the depth of his knowledge.[94] Similarly, in a famous citation, Abū Tammām is asked, 'Why don't you recite poetry that is known?' Abū Tammām responds indignantly, 'Why don't you know what is recited?'[95] Protests about the unprofessional evaluation of poetry help to illustrate the importance of standards of evaluation.

Shared standards in the composition and evaluation of poetry contribute to individual identity: not just as a way to be yourself, but as a way to be with other people. Emotional and intellectual life take shape through interaction in language and especially in refined rhetoric.[96] Subjectivity and creativity offer a context in which the individual poet can redefine himself, in conjunction with others, through the use of rhetoric. The redefinition of the self through professional identity facilitates social mobility for participants in patronage. The expression of the possibilities of patronage in poetry appears to be highly conventional. However, attitudes toward subjectivity and creativity suggest that critics viewed the nuanced complexity of elaborate rhetoric as a product of inner life.

If one can transform the self, others and the world through the use of elaborate rhetoric, then it makes sense that one can transform one's place in society. Al-Jāḥiẓ describes eloquence (*bayān*) as whatever tears the veil from consciousness (*ḍamīr*). The mind sets out as a pioneer for the spirit, knowledge is a pioneer for the mind and eloquence is the translation of that knowledge.[97] Rhetorical skills not only spring from intellectual, spiritual and emotional dimensions of inner life: they are the only way for this inner life to crystallize into something that can be shared in all of its complexity. Ibn Ṭabāṭabā observes that the poet knows poetry to be the product of his mind, the fruit of his intellect and the image of his knowledge, and that 'poetry displays what the self conceals and the listener finds splendor in what he arrives at, of what he knows by nature ... and the veil is removed from understanding.'[98] The inner life that crystallizes in refined rhetoric is not just the inner life of the speaker, it is also a new articulation of inner life for the listener. Al-Jurjānī observes that in figurative language, you [the listener or reader] are with the poet, though you are not the poet.[99] Refined rhetoric is a central feature of shared intellectual experience. In the context of patronage, the poet can say something about his own experience in relationships that enables his audience, including the patron, to see their own experiences in new ways.

The inner life that crystallizes in refined rhetoric is complemented by the communal life that is implied by encyclopedias of poets. While important in negotiating the relationship between ancients and moderns, and Arabs and non-Arabs in Arabic, they are even more important in Persian, where they form a larger proportion of prose writing. Some poets integrated the networking sites of politics and religion in their work or different cultures.[100] Writers of encyclopedias not only provide information about poets: they also imply arguments about how poetry links people. In addition to communal links among people who compose poetry, some encyclopedic compilations of poets appear in conjunction with other kinds of discourse. Shīr ᶜAlī Khān Lūdī intersperses biographies of poets with sections that imply an argument about the significance of poetry.[101] Poets fit into a scheme that has universal significance, given the section on the seven climes. The mastery of refined rhetoric in poetry complements exegesis as a way to approach the divine, or dream interpretation and physiognomy as a way to articulate hidden meanings. The refinement, altered states and alternative perspectives on experience that are involved in sharing poetry complement the same qualities as wine and music.

The subjectivity and creativity involved in poetry are not necessarily natural gifts, and may be the product of acquired skills. Ibn Ṭabāṭabā explains that some people with natural talent and good taste can dispense with metric rules, while others must have recourse to the rules of composition until this knowledge comes to be like a natural talent without artifice.[102] In other words, acquired skills in the refined rhetoric of poetry become like a second nature, absorbed until they become an integral feature of the poet's subjective deployment of creativity. For Shams-i Qays, rhetorical devices such as paronomasia are not only an indication of rhetorical skills, but also testimony of a person's intellectual ability in general.[103]

Innovation enables poetry to define subjectivity for the speaker as well as the listener. Ibn Rashīq compares creativity and imitation, and sees innovation as distinct from both creation and plagiarism.[104] In other words, innovation plays a mediating role between the individual and the community and defines the manneristic use of elaborate rhetoric to capture the dynamic and multifaceted experience of patronage. In some cases, and increasingly in later periods, as Alīshīr Navāʾī demonstrates in his biographical dictionary, poets made this mediating role more explicit by composing poems or verses as responses to the work of other poets.[105] The poet was under two distinct kinds of pressure – a classical heritage to be imitated and a personal and public craving for innovation: the result was mannerism.[106] In the context of panegyric poetry, we can identify a third and related social factor in mannerism: the need to articulate the shifting terms of patronage relationships and define new relationships against the backdrop of the broader discourse on patronage. In this case, mannerism is not a feature of form alone, but an aesthetic expression of social life. Poetry is not about imitating what already exists, but bringing into society something that never before existed.[107] It is in this sense that the technique of mannerism can be a technology of identity that evolves in the dynamic context of patronage. According to al-Jurjānī's theory, thought and fine rhetoric are two sides of the same process.[108] As a result, verbal technique and a social technology of identity are intertwined. *Badīᶜ* or elaborate rhetoric is the obverse of *taʾwīl* or interpretation.[109] Therefore, this technology of identity was not individual but communal. Capturing the complexity of patronage relationships in elaborate rhetoric implies that the audience will try hard to decipher it all.

The poet does not just make it up, which would alienate him from the community, or just copy something else, which would dissolve him into the community. While this approach to innovation may sound appealing, critics had to defend it. Ibn al-Muᶜtazz defends the innovative aspects of contemporary poetry by showing that what is good about this innovation is also good in the Qur'an and sayings of the Prophet. Al-Qāḍī al-Jurjānī defends the flaws in innovative poetry by showing that what is bad about this innovation is also bad in pre-Islamic and early Islamic poets.[110] Al-Qāḍī al-Jurjānī explains that the rivalry for excellence in poetry is about circulating meanings that are reworked in creative and innovative ways. Ibn al-Athīr emphasizes that the famous verse by the ancient poet ᶜAntar, 'Are there any meanings left to be had?' is not to be taken literally, for there is no shortage of new meanings to be innovated by the diligent student of poetry.[111] This question, which the poet poses at the beginning of a poem that became canonical in the medieval period, is rhetorical. It means, 'Are there any meanings left to be had? You bet there are.' As Ibn al-Athīr clarifies about poetry – echoing debates about innovation in legal thought – the door to innovation remains open until the end of time.[112]

Creativity and subjectivity in poetry are less about brand new ideas than they are about the articulation and configuration of existing motifs, and elaborations of these in rhetorical devices and figurative language. Discussions of these techniques in criticism are not merely technical. They demonstrate how refined rhetoric can be a technology of identity, enabling poets and their audience to gain new insights into their experiences and aspirations. The verse or short sequence of verses is a major focus of medieval critical attention; not because critics were not aware of or interested in whole poems, but because short segments afforded the opportunity to do a close reading of poetry as a technology of identity.

A multifaceted perspective is the key to this close reading of poetry as a technology of identity. Critics identify segmentation as a central feature of elaborate rhetoric. Shams-i Qays and Qudāma b. Jaᶜfar, among others, advocate for verses that can stand on their own, not relying on preceding and following verses; and Qudāma contrasts this with the concatenation of utterances in narrative,[113] which can generate multifaceted meaning through developments of plot and character. Critics of poetry are more interested in multifaceted perspectives generated through juxtaposition, comparison and contrast. These relations take shape through the articulation of motifs, configurations of them in syntax, constructions of them in rhetorical devices and the imagination of them in figurative language.

The technology of identity takes shape in a multifaceted perspective, and this perspective is all in the details. Al-Jurjānī observes in his description of a figure that is basically the enumeration of details, 'I mean that you have two or more descriptions and you look at them one at a time and consider them one at a time ... or that you look at one thing from more than one perspective.'[114] In discussing a range of figures that segment meaning, he points out that 'they say the first look is foolish because you see the description as a whole, and then you see the details when you look again.'[115] Vaṭvāṭ, Ibn al-Muᶜtazz and Qudāma

b. Ja^cfar, among others, discuss the technique of shifting from one point of view to another, or back and forth.[116] This segmentation of point of view contributes to a multifaceted perspective in description. Vaṭvāṭ, Ibn Wakīʿ, Shams-i Qays and Qudāma each mention other ways to create disjunctions between segments of expression, including digression to another topic, digression with a return to the original topic, and citation of a proverb or two.[117] The devices of parallel expressions, paronomasia and antithesis, discussed by al-Jurjānī and Qudāma, promote the interplay of conjunction, disjunction, and comparison between terms and their contexts.[118] Critics appreciate the technique of piling figures on top of each other, such as the combinations cited by Vaṭvāṭ, Rādūyānī and Qudāma, and devices for adding extra dimensions of meaning and interpretation such as several devices cited by Shams-i Qays.[119] Both al-Jurjānī and Qudāma b. Jaʿfar offer approaches to coping with apparent and actual contradictions in elaborate rhetoric, and they also observe that the audience must sift through meanings that may come to mind in an image in order to select the primary comparison.[120] Al-Jurjānī notes that the nice thing about images is that they give you a lot of different meanings in a small number of words, like a number of pearls from a single shell or varieties of fruits from a single branch, or like a number of branches from the trunk of a tree with fruit upon each branch.[121]

The multifaceted perspective that generates a technology of identity is in the details – but not just any details. Critics delight in images that reveal what is hidden. While some images can be obvious, others require interpretation and al-Jurjānī's discussion valorizes the factor of surprise in the distant comparison.[122] He cites al-Jāḥiẓ's emphasis on the aesthetic and intellectual value of long perception, in which he contrasts an animal's immediate pleasure in killing with the very different pleasure that comes from perseverance, as in the horse race or the competition between archers.[123] Ibn Ṭabāṭabā compares this pleasure with the pleasure in foods that are delicious but whose complexity is hidden, or complex fragrances, designs and musical rhythms.[124] Ibn al-Athīr compares innovative meanings to unsolved problems in arithmetic and algebra, so that when you come across one, you take it and turn it over front and back and look at its beginning and ending and consider its sides and middle parts, and after that your thinking leads you to that which is known.[125]

Like poetry itself, anthologies and other prosimetrical texts that present short segments of poetry can be a technology of identity that enables readers to gain insights into their experiences and aspirations. Re-use and recycling of poetry in both oral and written contexs can work this way.

Al-Qāḍī al-Jurjānī displays the analysis of plagiarism or intertextuality as yet another way to view verses as segments of meaning in a comparative way. Anthologies also demonstrate this type of implied analysis in which the reader does most of the work.[126] Anthologies helped members of the cultural elite to participate skillfully in gatherings.[127] In a similar way, the interest in biography derived from the ability of the reader or listener to compare distinct versions of the same individual's biography.[128] This type of do-it-yourself reading sometimes leaves modern readers puzzled or dissatisfied about the minimal or non-existent commentary, while medieval readers may have appreciated the flexibility that it entailed for the reader or listener. In the context of patronage, rhetorical complexity engenders a nuanced commentary on relationships. The audience is put to work, and in exchange for doing this they receive the benefit of engaging in the evaluation of others and their own experiences – to some extent in conjunction with the poet, and to some extent independently of the poet. While elaborate rhetoric may seem like a self-absorbed way to play mental games rather than communicate, critics show that elaborate rhetoric is actually quite other-centered. The result is an experience of subjectivity and creativity that is both communal and individual.

The Arabic or Persian poet became a cosmopolitan professional through his acquired skills in refined rhetoric. This professional identity was constituted by critical debates about its validity. Critics and poets formulated and questioned professional standards, disciplinary boundaries, the definition of creativity and the significance of individual and shared subjectivity. The result was a professional identity that facilitated social mobility. The final chapter examines to what extent social mobility based on this professional identity could provide an alternative to the more established categories of socio-economic, religious and ethnic identity.

9

THE SOCIALLY MOBILE PROFESSIONAL POET

In the medieval Middle East and Central Asia, skills in refined rhetoric gave poets an acquired professional identity. Poets encountered uncertainty as well as flexibility in the social order of patronage. They used the elaborate rhetoric of poetry to forge, transform and end the unequal relationships of patronage and to provide a commentary on this form of social order for their audience, including – but not limited to – the patron. The medieval Middle East was characterized by a high degree of social mobility.[1] Poetry also facilitated such mobility in Central Asia. Professional identity based on skills in refined rhetoric enabled people from diverse backgrounds to do business together. This discussion of the socially mobile, professional poet examines how people who composed poetry acquired a professional identity that complemented, and in some cases replaced or displaced, their socio-economic, religious or ethnic identity.

Social mobility through professional identity helps to explain the development of cosmopolitan, imperial culture around the Arabic language in the Abbasid Empire based in Iraq, and around the Persian language in the Ghaznavid Empire based in what is now Afghanistan. The price that poets sometimes paid to participate in patronage, in terms of socio-economic, religious or ethnic assimilation, illustrates an important point about cosmopolitan culture. The cosmopolitan cultures of the medieval Middle East and Central Asia, like their counterparts in other times and places, were as much about hegemony as they were about diversity. Medieval Middle Eastern and Central Asian portrayals of social mobility based on professional identity show that in many cases, the benefits of participating in patronage outweighed the costs.

Socio-economic identity

While critics emphasized the middle position of poets between rulers and common people, skills in poetry spread upward and downward. In the Middle East, the fourth-/tenth-century Arabic poet al-Sarī al-Raffāʾ began his career in the fabric mending trade. At the same time, the rulers Sayf al-Dawla, ʿIzz al-Dawla and al-Rāḍī, the royal family member Abū Firās, the ministers al-Ṣāḥib b. ʿAbbād and al-Muhallabī, and the secretary Abū Isḥāq al-Ṣābiʾ composed poetry in addition to their other work.[2] In Central Asia in the Timurid period, 'Poetry written according to rules and conventions originally established under court patronage spread throughout all the urban classes of society, from wealthy merchants to lowly craftsmen.'[3] The following investigation of the acquired identity from skills in rhetoric alongside socio-economic identity looks at the use of poetry by rulers, ministers and secretaries, mystics, playboys and bohemians, tradesmen, provincial people and the Bedouin, male and female slaves, as well as debates about the validity of refined rhetoric composed by people from marginalized socio-economic groups.

Numerous ruling elites cultivated skills in poetry and refined rhetoric in general. For example, the caliph al-Muktafī is listed in al-Marzubānī's biographies of poets.[4] Notices about ruler-poets, al-Ṣūlī's work on this topic in Arabic, Haravī's biographical collection on rulers who composed poetry in either Persian and Turkish or both, and Sām Mīrzā's opening chapter on rulers who were poets, demonstrate that political elites were interested in acquiring these skills.[5] The use of a poet's nickname by many of the ruling elite poets in Haravī's collection shows that these rulers assumed an alternative, professional identity based on their rhetorical skills.[6] Writers may depict ruling elites who were also poets in conjunction with the professional poets who worked with them, as if to emphasize the professional approval of their efforts. Al-Ṣūlī cites al-Buḥturī describing one patron who, in spite of his honor, was elegant and a poet.[7] Similarly, Abū Hiffān describes Abū Nuwās seeking a patron. He is told of a man who, if you praise him, will praise you back, and if you do invective on him will do invective back. Abū Nuwās inspects the man's poetry and finds it to be elegant and elaborate, and writes to him.[8] In Ottoman Turkish literary culture, sultans beginning with Murād II had their poetry compiled in collections.[9] While ruling elites hired poets to praise them, they also demonstrated their refinement by displaying their own skills in refined rhetoric.

The complementary relationship between poetry and prose developed in conjunction with the cultivation of both kinds of writing by elites who worked in the government.[10] Early critics compared poems to the letters used in secretarial work, and Ibn Ṭabāṭabā 'effaced the distinction between them.'[11] The genres of the *qaṣīda* and the letter 'influenced each other throughout their development.'[12] The minister al-Fatḥ b. Khāqān was one of the most knowledgeable people about poetry.[13] Ibn al-Jarrāḥ's biographical dictionary of poets refers to the poetry skills of secretaries.[14] Al-Ṣūlī cites a man who describes gatherings of secretaries in which the conversation revolves around explicating difficult poetry by Abū Tammām.[15] Al-Jāḥiẓ complains about the narrow focus of critics known for specializations in the fields of strange diction, grammar, legendary battles and genealogy. In contrast, he praises the broad intellectual interests of secretaries who possess skills in refined manners and rhetoric, and whose poetry is characterized by delightful craftsmanship, sweet diction, fine meanings, and the avoidance of excessive artifice.[16] Al-Marzubānī's biographies of poets include administrators such as al-Faḍl b. al-Rabīᶜ and al-Faḍl b. Sahl.[17] The poet Ḥammād ᶜAjrad began his career as a teacher before becoming famous as a poet.[18] ᶜAwfī and Sām Mīrzā include sections or notices on poets who were also ministers or religious scholars, imams or judges.[19] However, when the professional poet Khāqānī identifies an imam in his gathering by a poem that the imam composed, disapproval ensues, since it is inappropriate to refer to a man of religious learning in this way.[20] Many Ottoman Turkish poets had day jobs, and worked as secretaries, in trades such as surgery or pharmacy, or as members of mystical brotherhoods, musical performers or elite soldiers with or without agricultural land.[21] The literary interest in members of other professions who are also known for their expertise in poetry suggests the importance of these skills as an acquired professional identity that could complement those of other professions. While many of these people would not have been able to compete with professional poets, their composition of poetry demonstrated skills in refined rhetoric and gave them a professional identity in poetry that complemented and enhanced their other work. In addition to enhancing other writing skills, composing poetry is likely to have improved the social networking in their own professions.

Persian biographical collections in particular represent numerous people who are referred to as mystics. A dervish may be described as avoiding rulers or going into service in patronage, while in most cases the relevance of patronage is not specified.[22] While this role always implies an alternative lifestyle, some narratives display the transformation, such as the son of an architect who becomes a dervish, a minister's son who is also a dervish, and one whose father ruled a city and who left the army to be a dervish.[23] Stories of patronage or transformation emphasize the links between the routine and this alternative lifestyle. Some poets not only live as dervishes, they are also specialists in mystical sciences; others are known as lovers, emphasizing the connection between mysticism and poetry.[24]

Playboys and bohemians, whose activities were more of an avocation than a vocation, developed skills in poetry that complemented their work, or rather their play. Skills in poetry fit into their alternative networks and sometimes their ties that were more serious. Some biographers link poets' misbehavior to poetry. One bohemian could not write or compose poetry while intoxicated, and Sām Mīrzā points out that God is merciful and hopes that another playboy will follow the more lofty ideals in a short poem.[25] Some come around, such as one who drank constantly but would repent every few days, or another who had been wild but calmed down.[26] Ibn al-Muᶜtazz describes Muṭīᶜ b. Iyās as a bohemian poet and records a story in which he praises a patron, who offers to praise him back or reward him. Muṭīᶜ resents having to make this choice, and is loath to choose praise when he is in need and sends verses to express his dilemma. The patron laughs and sends him a reward. Ibn al-Muᶜtazz also records a story in which the caliph al-Mahdī praises the bohemian poet Wāliba, the mentor of the famous bohemian poet Abū Nuwās, describing him as someone who composes fine poetry, is refined in manners and rhetoric, and has a wide-ranging memory of poetry and related matters. When one of al-Mahdī's companions asks, 'Why don't you have him work here as a drinking companion?', al-Mahdī cites two obscene verses by Wāliba about how he has sex with his companions in a gathering. Al-Mahdī asks 'Do you want him to come and have sex with us, you bastard?'[27] Ibn al-Muᶜtazz observes that Salm al-Khāsir sold a Qur'an that he inherited to buy a musical instrument, but notes that he did this as a bohemian playboy, not because he was corrupt in his religion.[28] Al-Jāḥiẓ describes Ibrāhīm b. Hāniʾ as very bohemian and rebellious, but does so in passing, on the way to citing him in his book of rhetoric.[29] Bohemians use their skills in poetry and refined rhetoric to disrupt serious business and also to participate in it.

People who worked in trades and developed skills in poetry could display professional identity alongside their other work. Al-Thaᶜālibī refers to the poet al-Khubzʾaruzī: he has heard from more than one person that he was illiterate, worked in a shop in Basra and would recite short poems that people gathered round to hear. Ibn Lankak, in spite of his high rank, would go to his shop to hear him.[30] Al-Tawḥīdī cites Jaḥẓa, who heard of a tailor who composed poetry and went to hear him so that he could mock him. He asks him to recite and hears verses the beauty of which astounds him.[31] In his compilation of biographies, Rāzī refers to a poet who is a cobbler.[32] Other circumstances can help to explain how a person who works in a trade can produce refined rhetoric, such as one Arabic poet depicted by al-Iṣfahānī – a client who was possibly bought or freed, and who started out in the Persian imperial court before becoming a food-seller in Medina.[33] The references to poets who also work in trades in the encyclopedias of Sām Mīrzā (such as a butcher, a fabric seller and a paper seller) and ᶜAlīshīr (such as a tailor and a tentmaker) are interesting not only because they imply that people from different walks of life could express a more elite identity through refined rhetoric, but also because their trades are mentioned at all.[34] Merchants and soldiers also populate these books. If these other dimensions of identity pull people toward their other work, the affiliation of poetry takes on a hegemonic status by gathering together diverse people in a well-defined and well-documented group. Without an affiliation with poetry, some of these people might not appear in sources at all – there do not seem to be biographical dictionaries of butchers or merchants. Poetry, more than many other activities, afforded a way for a person to be somebody.

Some poets began their careers in other trades and later became full-time professional poets. Al-Thaᶜālibī describes the poet al-Sarī al-Raffāʾ starting out in the fabric mending trade and continuing with a successful career as a panegyric and descriptive poet.[35] Al-Tanūkhī cites a reference to the well-known poet Kuthayyir ᶜAzza working as a merchant.[36] Al-Iṣfahānī describes the poet Abū al-ᶜAtāhiya beginning his work as a musician and then selling pottery in Kufa until he succeeds as a poet.[37] He meets a group of young men exchanging verses, puts down his pottery and proposes to offer a half-verse for them to follow up with a matching half-verse, as a bet. The young men mock him, but when he offers the half-verse they cannot produce a matching half-verse, and he offers more verses that display his skill.[38]

Persian biographical dictionaries describe some ordinary people by trade, while others are simply designated 'common'. ᶜAlīshīr describes a couple of them as 'not bad', which makes him sound underwhelmed, but common people are not the only poets that he describes in this way, and one of them is well enough connected to do panegyric.[39] Sām Mīrzā places common people in the last chapter, after a chapter on Turks, which probably says something about his view of both. The affiliation with poetry ranges from one common person who, although common, sometimes composed poetry, to another who was both poor and common, and composed poetry in both Persian and Turkish.[40] Like people of higher status, some common people are dervishes.[41] The theme of common people who demonstrate refined rhetoric in Arabic, Persian or Turkish appears for hundreds of years, showing that refined rhetoric was a significant feature of cultural elite identity as a feature of social mobility.

Poverty and common people overlap, but other people are also described as poor. Sām Mīrzā admires one poet for not composing panegyric although he was poor, and he refers to a poor poet who had some good *qaṣīda*s, showing that poor people could be well connected enough to seek literary patronage.[42] One poor poet sells ghazal poems.[43] In some contexts, poverty relates directly to piety.

Upward mobility was sometimes offset by social mobility in a downward direction. Ibn al-Muᶜtazz describes one poet who was a cupper and who was also accused of heresy. The caliph al-Mahdī inspects his books and finds nothing, and hires him as a secretary until somebody finds evidence against him and he is thrown out, ending up as a beggar.[44] The more extensive stories about risk in patronage usually involve people with more professional involvement in poetry, perhaps because they matter enough to get in trouble.

Provincial people sometimes appear to be at a disadvantage in patronage, but they can succeed if they are able to demonstrate that they have mastered the refined rhetoric of poetry. Niẓāmī ᶜArūẓī focuses on the role of social mobility for the poet Farrukhī, first in his marriage to a woman whose expenses exceed his income as a provincial poet, and then in his move to the Ghaznavid capital. When the Ghaznavid administrator first sees him, he thinks he looks so provincial that he cannot believe he composed the poem that he proposes to offer to the ruler, and arranges a test. Niẓāmī offers material details about Farrukhī's upward mobility.[45] Rāzī includes the story, pointing out that Farrukhī was the son of a male slave.[46] Similarly, in one story of the great epic poet Firdawsī, ᶜUnṣurī, the leading panegyric poet of the Ghaznavid court, sizes up Firdawsī, decides that he looks too provincial, and turns away, saying, 'Only poets can come in here!' Firdawsī appeals for a chance and passes a test, at which point ᶜUnṣurī apologizes.[47]

While the anonymous Bedouin figure is the most widely cited Bedouin, some poets are named and identified as Bedouins. Ibn al-Jarrāḥ refers to the poet Abū Firᶜawn al-Sāsī as a Bedouin who came to Basra to beg and has fine poetry.[48] Similarly, Ibn al-Muᶜtazz mentions a Bedouin poet who moves to Baghdad.[49] Notices about named Bedouin poets often end with emigration from the provinces to the city. In contrast, Ibn al-Muᶜtazz also refers to ᶜUmāra b. ᶜAqīl as a Bedouin who left the desert for the city when poetry allowed him to make connections, and who went on to be a great poet who praised caliphs, ministers, elites and kings. He then took his enormous earnings and returned to the desert.[50] The Bedouin are sometimes identified with trades. Ibn al-Jarrāḥ describes the poet Abū Ṣalt, a client of the Banū Sulaym, as a Bedouin whose father made ovens.[51] Ibn Qutayba and al-Jāḥiẓ record the story of the poet al-ᶜUmānī, who enters to see the caliph al-Rashīd wearing a tall hat and simple shoes. Al-Rashīd says, 'You had better not recite poetry to me except in a great turban and smooth, rounded shoes'. The poet arrives the next time in Bedouin attire, citing his success with a wide range of rulers and elites, and is well rewarded.[52]

The figure of the anonymous Bedouin who uses refined rhetoric, sometimes for a reward, may refer less to actual Bedouin than it does to the broader interest in refined rhetoric as a way to get ahead.[53] This figure is often portrayed as an impoverished and itinerant beggar who is equipped with 'natural' eloquence that allows him to participate in patronage and to be an arbiter of ethical evaluation and a model for other poets. If this figure is an authority on first-rate rhetoric, then authority in refined rhetoric is in effect displaced from competition between different groups within the city. If it is natural for the Bedouin, it is not natural for urban Arabs. People could gain access to the wise (serious and comic) rhetoric of the Bedouin in prosimetrical texts and the oral circulation of stories and poetry. These factors put people in the city, Arab and non-Arab alike, on a more equal footing in their quest to master refined rhetoric. The Bedouin figure is both marginal and central, living at the boundaries of medieval Arabic urban cultural production, yet performing a central role in eloquence. Similarly, many of the urban people who used skills in refined rhetoric to get ahead were both marginal and central. Writers express ambivalence about the marginal yet central status of the Bedouin, possibly referring to the broader range of people who used refined rhetoric. The figure appears as an arbiter of ethical evaluation, like a panegyric poet. Al-Bayhaqī's chapter on the good qualities of men defines virtue with citations of praise attributed to this anonymous Bedouin figure. Likewise, his chapter on the bad qualities of men defines vice with citations of blame attributed to this figure.[54] Just as they criticize panegyric poets, writers criticize the figure of the Bedouin. Al-Jāḥiẓ describes the Bedouin figure as a tyrannical beggar who lies in both praise and blame.[55] Descriptions of him combine mockery of his poverty and rural background with admiration of his refined use of rhetoric. The Bedouin figure uses refined rhetoric for a broad range of themes, including serious themes of love, praise and blame, supplication, detailed description, virtue, wisdom and religion, as well as comic themes of the body that include begging and poverty, violations of manners and of religious rules. He appears in a broad range of contexts including citations of proverbs, poetry and prose description, as well as selections about the Bedouin figure in the form of notices or anecdotes. He is an exemplary figure of the outsider who is also an insider, so that he is perhaps less important as an emblem of the superiority or inferiority of the Arabs (who are not necessarily Bedouin, and do not necessarily remain Bedouin even if they start out as such) relative to non-Arabs, than as an emblem of the possibility of social mobility using skills in refined rhetoric.

In addition to provincial people, Bedouin and tradesmen, other poets are described as just being ordinary people. ᶜAwfī emphasizes in the notice on the poet ᶜAbd al-Wasīᶜ that he was crude and illiterate before he became a poet,[56] and al-Thaᶜālibī refers to the poet al-Khabbāz al-Baladī, pointing out that one of the amazing things about him is that he is illiterate, but his poetry is all charming.[57] Ibn Rashīq includes the example of a man who is a poor father of daughters, who succeeds because his wife urges him to try to get a foot in the door when the famous poet al-Aᶜshā is in town.[58]

Critics address the issue of social status in their instructions for composing poetry. Shams-i Qays offers the correct descriptive terms for people in a variety of positions in the social hierarchy, including ordinary people.[59] Similarly, Qudāma b. Jaᶜfar's book of rhetoric outlines the categories of praise in conjunction with the categories of people, including provincial and urban types, and referring to ordinary people (*sūqa*).[60]

While people of lower social status can be spoken about in accordance with the rules of rhetoric, writers express more ambivalence about people of lower social status who speak. Shams-i Qays refers to one rhetorical device as being common among both elites and ordinary people.[61] His comment implies continuity between the use of refined rhetoric by people of different status, and complements the references to ordinary people who compose poetry in biographical dictionaries. In contrast, Al-Jāḥiẓ, cited by Ibn Rashīq, warns against including low-class diction or strange and rough diction in poetry 'unless the speaker is a Bedouin, since rough people understand rough speech just as common (*sūqī*) people understand common mumbling, and speech, like people, comes in classes.'[62] While al-Jāḥiẓ marginalizes 'rough' uses of speech with respect to refined rhetoric in poetry, he makes a place for it in refined rhetoric in storytelling. He says, 'When you hear a funny Bedouin story, be careful that you don't tell it except with Bedouin diction and grammar, because if you change it and retell it with the diction of modern, settled people (*muwalladīn*), you lose the story. And likewise if you hear a funny story from commoners, or a low-class joke, do not change it to fine diction or increase its [rhetorical] virtue in your delivery, lest you spoil the pleasure of it.'[63] Although prosimetrical compilations are full of examples of Bedouin speech presented as an authoritative use of refined rhetoric, critics disagree about this authority. On the one hand, Ibn al-Muᶜtazz includes Bedouin speech, referring to ancient examples circulated orally and in writing, in his sources of legitimacy for the elaborate rhetoric of contemporary poetry;[64] on the other hand, Ibn Sinān al-Khafājī finds that eloquent Bedouin rarely distinguish between the emphatic letters *ḍād* and *ẓāʾ*, and suggests that they not be used as a source for language, 'for today they need to acquire language from settled people.'[65] The diverse perspectives on authoritative sources and uses of Arabic demonstrate ambivalence about the use of refined rhetoric for social mobility.

The inclusion of people of lower socio-economic status in biographies of poets reinforces the fact that refined rhetoric and professional identity can be acquired. Al-Jāḥiẓ cites Sahl b. Hārūn, who offers an approach to aesthetic evaluation of rhetoric that incorporates social background, a kind of affirmative action in the evaluation of rhetoric. He says, 'If you have two men speaking and one is high-class and wealthy and the other is a bit rough, and they speak with the same eloquence, people will be more impressed with the lower-class man because that which is less expected is more impressive.' Al-Jāḥiẓ conflates the evaluation of rhetoric based on socio-economic background with evaluation based on ethnicity. He observes, 'They are more impressed with the newcomer and they are attracted to the one who is far [different] from them, and they leave off the one who has more wealth, knowledge, and benefit, and that's why some people advance the foreigner over the native, and the one whose benefit is new over the one whose benefit is old.'[66] The literary interest in ordinary people with skills in refined rhetoric emphasizes the possibility of using these skills to complement or change socio-economic identity.

Some poets and writers seem to harbor antipathy toward the role of ordinary people in cultural production. Abū Tammām apparently believed that poetry is for the elite, not common people.[67] While this antipathy may not be conducive to the kind of social mobility that biographical dictionaries and some critical views imply, it suggests that these more elitist views were responses to social mobility and the participation of a wider range of people in the circulation of refined rhetoric. Perhaps because of the acceptance of people of lower socio-economic status in professional identity by way of rhetorical skills, a mystical narrative poem by Sanāʾī emphasizes low economic status in his rejection of poets who compose praise and blame. Their problem is that they are poor and desperate for food and clothes, and can be seen plying their trade before the baker and the butcher.[68] Ibn Rashīq observes that good food, fine drink and listening to music refine talent, purify mood, and assist in the composition in poetry. More specifically, he emphasizes that the best things for poetry are wealth, ease and desire, since 'ease allows him [the poet] to review his work at his leisure, and desire gets him moving. Poverty is the worst for poetry, for if he is poor and under the pressure of obligations, he is content with what comes out first and accepts it, not expanding on it to reach his goal.'[69] Al-Jurjānī repeatedly emphasizes that the knowledge of refined rhetoric is not available to just anyone, in an observation that may apply more to aspiring critics than to aspiring poets. He asserts, 'Do you not see that none but those whose intellect and perspicacity raise them above the common class can truly understand this?'[70] Al-Jurjānī also asserts that not all those who seek knowledge of refined rhetoric can attain it, just as not all who seek entry into a ruler's presence are allowed in.[71] Al-Khafājī's elitist views refer directly to poetry, since he includes a section on mistakes in poetry that involve non-standard dialects. However, the inclusion of famous poets in this litany of errors suggests that the distinction between refined rhetoric and non-standard dialects is not always clear.[72] Negative attitudes toward social mobility through skills in refined rhetoric demonstrate that some poets and writers viewed social mobility as a threat.

The distinction between ordinary people and elites also relates to the audience. Ibn Wakīʿ contrasts modern poets, who are like singers whose work is appreciated by elites and ordinary people alike, with ancient poets, who are like a singer with a rough voice whose work is only appreciated by those who know about music.[73] This changing audience of poetry implies that medieval refined rhetoric appealed to an expanding range of people.

Slaves, former slaves and descendants of slaves are sometimes portrayed as mastering the professional skills of refined rhetoric, and adding to or modifying their socio-economic identity. In many cases slaves were both outsiders and insiders, in some cases because they had free fathers and slave or foreign mothers. They could enhance the insider dimension of their identity through their skills. The canonical poet ᶜAntara is described by Ibn Qutayba as one of three 'strangers among the Arabs,' meaning sons of Arab fathers and African mothers.[74] Al-Tawḥīdī refers to an eloquent slave from the desert who was purchased for the caliph al-Wāthiq. The narrator and his companions write down his every word.[75] Al-Ṣūlī includes a notice on a poet who is a client (*mawlā*) of an Arab tribe and whose father was a freed slave of Coptic descent.[76] Al-Iṣfahānī also describes the poet and jester Abū Dulāma as a black client whose father was a slave.[77] Abū Dulāma plays a significant role in parody of the patronage network that is both a marginal feature of the network and a commentary upon it.[78] Ibn al-Muᶜtazz describes the poet Marwān b. Abī Ḥafṣa, a Jewish convert to Islam, as a client who was freed because of his efforts in a political crisis. Marwān declared that he had nothing to boast about in terms of honor, neither old nor new, except poetry.[79]

The portrayal of the poet Nuṣayb, a slave of East African descent who was freed in conjunction with his professional skills in poetry, is particularly detailed. The interest in his story displays an interest in social mobility. Ibn Abī al-Dunyā in his book on ethics describes a patron who is challenged for giving a mount and a robe in exchange for praise to Nuṣayb: 'All that for an Ethiopian?' The patron points out that mounts and clothes wear out, but praise lasts. This conventional view of praise for pay suggests that Nuṣayb's skills as a poet are defined in terms of the professional standards of patronage, and not his ethnic, socio-economic or racial identity.[80]

Nuṣayb also displays an explicit awareness of professional skills in social mobility. In his book about clever people, Ibn al-Jawzī records an anecdote in which Nuṣayb goes to eat with the caliph ᶜAbd al-Malik. When the caliph asks Nuṣayb if he has any quality to make him a good drinking companion, Nuṣayb responds, 'My color is dark, my hair is curly, my appearance is distorted, and I did not get to where I am in your respect for me through the honor of my father and mother, but rather through my mind and my voice'.[81]

In his chapter on Nuṣayb, al-Iṣfahānī offers a story of his career. Nuṣayb was an Ethiopian servant who was grazing camels for his masters when one strayed. He went as far as Fustat (in northern Egypt) looking for the animal. ᶜAbd al-ᶜAzīz, the heir to the caliph ᶜAbd al-Malik, was there, and Nuṣayb asked the man at reception if he could enter, for he had praised ᶜAbd al-ᶜAzīz. When he was announced, ᶜAbd al-ᶜAzīz thought that he was a jester and postponed his entry. Nuṣayb went to the door each morning and evening for four months and finally got in to recite his piece. The audience said, 'Give benefit to him'. Nuṣayb pointed out that he was owned. The patron sent the man at reception to check on his value. The man asked about the value of an African man with no defects with one skill after another, until he mentioned his skills in poetry. The value was high, but ᶜAbd al-ᶜAzīz paid it, and Nuṣayb asked for the value of the stray camel as well. ᶜAbd al-ᶜAzīz sent him away with instructions to buy himself and come back.[82] Nuṣayb also bought his mother and grandmother, and when one appreciative patron asks him what he wants, he says that he has black daughters and does not want black men for them, so the patron helps him to make other arrangements.[83] When an adversary composes invective upon him in which he describes him as black, Nuṣayb is encouraged to respond, but he declines, saying, 'I describe myself that way'.[84] Skills in refined rhetoric provided slaves, former slaves and their descendants with channels for social mobility. Negative attitudes toward their success show that this type of social mobility was open to debate.

In addition to notices about specific slaves with professional skills in poetry, writers refer to numerous anonymous or less well-known male and female slaves with proven skills in literacy or refined rhetoric. Al-Washshāᵓ has chapters on a range of marginal categories of people, including the well-known rhetorical skills of the Bedouin, as well as chapters on the skills of free women, male slaves, female slaves, Persians and other non-Arabs.[85] Ibn Abī Ṭāhir Ṭayfūr's book on the eloquence of women focuses on free women and especially pre-Islamic free women, but the broader context of compilations from this period shows that his interest in free women may reflect the widespread literary interest in the rhetorical skills of female slaves.[86] These references to the rhetorical skills of free women and slaves emphasize that refined rhetoric has value that is independent of the value of the speaker or writer. Refined rhetoric with inherent value facilitates social mobility.

There are numerous notices about female slaves writing.[87] However, in many cases, these female slaves are described writing in conjunction with descriptions of their bodies, or are writing upon clever gifts or upon their own bodies or clothes. This combination of writing with material objects or objectified bodies emphasizes not only the subjectivity associated with rhetorical skills and writing, but also the significance of rhetorical skills as an objectified commodity, or an aspect of the slave as such a commodity.

Poets, critics and other writers debated the possibility of people from marginalized socio-economic categories using refined rhetoric to get ahead. This issue is perhaps less important for people from marginalized socio-economic groups, and more important for the diversity of religious and ethnic backgrounds of free urban men. The following section investigates attitudes toward the relationship between professional skills in refined rhetoric, especially poetry, and religious identity.

Religious identity

Poets were often expected to affiliate with the version of Muslim faith of their patrons. However, skills in refined rhetoric in Arabic or Persian sometimes enabled individuals affiliated with other versions of Muslim faith, or other faiths, to participate in patronage. Others were able to participate by concealing their religious identity or converting. Tension in patronage that is expressed in terms of religion may not have been about religion. In many cases, accusations of religious offenses occurred when the offended party used the alleged offense in a personal or political conflict.[88] Like the stories of socio-economic identity in patronage, stories of religious identity demonstrate coexistence as well as tension in the social order of patronage. Because of the role of Arabic in religious discourse, the study of Arabic linguistics was a way for non-Arabs to be equal to Arabs in terms of religion.[89] While ministers in medieval Arab culture played a role in ideological conflicts, including the conflicts that surrounded religious beliefs, 'they rarely worked actively to secure victory for one of these.' Instead, 'They were only inclined to favor the expansion of Islamic culture at the expense of strict orthodoxy, which was defended by pious and popular circles.'[90] The fact that religious affiliations and beliefs are mentioned at all suggests that even when they do not entail any particular disadvantage for the poet, religion was relevant to patronage. The participation of poets with diverse religious beliefs demonstrates the capacity of professional identity to transcend religious boundaries, while the challenges that some poets face illustrate the tension between professional and religious identity. This discussion of religious identity investigates the attitudes of writers, critics and poets to this issue, with reference to non-religious sources of religious tensions, poets with multiple religious affiliations, conversion and concealing religious identity.

Attitudes toward religious identity in patronage include the views of writers, critics, and poets. The writers Ibn ᶜAbd al-Barr and Ibn Qutayba offer exemplary arguments for doing business across religious boundaries. One authority says, 'If Pharoah did good to me, I would return the favor'. Likewise, someone asks another authority if he would thank a Magian who does good to him, and he responds, 'Yes'.[91] The examples are extreme to make a point: Pharoah in medieval Islamic literary culture is about as bad as it gets short of the devil himself; and in comparison with the Christians and the Jews, the other major religious groups in the medieval Middle East, Magians, are usually situated beyond the pale. If one can do business with Pharoah and Magians, these writers imply, one can do business with just about anyone in the region, or beyond it.

Critics and poets demonstrate support for refined rhetoric as a basis for professional life, but religious identity remains relevant. Although the critic al-Aṣmaᶜī refused to recite poetry that referred to constellations on religious grounds, he insisted that religion and poetry were two separate spheres. However, it is hard to imagine how he would give a fair hearing on a poem that included constellations. Al-Aṣmaᶜī praised the ancient poet Labīd because of his conversion to Islam and his mention of Islam in poetry, but distinguishes this praise from his evaluation, and concludes that his poetry was no good.[92] Ibn Qutayba observes the great affection between the poets Kumayt and Ṭirmāḥ in spite of their differences: Kumayt was pro-Alid and Ṭirmāḥ was Kharijite, and each man strongly supported a different tribal confederation and each strongly supported a different region.[93] The friendship transcends many boundaries, and the boundaries are the reason why the friendship becomes a focus of attention.

Religion remains part of the discussion even when critics reject its relevance to their work. Al-Jumaḥī, Ibn Qutayba and others not only include but valorize the poetic production of the earliest Arabic poets, many of whose lives and careers include pre-Islamic polytheist, Christian or Jewish beliefs; as well as Muslim, Christian, or Jewish beliefs in the wake of the early Islamic movement. The fact that a life or career spans the pre-Islamic and Islamic periods is often noted in biographies, as in al-Jumaḥī's notice on the poet Ḥutayᵓa.[94] Al-Iṣfahānī observes that Nābigha of Banū Shaybān, who used to praise the caliphs, appears to have been Christian, because in his poetry he swears by the Bible, priests and the faith.[95] Al-Marzubānī includes notices on poets of various religious affiliations without mentioning any complications, such as the Kharijite poet ᶜAṭiyya b. Samura and the Christian Shīrawayh.[96]

Likewise, Ibn al-Muᶜtazz mentions a poet who was accused of ascribing to the free-thinking Iranian-related religious cultural movement known as *zandaqa*; another who became Jewish to marry a Jewish woman and then converted back to Islam; one who subscribed to Kharijite views; and one who prayed a hundred prostrations each day and lived ascetically.[97]

Poets may defend themselves against religious tension. Abū Tammām defends himself against a peer with an effective argument. One observer describes Abū Tammām doing a light version of prayer and asks him about it. Abū Tammām responds that life is hard; the observer wishes that he worked as hard on prayer as he does on poetry. In a more elaborate response, another observer enters the room where Abū Tammām is studying collections by the poets Muslim and Abū Nuwās, and asks him what he is reading. Abū Tammām tells the witness, 'This one is al-Lāt and this one is al-ᶜUzza', referring to two female deities who were worshipped by some Arabs before Islam – an impious or even blasphemous thing to say. Abū Tammām notes the equivalent skills of the early Islamic Christian poet al-Akhtal and his two Muslim peers, Jarīr and al-Farazdaq, as well as the success of the great pre-Islamic Arab poets, to justify his distinction between being a good Muslim and being a good poet.[98] Heresy could be a serious liability for poets, as is shown by the story of Ḥammād ᶜAjrad and two of his poet friends who were all accused of heresy, so that when people saw them, they said, 'Heretic! Kill him!'[99] However, it was not always taken so seriously. The poet ᶜAlī b. Khalīl al-Kūfī, a friend of Muṭīᶜ b. Iyās and other elegant types, is sought by the caliph al-Rashīd along with other alleged adherents to the *zandaqa* heresy. ᶜAlī hides out until the caliph catches up with him, and then recites a poem that leads al-Rashīd to cancel the charges and give him five thousand dirhams.[100] This poet talks his way out of tension, so that refined rhetoric is not just an alternative to religious identity, but a way to work around it.

Religious tension may emerge from other conflicts. When the Jewish poet Abān al-Lāḥiqī insults a competitor's lineage, the man responds that the sultan forgot to take the religious minority protection tax from Abān and his family, for they are Jewish and have the Torah and no Qur'an, and they memorize the Torah but not the Qur'an. Abān responds with poetry opposing idle gossip. His allies respond that Abān reads the Qur'an extensively and gives Muslim charity in accordance with custom and law, and they cite a poem of Abān's with a Qur'anic citation in the first line. His supporters also point out that he skips the parties of the Barmakids, a wealthy family of political elites, to avoid drinking and missing prayer, and that he has been seen praying all night. These supporters defend Abān not as a Jew but as an ally of the Muslims.[101] He uses his allies in the patronage network, and defends himself with a combination of his own refined rhetoric and theirs. Similarly, the administrator Abū Isḥāq al-Ṣābiʾ, a Sabean, visits the minister al-Muhallabī and explains his religion's dietary rules in the course of the visit. Al-Muhallabī admires his piety. Al-Ṣābiʾ's peers urge him to convert to Islam, and he does not do so. However, he is supportive of Muslim practice and memorizes the Qur'an.[102]

Competition in patronage is also implicated in generating religious tension in the following story: actual religious tension is juxtaposed to the illusion of religious tension that emerges out of competition. Abū Hiffān relates that adversaries convinced the caliph al-Rashīd to test Abū Nuwās in his faith. They ask him to spit on a picture of Mānī, the leader of the Manichean religion, but people know that he is an impious bohemian, not a heretic. Ḥamdawayh the heretic is brought forward and asked to spit on the picture, and says, 'Nice people do not spit'. Both men are sent away: Abū Nuwās to be disciplined for being a playboy and Ḥamdawayh to be imprisoned until he repents for his heresy. The servant mixes up the two punishments at first, prompting Abū Nuwās to slap the servant and complain to the caliph, and the caliph laughs and lets him go.[103] The illusory religious tension disappears when confused with actual religious tension, and gives way to comedy. The real heretic presumably went to prison.

Competition provides a context for religious tension in the following story, but the immediate issue is a poet's resistance to his patron. The Muslim poet Jarīr has trouble getting a foot in the door with the caliph and makes his way in through intercession with a governor. The caliph demands praise of the governor, but Jarīr resists, preferring to praise the caliph; he then agrees and includes the caliph in his praise of the governor. The caliph then turns to the Christian poet al-Akhtal and demands praise. After the praise, the caliph says, 'You are our poet, stand up and ride Jarīr!' Al-Akhtal prepares to obey, but the audience objects to the idea of a Christian riding a Muslim.[104] Religious bias actually defuses the situation, which was caused by other problems.

Religious tension may develop out of patronage as well as broader cultural tensions. Dawlatshāh records a story in which Firdawsī must praise the sultan Maḥmūd to get a foot in the door, and also praises the minister Maymandī, but ignores the ruler's favorite male slave, Ayāz, who then convinces Maḥmūd that Firdawsī is pro-Alid.[105] Although the immediate cause for the tension may be the dynamics of patronage, the friction between the Sunni ruler Maḥmūd of Ghazna and the great epic poet Firdawsī, who is accused of being pro-Alid, may refer to a conflict over the role of pre-Islamic Persian culture in Ghaznavid political ideology.

Poets may perform their religious identity in more than one way. The poet Kisāʾī is described as composing both panegyric and ascetic verse.[106] Ibn Qutayba observes that the poet Kumayt praises both the line of ʿAlī and their opponents the Umayyads. He speculates that the superiority of the poetry about the Umayyads indicates the poet's preference for benefit in this world rather than rewards in the next.[107] One poet endures punishment in this world because of his religious identity. ʿAlī b. Jahm is linked with a range of affiliations, including the Shi'ites, Christians and the theology of the Muʿtazila, so that his enemies conspire against him and he ends up crucified naked in Khurasan.[108]

A range of beliefs are attributed to al-Sayyid al-Ḥimyarī. Al-Iṣfahānī relates that both al-Sayyid al-Ḥimyarī and Kuthayyir display pro-Alid views in their poetry and statements, apparently without any impact on their work.[109] Al-Sayyid defends himself with rhetoric that is clever, if not refined. When a man confronts him about his adherence to the Kaysānī sect, which includes a belief in reincarnation, he admits to it, and the man asks if al-Sayyid will give him a gold coin in exchange for a hundred gold coins at the time of the reincarnation. Al-Sayyid agrees, and will give more, on the condition that the man confirms he will be reincarnated as a human. 'What else could I be?', the man asks. Al-Sayyid says, 'I fear you'll come back as a dog or a pig and I'll be out of my money', and the man is silenced.[110] In another notice, two men are having a dispute and decide that the first passerby will resolve it. Al-Sayyid passes by and the Shi'ite man hastens to say, 'We've differed and the first passerby should judge'. Al-Sayyid asks, 'About what?' The man says, 'I say that ʿAlī is the best of people after the Prophet.' Al-Sayyid responds, 'So what does this son of a bitch say?'

Similarly, but with more negative consequences, a range of beliefs are ascribed to the poet Bashshār, and some stories demonstrate the role of patronage in generating religious tension. Bashshār's invective of an elite and al-Mahdī may have been the cause of the efforts to attribute religious offenses to him.[111] Ibn al-Muʿtazz records that a rival told the caliph al-Mahdī that Bashshār was Kharijite and al-Mahdī killed him. Alternatively, he was accused of composing invective on al-Mahdī, who then killed him. In another version, which Ibn al-Muʿtazz prefers,

Bashshār is accused of heresy and killed, either by seventy lashes or beheading.[112]

The critic Ibn al-Muᶜtazz defends the poets al-Sayyid al-Ḥimyarī and Bashshār, not by denying the impact of marginal Muslim religious affiliations on the professional evaluation of their poetry, but by mentioning how their poetry demonstrates their belonging in the broader Muslim community. He observes that al-Sayyid composes praise of the Prophet.[113] This observation implies an argument for religious tolerance of unorthodox Muslim beliefs, since all Muslims agree about the Prophet. Ibn al-Muᶜtazz records verses by Bashshār and asserts that they show that he was a good Muslim.[114] Just as the non-Muslims Abū Isḥāq al-Ṣābiᵓ and Abān al-Lāḥiqī were accepted because their use of refined rhetoric incorporated Muslim beliefs, these heretical Muslim poets are supported by Ibn al-Muᶜtazz because their verse demonstrates their allegiance to orthodoxy.

For some poets, changing from one religious affiliation to another is the best way to cope with the pressures and demands of the patronage network. The story of Kaᶜb b. Zuhayr with the Prophet is an early example in which a poet's religious identity straddles the pre-Islamic and Islamic periods, and in which the poet's conversion is successful yet fraught with risk. Ibn Qutayba and al-Jumaḥī record versions of this story in which Kaᶜb's brother has already converted and Kaᶜb criticizes his conversion. The Prophet in turn sends the brother to warn Kaᶜb not to interfere. Kaᶜb approaches the Prophet by way of the Prophet's companion Abū Bakr, who later became caliph. Abū Bakr is neither identified with a tough stance on religious regulation of culture and society, as ᶜUmar appears to be in stories, nor implicated in the major early Islamic succession dispute, as ᶜUthmān and ᶜAlī are, so he may serve as a neutral figure. He is veiled, and announces himself as a man who has come to make an alliance with the Prophet in Islam and unveils himself. While one faction of early Muslims is rude and resentful of Kaᶜb's conversion, another faction is welcoming, and the Prophet also welcomes the newcomer, who recites his legendary poem upon conversion.[115] The widespread interest in this story suggests that it provides a significant context for thinking about the dynamics of patronage, refined rhetoric and other categories of identity.

Conversion may imply a need to cope with patronage. It demonstrates the difficulties that poets face in trying to do business across religious boundaries, as well as the acceptance of converts in the social order of patronage. ᶜAwfī refers to a poet who is described as young and successful, a client and a Muslim though his father was a fire worshipper, and very popular.[116] Rāzī includes a notice about a poet whose parents were Christian, but who used to insist that God is one, until he fled and became Muslim.[117] Ibn al-Muᶜtazz records that the Jewish client Marwān b. Abī Ḥafṣa was freed in conjunction with ᶜUthmān's political crisis, and converted to Islam by ᶜUthmān. In addition to his successful career as a poet, he was placed in charge of the Umayyad treasury, married an elite Muslim woman, and was known for his anti-Alid sentiments. Marwān's comment that he has no old or new source of pride other than poetry emphasizes the use of refined rhetoric to secure social mobility. However, his story shows that his conversion helped too.[118]

Conversion may be explicitly articulated as a response to the pressures and demands of patronage. The pro-Alid compiler al-Bayhaqī cites a confrontation between the caliph ᶜAbd al-Malik and al-Farazdaq when they see an Alid while on pilgrimage, and al-Farazdaq recites a poem about him, acknowledging his affection for the Alid line. The caliph prohibits him his reward, and al-Farazdaq seeks and obtains a reward to last a lifetime from a member of the Alid line.[119] When al-Buḥturī is asked if he has taken on the theological views of free will, based on some of his verses, he says, 'That was my religion in the days of the caliph al-Wāthiq, and then I left it under the caliph al-Mutawakkil'. His interlocutor says, 'This is bad religion that changes with the turns in power'.[120] In spite of the interlocutor's criticism, al-Buḥturī's success demonstrates the effectiveness of his subordination of religious allegiances to professional interests.

Conversion may also be about changes in lifestyle that affect a poet's patronage. In addition to being accused of being a heretic, Abū al-ᶜAtāhiya takes on the religious identity of an ascetic and refuses to compose love poetry, so that the caliph imprisons him in a house.[121] ᶜAwfī describes a poet who turns to asceticism and mysticism in his old age.[122] In his collection of biographies of rulers and other elites who are also poets, Haravī records the story of a Mongol ruler-poet who gives everything up and wanders around Christian-ruled Anatolia as a dervish and tradesman, only to return to the Muslim-ruled region to the southeast to find that his own allies are no longer in power.[123]

As an alternative to conversion, poets may pretend to adhere to one affiliation to facilitate patronage, while retaining another. Concealing religious affiliations usually leads to the poet's undoing. Stories of Sāliḥ b. ᶜAbd al-Qudūs imply that he may have attempted to conceal heretical beliefs. In one version, al-Mahdī brings him in on heresy charges and likes him and lets him go, then calls him back and confronts him with heretical verses that have been attributed to him. Sāliḥ admits to composing the verses and is simply killed, according to one account, or beheaded and his body crucified on a bridge in another account. In another story al-Rashīd brings him in on heresy charges and when he is confronted with heretical verses he claims that he did not compose them. Al-Rashīd observes that Sāliḥ recites the Qur'an and lets him go, then asks him to recite a poem and observes that it resembles the verses upon which the accusation was based, and has him killed. During his lifetime, Sāliḥ rises to pray along with his companions and they ask him why he does that, given his beliefs. Sāliḥ responds, 'It's the local custom and a habit of the body.' As he does in his defense of al-Sayyid al-Ḥimyarī and Bashshār, Ibn al-Muᶜtazz offers a sample of Ṣāliḥ's ascetic poetry and questions the accusation of heresy, citing a story in which a man sees Sāliḥ in a dream, laughing in heaven. The dreamer asks him how he escaped the punishment of a heretic, and he responds, 'I met my maker and he knew me to be innocent of those charges.'[124] In the story of a poet who is a cupper, recorded by Ibn al-Muᶜtazz, an initial accusation of heresy, of which the poet is cleared, leads to an inspection of his books, exoneration and a job as a secretary. The subsequent accusation of heresy, which causes him to lose his job and end up a beggar, suggests that he may have been a secret heretic all along.[125] In a more clear-cut case of pretense, the caliph al-Rashīd favors the poet Manṣūr al-Namarī because of his good poetry and his maternal lineage to al-ᶜAbbās b. ᶜAbd al-Muṭṭalib, as well as his support of the Abbasid line and rejection of the Alid line. However, when al-Rashīd learns of his secret support of the Alids through some verses, he orders him killed, though too late, since he has already died. Even before his death the poet had expressed his pro-Alid sentiments in riddles that went undetected in poetry dedicated to the Abbasids.[126]

Poets who get caught with the wrong religious affiliation, or for concealing the wrong affiliation, can often talk their way out of the problem by backing off. The poet Ibn Harma praises a member of the Alid line and favors them, but backs off when one of them rebels against the caliph al-Manṣūr. When he is accused of pro-Alid affinities and verses for the Alids are attributed to him, he disowns the verses and says that the composer of them did something to his own mother (better left unmentioned). His son turns to him and says, 'Dad, didn't you say those verses at such and such a time?' Ibn Harma replies, 'What's better, that I should do something to my mother (better left unmentioned) or that Ibn Qaḥtaba should take me away?'[127] The poet Ibn Mawlā denigrates the Alids in order to succeed with the Abbasid caliph and then praises an Alid, who confronts him about his earlier poetry for the caliph. Ibn Mawlā claims that his verse about 'the commander of the faithful and his people' refers to the caliph and the Alids.[128] The caliph attributes verses in favor of Kharijite beliefs (that leadership belongs with the most able Muslim regardless of lineage) to one client poet, but the poet claims that he did not say 'the caliph is *Shabīb* [referring to a Kharijite leader]', but rather 'the caliph is *nasīb* [referring to the love description at the beginning of a *qaṣīda*]', and the caliph likes the response and lets him go.[129] Saᶜdī records a story of a poet who, when faced with an accusation, admits to his religious pretenses in such a clever way that they cease to be a liability: the man pretends to be a supporter of ᶜAlī, and returns from the pilgrimage to offer a poem to the ruler. A drinking companion points out that his father is a Christian and he plagiarized the poem from another poet. When the king orders that he be beaten and exiled, the man says, 'You're right about me', and offers two verses about the unreliability of strangers. The king laughs and orders a gift.[130]

Critics and writers bring religion into the mix by talking about it even when they deny that it is relevant to the professional identity of poets. Religious identity in patronage is complicated by the non-religious sources of religious tension, as well as the attribution to poets of multiple religious affiliations. While many poets do business in spite of tensions, others have recourse to conversion and concealing their religious beliefs. Professional identity based on refined rhetoric did not efface religious tension, but it provided an alternative approach to relationships that competed with religious identity. Poets sometimes had to pay a price of religious assimilation of one kind or another in order to enjoy the benefits of social mobility based on refined rhetoric. The final section of this chapter investigates the implications of ethnic identity – or identity based on language, geography or both – for professional identity based on refined rhetoric and social mobility in patronage.

Ethnic identity

Professional identity based on refined rhetoric offered an alternative to ethnic identity. Ethnic, language-based identity was also intertwined with the use of refined rhetoric in Arabic and Persian for a professional identity. As a result, professional identity and ethnic identity overlap yet compete with one another. As with religious identity, poets sometimes had to pay the price of ethnic assimilation in order to take on a professional identity based on refined rhetoric. This discussion of ethnic identity examines critical attitudes toward Arabic, and its use by Arabs and non-Arabs, and toward Persian, and its use by Persians and non-Persians.

Arabic and Persian each provided a context in which people from different backgrounds could work together. Baghdad was multicultural before it became the cosmopolitan center of medieval Arabic culture, since its residents included Persians, Aramaens, Nabateans and Arabs who had settled there before the Islamic conquests of the region.[131] Persian and Turkish culture were intertwined and interdependent under the Ghaznavids.[132] In the Persianate Indian cultural capitals of Lahore and later Delhi, Turkic rulers presided over an administration and cultural elite that used Persian, wrote in Arabic in religious discourse, and coexisted with a larger population that used Hindavi.[133] Arabic poets such as Abū Tammām and al-Ṣanawbarī combined rare, Bedouin-like Arabic words and Persian words.[134] Persian poets such as Manūchehrī and ᶜIrāqī displayed their knowledge of Arabic in their poetry. Abū Tammām was knowledgeable about all of the cultures in his time and region, from ancient Arab and medieval Islamic culture to Persian, Indian and Greek cultural influences, and Manūchehrī incorporates motifs of Arab, Islamic, ancient Persian, Indian, Greek, Jewish and Christian culture in his poetry.[135]

Coexistence entailed competition. Efforts to focus on ancient Arabic criteria in poetry promoted Arab heritage in competition with the Persian pride movement, and the development of theories of the inimitability of the Qur'an, often using poetry as a counterpoint, was an effort to promote the Qur'an's superiority to Persian books of wisdom.[136] Motifs of Indian culture in Ghaznavid poetry must be viewed in the context of the Ghaznavid conquests of India.[137]

Being Arab and using Arabic were not the same thing, and critical attitudes toward Arabic demonstrated the role of other peoples and languages in defining the Arabic language. The medieval portrayal of the complex heritage of the Arabic language begins in pre-Islamic culture. The poet al-Nābigha goes in to see the caliph ᶜUthmān and says 'I've changed so that I dislike myself,' and wants to go out to the camels, drink their milk and smell the desert. ᶜUthmān admonishes him, saying that this type of Arab identity (*taᶜarrub*) is not appropriate in the wake of the expansion of Islam. Al-Nābigha says he didn't know, and would not have gone out to the desert this way without permission, and ᶜUthmān grants him permission to go.[138] The story begins with change and anxiety about it. It emphasizes that al-Nābigha was wrong to want to go out to the desert, but he goes anyway. His experience of the unfettered life in the desert is inscribed in his obedience to the caliph in the new world order.

Likewise, the medieval portrayal of Arabs and Persians working together in Arabic puts down roots in portrayals of the pre-Islamic Arabic poets and the Persian empire. The critics' portrayal of pre-Islamic Arabic poetry as pristinely apolitical is compromised by the interaction between poets and the Persians. Ibn Qutayba reports that Qubād the king of the Persians crowned the grandfather of Imruʾ al-Qays king of the Arabs, and that the Persian king Anūshirvān set up the son of Imruʾ al-Qays, Mundhir, in the city of Hira.[139] Ibn Rashīq makes al-Aʿshā's marketing of poetry to the Persian king, who rewarded him to please the Arabs in spite of his contempt for the poetry, a crucial step in the development of panegyric.[140] For Ibn Rashīq, this moment represents a kind of fall from grace for poetry.

The origins of Arabic poetry are not only bound up with the Persian empire, they have roots in very different versions of the Arabic language. Al-Jumaḥī rejects legends about the Arabic poetry of ʿĀd and Thamūd in ancient times and observes that the Arabic in which the Qur'an was revealed and which was spoken in the age of the Prophet, and the language of Ḥimyar in Yemen, are each distinct from the Arabic spoken in his own time.[141]

This other-centered approach to the definition of Arabic becomes more elaborate in al-Jāḥiẓ's analysis of medieval cross-cultural interaction. He seems fascinated by the contact zone in which speakers of Arabic and other languages interact. He records a number of deviations in diction, pronunciation and grammar that occur in the contemporary Arabic of Nabateans who have grown up in the agricultural region around Kufa, Khurasanis, and secretaries from Ahwaz, and offers a few jokes about second-language speakers, about a Sindi woman and a Nabatean man.[142] He discusses the strange sounds made by Persians and Magians.[143] Al-Jāḥiẓ rejects the assertion that anyone who can make himself understood is articulate, offering examples of Arabic speech that is understandable yet inarticulate, by a Nabati, a Farsi, a Khurasani and one of his own servants. He notes that such inarticulate speech is only comprehensible because of the listener's long exposure to it, and that the masters of Arabic do not deal with this type of speech any more than they deal with the gibberish of the Greek or the Slav.[144] He defines Basra as the nearest land of the Persians and the farthest land of the Arabs, and Kufa as the nearest land of the Nabateans and the farthest land of the Arabs, and observes the impact of Persian on the Arabic of Medina.[145] Al-Aṣmaʿī defines Arabic by explaining that the Greeks lack one letter, the Persians another, and the Syriac-speaking people a third.[146] Al-Jāḥiẓ cites examples of Persian words that find their way into Arabic poetry, including the Arabic poetry of Bedouin poets.[147] In all of these comments, al-Jāḥiẓ's ethnocentric attitude is also other-centered insofar as he arrives at conclusions about Arabic by listening to and remarking on languages that he does not know, and Arabic spoken by non-Arabs. While Arabic is Arabo-centric for al-Jāḥiẓ when it comes to pronunciation, diction and grammar, the issue of eloquence leads to a cross-cultural consultation. He gathers input from the peninsular Greek, the Anatolian Greek and the Indian, as well as an in-depth consultation and quest for a translation of an Indian essay on the topic, which is found and presented in Arabic, in conjunction with other consultations with imported Indian doctors.[148]

The critic Ibn Sinān al-Khafājī turns this type of thinking into a complicated narrative of Arabic superiority articulated through discussions of other languages. The result is a kind of comparative supremacist linguistics. Al-Khafājī asserts that no language matches Arabic in the abundance of singular nouns, and makes specific observations about Greek. He cites a Greek king who listens to a translation of Arabic poetry by al-Mutanabbī, famous for his heroic poetry about Arab Muslim battles with Greek Christians, and completely misses the point of the imagery. Al-Khafājī also observes that Dāwūd al-Mutrān (a Christian name), who knows both Arabic and Syriac, concludes that speech translated from Arabic to Syriac becomes ugly, while speech translated in the opposite direction becomes beautiful; apparently, everyone says this about Arabic and other languages. As Al-Khafājī explains, 'The thing is, we Arabs have metaphors and diction that others simply do not have'. Another virtue is that Arabic avoids difficult sounds and combinations of sounds, unlike other languages such as Armenian and Zanj, the language of East Africa. He cites the conventional argument that Arabic is special or superior because it has the emphatic letter *ḍād,* not present in other languages, and notes that the emphatic letter *ḥā*ʾ is not unique to Arabic, since he has encountered it in Syriac, Ethiopic and Hebrew, and other unusual letters are used in a few other languages as well.

Al-Khafājī's comparative supremacist linguistics of Arabic gives way to a more critical discourse. He notes that Armenian has considerably more letters than Arabic. He addresses this problem by observing that many of these numerous letters are similar, and then notes that emphatic *ḍād* and *ẓā*ʾ are also similar in Arabic – which seems like a problem for the special status of the language of *ḍād*. This problem of the *ḍād* and the *ẓā*ʾ that he encounters in his inspection of Armenian leads him to the problem of these letters in Arabic. The eloquent Arabic of the Bedouin, often considered the ultimate source for Arabic, apparently fails to distinguish between *ḍād* and *ẓāʾ*. Ibn Sinān al-Khafājī concludes that these days, the eloquent Bedouin need to acquire their Arabic language from settled people and by way of systematic grammar.[149]

Just as he constructs Arabic language superiority and then complicates it, Ibn Sinān constructs the superiority of the Arabs and then does the same thing, since other people deserve to know Arabic too. The Arabs' fine minds, daring, heroism, generosity and adherence to religion are unmatched, so that their proverbs, ethical insights and excellent yet rough-hewn poetry enable the reader to dispense with the Greeks. However, the Arabs' transmission of religion initiated a range of fields of knowledge that opened up to anyone (presumably Arab or non-Arab) who mixes with scholars and reads books. Like al-Jāḥiẓ, Ibn Sinān's ethnocentric discussion of Arabic is also other-centered in important ways. Each of these critics demonstrates the way cosmopolitan discourse intertwines hegemony and diversity, since you have to make contact and work with other people to dominate them.[150]

Other writers contribute to the portrayal of Arabic in an ethnocentric yet other-centered way. In his chapters on the eloquence of distinct populations, al-Washshāʾ includes non-Arabs, especially Persians, as well as Bedouin.[151] The organization of topics offers an argument about the way the world is organized, and here both Persians and Bedouin fit into Arabic eloquence. Ibn al-Athīr explains that one does not need to live in the desert to produce good poetry, though poets from settled communities do not simply imitate the Greeks. This analysis situates Arabic somewhere between the desert and the Greeks, and implies that the field extends between the ancient poets and the Bedouin on the one hand, and the moderns in cosmopolitan cities on the other.[152] In the context of polemics between Persian and Arabic as sources of cultural authority, Ibn Qutayba explains that Persians who are proud of their ancient wisdom literature, attributed to figures such as the minister Buzurjmihr or the king Anūshirvān, should have a look at the poetry of the Arabs, where they will find the same kind of ideas, if not better. He follows up with selections of wisdom or proverbs in poetry.[153] In more general statements, everyone is brought in together: people derive status from family or from deeds, or from both or neither, for all people were created from dust that has run in the sewers and mixed with filth, and when they return to God, none of their worldly accomplishments will do them any good, except piety.[154]

Two statements are often cited about the status of Arabic and non-Arabs. First, Ibn Qutayba explains that God did not restrict eloquence in poetry to any one people or age. Second, Ibn al-Rūmī confronts an audience member who mocks his skills in poetry, suggesting that an Arab slept with Ibn al-Rūmī's mother. Ibn al-Rūmī responds, 'That must mean that as for those Arabs who do not compose poetry, non-Arabs must have slept with their mothers'.[155] Ibn Qutayba is clearly responding to the circulation of the opposite view, and Ibn al-Rūmī's joke makes the confrontation of these views explicit enough. Integrating analyses such as those by al-Jāḥiẓ and Ibn Sinān represent attempts to make sense of the contradiction of diversity and hegemony in the professional use of Arabic.

In addition to broad theoretical analyses, writers offer stories about specific people to deal with the diversity and hegemony of professional identity rooted in Arabic. Persians are a major focus of these discussions. Medieval Islamic culture in an Arabic context drew heavily on the Iranian tradition of kingship augmented by eloquence.[156] Poets display a multifaceted approach to ethnic identity: Bashshār grew up among Arab tribes but participated in the discourse of Persian pride or *shu*ᶜ*ubiyya*, and Abū Nuwās displays Persian pride in an explicit way in one poem, but his interest in literary change derives more from his effort to make poetry fit into cosmopolitan life than it does from his interest in Persian pride.[157] The client Khālid b. Barmak, who is descended from a Buddhist family of Central Asia, is so skilled in rhetoric that the caliph Abū al-ᶜAbbās thinks he is an Arab. When the caliph asks who he is from, Khālid cites the Arab poet who said, 'I am from no other party than the people of Aḥmad (the Prophet), and I am from no other branch than the branch of righteousness'.[158] Khālid al-Barmakī becomes annoyed when he is asked to attend to some beggars, and retorts that many of those who come seeking benefit are actually noble or even better than those from whom they seek benefit, with more refined manners, so they should be called visitors, not beggars. This view may reflect his concern about the status of protégés from non-Arab ethnic groups. The non-Arab poet Bashshār praises him for this in some versions of the notice.[159] While some non-Arab Arabic poets, such as Ismāᶜīl b. Yasār, are portrayed deploying their skills mainly to praise the Persians and blame the Arabs, most references to ethnic identity do not involve such a contentious perspective.[160]

While Persians are a major focus, they are part of a wider variety of people involved in Arabic. A number of poets are identified as being Farsi, Khurasani, Bedouin, Persianized Turkish, African or simply as non-Arab clients.[161] Several particularly important poets and critics are depicted as non-Arab slaves or clients, including the Arab-African poet ᶜAntar, the critic Khalaf al-Aḥmar from the Central Asian province of Farghana and the Khurasani poet Bashshār.[162] Other poets are depicted as Azerbayjani, Khurasani, and a non-Arab who has been honored by a leader of the Soghdians.[163] One Arabic poet is described as a descendant of a Persian minister of the Persian king Ardashīr.[164] One Arabic poet from India experiences a misunderstanding.[165] Ibn Qutayba's description of a Sindi poet refers to poetry that is good in spite of the poet's unclear accent.[166] The literary interest in diverse people and sources of Arab music complements the discussions of diversity among poets.[167]

In addition to language-based ethnic identity, tribal ethnic identity influences the dynamics of patronage. Al-Ṣūlī cites an encounter in which a member of a patron's gathering is disappointed to learn that Abū Tammām is not affiliated with the tribal confederations of Rabīᶜ or Nizār.[168] Professional skills in refined rhetoric forged bonds and articulated differences across tribal boundaries within the Arab community. The issue of tribal identity calls attention to the fact that Arabic speakers, like speakers of other languages, had to acquire skills in order to use refined rhetoric in Arabic.

Arabic does not just encounter other languages and cultures, especially Persian: its development in the medieval discourse on refined rhetoric is bound up with these other languages and cultures. Ethnocentric discourse becomes other-centered. In his book of rhetoric, Ibn al-Athīr praises the Persian *Shāhnāma* or *Book of Kings*, saying 'it's the Qur'an of their people, and in spite of the breadth of the Arabic language it has nothing like it, though the Persian language in comparison to Arabic is like a drop in the sea.'[169] Similarly, the development of Persian in the medieval discourse on refined rhetoric is bound up with other languages and cultures, especially Arabic at first, and later Hindavi and Ottoman Turkish. Perspectives on Arabic and Persian as cultures that could be joined by anyone who masters refined rhetoric support the view of Ibn al-Muqaffaᶜ, a Persian minister who wrote in Arabic and translated part of the Indian *Panchatantra* from Pahlavi Persian into Arabic. He explains that a man's religion or ethical status is not a stable condition, but rather is constantly in flux.[170]

Most Persian poets before the renaissance of Persian literature composed poetry in both Arabic and Persian. Translations were a crucial form of interaction between the two languages, allowing the movement of ideas, form and content that contributed to the emergence of a new Persian literary tradition in the Islamic period.[171] New Persian literary culture combined ancient Persian, Arabic, Islamic and other cultural influences.

Medieval Persian discourse on refined rhetoric has roots that take it back to the beginning of human time. In legends about the beginning of Persian poetry, Persian poetry appears in conjunction with and in counterpoint to Arabic poetry. These stories of Arabic poetry emphasize the complex relationship between Arabic and Islam. ᶜAwfī's biographical collection of poets begins with the legendary origins of Persian poetry in Adam's verses in the wake of Cain's murder, and then discusses the origins of Arabic poetry. This story implies that the essence of poetry lies in loss and grief, the desire expressed by the poet about the uncertainty of relationships. A later account points out that Adam would have spoken Syriac and translated into Arabic, but assigns the first Arabic speech to the grandson of the prophet Hūd, and the role of the first poet to a Yemeni named Ashᶜar, whose name is derived from the Arab words for poetry and poet. While this narrative splits poetry off from the Islamic function of Arabic, another narrative splices them together again. Labīd b. Aswad al-Bāhilī is said to have hung a poem in the Kaᶜba. The first verse, about how everything but God is pointless, is cited.[172] In the Arabic tradition, Labīd b. Rabīᶜa, an ancient poet who converts and who composed one of the poems known as the *muᶜallaqāt* ('hung up', in the Ka'ba), became a figure of the conjunction and disjunction between the ancients and the early Muslims, but this story is about a different Labīd. When the chapter 'Iqraᵓ' or 'Read' is revealed, this Persianate ancient Arabic poet says, 'This is not the speech of humankind', and removes his poem so as to replace it with the chapter, and converts to Islam. However, one reason for the precedence of the Arabs over the Persians is the presence of Arabic poets before Islam, while the authorities on Persian poetry could not find anyone other than Bahrām.[173]

The ancient Persian king Bahrām Gūr, who was raised in Arabia, begins the history of Persian poetry.[174] This part of the legend works on several levels.[175] First, Bahrām learned how to be king from the Bedouin; second, he spent time in his palace whose parts corresponded to regions on earth, heavenly bodies and days of the week – good preparation to be the legendary initiator of poetry with its aspirations to universality. Although distracted from work, Bahrām stored up knowledge about life, listening to the tales of princesses from around the known world. Third, he complemented this with more practical knowledge, which he gained by traveling in his kingdom and encountering people from all walks of life – the inverse of a patron who is approached by his subjects. It is only by listening to the complaints of ordinary people that he learns of his minister's nefarious deeds, and manages to stave off an invasion and restore prosperity just in the nick of time. As a ruler who saved the day by attending to the needs of his people, he resembles a patron who attends to poets.

ᶜAwfī continues with the story of a man named ᶜAbbās who had rhetorical skills in Arabic and Persian, praising the caliph al-Maᵓmūn in Persian in Marv. The story reflects the fact that Persians made significant gains in administrative careers under this caliph. In this legend, after a hiatus, Persian poetry begins anew in a more thoroughly and independently Persian context under the Persian provincial rulers the Saffarids, who establish autonomy from the caliphate; and the more successful Persian provincial rulers, the Samanids of Central Asia, who initiate the Persian–Turkish alliance that enabled Persian literary culture to flourish and spread throughout South Asia and the Ottoman Empire.[176] At this point, legend has given way to history. After the Samanids, the Ghaznavid dynasty became the first group of political elites to offer extensive patronage of Persian poetry.

Dawlatshāh offers a more detailed story of the patronage of Persian by the Tahirids in the Middle East. A governor is so delighted with a Persian romance that was prepared for the ancient king Anūshīrvān that he commands the Qur'an and sayings of the Prophet be thrown in the water. However, he later commands that the writings of the Persians be burnt, so that Persian literary production disappears again until the Samanids. The only way to explain the disappearance of Persian literature in the early Islamic period is to also throw away the most important texts written in Arabic.

Dawlatshāh offers a more detailed version of the surfacing of Persian poetry under the Saffarids, describing them as the first to rebel against the caliphs among the Persians. In this story, Persian literature reappears in conjunction with rebellion. In this famous legend, Yaᶜqūb b. Layth watches his son play with a ball that rolls along, and then summons his administrators to get to work on formulating a poetic meter from this motion, leading to the epigram genres. This is perhaps a legendary equivalent of the widespread emphasis on the natural quality of the Bedouin's eloquence in Arabic. Dawlatshāh expresses an ethnocentric yet other-centered approach to the genesis of New Persian poetry in his depiction of the fourth-/tenth-century poet Rūdakī. Just as the Saffarids bring forth all-natural Persian meters, Rūdakī's work in poetry relates closely to his work in music. While these natural approaches to Persian are ethnocentric, Rūdakī is also described in conjunction with his rendition of *Kalīla and Dimna* in Persian verse.[177] The text is Indian and, after its translation from Pahlavi to Arabic, it circulated in Arabic before Rūdakī worked on it. The reference to this text is both ethnocentric and other-centered. Similarly, Rūdakī and other Samanid poets integrated Arabic references to the Qur'an with references to Persian legend.[178] In this way, these poets appropriate Islamic culture for the development of Persian literary culture and look outward to the broader Muslim community.

Legends with an other-centered angle on the ethnocentric development of Persian give way in biographical dictionaries to notices that sometimes include non-Persian poetry and poets. ᶜAwfī's biographical compilation includes Arabic citations, Dawlatshāh's includes Arabic poets, and Turkish examples appear in Haravī's compilation.[179] As the penultimate chapter of the book, the group of Turkish poets is both integrated into the larger group and marginalized. Sām Mīrzā's penultimate chapter, before the final chapter on common people, deals with Turkish poets, beginning with a long entry on the poet and writer of a biographical dictionary in Chagatai Turkish with Turkish and Persian verses, ᶜAlīshīr Navāʾī, and continuing with poets whose range of activities sounds much like the lives of the Persian poets earlier in the book, including one with Persian and Turkish collected poems.[180] In addition to his interest in Arabic poetry, Rūmī included Turkish verses that were some of the earliest examples of metered verse in Turkish, as well as Greek words.[181] As with Persian and Arabic poets, Turkish is about the use of refined rhetoric, not necessarily the language spoken at home or by everyone from that ethnic background. This group is complemented by occasional Turkish verses earlier in Sām Mīrzā's book, a reference to pre-Islamic Turkish culture, a reference to a translation project of the Persian *Book of Kings* into Turkish, and a poet in the 'common people' section who has Persian and Turkish collected poems.[182] Alīshīr's own Chagatai Turkish encyclopedia of poets, including verses in Persian and Turkish, gets translated into Persian in Herat and Istanbul within a century of its composition.[183] Most of the poetry is Persian, but there is a significant amount of Turkish poetry included, as well as a few bilingual poets. Shūshtarī's more general encyclopedia concludes with two chapters on poets: one on Arabic poets and one on Persian poets.[184] ᶜAwfī refers to a poet born in Lahore and raised in Samarqand, as well as the tri-lingual production of Masᶜūd-i Saᶜd-i Salmān in Arabic, Persian and Hindustani, while Rāzī's compilation was produced in India and includes poets who work in Arabic and Turkish as well as Persian.[185] Similarly, biographical dictionaries of Ottoman Turkish poets compare them to

Persian poets, and include those who compose poetry in both Persian and Turkish.[186]

Persian rhetoric books draw on both Persian and Arabic examples to articulate an other-centered discourse on refined rhetoric in Persian. Vaṭvāṭ includes Arabic citations from the Qur'an, prose, poetry, the *maqāma* or series of stories in rhymed prose, and proverbs.[187] He also refers to a rhetorical device that consists of alternating between Arabic and Persian, as well as one known as translation from Arabic to Persian or vice versa.[188] Shams-i Qays praises Vaṭvāṭ's bilingual book of rhetoric and proposes the need for a study that focuses on Persian poetry.[189] In his section on the beauties of poetry he opens with a device that consists of using Arabic terms in Persian poetry, conversation, and correspondence, and describes this device using the image of a fine robe with colored stripes in which there is no separation between the warp and the weft.[190] In his second device, he includes citations from the Qur'an and Persian poetry, and chooses Persian poetry that is mostly by Vaṭvāṭ or Masᶜūd-i Saᶜd-i Salmān – both known for their use of Arabic as well as Persian.[191] Rādūyānī offers Persian translations of the Arabic terms used in Persian rhetoric.[192] He also includes a device for people who know the legends of the Persians and the verses of the Qur'an.[193]

Other genres of medieval Persian writing display or advocate the use of Persian complemented by Arabic. Saᶜdī's *Gulistān*, *The Rose Garden*, is a book of prose and verse in Persian and Arabic, and Kaykāvūs b. Iskandar advises aspiring drinking companions to master both languages.[194] Mystical poetry by ᶜIrāqī includes selections of Arabic in several genres.

Transnational themes complement the transnational definition of refined rhetoric in Persian. Niẓām al-Mulk advises rulers and administrators to combine different ethnic groups in the army, and this is just what the Ghaznavids do in their military incursions in Central, West and South Asia.[195] Niẓāmī Ganjavī's medieval mystical rendition of Firdawsī's medieval version of the ancient epic of Bahrām Gūr emphasizes the role of distracting images of women from seven regions of the world and the effort to avert war with China.[196] Transnational themes help to articulate the intersection of diversity and hegemony in cosmopolitan imperial culture.

Several features of medieval Arabic and Persian literary culture complement the intersection of ethnic identity and refined rhetoric in patronage. The *maqāma* resembles geographical literature, since its concatenated stories take place in different locations.[197] Like the panegyric poet, the trickster figure seeks patronage with elaborate sermons in a wide range of cities: hailing from the margins of Muslim-ruled territory, he resembles a panegyric poet who uses refined rhetoric to get a foot in the door. Like the figure of the Bedouin, the rhetorical skills of the trickster and the poet make them insiders, while their mobility means that they are, in other ways, outsiders. This insider-outsider status resembles the role of the panegyric poet, especially the poet who crosses boundaries of socio-economic, religious or ethnic identity, but also all poets who move from one patron to the next.

Travel facilitates the other-centered performance of ethnocentric identity. Al-Thaᶜālibī describes movement from place to place by poets such as al-Mutanabbī and al-Babbaghāᵓ.[198] Al-Ṣūlī mentions Abū Tammām's trips to Armenia and Khurasan to praise elites involved in military conflicts near the borders of the Abbasid Empire, as well as his travel to Basra and Ahwaz to praise whomever he could find there.[199] The poet Khāqānī's *masnavī* or narrative poem revolves around his travel in 'the two Iraqs', approximately Iran and Iraq, with plenty of stops to praise patrons, and plenty of imagery of the motion of the sun as a figure of the natural and beneficial activity of travel.[200] The ancient Persian king who is the hero of the poet Asadī's epic, the *Garshāsbnāma* or *Legend of Garshāsb*, embarks on a journey in which he develops through travel in India, distant islands, North Africa, Anatolia and Central Asia.[201] In the case of the poet Shahīdī Qumī, travel is intertwined with different ways of using poetry, since he worked as a poet for a regional ruler, a leader in literary culture under a more ambitious ruler, and in 'freelance' movement among different literary centers; and because he came from the first generation of Iranian-born poets who moved to work in Indian courts.[202]

The ethnocentric yet other-centered quality of the medieval discourse on Arabic and Persian refined rhetoric helps to explain the use of these languages for social mobility. The discourse on refined rhetoric in each language displays the opportunities for and barriers to mobility across bondaries of ethnic identity. Professional identity based on refined rhetoric often coexisted and sometimes conflicted with other categories of identity, including socio-economic, religious and ethnic identity. The cosmopolitan cultures of the medieval Middle East and Central Asia were both diverse and hegemonic. As a result, professional identity based on refined rhetoric served as a way to get ahead and as a form of social control.

CONCLUSION

This project began as an investigation of the intersection between assertions of success and allusions to risk in medieval Arabic and Persian panegyric poetry by Abū Tammām, al-Buḥturī, ᶜUnṣurī and Farrukhī. Conventional motifs, their configuration in syntax and their elaboration in rhetorical devices and figurative language provide a commentary on the uncertainty of patronage. Stories about literary patronage complement the portrayal in poetry of uncertainty in patronage relationships. In particular, stories about poets illustrate ambivalence regarding the validity of poetry that is exchanged for pay.

Attitudes toward the craft of poetry show how poets came to possess a professional identity based on refined rhetoric. Poets could have recourse to this as an alternative to more limited categories of socio-economic, religious and ethnic identity. Elaborate rhetoric enabled poets to place patrons in the hegemonic universality of imperial culture, and to demonstrate that patronage relationships were contingent and subject to change. In the imperial cultures of Arabic in the Abbasid Empire of the Middle East, and Persian in the Ghaznavid Empire of Central Asia, the experiences of poets show that refined rhetoric in Arabic and Persian was a path to social mobility. Refined rhetoric in Arabic and Persian became a crucial feature of the literary heritage of each language, and continued to be a basis for professional identity and social mobility after the Abbasids and the Ghaznavids lost control of the region. The experiences of poets and attitudes toward refined rhetoric illustrate the intersection of hegemony and diversity in cosmopolitan culture. Poets had a lot to gain through social mobility, but they often had to pay a price for their success.

Panegyric poetry provided a particularly salient example of poetry for professional identity – or refined rhetoric as a way to be somebody.

However, panegyric was by no means the only way that poets could use refined rhetoric to define their identity in a social network. After the canonical Arabic panegyric of Abū Tammām and al-Buḥturī, an emerging genre of short descriptive poetry became prominent in the work of Arabic poets such as Kushājim, al-Ṣanawbarī, and al-Sarī al-Raffāᵓ.[1] This poetry focused on things, bodies and locations and circulated in less formal settings than panegyric, which continued to flourish. After the canonical Persian panegyric of ᶜUnṣurī and Farrukhī, a mystical turn took place that defined the work of Persian poets such as Sanāᵓī, ᶜIrāqī and ᶜAttār.[2] Mystical poetry turned from the beloved to the divine, although panegyric continued to be a part of many poets' careers. Changing circumstances of patronage lead to literary change,[3] and shaped the development of mannerist rhetoric in medieval Arabic and Perisan panegyric. Very brief panegyric was used, often in less formal settings.[4] The turn away from the serious business of political life in short descriptive and in mystical poetry complemented the use of very brief panegyric. Professional identity based on refined rhetoric, which was developed in the context of panegyric, became a model for descriptive and mystical poetry as approaches to refined rhetoric in social life. As in panegyric, poets could socialize around their elaborate descriptions in short descriptive poetry and related prosimetrical works, or around insightful lyric and narrative poetry in mystical discourse.

These were not the only things that were going on in literary culture, but they were important developments that came from panegyric. Panegyric poets investigated what it meant to be inside and outside of the social order of patronage; short descriptive poets explored the relationship between the interior of their pleasure scenes and the world beyond them; likewise, mystical poets considered the relationship between the enlightened interior of their social circle and the world outside it. In panegyric, short descriptive and mystical poetry, poets could use refined rhetoric to work with a network of like-minded people.

NOTES

Introduction

1 Mottahedeh, Roy P., *Loyalty and Leadership in an Early Islamic Society* (Princeton, New Jersey, 1980), pp. 4–5; does not refer to China.

In this project, I benefited from a number of opportunities to make presentations and receive feedback. On material relating to Chapters 4–7: the Middle East Studies Association in fall 2000 and 2002; University of California, Berkeley in spring 2004; the International Society for Iranian Studies in summer 2008. On material relating to Chapters 1, 2, 8 and 9: the American Research Center in Egypt in summer 2003; Cornell University in spring 2006; California State University, Sacramento in spring 2007; the American Oriental Society in spring 2007 and spring 2008; and the Middle East Studies Association in fall 2007.

A work that focuses in part on Farrukhī, one of the poets studied in Chapters 3–7 of this book, came out after the manuscript was completed in October 2008: Tetley, G. E., *The Ghaznavid and Seljuq Turks: Poetry as a Source for Iranian History* (London, 2009). A work that focuses in part on al-Buḥturī, another poet studied in Chapters 3–7, is still to be published, and the author shared a final manuscript on 7 December, 2009: Ali, Samer M., *Arabic Literary Salons in the Islamic Middle Ages* (Notre Dame, Indiana, 2010).

2 Arabic and Persian literature do not fit together neatly, any more than other literary cultures that interact with each other over many centuries. Reading texts from different cultures together can allow us to pick up nuances in each that might otherwise remain hidden (Amer, Sahar, *Crossing Borders: Love Between Women in Medieval French and Arabic Literatures* (Philadelphia, 2008)). This project is not about influence or perfect parallels, but about reading two groups of texts together to seek insights into each, and to get a better picture of the commentary on patronage in medieval Muslim societies.

3 Crises of patronage may define entire poems in explicit ways. Suzanne Stetkevych examines several well-known Arabic poems as expressions of supplication in the context of requests for pardon, and Beatrice Gruendler analyzes a poem by Ibn al-Rūmī that conveys the poet's most serious grievance against the patron (Gruendler, Beatrice, *Medieval Arabic Praise Poetry: Ibn al-Rumi and the Patron's Redemption* (London, 2003), pp. 182–95; Stetkevych, Suzanne, *The Poetics of Islamic Legitimacy: Myth, Gender, and Ceremony in the Classical Arabic Ode* (Bloomington, Indiana, 2002)).

Sunil Sharma examines Persian prison poems by Masᶜūd-i Saᶜd-i Salmān and observes that the crisis of imprisonment is bound up with panegyric elements (Sharma, Sunil, *Persian Poetry at the Indian Frontier: Masᶜūd-i*

Sa^c^d-i Salmān of Lahore (Delhi, 2000), p. 72). Julie Meisami discusses a series of Arabic and Persian *qaṣīda*s that are associated with specific problems: a dead slave, an aborted military campaign, a particularly negative theme in a holiday poem and several poems that consist of a request for pardon or censure (Meisami, Julie, *Structure and Meaning in Medieval Arabic and Persian Poetry: Orient Pearls* (London, 2003), pp. 144–55). Samer Ali discusses two poems by al-Buḥturī in relation to an Abbasid patricide and political crisis (Ali, Samer Mahdy, 'Praise for murder? Two odes by al-Buḥturī surrounding an Abbasid patricide' in Beatrice Gruendler and Louise Marlow (eds), *Writers and Rulers: Perspectives on their Relationship from Abbasid to Safavid Times* (Wiesbaden, 2004), pp. 1–38). In medieval Arabic biography, the literary effects are a way of negotiating crises in the groups to which individual subjects belong (Cooperson, Michael, *Classical Arabic Biography: The Heirs of the Prophets in the Age of al-Ma'mun* (Cambridge, 2000), p. xii).

4 The mostly positive biographical anecdotes about Arabic poets are not necessarily representative of the practice of patronage (Gruendler, Beatrice, 'Verse and taxes: the function of poetry in selected literary *Akhbār* of the third/ninth century', in Philip F. Kennedy (ed), *On Fiction and Adab in Medieval Arabic Literature* (Wiesbaden, 2005), pp. 85–123, p. 107). In epic, there is a difference between a text that supports sovereignty and a text that is about sovereignty (Davis, Dick, *Epic and Sedition: The Case of Ferdowsi's Shahnameh* (Fayetteville, Arkansas, 1992), p. xiv). This difference matters in panegyric as well. The medieval Arabic panegyric poem is 'not so much a statement of legitimacy as a bid for, or claim to, legitimacy' (Stetkevych, *Poetics*, p. 101). Paul Losensky observes of medieval Persian poetry commissioned by a ruler that 'Even when literary production was initiated by the court ... the play of signification could easily trespass ideological boundaries' (Losensky, Paul 'The equal of heaven's vault', in Gruendler and Marlow (eds), *Writers and Rulers*, pp. 195–216, p. 214).

5 In fact, a wide range of Persian poetry is about complaints, ranging from the crisis of imprisonment, to love poetry, complaints to unjust patrons or general grievances about fate and unfaithful friends (Beelaert, Anna Livia Fermina Alexandra, *A Cure for the Grieving: Studies on the Poetry of the 12th Century Persian Court Poet Khāqānī Širwānī*, Proefschrift (Leiden, 2000)). The present analysis demonstrates that poets express the uncertainty about patronage as a default setting in refined rhetoric, not as a reaction to a particular situation of perceived injustice.

6 Richard Firth Green makes this point about medieval English patronage networks (Green, Richard Firth, *Poets and Princepleasers: Literature and the English Court in the Late Middle Ages* (Toronto, 1980), p. 148).

7 Medieval Arabic panegyric poetry is an accurate model of the ideals of sovereignty rather than an inaccurate description of an actual ruler (Ḍayf, Shawqī, *al-^c^Aṣr al-^c^Abbāsī al-thānī* (Cairo, 1973), p. 161). Medieval Arabic panegyric poetry is not a misleading portrayal of an actual patron, but an identification of the actual patron with an ideal role of kingship (Sperl, Stefan, 'Islamic kingship and Arabic panegyric poetry in the early 9th century', *Journal of Arabic Literature* 8 (1977), pp. 20–35, p. 34). In poetry dedicated to the Fatimid imam, al-Mu'ayyad al-Shīrāzī portrays the qualities that any imam must possess (Qutbuddin, Tahera, *Al-Mu'ayyad al-Shīrāzī and Fatimid Da^c^wa Poetry: A Case of Commitment in Classical Arabic Literature*

(Leiden, 2005), p. 145). Ottoman *gazel* offers insights into how participants in Ottoman culture viewed themselves and their society, rather than information about specific individuals (Andrews, Walter G., *Poetry's Voice, Society's Song: Ottoman Lyric Poetry* (Seattle, 1985), p. 187).

8 The epic hero, who is known only through the text, contrasts with the 'hero' of panegyric, who is known to differ from his portrayal in poetry; the Ghaznavid ruler Sultan Maḥmūd, a great patron of panegyric, did not go to war himself and sent his men to raid defenseless Indian communities (Shamīsā, Sīrūs, *Anvāᶜ-i adabī* (Tehran, 1370/1993), p. 310). In Persian panegyric, 'by calling attention to the tension (not to say the discrepancy) between ideals of kingship and the limitations of the current ruler, such poems invite a rededication to those ideals on the part of the prince and those who advise him, as well as suggesting an ethical judgment of the realities' (Meisami, Julie Scott, 'Ghaznavid panegyrics: some political implications', *Iran* 28 (1990), pp. 31–44, p. 42).

9 Samer Ali examines the social dimensions of prestige, networking and intimacy as a way to understand medieval Arabic literary salons (Ali, *Literary Salons*, chapter 2).

10 Althusser, Louis, 'Ideology and ideological state apparatuses (notes toward an investigation)' in *Lenin and Philosophy and Other Essays*, tr. Ben Brewster, London, 1971), pp. 121–73.

11 Eagleton, Terry, *Criticism and Ideology: A Study in Marxist Literary Theory*, new edition (London, 2006), p. 72.

12 Butler, Judith, *Bodies that Matter: On the Discursive Limits of 'Sex'*, New York, 1993), p. 22.

13 Laclau, Ernesto and Chantal Mouffe, *Hegemony and Socialist Strategy: Towards a Radical Democratic Politics*, second edition (London, 2001), p. xiii.

14 Lecture at Cornell University, spring 2006.

15 Barchiesi, Alessandro, *The Poet and the Prince: Ovid and Augustan Discourse* (Berkeley, California, 1997), pp. 6, 44.

16 de Lauretis, Teresa, *Technologies of Gender: Essays on Theory, Film, and Fiction* (Bloomington, Indiana, 1987).

17 On the gaze as a technology of social position, see Morales, *Helen, Vision and Narrative in Achilles Tatius' Leucippe and Clitophon* (Cambridge, 2004).

18 Irigaray, Luce, *To Be Two*, tr. Monique M. Rhodes and Marco F. Cocito-Monoc (New York, 2000); Butler, *Bodies*.

19 Sharlet, Jocelyn, 'Inside and outside the pleasure scene in descriptive poetry about locations by al-Sarī al-Raffāʾ al-Mawṣilī', *Journal of Arabic Literature* 40/2 (2009), pp. 133–69.

20 The term 'mystical turn' is from a lecture by Dick Davis at UC Davis in November 2008. On the beginning of the mystical turn, see De Bruijn, J. T. P., *Of Piety and Poetry: The Interaction of Religion and Literature in the Life and Works of Ḥakīm Sanāʾī of Ghazna* (Leiden, 1983).

Chapter 1

1 Two views of poetry emerged in Arabic-Islamic culture: one that considered poetry a source of knowledge of the Arabic language, the study of which was central for any Muslim's education; another that considered poetry to be in

contradiction with Islamic culture (Ouyang, Wen-Chin, *Literary Criticism in Medieval Arabic-Islamic Culture: The Making of a Tradition* (Edinburgh, 1997), p. 60). Franklin Lewis discusses some of the praise and blame of panegyric (Lewis, Franklin, 'Sincerely flattering panegyric: The shrinking Ghaznavid qasida' in Franklin Lewis and Sunil Sharma (eds), *The Necklace of the Pleiades: Studies in Persian Literature Presented to Heshmat Moayyad on his 80th Birthday* (Amsterdam, 2007).

2 Bowditch, Phebe Lowell, *Horace and the Gift Economy of Patronage* (Berkeley, California, 2001), p. 48; Kurke, Leslie, *The Traffic in Praise: Pindar and the Poetics of Social Economy* (Ithaca, New York, 1991), p. 192.

3 Mauss, Marcel, *The Gift: The Form and Reason for Exchange in Archaic Societies*, tr. W. D. Halls (London, 1990), p. 13.

4 Shershow, Scott Cutler, *The Work and the Gift* (Chicago, 2005).

5 Van Gelder, G. J., 'The apposite request: A small chapter in Persian and Arabic rhetoric', *Edebiyat* 12 (2001), p. 113.

6 Al-Rāghib al-Iṣbahānī, Abū al-Qāsim Ḥusayn b. Muḥammad, *Muḥāḍarāt al-udabāʾ wa-muḥāwarāt al-shuʿarāʾ wal-bulaghāʾ*, 2 vols. (Beirut, 1961, 1980), p. 1:80.

7 Al-Rāghib al-Iṣbahānī, *Muḥāḍarāt*, p. 1:391.

8 Ibn Abī al-Dunyā, ʿAbd Allāh b. Muḥammad Abū Bakr al-Qurashī al-Baghdādī, *Kitāb makārim al-akhlāq*, ed. James A. Bellamy (Wiesbaden, 1393/1973), p. 29.

9 Al-Tawḥīdī, Abū Ḥayyān ʿAlī b. Muḥammad, *Akhlāq al-wazīrayn: mathālib al-wazīrayn al-Ṣāḥib b. ʿAbbād wa Ibn al-ʿAmīd*, ed. Muḥammad b. Tāwīt al-Ṭanjī (Beirut, 1412/1992), p. 7.

10 Al-Rāghib al-Iṣbahānī, *Muḥāḍarāt*, p. 1:79.

11 Al-Jumaḥī, Muḥammad b. Salām, *Ṭabaqāt fuḥūl al-shuʿarāʾ*, ed. Maḥmūd Muḥammad Shākir, 2 vols. (Jidda, 1974), p. 2:336.

12 Al-Ghuzūlī, ʿAlāʾ al-Dīn ʿAlī b. ʿAbd Allāh Al-Bahāʾī, *Maṭāliʿ al-budūr fī manāzil al-surūr* (Cairo, 1419/2000), p. 1:236.

13 Al-Rāghib al-Iṣbahānī, *Muḥāḍarāt*, p. 1:79.

14 Al-Rāghib al-Iṣbahānī, *Muḥāḍarāt*, p. 1:380.

15 Ibn Qutayba, Abū Muḥammad ʿAbd Allāh b. Muslim, *Faḍl al-ʿArab wa-al-Tanbīh ʿalā ʿUlūmihā*, ed. Walīd Maḥmūd Khāliṣ (Abu Dhabi, 1998), p. 182.

16 Al-Jumaḥī, *Ṭabaqāt*, p. 2:416. Al-Iṣfahānī, Abū al-Faraj, *Kitāb al-aghānī*, ed. ʿAbd A. ʿAlī Muḥannā, 27 vols. (Beirut, 2002/1422), p. 3:216.

17 Naṣīr al-Dīn Ṭūsī, *Akhlāq-i Nāṣirī*, ed. Mujtabā Mīnuvī and ʿAlīriḍā Ḥaydarī (Tehran, 1352), p. 223–4. *Adab* relates to raising children in earlier Arabic sources (Ali, *Literary Salons*, chapter 2).

18 Al-Bayhaqī, al-Shaykh Ibrāhīm b. Muḥammad, *al-Maḥāsin wal-masāwī*, ed. ʿAdnān ʿAlī (Beirut, 1420/1999), p. 313.

19 Al-Tawḥīdī, Abū Ḥayyān ʿAlī b. Muḥammad, *al-Baṣāʾir wal-dhakhāʾir*, ed. Wadād al-Qāḍī, 10 vols. (Beirut, 1406/1988). pp. 1:100, 2:60.

20 Al-Tawḥīdī, *Baṣāʾir*, p. 2:61.

21 Al-Rāghib al-Iṣbahānī, *Muḥāḍarāt*, p. 1:80. Al-Bayhaqī, *Maḥāsin*, p. 316.

22 Al-Tawḥīdī, *Akhlāq*, p. 74.

23 Al-Māwardī, ʿAlī b. Muḥammad b. Ḥabīb Abū al-Ḥasan al-Baṣrī, *Naṣīḥat al-mulūk*, ed. Fuʾād ʿAbd al-Munʿim Aḥmad (Alexandria, 1988), p. 199.

24 Al-Māwardī, *Naṣīḥat al-Mulūk*, p. 199.

25 Al-Rāghib al-Iṣbahānī, *Muḥāḍarāt*, p. 1:381.

26 Al-Rāghib al-Iṣbahānī, *Muḥāḍarāt*, p. 1:381.

27 Al-Rāghib's version, al-Rāghib al-Iṣbahānī, *Muḥāḍarāt*, p. 1:81; al-Tawḥīdī, *Baṣā'ir*, p. 7:113; al-Bayhaqī, *Maḥāsin*, p. 316.

28 Al-Bayhaqī, *Maḥāsin*, p. 316.

29 Al-Māwardī, ᶜAlī b. Muḥammad b. Ḥabīb Abū al-Ḥasan al-Baṣrī *Adab al-wazīr al-maᶜrūf bi-qawānīn al-wizāra wa-siyāsat al-mulk*, ed. Ḥasan al-Hadī Ḥusayn (Cairo, 1348/1929), p. 53.

30 Al-Māwardī, ᶜAlī b. Muḥammad b. Ḥabīb Abū al-Ḥasan al-Baṣrī, *Adab al-dunyā wal-dīn*, ed. Muṣṭafā al-Saqā (Cairo, 1393/1973), p. 234.

31 Al-Bayhaqī, *Maḥāsin*, p. 315.

32 Al-Jāḥiẓ, Abū ᶜUthmān ᶜAmr b. Baḥr, *Al-Bukhalā' lil-Jāḥiẓ*, ed. Ṭahā al-Hajirī (Cairo, 1981), p. 181.

33 ᶜAwfī, Muḥammad, *Lubāb al-albāb*, ed. Saᶜīd Nafīsī (Tehran, 1363/1984), p. 12.

34 Saᶜdī, *Gulistān-i Saᶜdī*, ed. Khalīl Khaṭīb Rahbar (Tehran, 1969), p. 536.

35 Sanā'ī, *Kitāb ḥadīqat al-ḥaqīqa wa-sharīᶜat al-ṭarīqa*, ed. Mudarris Raḍavī (Tehran, 1940), pp. 45–6.

36 Al-Ṣūlī, Abū Bakr Muḥammad b. Yaḥyā, *Akhbār al-Buḥturī*, ed. Ṣāliḥ al-Ashtar (Damascus, 1964/1384), p. 112.

37 Al-Ṣūlī, Abū Bakr Muḥammad b. Yaḥyā, *Akhbār Abī Tammām*, ed. Khalīl Maḥmūd, Muḥammad ᶜAbduh ᶜAzzām, and Naẓir al-Islām al-Hindī (Cairo, 1356/1937), p. 254.

38 Ibn al-Muᶜtazz, *Ṭabaqāt al-shuᶜarā'*, ed. ᶜAbd al-Sattār Aḥmad Farrāj (Cairo, 1968), p. 107.

39 Al-Ābī, Abū Saᶜd Manṣūr b. al-Ḥusayn, *Nathr al-Durr*, ed. Muḥammad ᶜAlī Qurna, 9 vols. (Cairo, 1980), p. 7:170.

40 Al-Jāḥiẓ, Abū ᶜUthmān ᶜAmr b. Baḥr, *al-Bayān wal-tabyīn*, ed. ᶜAbd al-Salām Hārūn, 4 vols. (Beirut, n.d.), p. 1:241.

41 Al-Marzūqī, Abū ᶜAlī Aḥmad b. Muḥammad b. al-Ḥasan, *Sharḥ dīwān al-ḥamāsa*, ed. Aḥmad Amīn and ᶜAbd al-Salām Hārūn, 2 vols. (Beirut, 1411/1991), p. 17.

42 Al-Tawḥīdī, Abū Ḥayyān ᶜAlī b. Muḥammad, *al-Ṣadāqa wa al-Ṣadīq*, ed. Ibrāhīm al-Kīlānī (Beirut, 1998/1419).

43 Al-Tawḥīdī, *Akhlāq*, p. 35.

44 Ibn Rashīq, Abū ᶜAlī al-Ḥasan al-Qayrawānī, ed. Muḥammad ᶜAbd al-Qādir Aḥmad ᶜAtā, *al-ᶜUmda fī maḥāsin al-shiᶜr wa-ādābih*, 2 vols. in 1 (Beirut, 1422/2001), p. 89.

45 Sām Mīrzā Ṣafavī, *Tadhkirah-yi Tuḥfah-yi Sāmī*, ed. Rukn al-Dīn Humāyūn Farrukh, (Tehran, 1384/2005), p. 298.

46 ᶜAlīshīr Navāᶜī, *Tadhkirah-yi Majālis al-Nafā'is* (ninth century), tr. from Chagatay Turkish to Persian, first version tr. Muḥammad Fakhrī Hirātī, second version tr. Muḥammad Qazvīnī (both tenth century) collated with three Turkish versions by the editor, ed. ᶜAlī Aṣghar Hikmat (Tehran, 1363/1984), p. 54.

47 Al-Jāḥiẓ, *Bukhalā'*, p. 181.

48 Al-Tawḥīdī, *Baṣā'ir*, p. 9:14.

49 Al-Tawḥīdī, *Baṣā'ir*, p. 4:32.

50 Sām Mīrzā, *Tuḥfa*, p. 296.

51 Al-Jahshiyārī, Abū ᶜAbd Allāh Muḥammad b. ᶜAbdūs, *Kitāb al-wuzarā' wal-kuttāb* (Cairo, n.d.), p. 131.

52 Al-Ḥuṣrī, Abū Isḥāq Ibrāhīm b. ᶜAlī al-Qayrawānī, *Zahr al-ādāb wa-thamr al-albāb*, ed. ᶜAlī Muḥammad al-Bajāwī, 2 vols. (Cairo, 1953), p. 2:816.

53 Al-Rāghib al-Iṣbahānī, *Muḥāḍarāt*, p. 1:389.
54 Al-Ṣūlī, *Akhbār Abī Tammām*, p. 124.
55 Al-Iṣfahānī, *Aghānī*, p. 10:104.
56 Al-Ṣūlī, *Akhbār Abī Tammām*, p. 105.
57 Al-Ṣūlī, *Akhbār al-Buḥturī*, p. 86.
58 Al-Iṣfahānī, *Aghānī*, p. 3:216.
59 Ibn al-Mu^ctazz, *Ṭabaqāt*, p. 43; Ibn ^cAbd Rabbihi, Aḥmad ibn Muḥammad Abī ^cUmar al-Andalusī, *Kitāb al-^ciqd al-farīd,* ed. Muḥammad al-Tūnjī, 7 vols. (Beirut, 2001), p. 1:303.
60 Ibn Qutayba, Abū Muḥammad ^cAbd Allāh b. Muslim, *al-Shi^cr wal-shu^carā^ɔ*, ed. Aḥmad Muḥammad Shākir, 2 vols. (Cairo, 1421/2001), p. 1:483.
61 Ibn al-Jawzī, Abū al-Faraj, *Akhbār al-adhkiyā^ɔ*, ed. Muḥammad Mursī al-Khūlī (Cairo, 1970), p. 161.
62 al-Ṣābi^ɔ, Ghars al-Ni^cma Abū al-Ḥasan Muḥammad b. Hilāl, *al-Hafawāt al-nādira*, ed. Ṣāliḥ al-Ashtar (Beirut, 1967), p. 6.
63 Al-Ṣābi^ɔ, *Hafawāt*, p. 26.
64 Al-Ṣābi^ɔ, *Hafawāt*, p. 135.
65 Ibn al-Jawzī, Abū al-Faraj, *Akhbār al-ḥamqā wal-mughaffalīn min al-fuqahā^ɔ wal-mufassirīn wal-ruwāt wal-muhaddithīn wal-shu^carā^ɔ wal-muta^ɔaddabīn wal-kuttāb wal-mu^callimīn wal-tujjār wal-mutasabbibīn wa-ṭawā^ɔif tattaṣil lil ghafla bi-sabab matīn* (Beirut, 1997/1418), p. 124.
66 Qudāma b. Ja^cfar, Abū al-Faraj, ed. Kamāl Muṣṭafā, *Naqd al-shi^cr* (Cairo, 1963, 1979), p. 190.
67 Ibn al-Athīr, Ḍiyā^ɔ al-Dīn, *al-Mathal al-sā^ɔir fī adab al-kātib wal-shā^cir*, ed. Aḥmad al-Ḥawfī and Badawī Ṭabāna, 3 vols. (Riyāḍ, 1404/1984), p. 3:215.
68 Shams-i Qays al-Rāzī, *al-Mu^cjam fī ma^cāyīr ash^cār al-^cAjam*, ed. Muḥammad b. ^cAbd al-Wahhāb Qazvīnī and Mudarris Raḍavī (Tehran, 1959), p. 409.
69 Shams-i Qays, *Mu^cjam*, p. 407.
70 Al-Tawḥīdī, *Baṣā^ɔir*, p. 3:91.
71 Al-Ṣābi^ɔ, *Hafawāt*, pp. 27, 29.
72 Al-Ṣābi^ɔ, *Hafawāt*, pp. 39, 350.
73 Al-Ṣābi^ɔ, *Hafawāt*, p. 131.
74 Ibn al-Jawzī, *Ḥamqā*, p. 124.
75 Ibn Rashīq, *^cUmda*, p. 230.
76 Al-Ṣābi^ɔ, *Hafawāt*, p. 74.
77 Shams-i Qays, *Mu^cjam*, p. 358.
78 Al-Ṣūlī, Abū Bakr Muḥammad b. Yaḥyā, *Adab al-kuttāb*, ed. Aḥmad Ḥasan Basaj (Beirut, 1415/1994), p. 166.
79 Al-Ṣūlī, *Adab al-kuttāb*, p. 164.
80 Al-Tawḥīdī, *Akhlāq*, p. 43.
81 Al-Ṣūlī, *Akhbār Abī Tammām*, p. 231.
82 Ibn al-Jawzī, *Adhkiyā^ɔ*, p. 165.
83 Vaṭvāṭ, Rashīd al-Dīn Muḥammad, *Ḥadāyiq al-sihr fī daqāyiq al-shi^cr*, ed. ^cAbbās Iqbāl, (n.p., 1362/1984), p. 36; Rādūyānī, Muḥammad b. ^cUmar, *Tarjūmān al-balāgha*, ed. Aḥmad Atash (Tehran, n.d.), p. 94; Qudāma b. Ja^cfar, *Naqd al-shi^cr*, p. 69.
84 Al-Rāghib al-Iṣbahānī, *Muḥāḍarāt*, p. 1:92.
85 Ibn al-Athīr, *Mathal*, p. 1:92.
86 Al-Bayhaqī, *Maḥāsin*; Al-Tha^cālibī, *Al-Laṭā^ɔif wal-ẓarā'if* (Beirut, 1990); al-Khwārazmī, Abū al-Wafā^ɔ Rayḥān b. ^cAbd al-Wahīd, *Kitāb al-manāqib wal-*

mathālib (Damascus, 1999); Al-Rāghib al-Iṣbahānī, *Muḥāḍarāt*, pp. 1:221 and 240, 1:606.

87 Al-Thaᶜālibī *Taḥsīn al-qabīḥ wa-taqbīḥ al-ḥasan*, ed. Shākir al-ᶜAshūr (Baghdād, 1981/1401).

88 McKinney, Robert C., *The Case of Rhyme Versus Reason: Ibn al-Rumi and his Poetics in Context* (Leiden, 2004), p. 157; Al-Marzubānī, Abū ᶜUbayd Allāh Muḥammad b. ᶜImrān b. Mūsā, *Muᶜjam al-shuᶜarā'*, ed. ᶜAbd al-Sattār Aḥmad Farrāj (no publication details available), p. 189.

89 Al-Māwardī, *Naṣīḥat al-mulūk*, p. 108.

90 Al-Rāghib al-Iṣbahānī, *Muḥāḍarāt*, p. 1:377.

91 Ibn al-Athīr, *Mathal*, p. 3:221.

92 Al-Khafājī, Ibn Sinān, *Sirr al-faṣāḥa*, ed. al-Nabawī ᶜAbd al-Waḥīd Shaᶜlān (Cairo, 2003), pp. 235, 385, 408.

93 Al-Jumaḥī, *Ṭabaqāt*, pp. 2:470–1.

94 Al-Ṣūlī, *Akhbār Abī Tammām*, p. 126.

95 Ibn Rashīq, *ᶜUmda*, pp. 228–9.

96 Sanā'ī, *Ḥadīqat al-ḥaqīqa*, p. 647.

97 Sanā'ī, *Ḥadīqat al-ḥaqīqa*, p. 688. Franklin Lewis discusses several examples of mystical anti-panegyric sentiment in work by Sanā'ī and Rūmī (Lewis, 'Panegyric').

98 Al-Rāghib al-Iṣbahānī, *Muḥāḍarāt*, p. 1:382.

99 Al-Ṣūlī, Abū Bakr Muḥammad b. Yaḥyā, *Akhbār al-shuᶜarā' al-muḥdathīn min kitāb al-awrāq*, ed. J. Heyworth Dunne (Beirut, 1982/1401), p. 4.

100 Ibn al-Jarrāḥ, Muḥammad b. Dāwud Abū ᶜAbd Allāh, *al-Waraqa*, ed. ᶜAbd al-Wahhāb ᶜAzzām and ᶜAbd al-Sattār Aḥmad Farrāj (Cairo, 1967), p. 85.

101 Abū Hiffān, ᶜAbd Allāh b. Aḥmad b. Ḥarb al-Mihzamī, *Akhbār Abī Nuwās*, ed. ᶜAbd al-Sattār Aḥmad Farrāj (Cairo, 1953), p. 71.

102 Ibn al-Muᶜtazz, *Ṭabaqāt*, p. 57.

103 Ibn al-Jarrāḥ, *Waraqa*, pp. 84–5. Beatrice Gruendler suggests that the story of the poet composing invective on himself, and Abān praising himself, cited above, show that patrons were open to experimentation and ready to be surprised and amused (Gruendler, Beatrice, 'Meeting the patron: An *Akhbār* type and its implications for *Muḥdath* poetry', in S. Günther (ed), *Ideas, Images, Methods of Portrayal: Insights into Arabic Literature and Islam* (Wiesbaden, 2005), pp. 59–88, p. 74).

104 Ibn al-Muᶜtazz, *Ṭabaqāt*, p. 125.

105 Al-Tawḥīdī, *Baṣā'ir*, p. 3:120.

106 Ibn al-Jawzī, *Adhkiyā'*, p. 163.

107 Ibn ᶜAbd Rabbihi, *ᶜIqd*, p. 2:114.

108 Al-Tawḥīdī, *Baṣā'ir*, p. 1:28.

109 Aside from chapters and notices in books on other topics, see al-Jāḥiẓ, *Bukhalā'*; Al-Baghdādī, al-Khaṭīb Abū Bakr Aḥmad b. ᶜAlī, *Kitāb al-bukhalā'*, ed. Bassām ᶜAbd al-Wahhāb al-Jābī (Beirut, 1461/2000); Al-Baghdādī, al-Khaṭīb Abū Bakr Aḥmad b. ᶜAlī, *Al-Ṭatfīl wa-hikāyat al-ṭufayliyyīn wa-akhbārihim wa-nawādir kalāmihim wa-ashᶜārihim*, ed. Bassām ᶜAbd al-Wahhāb al-Jābī (Beirut, 1999).

110 Al-Baghdādī, *Bukhalā'*, p. 154.

Chapter 2

1 In medieval Arabic narrative that is presented as factual, selection and re-organization are aspects of creativity, and are used to re-read and transform existing material for the author's own goals (Cheikh-Moussa, Abdallah, 'Mouvance narrative et polysémie dans la littérature d'*adab*: le cas d'Abū Ḥayya al-Numayrī/Abū al-Aġarr al-Nahšalī' in Frédéric Bauden, Aboubakr Chraïbi and Antonella Ghersetti (eds), *Le répertoire narrative arabe médiéval: transmission et ouverture* (Liège, 2008), pp. 47–61, p. 59). Medieval Arabic prose writers valorized the combination of reality and fiction for literary, philosophical, and ethical ends (Geries, Ibrahim '*L'adab et le genre narratif fictif*' in Stefan Leder (ed), *Story-telling in the framework of non-fictional Arabic literature* (Wiesbaden, 1998), pp. 168–95, p. 195). In Arabic, narratives convey information about the beliefs and attitudes of those who transmitted them (Ali, *Literary Salons*, chapter 2). Arabic writers used storytelling techniques also found in folklore to shape their beliefs and attitudes (Hamori, Andras, 'Going down in style: the Pseudo-Ibn Qutayba's story of the fall of the Barmakis', *Princeton Papers in Near Eastern Studies* 3 (1994), pp. 89–125). In medieval Persian biographies, ᶜAṭṭār 'gives shape and meaning to a dispersed body of formerly discrete stories and sayings' (Losensky, Paul, 'Words and deeds: message and structure in ᶜAṭṭār's *Tadhkirat al-awliyaʾ*' in Lewis Lewisohn and Christopher Shackle (eds), *ᶜAṭṭār and the Persian Sufi Tradition: The Art of Spiritual Flight* (London, 2006)).

2 In medieval Arab culture etiquette is about bringing out the social distance between the ruler and his subjects (Sadan, Joseph, 'The "nomad versus sedentary" framework in Arabic literature', *Fabula* 15 (1974), pp. 59–86, p. 68). In Roman culture, the 'affect-laden language' that is used in patronage networks may imply an effort to neutralize status differences (White, Peter, *Promised Verse: Poets in the Society of Augustan Rome* (Cambridge, Massachusetts, 1993), p. 14). The genre of Persian political advice is not just about influencing the ruler himself, it is also about making society coherent (de Fouchécour, Charles-Henri, *Moralia: Les notions morales dans la littérature persane du 3/9 au 7/13 siècle* (Paris, 1986), p. 358). Samer Ali proposes that in a hierarchical society where most public and private associations were defined by patronage or clientage, Arabic literary salons afforded people a form of intimacy and equality (Ali, *Literary Salons*, chapter 2). The unequal relationships of patronage in this poetry involved intimacy as well as distance, but not equality.

3 Althusser, 'Ideology', p. 137.

4 Arendt, Hannah, *On Violence* (New York, 1969), p. 52.

5 Derrida, Jacques, *Acts of Literature*, ed. Derek Attridge (New York, 1992), p. 203.

6 Ibn Rashīq, *ᶜUmda*, p. 210.

7 Al-Māwardī, *Adab al-wazīr*, p. 2.

8 Al-Jāḥiẓ, *Bayān*, p. 1:54.

9 *Kitāb al-Tāj fī akhlāq al-mulūk*, ed. Fawzī ᶜAtawī (Beirut, 1970), p. 54–6.

10 Shams-i Qays, *Muᶜjam*, p. 451. Ibn Ṭabāṭabā, Muḥammad b. Aḥmad Al-ᶜAlawī, *ᶜIyār al-shiᶜr*, ed. Muḥammad Zaghlūl Salām (Alexandria, 1980), p. 44.

11 Shams-i Qays, *Muᶜjam*, p. 409.

12 Kaykāvūs b. Iskandar b. Qābūs b. Vashmgīr, *Qābūsnāma*, ed. Ghulāmḥusayn Yūsufī (Tehran, 1345/1967), p. 191.
13 Niẓām al-Mulk, Abū ᶜAlī Ḥasan Ṭūṣī, *Siyar al-mulūk*, ed. Hubert Dark, Tehran, 1378/2000), pp. 17, 31–41; Firdawsī, *Shāhnāma-yi Firdawsī*, ed. Saᶜīd Ḥamīdiyān, 9 vols. in 4. (Tehran, 1374/1996); Niẓāmī Ganjavī, *Kuliyyāt-i Khamsa-yi Niẓāmī*, ed. Vahīd Dastgardī. 2 vols. (Tehran, 1374/1995).
14 Al-Thaᶜālibī *Tuḥfat Al-Wuzarāᵓ*, ed. Ḥabīb ᶜAlī al-Rāwī and Ibtisām Marhun al-Saffār (Baghdād, 1977), p. 72. Beatrice Gruendler discusses several examples of jealous peers in medieval Arabic literary patronage (Gruendler, 'Meeting the patron', p. 67).
15 Kaykāvūs b. Iskandar, *Qābūsnāma*, p. 198.
16 Al-Jahshiyārī, *Wuzarāᵓ*, p. 90.
17 Al-Jahshiyārī, *Wuzarāᵓ*, p. 19.
18 *Kitāb al-tāj*, pp. 31–8.
19 Al-Māwardī, *Adab al-wazīr*, p. 26.
20 Sanāᵓī, *Ḥadīqat al-ḥaqīqa*, p. 647.
21 Al-Ṣūlī, *Akhbār al-Buḥturī*, pp. 189–90.
22 Al-Ḥuṣrī, *Zahr*, p. 1:319. Ibn ᶜAbd Rabbihi, *ᶜIqd*, p. 1:249.
23 Al-Bayhaqī, *Maḥāsin*, p. 192–3.
24 Beatrice Gruendler discusses the threshold in medieval Arabic literary patronage (Gruendler, 'Meeting the patron', p. 62).
25 Al-Ghuzūlī, *Maṭāliᶜ al-budūr*, p. 1:31.
26 Al-Jāḥiẓ, Abū ᶜUthmān ᶜAmr b. Baḥr *Rasāᵓil al-Jāḥiẓ*, ed. ᶜAbd al-Salām Hārūn, 4 vols. in 2 (Beirut, 1991/1411), p. 2:56.
27 Al-Tanūkhī, al-Qāḍī Abū ᶜAlī al-Muḥsin b. ᶜAlī, *al-Mustajād min faᶜalāt al-ajwād*, ed. Yūsuf al-Bustānī (Cairo, 1985), p. 146.
28 Al-Thaᶜālibī, *Tuḥfat al-wuzarāᵓ*, p. 100.
29 Al-Jāḥiẓ, *Rasāᵓil*, p. 2:31.
30 Ibn Abī al-Dunyā, *Makārim*, p. 232.
31 Ibn ᶜAbd Rabbihi, *ᶜIqd*, p. 1:240.
32 Al-Jahshiyārī, *Wuzarāᵓ*, p. 166.
33 Al-Ṣūlī, *Akhbār Abī Tammām*, p. 211.
34 Al-Tawḥīdī, *Baṣāᵓir*, p. 3:71.
35 Al-Tawḥīdī, *Baṣāᵓir*, p. 9:70.
36 Al-Ṣūlī, *Akhbār al-Buḥturī*, p. 117.
37 Al-Bayhaqī, *Maḥāsin*, p. 171.
38 Beatrice Gruendler discusses several examples of intercession in medieval Arabic literary patronage (Gruendler, 'Meeting the patron', p. 66).
39 Niẓāmī ᶜArūẓī, Aḥmad b. ᶜAmr b. ᶜAlī Samarqandī, *Chahār Maqāla*, ed. Muḥammad Muᶜīn (Tehran, 1334/1955), pp. 71–81.
40 Niẓāmī ᶜArūẓī, *Chahār Maqāla*, pp. 81–6.
41 Dawlatshāh-i Samarqandī, *Tadhkira-yi Dawlatshāh-i Samarqandī*, ed. Muḥammad ᶜAbbāsī (Tehran, 1337/1958), p. 58.
42 Ibn Abī al-Dunyā, *Makārim*, p. 213.
43 Rūmī, *Masnavī-yi Maᶜnavī*, ed. Reynold Nicholson (n.p., 1374/1995), pp. 587–91.
44 Al-Jāḥiẓ, *Rasāᵓil*, pp. 4:254–5.
45 In ancient Greek literature, 'Supplication is an appeal for limitations to the use of power, for a relation of exchange to bound the relation of dominance' (Goldhill, Simon, *The Poet's Voice: Essays on Poetics and Greek Literature* (Cambridge, 1991), p. 73).

46 Foucault, Michel, *The History of Sexuality: Volume I: An Introduction*, tr. Robert Hurley (New York, 1990), p. 101.
47 The act of representation is a voice of authority that is clearly a claim of power (Brummett, Barry, *The World and How We Describe It: Rhetorics of Reality, Representation, Simulation* (Westport, Connecticut, 2003), p. 6).
48 In medieval Muslim political advice literature, 'authors had freedom to negotiate their own relationship with the royal or influential figures to whom they presented their work' (Marlow, Louise, 'The way of viziers and the lamp of commanders (*Minhāj al-wuzarāʾ wa-sirāj al-umarāʾ*) of Aḥmad al-Isfahbādhī and the literary and political culture of early fourteenth-century Iran' in Gruendler and Marlow (eds), *Writers and Rulers,* pp. 169–94, p. 170).
49 Ibn Qutayba, Abū Muḥammad ᶜAbd Allāh b. Muslim, *ᶜUyūn al-akhbār*, ed. Yūsuf ᶜAlī Ṭawīl, 2 vols. (Beirut 1986, 1988), p. 1:169.
50 Al-Ḥuṣrī, *Zahr*, p. 2:648.
51 Al-Thaᶜālibī, *Yatīmat al-dahr fī maḥāsin ahl al-ᶜaṣr*, ed. Mufīd Muḥammad Qamīḥa, 6 vols. (Beirut, 1420/2000), p. 3:269.
52 ᶜAwfī, *Lubāb*, p. 255.
53 Al-Ṣāḥib ibn ᶜAbbād called for repetition of many of the verses in two performances (al-Thaᶜālibī, *Yatīma*, pp. 3:228–9). In two well-known notices, one patron interrupted Abū Tammām to offer positive comments, and another interrupted him to announce that he must stand for the rest of the performance, prompting Abū Tammām to stand as well (al-Ṣūlī, *Akhbār Abī Tammām*, p. 168). This interference is both supportive of the poet and coercive, so that it complicates the use of poetry to offer a professional evaluation of the patron.
54 Al-Ḥuṣrī, *Zahr,* p. 1:554.
55 Ibn ᶜAbd Rabbihi, *ᶜIqd*, p. 2:111.
56 Al-Iṣfahānī, *Aghānī*, p. 7:54.
57 Al-Ṣūlī, *Akhbār al-Buḥturī*, p. 117.
58 Andras Hamori makes this point in a discussion of stories about the fall of the Barmakids (Hamori, 'Going down in style', p. 107).
59 Ibn al-Muqaffaᶜ, *Āthār Ibn al-Muqaffaᶜ* (Beirut, 1986), pp. 39, 46.
60 Kaykāvūs b. Iskandar, *Qābūsnāma*, p. 198.
61 Kaykāvūs b. Iskandar, *Qābūsnāma*, p. 191.
62 Al-Thaᶜālibī, *Yatīma*, p. 3:253.
63 Qudāma b. Jaᶜfar, *Naqd al-shiᶜr*, p. 69.
64 Al-Tawḥīdī, *Baṣāʾir*, p. 3:120.
65 Al-Tawḥīdī, *Baṣāʾir*, p. 9:84.
66 Al-Iṣfahānī, *Aghānī*, p. 1:119.
67 Abū Hiffān, *Akhbār Abī Nuwās*, pp. 70–1.
68 Abū Hiffān, *Akhbār Abī Nuwās*, pp. 72–3.
69 Al-Tawḥīdī, *Baṣāʾir*, p. 9:158.
70 Al-Ṣūlī, *Akhbār al-Buḥturī*, p. 90.
71 Al-Ḥuṣrī, Abū Isḥāq Ibrāhīm b. ᶜAlī al-Qayrawānī, *Jamᶜ al-jawāhir fil-mulaḥ wal-nawādir*, ed. ᶜAlī Muḥammad al-Bajāwī (Cairo, 1953/1372), p. 112.
72 Al-Ḥuṣrī, *Jamᶜ al-jawāhir*, pp. 158–9.
73 Al-Ḥuṣrī, *Jamᶜ al-jawāhir*, p. 283.
74 Al-Iṣfahānī, *Aghānī*, p. 4:33.
75 ᶜAwfī, Muḥammad, *Guzīda-yi javāmiᶜ al-ḥikāyāt va lavāmiᶜ al-rivāyāt*, ed. Jaᶜfar Shiᶜār (Tehran, 1363/1984), p. 284.

76	Al-Jumaḥī, *Ṭabaqāt*, p. 2:338.
77	Al-Ṣūlī, *Awrāq*, p. 86.
78	Al-Iṣfahānī, *Aghānī*, p. 3:179.
79	Al-Ṣūlī, *Awrāq*, p. 2.
80	Ibn al-Muʿtazz, *Ṭabaqāt*, p. 336.
81	ʿAwfī, *Lubāb*, pp. 297, 441.
82	Dawlatshāh, *Tadhkira*, p. 88. Niẓāmī ʿArūzī, *Chahār Maqāla*, pp. 89–90.
83	ʿAṭṭār, Farīd al-Dīn Nīshābūrī, *Manṭiq al-ṭayr*, ed. Muḥammad Rawshan (Tehran, 1374/1995), p. 77.
84	ʿAṭṭār, *Manṭiq al-ṭayr*, p. 134.
85	ʿAṭṭār, Farīd al-Dīn Nīshābūrī, *Ilāhīnāma*, ed. Fuʾād Rūḥānī (Tehran, 1339/1961), p. 198.
86	Saʿdī, *Gulistān*, p. 171.
87	Firdawsī, *Shāhnāma*.
88	Iṣfahānī, *Aghānī*, pp. 7:56, 7:78.
89	ʿAwfī, *Javāmiʿ al-ḥikāyāt*, p. 298.
90	In French court culture, 'The actual order of rank within court society constantly fluctuated. The balance within the society was, as we have said, very precarious. Now small, almost imperceptible tremors, now large scale convulsions incessantly changed the positions of people and the distance between them. ... it was dangerous to be discourteous to a person whose stock was rising. It was no less dangerous to be unduly amiable to a person who was sinking in the hierarchy' (Elias, Norbert, *The Court Society*, tr. Edmund Jephcott (Oxford, 1983), p. 91). Similarly, in medieval English court culture, 'The courtier's life, dependent as it was on favour and patronage, could never have been wholly sure. ... Moreover, not only might a well-placed servant suddenly find himself fallen from grace, but he had also to face the fact that his fortunes were inextricably mixed with those of his master' (Green, *Poets and Princepleasers*, p. 148). The emphasis on uncertainty sometimes obscures the importance of flexibility in patronage.
91	Douglas, Mary, *Purity and Danger: An Analysis of Concepts of Pollution and Taboo* (New York, 1966), p. 9.
92	Ibn Qutayba, *ʿUyūn*, p. 1:1:56.
93	Ibn Qutayba, *ʿUyūn*, p. 1:1:56.
94	Al-Thaʿālibī, *Tuḥfat al-wuzarāʾ*, p. 118.
95	Al-Māwardī, *Adab al-wazīr*, p. 22.
96	Al-Māwardī, *Adab al-wazīr*, p. 23.
97	ʿAwfī, *Lubāb*, p. 18.
98	Kaykāvūs b. Iskandar, *Qābūsnāma*, p. 198.
99	Ibn al-Muqaffaʿ, *Āthār*, pp. 286, 290. Ibn al-Muqaffaʿ analyzes the incommensurability of pragmatic interests and ethical values (Hamori, Andras, 'Prudence, virtue, and self-respect in Ibn al-Muqaffaʿ' in Angelika Neuwirth and Andreas Christian Islebe (eds), *Reflections on Reflections: Near Eastern Writers Reading Literature* (Wiesbaden, 2006)).
100	Ibn ʿAbd al-Barr al-Qurṭubī, Abū ʿUmar Yūsuf ibn ʿAbd Allāh, *Bahjat al-majālis wa-uns al-mujālis wa-shahdh al-dhāhin wal-hājis*, ed. Muḥammad Mursī al-Khūlī, 3 vols. (Beirut, 1982), p. 2:519.
101	Al-Thaʿālibī, *Tuḥfat al-wuzarāʾ*, p. 121.
102	Al-Thaʿālibī, *Tuḥfat al-wuzarāʾ*, p. 121.
103	Ibn Rashīq, *ʿUmda*, p. 2:77.
104	Al-Ābī, *Nathr al-durr*, p. 4:232.

105 Al-Ābī, *Nathr al-durr*, p. 4:231.
106 Al-Tha^{c}ālibī, *Tuḥfat al-wuzarā*ʾ, p. 124.
107 Sa^{c}dī, *Gulistān*, p. 87.
108 Rūmī, *Masnavī*, pp. 611–13.
109 Ibn ^{c}Abd al-Barr, *Bahjat al-majālis*, p. 1:312.
110 Ibn ^{c}Abd Rabbihi, *^{c}Iqd*, p. 1:244.
111 Al-Tawḥīdī, *Baṣāʾir*, p. 9:104.
112 Ibn al-Muqaffa^{c}, *Āthār*, p. 47.
113 Ibn Qutayba, *Shi^{c}r*, p. 1:154.
114 Al-Jahshiyārī, *Wuzarā*ʾ, p. 127.
115 Al-Ḥuṣrī, *Jam^{c} al-jawāhir*, pp. 299–300.
116 Al-Ḥuṣrī, *Zahr*, p. 1:555.
117 Ibn Qutayba, *Shi^{c}r*, p. 2:803.
118 Shams-i Qays, *Mu^{c}jam*, pp. 452–3.
119 Ibn Rashīq, *^{c}Umda*, p. 204.
120 Niẓāmī ^{c}Arūẓī, *Chahār Maqāla*, p. 66.
121 Niẓāmī ^{c}Arūẓī, *Chahār Maqāla*, p. 86.
122 ^{c}Awfī, *Lubāb*, p. 310.
123 Dawlatshāh, *Tadhkira*, p. 82.
124 Sa^{c}dī, *Gulistān*, pp. 48–9.
125 Al-Ḥuṣrī, *Zahr*, p. 1:340.
126 Al-Tha^{c}ālibī, *Yatīma*, p. 1:61.
127 ^{c}Awfī, *Javāmi^{c} al-ḥikāyāt*, p. 298.
128 Ibn ^{c}Abd Rabbihi, *^{c}Iqd*, p. 2:112.
129 Al-Tanūkhī, al-Qāḍī Abū ^{c}Alī al-Muḥsin b. ^{c}Alī, *Kitāb al-faraj ba^{c}d al-shidda*, ed. ^{c}Abbūd al-Shāljī, 5 vols. (Beirut, 1978/1398), p. 1:380.
130 Ibn al-Mu^{c}tazz, *Ṭabaqāt*, p. 54.
131 Al-Iṣfahānī, *Aghānī*, p. 10:250.
132 Ibn al-Mu^{c}tazz, *Ṭabaqāt*, p. 320.
133 Al-Jumaḥī, *Ṭabaqāt*, p. 2:318.
134 Al-Tanūkhī, *Faraj*, p. 1:356.
135 Al-Tanūkhī, *Mustajād*, p. 51.
136 Al-Tanūkhī, *Mustajād*, pp. 59–67.
137 Ibn Abī al-Dunyā, *Makārim*, p. 154.
138 Al-Rāghib al-Iṣbahānī, *Muḥāḍarāt*, p. 1:389.
139 Al-Jumaḥī, *Ṭabaqāt*, p. 2:420.
140 Ibn al-Mu^{c}tazz, *Ṭabaqāt*, p. 171.
141 Al-Rāghib al-Iṣbahānī, *Muḥāḍarāt*, pp. 1:389, 1:555.
142 Al-Bayhaqī, *Maḥāsin*, p. 186.
143 Al-Ṣūlī, *Awrāq*, p. 55.
144 Ibn al-Mu^{c}tazz, *Ṭabaqāt*, pp. 158–9.
145 Ibn al-Jarrāḥ, *Waraqa*, p. 97.
146 Ibn al-Mu^{c}tazz, *Ṭabaqāt*, p. 107.
147 Ibn al-Mu^{c}tazz, *Ṭabaqāt*, p. 202.
148 Al-Iṣfahānī, *Aghānī*, p. 2:241.
149 Al-Marzubānī, *Mu^{c}jam*, p. 28.
150 Ibn Qutayba, *Shi'r*, p. 1:181.
151 Ibn al-Mu^{c}tazz, *Ṭabaqāt*, p. 40.
152 ^{c}Awfī, *Javāmi^{c} al-ḥikāyāt*, pp. 278–82.
153 Al-Iṣfahānī, *Aghānī*, p. 2:241.
154 Al-Jahshiyārī, *Wuzarā*ʾ, p. 111. Al-Iṣfahānī, *Aghānī*, p. 3:241.

155 Ibn Rashīq, *ᶜUmda*, pp. 62, 81.
156 Samer Ali discusses two poems that show al-Buḥturī's shifting affiliations in the wake of al-Mutawakkil's assassination and concludes that they complement the destruction of one order and the creation of a new one (Ali, 'Praise for murder'). I think that what poets in this situation have in common, including the unusually powerful poet al-Buḥturī, is loyalty not to patrons but to their profession in the flexible and uncertain social order of patronage.
157 Al-Ṣūlī, *Akhbār al-Buḥturī*, p. 112.
158 Al-Rāghib al-Iṣbahānī, *Muḥāḍarāt*, p. 1:374. Al-Ṣūlī, *Akhbār al-Buḥturī*, p. 103.
159 Al-Ṣūlī, *Awrāq*, p. 76.
160 Al-Iṣfahānī, *Aghānī*, p. 3:51.
161 Abū Hiffān, *Akhbār Abī Nuwās*, p. 23.
162 Al-Iṣfahānī, *Aghānī*, p. 5:180.

Chapter 3

1 Sperl, Stefan and Christopher Shackle (eds), *Qasida Poetry in Islamic Asia and Africa* (Leiden, 1996).
2 This summary is compiled from the biographies by Mannāᶜ, Hāshim Ṣāliḥ, *Abū Tammām al-Ṭāʾī, 188-231 H: ḥayātuhu wa-shiᶜruhu* (Beirut, 1994) and Bearman, *EI*. For more detailed information about the careers of Abū Tammām and al-Buḥturī, see Cooperson, Michael and Shawkat M. Toorawa, *Arabic Literary Culture, 500–925* (Detroit, 2005).
3 Bearman, *EI*, 2008; Al-Buḥturī, *Dīwān al-Buḥturī*, ed. Ḥasan Kāmil al-Ṣīrafī, 5 vols. (Cairo, 1963–72), p. 1:193.
4 Mannāᶜ, *Abū Tammām*; Bearman, *EI*, 2008.
5 Aḥmad b. Abī Duʾād' in Bearman, *EI*, 2008.
6 Al-Buḥturī, *Dīwān*, p. 1:158.
7 Al-Buḥturī, *Dīwān*, p. 1:632.
8 Al-Buḥturī, *Dīwān*, p. 1:169.
9 Al-Buḥturī, *Dīwān*, p. 1:193.
10 'Al-Ḳāsim b. ᶜĪsā b. Idrīs, Abū Dulaf' in Bearman, *EI*, 2008; Al-Buḥturī, *Dīwān*, p. 1:71.
11 'Al-Ḥasan b. Sahl' in Bearman, *EI*, 2008.
12 Al-Buḥturī, *Dīwān*, p. 1:158; Al-Ḳāsim b. ᶜĪsā b. Idrīs', Abū Dulaf' in Bearman, *EI*, 2008.
13 'Al-Maʾmūn, Abū l-ᶜAbbās ᶜAbd Allāh b. Hārūn al-Rashīd' in Bearman, *EI*, 2008.
14 Mannāᶜ, Hāshim Ṣāliḥ, *Al-Buḥturī: ḥayātuhu wa-shiᶜruhu* (Beirut, 2002), p. 13.
15 Bearman, *EI*, 2008.
16 Mannāᶜ, *Al-Buḥturī*; Bearman, *EI*, 2008.
17 'Al-Fatḥ b. Khāḳān' in Bearman, *EI*, 2008.
18 Al-Buḥturī, *Dīwān*, p. 1:23.
19 Al-Buḥturī, *Dīwān*, p. 1:93.
20 Al-Buḥturī, *Dīwān*, p. 1:134.
21 Al-Buḥturī, *Dīwān*, p. 1:115; 'Ismāᶜīl b. Bulbul, Abū'l-Saḳr' in Bearman, *EI*.
22 Al-Buḥturī, *Dīwān*, p. 1:58.
23 Al-Buḥturī, *Dīwān*, p. 1:408.

24 'Al-Mu^c^tazz Bi-llah' in Bearman, *EI*.
25 de Blois, François, *Persian Literature: A Bio-bibliographical Survey*, vol. 5: *Poetry of the Pre-Mongol Period* (London, 1970); Browne, Edward Granville, *A Literary History of Persia*, 4 vols. (London, 1964–9).
26 Niẓāmī ^c^Arūẓī, *Chahār Maqāla*, p. 66.
27 Lūdī, Shīr ^c^Alī Khān, *Tadhkirah-yi Mir*ʾ*āt al-Khayāl*, ed. Ḥamīd Ḥasanī (Tehran, 1377), p. 20.
28 Bosworth, Clifford Edmund, *The Ghaznavids: Their Empire in Afghanistan and Eastern Iran 994–1040* (Edinburgh, 1963), p. 232.
29 'Maḥmūd b. Sabuktegīn' in Bearman, *EI*.
30 Bosworth, *Ghaznavids*, pp. 89, 175.
31 Bosworth *Ghaznavids*, pp. 39–41.
32 Dawlatshāh, *Tadhkira*, p. 58.
33 Perhaps this is why Shamīsā refers to panegyric as false epic.
34 Lūdī, *Mir*ʾ*āt*, pp. 21–2.
35 For a detailed history of the poet and his patrons, see Tetley, *Turks*.
36 Yūsufī, Ghulām Ḥusayn, *Farrukhī Sīstānī: baḥthī dar sharḥ-i aḥvāl va rūzgār va shi*^c^*r-i u* (Tehran, 1989); de Blois, *Persian Literature*.
37 Yūsufī, Ghulām Ḥusayn, *Kāghaz-i Zarr: Yāddashthā-yi dar Adab va Tārīkh* (Tehran, 1363/1984), pp. 34–43.
38 Yūsufī, *Kāghaz-i Zarr*, pp. 51–5.
39 Yūsufī, *Kāghaz-i Zarr*, p. 147.
40 'Mas^c^ūd b. Maḥmūd, Abū Sa'id, Shihāb al-Dawla, Djamāl al-Milla' in Bearman, *EI*.

Chapter 4

1 Medieval writers used small segments of composition that the author reorganized in a way that was both intertextual and creative (Carruthers, Mary J., *The Book of Memory: A Study of Memory in Medieval Culture* (Cambridge, 1990), p. 199).
2 Ghulām-Ḥusayn Yūsufī refers to the depiction of diverse emotions in his discussion of the love introduction by Farrukhī, and Philip Kennedy describes a kind of patchwork of erotic moods in his discussion of wine poetry by Abū Nuwās (Kennedy, Philip F., *The Wine Song in Classical Arabic Poetry: Abu Nuwas and the Literary Tradition* (Oxford, 1997), p. 62; Yūsufī, *Farrukhī*, p. 446).
3 Jerome Clinton suggests that the rapid shift from one motif to another in the Persian garden *nasīb* by Manūchihrī may be intended to convey the dynamic quality of the garden itself, and to draw the audience into an experience of that dynamic quality, 'One feels at first that this piece is poorly ordered, that some copyist has juggled the lines, and that, for example, the aspects of wind, rain and clouds should all be gathered together instead of scattered throughout the poem, as might the lines which describe the birds as singing or reciting … However, I think Manūchihrī may have been trying for a different effect here, and so arranged his lines as to emphasize the various and continuously changing faces of the garden. He keeps the reader's head spinning by pointing now to the clouds, now to the plains, then back to the clouds, and down to the flowers and shrubs' (Clinton, Jerome, *The Dīvān of Manuchihrī Dāmghānī: A Critical Study* (Minneapolis, Minnesota, 1972, pp. 105–6).

Fatemeh Keshavarz, in her study of Persian mystical lyric by Rūmī, notes that the potential productivity of segmented or fragmented composition has been largely ignored, 'Curiously, in all the debates concerning unity in the ghazal and the seemingly unresolvable problem presented by fragmentation, no attention has been paid to the fact that the strength of this genre and its suitability for lyric expression may indeed stem from this supposed weakness' (Keshavarz, Fatemeh, *Reading Mystical Lyric: The Case of Jalal al-Din Rumi* (Columbia, South Carolina, 1998), p. 144).

4 In medieval Arabic and Hebrew descriptive poetry, Andras Hamori observes, 'There end is to be compared; we do the comparing. We are imprisoned in time, every bit as much as the things that surround us; to compare, to sort out the relations about us, to actively experience our being in time is making the best of it' (Hamori, Andras, *On the Art of Medieval Arabic Literature* (Princeton, New Jersey, 1974), p. 98).

5 Beatrice Gruendler and G. J. H. Van Gelder make this observation about Arabic poetry (Gruendler, Beatrice, '*Qasida*: its reconstruction in performance' in Michael Cooperson (ed), *Classical Arabic Humanities in Their Own Terms: Festschrift for Wolfhart Heinrichs on his 65th Birthday* (Boston, 2008), pp. 325–93, p. 372, Van Gelder, Geert, *Beyond the Line: Classical Arabic Literary Critics on the Coherence and Unity of the Poem* (Leiden, 1982), p. 203). On breaking down whole poems into short segments to set them to music, see Kilpatrick, Hilary, *Making the Great Book of Songs: Compilation and the Author's Craft in Abū l-Faraj al-Iṣbahānī's Kitāb al-aghānī* (London, 2003), p. 55.

6 Gruendler, Beatrice, 'Motif vs. Genre: Reflections on the *Diwan al-Ma'ani* of Abu Hilāl al-'Askari' in Thomas Bauer and Angelika Neuwirth (eds), *Ghazal as World Literature I: Transformations of a Literary Genre* (Beirut, 2005), pp. 57–86, p. 83.

7 G. J. H. Van Gelder discusses this issue in Arabic rhetoric (Van Gelder, *Beyond the Line*, p. 201). Some passages in medieval Arabic literary criticism that have been understood as referring to the coherence of entire poems have been misinterpreted (Bakkār, Yūsuf Ḥusayn, *Binā' al-qaṣīda al-ᶜArabiyya* (Cairo, 1979), p. 487). While other passages do refer to the coherence of entire poems, the poetry itself does not necessarily reflect these theoretical views (ᶜAṭwān, Ḥusayn, *Muqaddimat al-qaṣīda fī al-ᶜaṣr al-ᶜAbbāsī al-awwal* (Cairo, 1974), pp. 250–1).

8 Qudāma b. Jaᶜfar, quoted in Ḥinnawī, al-Muḥammadī ᶜAbd al-ᶜAzīz, *Shiᶜr al-Sarī al-Raffā' fī ḍaw' al-maqāyīs al-balāghiyya wal-naqdiyya* (Cairo, 1405/1984), p. 88.

9 Raymond Scheindlin on the Andalusian Arabic poet al-Muᶜtamid b. ᶜAbbād (Scheindlin, Raymond P., *Form and Structure in the Poetry of Al-Muᶜtamid ibn ᶜAbbād* (Leiden, 1974), p. 60).

10 Alessandro Barchiesi on Latin literature, but he refers to politics, not social life (Barchiesi, *Poet and Prince*, pp. 271–2). Success and praise can only be comprehended in relation to failure and blame, Patricia Bulman observes about Pindar (Bulman, Patricia, *Phthonos in Pindar* (Berkeley, California, 1992), p. 3).

11 Nādir Vazīnpūr on Persian panegyric and Michael Glünz on the 7th-/13th-century Persian poet Kamāl al-Dīn Iṣfahānī (Vazīnpūr, Nādir, *Madḥ, dāgh-i nang bar sīmā-yi adab-i fārsī: bar-rasī-yi intiqādī va taḥlīlī az ᶜilal-i madīḥa-sarā-yi shāᶜirān-i īrānī* (Tehran, 1374/1995), p. 79); Glünz, Michael, *Die*

panegyrische Qaṣīda bei Kamāl ud-Dīn Ismāʿīl aus Iṣfahān, Beirut, 1993), p. 39). Many poems say next to nothing that is specific about the person to whom they are dedicated (Peter White on Latin poetry and patronage, White, *Promised Verse*, p. 22). If there is a specific significance of this exemplary description for the patron, the poem, though publicly circulated, resembles a private letter (Orsatti, P., 'Anvari's qasides as letters and the problem of identifying the addressee' in Daniela Meneghini (ed), *Studies on the Poetry of Anvarī* (Venice, 2006), p. 79). This exemplary quality is like a search for concrete experience in the realm of symbolic connotation, a reduction of story to symbol, or a ritual re-enactment of an archetype (Stetkevych, Jaroslav, 'The Arabic qaṣīdah: from form and content to mood and meaning', *Harvard Ukrainian Studies* 3–4 (1979–80), p. 782). In a study of the Ottoman Turkish poet Nedim, Kemal Silay asserts that in medieval Ottoman Anatolia, the individual poet spoke not for himself but for the world view of his social class (Silay, Kemal, *Nedim and the Poetics of the Ottoman Court: Medieval Inheritance and the Need for Change* (Bloomington, Indiana, 1994), p. 13). Michael Cooperson proposes that the primary concern of medieval Arabic biographers was not the commemoration of individual lives, but rather the demonstration of a group's legitimacy through the examples of individual members of that group (Cooperson, *Arabic Biography*, p. xii).

12 Adorno, Theodor W., 'Lyric Poetry and Society', *Telos* 20 Summer (1974), pp. 56–71, p. 57.

13 The love introduction in the pre-Islamic Arabic *qasida* could be understood as a manifestation of competitive virtue, or as a manifestation of pessimism and doubt about the validity of competitive virtue (Montgomery, James, 'Dichotomy in Jāhilī poetry', *Journal of Arabic Literature* 17 (1986), pp. 1–20, p. 9). This dimension of the ancient love introduction informs the function of this section in medieval Arabic panegyric.

14 Sīrūs Shamīsā asserts that the beloved in the Persian love introduction and the independent love poem is a boy 90 per cent of the time, and suggests that modern readers 'must accept this reality without intolerance,' and observes that in medieval culture this was not problematic, at least not in the court, or it would not have been spoken of so openly (Shamīsā, Sīrūs, *Sayr-i ghazal dar shiʿr-i Fārsī* (Tehran, 1362/1984), pp. 34, 38). In a study of Ottoman culture, Walter Andrews and Mehmet Kalpakli explain that the beloved is usually a young male, and that there is little difference between descriptions of male and female beloveds. They note that this ambiguity about the gender of the beloved characterizes medieval love poetry in Europe as well as the Middle East (Andrews, Walter and Mehmet Kalpakli, *The Age of Beloveds: Love and the Beloved in Early-Modern Ottoman and European Culture and Society* (Durham, North Carolina, 2005), p. 54).

15 Bettini, Maurizio, *The Portrait of the Lover*, tr. Laura Gibbs, (Berkeley, California, 1999), p. 52.

16 Morales, *Vision and Narrative*, p. 122.

17 Meisami, Julie, 'The body as garden: nature and sexuality in Persian Poetry', *Edebiyat* 6 (1996), pp. 245–74, p. 247.

18 Beatrice Gruendler on Ibn al-Rūmī (Gruendler, *Ibn al-Rūmī*, p. 15). ʿAbd al-Fattāḥ al-Nāfiʿ draws on the medieval Arabic critic al-Thaʿālibī to explore the Arabic poet al-Mutanabbī's use of the vocabulary of love in his description of the patron in the praise section (Nāfiʿ, ʿAbd al-Fattāḥ Ṣāliḥ, *Lughat al-ḥubb fī shiʿr al-Mutanabbī* (Amman, 1983/1403). Al-Mutanabbī in effect

makes an implicit aspect of panegyric into a more explicit one. The patron could recognize himself in the love introduction and also enjoy the description of a beautiful young person (On Farrukhī: Borg, Gabrielle van den, 'The Nasībs in the divan of Farrukhī Sīstānī: poetical speech versus the reflection of reality', *Edebiyat* 9 (1998), pp. 17–34, p. 29).

19 On love and professional life, see Algazi and Drory.

20 Lucien Dallenbach discusses the mise-en-abyme in other literary contexts (Dallenbach, Lucien, *The Mirror in the Text*, tr. Jeremy Whiteley with Emma Hughes (Chicago, 1989), p. 8).

21 On Persian, Shamīsā, *Ghazal*, p. 26; On Arabic, Bauer, Thomas, *Liebe und Liebesdichtung in der arabischen Welt des 9. und 10. Jahrhunderts: eine literatur- und mentalitätsgeschichtliche Studie des arabischen Gazal* (Wiesbaden, 1998), p. 185.

22 Morales, *Vision and Narrative*, p. 162.

23 Francette Pacteau on French love poetry about women (Pacteau, Francette, *The Symptom of Beauty* (Cambridge, Massachusetts, 1994), p. 66).

24 Sherry Ortner on women, nature, and culture in general (Ortner, Sherry B., 'Is female to male as nature is to culture?' in Michelle Zimbalist Rosaldo and Louise Lamphere (eds), *Woman, Culture, and Society* (Stanford, California, 1974), pp. 67–88, p. 88).

25 Dorothy Yamamoto on medieval English literature (Yamamoto, Dorothy, *The Boundaries of the Human in Medieval English Literature* (Oxford, 2000), p. 207).

26 Barthes, Roland, *A Lover's Discourse: Fragments*, tr. Richard Howard (New York, 1978), p. 13.

27 Freud, Sigmund, 'Beyond the Pleasure Principle' in *The Standard Edition of the Complete Psychological Works of Sigmund Freud*, tr. James Strachey with Anna Freud, Alix Strachey, and Alan Tyson, vol. 18 (1920–2), *Beyond the Pleasure Principle, Group Psychology, and Other Works* (London, 1955), pp. 3–64, pp. 15–18; Lacan, Jacques, *The Four Fundamental Concepts of Psycho-analysis*, ed. Jacques-Alain Millers, tr. Alan Sheridan (New York, 1981), p. 62.

28 Farrukhī, *Dīvān*, p. 4:74. Muḥammad b. Maḥmūd b. Sabuktegīn.

دوست دارم کودک سیمین بر بیجاده لب   هر کجا زیشان یکی بینی مرا آنجا طلب

29 ᶜUnṣurī, *Dīvān*, p. 19:214. Naṣr b. Sabuktegīn.

چیست آن جعد سلسله که همی   بوی عنبر ده است وعنبر نیست

30 Al-Buḥturī, *Dīwān*, p. 3:1724:4–5. Al-Muᶜtazz.

ذكرتُ بها قضيبَ البانِ لمّا   بدتْ تختالُ في الحُسْنِ اختيالا

تُشاكِلُهُ اهتزازاً وانعطافاً   وتَحكيهِ قواماً واعتدالاَ

31 Farrukhī, *Dīvān*, p. 23:477. Aḥmad b. Ḥasan Maymandī.

دل بر تو بستم و بتو بس کردم از جهان   وندر جهان زمن دل من دیدن تو خواست

32 ᶜUnṣurī, *Dīvān*, p. 28:321. Maḥmūd b. Sabuktegīn.

شادی اندر جان من مأوی گرفت از عشق او   شاد باشد جان آنکس کش چنو جانان بود

33 Al-Buḥturī, *Dīwān*, p. 3:1724:1. Al-Muᶜtazz.

سلاها كيفَ ضيَّعتِ الوصالا   وبَتَّتْ من مَوَدَّتنا الحِبالا

34 Abū Tammām, *Dīwān*, p. 1:161:15–16. Abū Saᶜīd al-Thaghrī.

طابَ فيه المَديحُ والتذَّ حتّى   فاقَ وَصْفَ الديارِ والتشبيبا

لو يُفاجا رُكنُ النسيبِ كَثِيرٌ   بمعانيهِ خالَهنَّ نسيبا

35 Abū Tammām, *Dīwān*, p. 3:1651. Isḥāq b. Ibrāhīm b. Ḥusayn b. Muṣcab.

أَصغَى إلى البين مُغترًّا فلا جرَما   أنَّ النوَى أسأَرَتْ فى قلبه لَمَما

36 Al-Buḥturī, *Dīwān*, p. 3:1724:2. Al-Muctazz.

وأضحتْ بالشآمِ ترى حَراماً   مواصَلتي وهِجراني حلالا

37 Abū Tammām, *Dīwān*, p. 3:160:5. Banū cAbd al-Karīm al-Ṭaiyyīn.

أَظُنُّ الدمْعَ فى خدِّى سيَبقَى   رُسوماً مِن بُكائِى فى الرُسومِ

38 Stetkevych, Jaroslav, *The Zephyrs of Najd* (Chicago, 1993), p. 114.

39 Farrukhī, *Dīvān*, p. 5–6: 95–7. Muḥammad b. Maḥmūd b. Sabuktegīn.

عامل بصره بنام تو همي خواهد خراج   خاطب بغداد بر نامت همي خواند خطب

گرت فرمان آيد زسلطان كه خالى كن عراق   گردن گردنكشانرا نرم گردان چون عصب

نامهٔ فتح تو از شام و ديگر ز مصر   منزلى زان تو حلوان باشد وديگر حلب

40 Jeanne Addison Roberts explains that in Shakespeare, the wild and its animal life 'provide insights into the structure of male culture, which is defined and threatened by them' (Roberts, Jeanne Addison, *The Shakespearean Wild: Geography, Genus, and Gender* (Lincoln, Nebraska, 1991), p. 4).

41 Michael Sells explains, in a study of a pre-Islamic description of a camel with water imagery, that the violent motion of water is essential to life yet destructive, a source of life and a flood (Sells, Michael A., 'Along the edge of mirage: The mufaḍḍaliyah of al-Mukhabbal as-Sacdī, an interpretation', in Mustansir Mir (ed), *Literary Heritage of Classical Islam: Arabic and Islamic Studies in Honor of James A. Bellamy* (Princeton, New Jersey, 1993), pp. 119–38, p. 132). Nature is a movement from the nameless and undefined sphere of nature to the naming and definition associated with human experience. (On the nature imagery of the Andalusian Arabic poet Ibn Khafāja: Foulon, Brigitte, 'Les représentations paysagères dans la poésie descriptive d'Ibn Ḫafāğa: Analyse de la structure hypsométrique du paysage et de l'action des météores', *Arabica* 52 (2005), pp. 66–108, p. 81.) 'The description of nature for this man [of the court] will reflect something of his "life work"' (de Fouchécour, Charles-Henri, *La description de la nature dans la poésie lyrique persane du XIe siècle: inventaire et analyse des thèmes* (Paris, 1969), p. iv).

42 Abū Tammām, *Dīwān*, p. 3:163:19. Banū cAbd al-Karīm al-Ṭāiyyīn.

إذا نَزَلَ النزيعُ بِهم قَرَوْه   رياضَ الريفِ من أُنُفٍ جَميمِ

Also see Abū Tammām, *Dīwān*, p. 3:164:27 for the same patrons:

When they descend at a location, they make it into a verdant
meadow with traces like the traces of the clouds.

إذا نَزَلوا بِمحَلٍ رَوَّضوه   بآثارٍ كآثارِ الغُيُومِ

43 Al-Buḥturī, *Dīwān*, p. 3:1734:21. Al-Fatḥ b. Khāqān.

خلائقُ كالغيوثِ تفيضُ منها   مواهِبُ مثلُ جمّاتِ السُّيولِ

44 Farrukhī, *Dīvān*, p. 5:89. Muḥammad b. Maḥmūd b. Sabuktegīn.

تو دلى دارى چو دريا وكفى دارى چو ابر   زان همى پاشى جواهر زين همى بارى ذهب

45 Al-Buḥturī, *Dīwān*, p. 3:1718:20. Al-Shāh b. Mīkāl.

أشيمُ منهم بُروقَ الخُلَّباتِ فهلْ   شخْصٌ يُخبِّرُنا عن بارِقِ الخالِ

46 Abū Tammām, *Dīwān*, p. 3:163:25. Banū cAbd al-Karīm al-Ṭaiyyīn.

لَهُمْ غُرَرٌ تُخالُ إذا استنارتْ   بواهِرُها ضرائرَ للنجومِ

47 Al-Buḥturī, *Dīwān*, p. 3:1721:15. Al-Muᶜtazz.

إذا بدا وجلالُ المُلْكِ يَغْمُرُهُ   حَسِبْتهُ البَدْرَ وفَّى حُسْنَهُ الكَمَلُ

Also al-Buḥturī, *Dīwān*, p. 3:1726, 26 for the same patron:

I saw felicity and blessings when I saw the brightness of your face and the crescent moon.

رأيتُ اليُمْنَ والبَرَكاتِ لمّا   رأيتُ بياضَ وجهِكَ والهلالا

48 Abū Tammām, *Dīwān*, pp. 3:151–2, 7–10. Al-Maᵓmūn.

ولقد أَراكِ فهَل أَراكِ بغِبْطَةٍ   والعَيشُ غَضٌّ والزمان غُلامُ

أعوامَ وَصْلٍ كان يُنسِى طُولَها   ذِكْرُ النوَى فكأنها أيّامُ

ثمّ انبرتْ أيّامُ هَجْرٍ أردَفَتْ   بجَوًى أسىً فكأنها أعوامُ

ثمّ انقضتْ تلكَ وأهلُها   فكأنّها وكأنّهمْ أحلامُ

49 Al-Buḥturī, *Dīwān*, p. 3:1850, 15. Al-Khiḍr b. Aḥmad. Abū ᶜAmir al-Khiḍr b. Aḥmad b. ᶜUmar b. al-Khaṭṭāb al-Taghlibī was from a ruling family of Rabīᶜa. He served as governor of Mosul under al-Muᶜtamid in 261/874, the year in which all five of al-Buḥturī's panegyrics for him were composed (Al-Buḥturī, *Dīwān*, p. 1:340).

تَسهُلُ أخلاقُهُ ونحنُ على   حالٍ من الدهر وَعْرَةِ الحِيلِ

50 ᶜUnṣurī, *Dīvān*, p. 30, 345. Maḥmūd b. Sabuktegīn. Maḥmūd b. Sabuktegīn ruled the Ghaznavid Empire 388/998–421/1030. His father Sabuktegīn was a leading Turkish slave soldier for the ruler of the preceding dynasty, the Samanids. Sabuktegīn gained autonomy in the city of Ghazna, which was at the eastern edge of the Samanid region. Maḥmūd became leader of the Khurasani troops under the Samanids. After his father died and designated Maḥmūd's younger brother heir, Maḥmūd was able to take over his father's region and eventually overthrow the Samanids. He obtained the caliph's nominal permission to rule Khurasan and Ghazna, including the titles Yamīn al-Dawla and Amīn al-Milla. He is best known for his enormous imperialist conquests in South Asia, which yielded great wealth for the Ghaznavid Empire, although the widespread conversion of Hindus to Islam in South Asia occurred in conjunction with conquests by later rulers. In addition, Maḥmūd collected tribute from the remaining Saffarids in southern Iran and competed for hegemony with the Buyids in northern Iran. Maḥmūd's court was the first Muslim court to offer extensive patronage to Persian poets ('Maḥmūd b. Sabuktegīn' in Bearman, *EI*, 2008).

کرد محکم کردگار اندر بقای جاودان   دولتش را تا رسومش ملک را بنیان بود

51 Farrukhī, *Dīvān*, p. 24, 486–7. Aḥmad b. Ḥasan Maymandī.

ای خواجگان دولت سلطان بهر نماز   او را دعا کنید که او در خور دعاست

با دشمنان دولت او دشمنی کنید   از بهر آنکه دولت او دولت شماست

52 ᶜUnṣurī, *Dīvān*, p. 34, 382. Maḥmūd b. Sabuktegīn.

سال نو در باغ نو نو دولت وشادی بود   هر دو نو مر دولت نو را همی ارکان شود

53 Glünz, *Panegyrische*, p. 43.

54 Farrukhī, *Dīvān*, p. 6, 111. Muḥammad b. Maḥmūd b. Sabuktegīn. Following the death of Maḥmūd, Abū Aḥmad Muḥammad b. Maḥmūd Ghaznavī Niẓām al-Dīn Jalāl al-Dawla ruled from spring to early fall in 421/1030 and was then taken prisoner by his brother Masᶜūd when he took over (Farrukhī, p. 41). Although things didn't work out in the long run, Maḥmūd had designated Muḥammad, not Masᶜūd, as his heir, although this preference was surprising

for contemporaries and later writers due to Mas^cūd's more extensive experience (Bosworth, *Ghaznavids*, pp. 183, 228). And although his reign was brief, silver coins minted in his name exist (Bosworth, *Ghaznavids*, p. 79). Muḥammad rejected the possibility of sharing power with Masᶜūd, and he lacked the support of other members of the ruling family (Bosworth, *Ghaznavids*, pp. 228–9). In the wake of Muḥammad's loss of power, Masᶜūd purged the elite of men who had supported Muḥammad as well as others who had not but whom he suspected of doing so (Bosworth, *Ghaznavids*, p. 232).

ای محمد سیرت ونامت محمد هر که او   از محمد باز گردد باز گشت از دین رب

55 ᶜUnṣurī, *Dīvān*, p. 20, 230. Abū al-Muẓaffar Naṣr b. Sabuktegīn. Abū al-Muẓaffar Naṣr b. Sabuktegīn was the brother of Maḥmūd b. Sabuktegīn and the general of the Ghaznavid army in Khurasan after Maḥmūd took power. (Farrukhī, p. 42) Naṣr was also appointed military governor over the restive province of Sīstān after the Ghaznavids defeated the last Saffarid ruler there, and he founded a Ḥanafī religious college in Nishapur (Bosworth, *Ghaznavids*, pp. 89, 175). He died young, before Maḥmūd, i.e. before 421/1030 (Farrukhī, *Dīvān*, p. 42).

خطبهٔ ملک را بگرد جهان   بجز از تخت شاه منبر نیست

56 ᶜUnṣurī, *Dīvān*, p. 20, 229. Abū al- Muẓaffar Naṣr b. Sabuktegīn.

دست او روز جود پنداری   چشمهٔ کوثر است وکوثر نیست

57 Al-Buḥturī, *Dīwān*, p. 3:1725, 11. Al-Muᶜtazz. Abū ᶜAbd Allāh Muḥammad b. Jaᶜfar al-Muᶜtazz billāh was an Abbasid caliph who reigned 252–5/866–9. He was the son of the caliph al-Mutawakkil and his favorite concubine, Qabīḥa. Al-Mutawakkil had planned that his sons al-Muntaṣir, al-Muᶜtazz, and al-Muᵓayyad should rule in succession.

While al-Muntaṣir ruled briefly after al-Mutawakkil, the next caliph became al-Muᶜtazz's cousin, al-Mustaᶜīn, and al-Muᶜtazz was imprisoned. Turkish military elites ended the caliphate of al-Mustaᶜīn and brought al-Muᶜtazz from prison to the throne. Although al-Muᶜtazz promised to protect al-Mustaᶜīn, he broke his promise and had him killed later the same year, and he also forced his brother al-Muᵓayyad to give up his right to succession and then killed him too. With the help of his minister, al-Muᶜtazz reduced the influence of the Turkish military elite temporarily, but al-Muᶜtazz was eventually removed from power by the Turkish military elite along with troops from Farghānā in Central Asia and Northern Africa. He died in captivity at the age of 24, and the Turkish military elite placed al-Muhtadī on the throne.

Al-Muᶜtazz's lack of control in the central cities of Baghdad and Samarra made it possible for provincial rulers and opposition movements to flourish, including the beginning of autonomy in Egypt, Kharijite rebellions in northern Iraq, Alid rebellions in Arabia and northern Iran, the beginning of the Zanj revolt in Basra, and most importantly the progress of the Saffarid provincial ruler in southern Iran ('Al-Muᶜtazz Bi-llah' in Bearman, *EI*, 2008).

أميرَ المؤمنين وأنتَ أَرضى   عِبادِ اللهِ عندَ اللهِ حالا

58 ᶜUnṣurī, *Dīvān*, pp. 20, 224. Abū al- Muẓaffar Naṣr b. Sabuktegīn.

شاه را مخبری بداد خدای   کش از آن بیش هیچ منظر نیست

59 Abū Tammām, *Dīwān*, p. 3:178, 11. Aḥmad b. Abī Duᵓād. Aḥmad b. Abī Duᵓād b. Jarīr Abū ᶜAbd Allāh worked as an advisor to the caliph al-Maᵓmūn and chief judge for al-Muᶜtaṣim. Ibn Abī Duᵓād was a Ḥanafī but was better

known as an adherent of Muᶜtazilī theology who oversaw the persecution of the jurist Aḥmad b. Ḥanbal during the inquisition that took place between 218/833 and 234/848–9. His participation in the apostasy trial of the caliph's general al-Afshīn in 225–6/839–41 and the execution of Aḥmad b. Naṣr al-Khuzāᶜī over theological issues probably grew out of questions about these individuals' loyalty to the caliph rather than religious and theological affiliations. In addition, Ibn Abī Duᵓād competed as a political elite with the Turkish miltary elite. He was a member of the group that contained members of both elites that selected the caliph al-Mutawakkil, who gradually purged most of the group that selected him, including Ibn Abī Duᵓād. Ibn Abī Duᵓād died in 240/854 of complications of a stroke ('Aḥmad b. Abī Duᵓād' in Bearman, *EI*, 2008).

جَزى اللهُ كفًّا مِلْؤُها مِن سَعادةٍ   سَرَتْ فى هلاكِ المالِ والمالُ نائمُ

In addition to سرتْ there is a manuscript that refers to سعتْ.

60 Farrukhī, *Dīvān*, pp. 24, 490. Aḥmad b. Ḥasan Maymandī. Aḥmad b. Ḥasan Maymandī Abū al-Qāsim served as minister twice: once under Maḥmūd from 404/1013 to 415/1024, and a second time under Masᶜūd from 422/1031 until he died in 424/1032. His father was a governor of Bust and Maymandī was a nursing brother of Maḥmūd and studied together with him as a boy. He became minister the first time after the previous minister was deposed and imprisoned, and he was later deposed, his money confiscated, and imprisoned in southern Kashmir. After Maḥmūd died and Masᶜūd took over, Maymandī reluctantly resumed work as a minister until the end of his life two years later (Yūsufī, *Kāghaz-i Zarr*, pp. 34–43).

اندر سلامتش همه کس را سلامتست   واندر بقاش دولت اسلام را بقاست

61 Al-Buḥturī, *Dīwān*, p. 3:1722, 24. Al-Muᶜtazz.

وكان كالعِجْلِ غُرَّ الجاهلونَ به   وكنتَ موسى هَدى القومَ الأُلى جَهِلوا

62 Abū Tammām, *Dīwān*, p. 3:169,12. Isḥāq b. Ibrāhīm. This is Isḥāq b. Ibrāhīm b. Muṣᶜab according to the editor of Abū Tammām's diwan and Isḥāq b. Ibrāhīm b. al-Ḥusayn b. Muṣᶜab b. Zurayq b. Māhān according to the more detailed information in al-Buḥturī's diwan. Isḥāq came from a powerful elite family, and al-Maᵓmūn put him in charge of Baghdad after he removed ᶜAbd Allāh b. Ṭāhir in 215/830, and then he also put Isḥāq in charge of neighboring regions. He remained chief of police in Baghdad under al-Maᵓmūn, al-Muᶜtaṣim, al-Wāthiq, and al-Mutawakkil for over twenty years. Al-Muᶜtaṣim also sent him to fight the Khurramī rebels in 218/833, and he died under al-Mutawakkil in 235/849 (Al-Buḥturī, *Dīwān*, p. 1:71).

قَرَّت بقُرّانَ عَينُ الدين وانتشرتْ   بالأشتَرَينِ عُيونُ الشِّرْكِ فاصطُلِما

63 Al-Buḥturī, *Dīwān*, p. 3:1722, 26. Al-Muᶜtazz.

فالدينُ في كلِّ أُفْقٍ ضاحِكٌ بِهجٌ   والكُفْرُ في كل أرضٍ خائفٌ وَجِلُ

64 Abū Tammām, *Dīwān*, p. 3:154, 27. Al-Maᵓmūn. Abū al-ᶜAbbās ᶜAbd Allāh b. Hārūn al-Rashīd al-Maᵓmūn was declared second heir to Hārūn al-Rashīd after his half-brother al-Amīn in 183/799. In the meantime, al-Maᵓmūn was placed in charge of the eastern province of Khurasan, and a third brother was designated heir and given the western frontier with Byzantium. When al-Amīn added his son to the list of heirs to the caliphate in 194/810, a conflict ensued between al-Amīn and al-Maᵓmūn. When al-Amīn moved his son up to first place in succession in place of al-Maᵓmūn and listed a second son in second place in place of the third brother in the following year, the conflict

intensified and involved the interests of a wide range of political and military elites as well as the ordinary people of Baghdad. After Ibrāhīm b. al-Mahdī struggled as caliph for two years, al-Ma'mūn took over in 204/819, using the title of Imam. Al-Ma'mūn is best known for his increasing integration of diverse cultures, especially Persian and Greek, into the Abbasid Empire, his increasing reliance on military power from the northeast, and his adherence to Mu'tazilī theology ('Al-Ma'mūn, Abū l-'Abbās 'Abd Allāh b. Hārūn al-Rashīd' in Bearman, *EI*, 2008).

لمّا رأيتَ الدينَ يَخْفِقُ قلبُهُ والكُفْرُ فيه تَغَطْرُسٌ وعُرامُ

65 Al-Buḥturī 3:1735, 31. Al-Fatḥ b. Khāqān. Al-Fatḥ b. Khāqān was descended from the Turkish ruling family in Farghānā in Central Asia, and led the Turkish troops from Central Asia for the caliph al-Mu'taṣim. He was educated with al-Mu'taṣim's son al-Mutawakkil, and became his secretary, and also held other positions in his administration. He was an author of literary works that are not extant, owner of a major library, and a major patron of literature. Al-Fatḥ was assassinated with al-Mutawakkil in 247/861 ('Al-Fatḥ b. Khāḳān' in Bearman, *EI*, 2008).

كفاكَ اللهُ ما تَخشى وغَطّى عليكَ بظِلٍّ نِعْمتِهِ الظليلِ

66 Cited by G. J. H. Van Gelder. Van Gelder compares this view to the theological view that the existence of praise and blame proves the existence of free will (Van Gelder, G. J. H., *The Bad and the Ugly: Attitudes Toward Invective Poetry (Hijā') in Classical Arabic Literature* (Leiden, 1988), pp. 69–70).

67 'Unṣurī, *Dīvān*, p. 30, 343. Maḥmūd b. Sabuktegīn.

چون گشاد کف او را راد خواندی راستی نام رادی رود وابر وبحر را بهتان بود

68 Al-Buḥturī 3:1722, 20. Al-Mu'tazz.

يا مَن له أوّلُ العلْيا وآخِرُها ومَن بجودِ يديه يُضرَبُ المَثَلُ

69 Al-Buḥturī, *Dīwān*, p. 3:1718, 18. Al-Shāh b. Mīkāl was one of the generals who served al-Musta'īn, al-Mu'tazz, and other caliphs until al-Muktafī, and he passed away in 302/914 (Al-Buḥturī, *Dīwān*, p. 2:688).

عليه سيما من العلياء بان بها من غافلين عن العلياء أغفال

70 'Unṣurī, *Dīvān*, p. 34, 379 and 381. Maḥmūd b. Sabuktegīn.

هر کجا خذلان بود با عدل او نصرت شود هر کجا نصرت بود بی عزم او خذلان شود ...

ای خداوند خداوندان ملک وسروری سروری وملک بی تدبیر تو خسران شود

71 Al-Buḥturī, *Dīwān*, p. 3:1735, 30. Al-Fatḥ b. Khāqaān.

وَقَتْ نَفْسَ الجَوادِ من المنايا ومحذوراتِها نَفْسُ البخيلِ

72 'Unṣurī, *Dīvān*, p. 5, 64. Naṣr b. Sabuktegīn.

بر آثارش بقارا اعتمادست بر انگشتش سخارا اتکالا

73 Abū Tammām 3:181, 23. Ibn Abī Du'ād.

له من إيادٍ قِمَّةُ المجدِ حَيثما سَمتْ ولها منه البِنا والدعائمُ

74 Farrukhī, *Dīvān*, p. 5, 90–1 and 93. Muḥammad b. Maḥmūd b. Sabuktegīn.

در هنر شاگرد خویشی چون نکوتر بنگری فضلهای خویشتن را هم تو بودستی سبب

هم خداوند سخایی هم خداوند سخن هم خداوند حسامی هم خداوند حسب ...

پادشاهی چون تو نی از پادشاهان جهان پادشاهی را به تست ای پادشاه زاده نسب

75 Myth and legend in praise is a kind of internal model of the larger panegyric theme. (On Greek panegyric: Felson, Nancy, 'The poetic effects of deixis in Pindar's *Ninth Pythian Ode*', *Arethusa* 37 (2004), pp. 365–9.)

76 ᶜUnṣurī, *Dīvān*, pp. 5, 70–1. Naṣr b. Sabuktegīn.

سلیمان باد را گر بسته کردی بزیر تخت وقت ارتحالا

امیر اندر سفر هم بسته دارد سر باد وزان اندر دوالا

77 Abū Tammām, *Dīwān*, p. 3:162, 18. Banū ᶜAbd al-Karīm al-Ṭaᵓiyyīn. Abū Tammām also asserted his affiliation to a different line of Ṭayyiᵓ. Al-Ṣūlī reports that at the beginning of his career, Abū Tammām was affiliated with Banū ᶜAbd al-Karīm al-Ṭaᵓiyyīn in Homs and offered panegyric to them, and also composed invective on an opponent, ᶜUtba b. Abī ᶜUṣaym, who composed invective on them. A member of the ᶜAbd al-Karīm family reports that when ᶜUtba heard Abū Tammām's work, he was so impressed that he told the family that Abū Tammām could not remain in Homs with ᶜUtba. He moved on to Egypt, Damascus and Baghdad (Abū Tammām, *Dīwān*, p. 4:605–6).

فإن شَهِدَ المقامةَ يومَ فصْلٍ رأيتَ نَظيرَ لُقمانِ الحكيمِ

78 Farrukhī, *Dīvān*, p. 5, 86–8. Muḥammad b. Maḥmūd b. Sabuktegīn.

بهمن آنگه روستم را چند گه شاگرد شد تا خصالش بیخلل گشت وفعالش منتخب

همچنان کیخسرو واسفندیار گرد را رستم دستان همی آموخت فرهنگ وادب

تو هم از خردی بدانستی همه فرهنگها نا کشیده ذل شگردی ونادیده تعب

79 Arendt, *On Violence*, p. 4.

80 Abū Tammām, *Dīwān*, p. 3:156, 37. Al-Maᵓmūn.

آسادُ مَوت مُخدِراتٌ ما لها إلاَّ الصوارمَ والقنا آجامُ

81 Al-Buḥturī, *Dīwān*, p. 3:1723, 33. Al-Muᶜtazz.

تورَّدوا النَّقْعَ لا حَيْدٌ ولا كَشَفٌ وباشروا الموتَ لا ميلٌ ولا عُزُلُ

82 ᶜUnṣurī, *Dīvān*, p. 27, 320. Maḥmūd b. Sabuktegīn.

رامش افزایی کند وقتی که در مجلس بود لشکر آرایی کند روزیکه در میدان بود

83 Abū Tammām 3:181, 26. Ibn Abī Duᵓād.

إذا سيفُهُ أضحى على الهامِ حاكِماً غدا العَفْوُ منه وهو فى السيفِ حاكِمُ

84 Margaret Larkin's citation of al-Jurjānī and commentary on it (Larkin, Margaret, *The Theology of Meaning: ᶜAbd al-Qāhir al-Jurjānī's Theory of Discourse* (New Haven, Connecticut, 1995), pp. 55, 60, 119).

85 de Man, Paul, *Allegories of Reading: Figural Language in Rousseau, Nietzsche, Rilke, and Proust* (New Haven, Connecticut, 1979), p. 9.

86 Al-Buḥturī, *Dīwān*, p. 4:2096, 7. Ibn Bisṭām.

هل الشَّبابُ مُلِمٌّ بى فراجِعةٌ أيّامُهُ لى في أعْقابِ أيّامى

87 Farrukhī, *Dīvān*, p. 45, 901. Abū Bakr Ḥaṣīrī.

چه فسون کردی بر من که بتو دادم دل دل چرا دادم خیره بفسون تو بباد

88 Farrukhī, *Dīvān*, p. 27, 568. Abū al-Ḥasan ᶜAlī b. Faḍl b. Aḥmad known as Ḥajjāj. This is the son of the minister Isfarāᵓinī.

هم دل خلق نگه دارد وهم مال امیر کار فرمای چنین در همه آفاق کجاست

89 Abū Tammām, *Dīwān*, p. 3:43, 37. Al-Ḥasan b. Wahb.

فمتى أُرَوّى مِن لِقائكَ هِمَّتى ويُفيقُ قَولى مِن سِواكَ ومِقْوَلى

90 Al-Buḥturī, *Dīwān*, p. 4:2151, 19–20. Ibn al-Fayyāḍ. ᶜAlī b. Muḥammad b. al-Ḥusayn al-Fayyāḍ Abū al-Ḥasan was a secretary to Isḥāq b. Kundāj. He was from a Persian family. Al-Ṣīrafī dates al-Buḥturī's poems to him to 269/882 (Al-Buḥturī, 1:607).

أبعدَ ما أعلَقَ الأقوامُ مِيسمَهم بصفحتي وقتلتُ الأرض عرفاناً

يَرجو البَخيلُ اغترارِى أو مُخادَعَتى حتّى أسوقَ إلَيه المدْحَ مَجّانا

91 Al-Buḥturī, *Dīwān*, p. 4:2254, 17. Al-Mutawakkil.

راموا النَّجاةَ وكيف تَنْجُو عُصْبَةٌ مَطلوبَةٌ باللهِ والسلطانِ

92 Al-Buḥturī, *Dīwān*, p. 4:2274, 31. Al-Mu^ctazz.

كيف لم يَقْبَلوا الأمانَ وقد كا نت حَياةٌ لِمثلهم فى الأمانِ

93 Farrukhī, *Dīvān*, p. 40, 786. Muḥammad b. Maḥmūd b. Sabuktegīn.

آن همت وآن دولت وآن راى كه اوراست او را كه خلاف آرد وبا او كه برآيد

94 Benveniste, Emile, *Problems in General Linguistics*, tr. Mary Elizabeth Meek (Coral Gables, Florida, 1966), p. 73.

95 Abū Tammām, *Dīwān*, p. 2:81, 5. Muḥammad b. Al-Haytham b. Shubāna.

فلا تحسبا هنداً لها الغَدْرُ وَحْدَها سجِيَّةَ نَفسٍ كلُّ غانيةٍ هِندُ

96 Farrukhī, *Dīvān*, p. 352, 7080. Muḥammad b. Maḥmūd b. Sabuktegīn.

نكند كندى وقتى كه كند پاداشن نكند تندى وقتى كه دهد بادافراه

97 Al-Buḥturī, *Dīwān*, p. 1:267, 12. [c]Abd al-Raḥmān b. Nahīk.

ما أَمَلِى فيك بالضعيفِ ولا ظَنّى فى نُجْحِهِ بمكذوبِ

98 Al-Buḥturī, *Dīwān*, p. 3:1851, 20. Al-Khiḍr b. Aḥmad.

لا يخلِطُ الغَدْرَ بالوفاءِ ولا يَبيعُ إلْفَ الخُلاّنِ بالمَلَلِ

99 [c]Unṣurī, *Dīvān*, p. 236, 2291. Naṣr b. Sabuktegīn.

جهان بى تو تاراج اهريمن است بره گرگ درّد چو نبود شبان

100 Al-Buḥturī, *Dīwān*, p. *Dīwān*, p. 3:1904, 32. Khālid b. Yazīd al-Shaybānī.

لولا نداهُ ولولا سيفُ نِقمَتِه دارتْ رحى الدينِ والدنيا على ثَكَلِ

101 Farrukhī, *Dīvān*, p. 362, 7299. Maḥmūd b. Sabuktegīn.

اى آنكه ملک هرگز بر تو بدل نجويد اى آنكه خسروى را از خسروان تو شايى

102 Farrukhī, *Dīvān*, p. 349, 7023. Yūsuf b. Sabuktegīn.

من كه معروف شدستم به پرستيدن او به پرستيدن هر كس نكنم پشت دوتاه

103 Al-Buḥturī, *Dīwān*, p. 2:1147, 4. Muḥammad b. al-[c]Abbās al-Kilābī. Muḥammad b. al-[c]Abbās al-Kilābī Abū Mūsā was a general of Ibn Ṭūlūn who fought and lost at Aleppo in 268/881. When Khumārawayh took over, Muḥammad b. al-[c]Abbās al-Kilābī was appointed over Aleppo in 271/884 (Al-Buḥturī, *Dīwān*, p. 2:680).

يا عَلْوَ لو شِئتِ أَبدلتِ الصُّدودَ لنا وَصْلاً ولانَ لِصَبٍّ قَلبُكِ القاسي

104 Abū Tammām 1:75, 1. Mālik b. Ṭawq al-Taghlibī. Mālik b. Ṭawq b. Mālik b. [c]Itāb al-Taghlibī was the ruler of al-Rahbah, between al-Raqqah and Baghdad on the Euphrates during al-Ma[c]mūn's rule, and he supervised Damascus under al-Mutawakkil. He died in 260/873 (Al-Buḥturī, *Dīwān*, p. 1:78).

لو أنَّ دهراً ردَّ رجْعَ جَوابِ أو كفَّ من شأوَيهِ طُولُ عِتابِ

لعذلتُهُ في دمنتين بأمرة مَمحوَّتين لزينبٍ وربابِ

105 [c]Unṣurī, *Dīvān*, p. 55, 680. Dabīrsiyāqī does not list a patron for this poem.

گر نبودى عزم او دولت نبودى پيشرو ور نبودى حزم او ملكت نبودى استوار

106 Al-Buḥturī, *Dīwān*, p. 2:1300, 29. Al-Mutawakkil. Al-Mutawakkil was the son of al-Mu[c]taṣim and was born in 206/822. When his brother al-Wāthiq died leaving no designated successor, a group of administrative and Turkish military elites appointed al-Mutawakkil caliph. He purged some of the group that appointed him and replaced the Turkish military elites with his sons as supervisors of most of the provinces. He attempted to recruit new troops to

undermine the power of the Turkish troops, including Arabs, Iranians, and Armenians, and established a new palace center near but not in Samarra in 245/859. In addition, he sought the wide support of those who advocated hadith transmission as the central feature of religion, ending the hegemony of the theological and rationalist Mu^ctazila at court. Due to his opposition to the Turkish military elite, they and his son al-Muntaṣir assassinated him in 247/861 ('Al-Mutawakkil Abū al-Faḍl Dja^cfar b. Muḥammad' in Bearman, *EI*, 2008).

فلولا أميرُ المؤمنين وطَولُهُ   لَعادَتْ جُيوبٌ والدِّماءُ رُدوعُها

107 Abū Tammām, *Dīwān*, p. 1:173, 54. Abū Sa^cīd al-Thaghrī.

وإذا الصُّنْعُ كان وَحْشاً فَمُلِّـ   ـيتَ بِرغمِ الزمانِ صُنعاً رَبيبا

108 Al-Buḥturī, *Dīwān*, p. 2:1078, 12. Isḥāq b. Nuṣayr. Isḥāq b. Nuṣayr al-^cIbādī al-Naṣrānī Abū Ya^cqūb was a secretary in the Egypt administration under Khumārawayh b. Aḥmad b. Ṭūlūn, and he died in 298/910 (Al-Buḥturī, *Dīwān*, p. 2:815).

إنْ أَعْجَزَ القومَ حَمْلُ الحقِّ قامَ به   ثَبْتَ المَقامِ جَهيراً غَيرَ مغمورِ

109 ^cUnṣurī, *Dīvān*, p. 34, 377. Maḥmūd b. Sabuktegīn.

شود گر زآهن تن کند بدخواه او در کارزار   باد خوش چون بر تن او بگذرد سوهان

110 Farrukhī, *Dīvān*, p. 203, 4065. Mas^cūd b. Maḥmūd b. Sabuktegīn.

گر کسی بر دل جز طاعتش اندیشه کند   موی گردد بمثل بر تن آن کس غماز

111 Al-Buḥturī, *Dīwān*, p. 2:1101, 32. Al-Khiḍr b. Aḥmad al-Taghlibī.

إذا جالتْ الأفكارُ فيك تَبيَّنتْ   بأنَّك لا تَحوِى مَكارِمَكَ الفِكَرُ

112 Andras Hamori on the Arabic poet al-Mutanabbī (Hamori, Andras, *The Composition of Mutanabbi's Panegyrics to Sayf al-Dawla* (Leiden, 1992), pp. 1–2).

113 Al-Buḥturī, *Dīwān*, p. 2:998, 5. Ibn Bisṭām Abū al-^cAbbās. Aḥmad b. Muḥammad b. Bisṭām was appointed governor of Syria by al-Muwaffaq. The minister al-Qāsim b. ^cUbayd Allāh b. Sulaymān b. Wahb imprisoned Ibn Bisṭām in his house over a personal conflict and later relented and appointed him to Amed and its environs, and then regretted his decision. After al-Qāsim died, Ibn Bisṭām was appointed to a position in Egypt that he occupied until he died in 297/909 (Al-Buḥturī, *Dīwān*, p. 1:134).

يَحُلُّ غُرورُ الوَعْدِ منها عزيمتى   وأحلى مَواعيدِ النِّساءِ غُرورُها

114 Al-Buḥturī, *Dīwān*, p. 2:1079, 8. Aḥmad b. Ayyūb. This may be Aḥmad b. Ayyūb al-Ramlī, as in Ramla in Palestine (Al-Buḥturī, *Dīwān*, p. 1:112).

أَيِسَ العاذلونَ مِن بُرْءِ سُكْرى   إنَّ سُكْرَ العزامِ أقتَلُ سُكْرِ

115 Farrukhī, *Dīvān*, p. 274, 5432. Muḥammad b. Maḥmūd b. Sabuktegīn.

کسیکه سایهٔ فرخ برو فکند همای   به مهتری وبه میری رسد زکار گران

116 Al-Buḥturī, *Dīwān*, p. 2:694, 11. ^cUbayd Allāh b. Yaḥyā b. Khāqān. ^cUbayd Allāh b. Yaḥyā Abū al-Ḥasan was the son of al-Fatḥ b. Khāqān's brother. He was born in 209/824 and was appointed secretary by al-Mutawakkil in 236/850. Al-Mutawakkil later appointed him minister and he held that position until al-Mutawakkil was assassinated in 247/861. ^cUbayd Allāh was exiled under al-Musta^cīn in 248 and reappointed minister under al-Mu^ctamid in 256/870 until he died in a riding accident in 263/876 (Al-Buḥturī, *Dīwān*, p. 1:516).

فَلِفِضَّةِ السيفِ المُحَلَّى حُسنُه   مُتقلَّداً ومَضاؤُهُ لِحديدِهِ

117 See Elias, *Court Society*.

118 ᶜUnṣurī, *Dīvān*, p. 78, 955. Yūsuf b. Sabuktegīn Abū Yaᶜqūb. Yūsuf was the brother of Maḥmūd b. Sabuktegīn and an experienced soldier. At first he supported the rule of Muḥammad b. Maḥmūd, and was in charge of Khurasan. He later deserted to Masᶜūd and supported him. When he took over, Masᶜūd sent Yūsuf on a mission far from the capital so that he could consolidate his power without competition, and when Yūsuf returned, Masᶜūd had him imprisoned (Bosworth, *Ghaznavids*, p. 232).

مثل زنند که جویندهٔ خطر بی حزم   از آرزوی خطر در شود بچشم خطر

119 Abū Tammām, *Dīwān*, p. 2:357, 31. Nūḥ b. ᶜAmr.

وإنما الفتْكُ لذى لأمةٍ   شبعانَ أو ذي كَرَمٍ جائعِ

120 Abū Tammām, *Dīwān*, p. 1:140–41, 10–11. Al-Ḥasan b. Sahl. Al-Ḥasan b. Sahl started work in the service of the powerful administrative family of the Barmakids under Hārūn al-Rashīd. He helped al-Maʾmūn against his brother al-Amīn, and al-Maʾmūn put him in charge of taxation in the provinces that he controlled. Al-Maʾmūn assigned him to establish order in Iraq after al-Maʾmūn was settled in Baghdad, and al-Ḥasan helped to put down Alid and popular revolts. After the mysterious death of his brother, the minister al-Faḍl b. Sahl, he retired from politics to his family home in Wasit, married his daughter to al-Maʾmūn, and died in 236/850 ('Al-Ḥasan b. Sahl' in Bearman, *EI*, 2008).

ومَن لم يُسلِّمْ للنوائبِ أَصبحتْ   خلائقُهُ طُرّاً عليه النوائبا

وقد يَكْهَمُ السيفُ المسمَّى مَنيَّةً   وقد يَرجعُ المرءُ المُظَفَّرُ خائبا

121 Farrukhī, *Dīvān*, p. 39, 773. Muḥammad b. Maḥmūd b. Sabuktegīn.

دل عاشق آنست که بی عشق نباشد   ای وای دلی کو ز پی عشق بر آید

122 Al-Buḥturī, *Dīwān*, p. 2:1311, 11. Al-Mutawakkil.

أَعطاكُموها اللهُ عن عِلْمٍ بكمْ   واللهُ يُعطِى مَن يشاءُ ويَمنعُ

123 Farrukhī, *Dīvān*, p. 276, 5485. Muḥammad b. Maḥmūd b. Sabuktegīn.

هر که را دولت جوان باشد بهر کامی رسد   ایزد او را دولتی داده ست پیروز وجوان

124 Al-Buḥturī, *Dīwān*, p. 2:766, 13. Muḥammad b. Ḥumayd al-Ṭūsī Abū Nahshal. He is referred to as Abū Nahshal on 1:39. Muḥammad b. Ḥumayd al-Ṭūsī al-Ṭāʾī is the son of the general Ḥumayd al-Ṭūsī who was killed in the Abbasid conflict with the Khurramī rebel Bābak in 214/829. Al-Marzubānī refers to Muḥammad b. Ḥumayd and his two brothers as literary types and poets. Al-Buḥturī's poetry for Muḥammad b. Ḥumayd dates to 230/844 (Al-Buḥturī, *Dīwān*, p. 1:39).

وكم لك فى الناسِ من حاسدٍ   وفى الحَسَدِ النَّزْرِ حَظُّ الحَسودِ

125 Benveniste, *Linguistics*, p. 224.

126 Abū Tammām 2:59, 1. Abū al-ᶜAbbās Naṣr b. Manṣūr b. Bassām. Al-Ṣūlī records a report in which Abū Tammām recites this poem for Naṣr b. Manṣūr and when he gets to a certain point, Naṣr warns Abū Tammām against praising that is out of place for a patron, and awards him a yearly payment and a robe. The report indicates that Naṣr died after that in 227/841 (Al-Ṣūlī, *Akhbār Abī Tammām*, p. 266). Al-Buḥturī praised a man who appears to be Naṣr's brother or son, Muḥammad b. Manṣūr b. Bassām or Muḥammad b. Naṣr b. Manṣūr b. Bassām, and who is described as a refined ladies' man with a son who is talented in invective and who spares no one, not even his own family members (Al-Buḥturī, *Dīwān*, p. 1:237).

أأطلالَ هندٍ ساءَ ما اعتَضْتِ من هِندِ   أقايَضْتِ حُورَ العِينِ بالعُونِ والرُّبْدِ

127 Farrukhī, *Dīvān*, p. 319, 6429. Abū Bakr Ḥaṣīrī. Abū Bakr ᶜAbd Allāh b. Yūsuf Sīstānī, known as Abū Bakr Ḥaṣīrī, was a drinking companion of Maḥmūd b. Sabuktegīn. Apparently he came from an elite family in Sīstān, and assisted Maḥmūd in subduing heretics and innovators in religion. He was an enemy of the minister Maymandī, who caused trouble for him during his second round as minister. When Maḥmūd was leaning toward appointing his son Muḥammad heir rather than the more experienced son Masᶜūd, Abū Bakr Ḥaṣīrī sided with Masᶜūd and was an intermediary in his return to power. His son Abū al-Qāsim was also successful in the Ghaznavid court (Yūsufī, *Kāghaz-i Zarr*, pp. 51–5).

چند ازین تنگدلی ای صنم تنگ دهان   هر زمانی مکن ای روی نکوروی گران

Also see ᶜUnṣurī, *Dīvān*, p. 286, 2707 for Aḥmad b. Ḥasan Maymandī, where the vocative address of the companion as a body is bound up with the motifs of telling tales and magic:

> O curly locks of the companion (O companion with curly locks?), because of the abundance of tales that you tell, the tale is yours, if you form an alliance with magicians

ای شکسته زلف یار از بسکه تو دستان کنی   دست دست تست اگر باساحران پیمان کنی

The vocative makes him present and distant, framing the intimacy implied by the body and the motif of verbal communication. The motif of an alliance with magicians refers to the allure of the companion, while it also makes him less accessible.

128 Farrukhī, *Dīvān*, p. 362, 7299. Maḥmūd b. Sabuktegīn.

ای آنکه ملک هرگز بر تو بدل نجوید   ای آنکه خسروی را از خسروان تو شایی

129 ᶜUnṣurī, *Dīvān*, p. 236, 2290. Naṣr b. Sabuktegīn.

ایا پاکدین شاه دانش گزین   زدین تو اهل هوا را هوان

130 Al-Buḥturī, *Dīwān*, p. 1:458, 13–14. Abū Muslim al-Kajjī. Abū Muslim Ibrāhīm b. ᶜAbd Allāh b. Muslim al-Baṣrī al-Kajjī was a hadith transmitter. He was born in 200/815 and moved to Baghdad, and he was appointed governor in Syria. He died in Baghdad in 292/904, and was taken to Basra to be buried (Al-Buḥturī, *Dīwān*, p. 1:457). His entry as a hadith transmitter refers to al-Buḥturī's praise in conjunction with his work as a governor in Syria, not as a hadith transmitter (Al-Baghdādī, al-Khaṭīb Abū Bakr Aḥmad b. ᶜAlī, *Tārīkh Baghdād aw Madīnat al-Salām*, ed. Muṣṭafā ᶜAbd al-Qādir ᶜAṭā, 23 vols. (Beirut 1417/1997), 6:121).

يا أبا مسلمٍ تَلفَّتْ إلى الشَرْ   قِ وأشْرِفْ للبارقِ اللمَّاحِ
مُستطيراً يقومُ في جانِبِ اللَّيـ   ـلِ على عَرَضِهِ مقامَ الصباح

131 Abū Tammām, *Dīwān*, p. 2:114–15, 22–3. Abū al-Mughīth al-Rāfiqī Mūsā b. Ibrāhīm. Al-Ṣūlī reports that after he was disappointed by his patron in Egypt and composed invective on him after his death, Abū Tammām moved to Damascus and praised Abū al-Mughīth al-Rāfiqī. He was again disappointed and responded with invective, and then moved on to seek the patronage of caliphs, beginning with an unsuccessful effort with al-Maᵓmūn when he was in Syria (Abū Tammām, *Dīwān*, p. 4:605). While Abū al-Mughīth was governor of Homs, the people of the city deposed him and the tax collector. Al-Mutawakkil responded by appointing a new governor and threatening military action if the people did not accept him. When they rose up against

the second governor, the caliph ordered that three of their leaders be whipped and, if they died, crucified upon their doors (Al-Buḥturī, *Dīwān*, p. 1:193).

أموسى بنَ إبراهيمَ دَعْوَةَ خامسٍ   به ظَمَأُ التثريبِ لا ظَمَأُ الوِرْدِ

جَليدٌ على عَتْبِ الخُطوبِ إذا التوَتْ   وليسَ على عَتْبِ الأَخِلاَّءِ بالجَلْدِ

132 Al-Buḥturī, *Dīwān*, p. 2:1074, 1. Al-Mu^ctazz.

كم لَيلَةٍ بيكِ بِتُّ أُسهَرُها   ولَوعةٍ في هواكِ أُضْمِرُها

133 Farrukhī, *Dīvān*, p. 374, 7574. Muḥammad b. Maḥmūd b. Sabuktegīn.

زهی خسروی کینهمه روشنایی   زرای تو گیرد همی نو بهاری

134 Farrukhī, *Dīvān*, p. 123, 2413. Muḥammad b. Maḥmūd b. Sabuktegīn.

آفرین بر یمین دولت باد   آن بلند اختر بزرگ آثار

135 Abū Tammām, *Dīwān*, p. 2:93, 41. Muḥammad b. al-Haytham Shubāna.

وكم لكَ عِندى مِن يدٍ مستهِلَّةٍ   عليَّ ولا كُفرانَ عندى ولا جَحْدُ

136 Al-Buḥturī, *Dīwān*, p. 2:972, 28. Muḥammad b. Badr. Muḥammad b. Badr Abū al-ᶜAbbās is from the tribe of Banū al-Ḥārith b. Kaᶜb on his father's side and Persian on his mother's side (Al-Buḥturī, *Dīwān*, p. 1:225).

حَبذا أنتَ مِن كريمٍ وإنْ كِدْ   تَ تُدانى شأْنى وتُخْمِلُ ذِكرى

137 Abū Tammām, *Dīwān*, p. 2:92, 33–4. Muḥammad b. al-Haytham b. Shubāna Abū al-Ḥusayn.

وكم أمطرتْهُ نَكبَةٌ ثُمَّ فُرِّجتْ   ولله فى تفريجِها ولَكَ الحَمدُ

وكم كان دهراً للحوادثِ مُضْغةً   فأضحَتْ جميعاً وهى عن لحمِهِ دُرْدُ

138 Al-Buḥturī, *Dīwān*, p. 3:1436, 43. Abū al-Ḥusayn Muḥammad b. Ṣafwān al-ᶜUqaylī. Muḥammad b. Ṣafwān's father was well known as a leader of the lands of the Muḍar tribal confederation, and his grandfather was appointed over Armenia and was influential in the court of al-Manṣūr. His father Ṣafwān rebelled in support of al-Muᶜtazz during the rule of al-Mustaᶜīn and died in captivity at Samarra in 253/867 (Al-Buḥturī, *Dīwān*, p. 3:1432).

للهِ أنتَ رحى هَيجاءَ مُشعَلَةٍ   إذا القنا مِن صُباباتِ الطُّلى رَعَفا

139 Abū Tammām, *Dīwān*, p. 2:189, 22. ᶜUmar b. ᶜAbd al-ᶜAzīz al-Ṭāʾī.

لله درُّ بَنِى عبد العزيزِ فكم   أردَوا عزيزَ عِدىً فى خدِّهِ صَعَرُ

140 Al-Buḥturī, *Dīwān*, p. 1:411, 3. Isḥāq b. Kundāj. Isḥāq was from Khazar and became one of the most well-known generals under al-Muᶜtamid, who sent him to fight the Zanj revolt in 259/872. He fought the Kurds north of Mawsil, encountered a Kharijite leader and killed him, defeated a Taghlibī leader at Nisibin and took over the region, which al-Muᶜtamid acknowledged by placing him in charge of Mawsil. When al-Muᶜtamid tried to go to Egypt and was threatened by Ibn Ṭūlūn on the way there, Isḥāq captured the troops who were after him and safely returned al-Muᶜtamid to the palace in Samarra. He was later placed in charge of Ibn Ṭūlūn's region and the police as far as Tunisia. He was defeated in several battles and finally captured by Khumārawayh, with whom he was reconciled (Al-Buḥturī, *Dīwān*, p. 1:408).

شمسٌ أضاءَتْ أمامَ الشمس إذْ بَرَزَتْ   تَسيرُ فى ظُعُنٍ منهم وأحداجِ

141 Abū Tammām, *Dīwān*, p. 2:184, 4. ᶜUmar b. ᶜAbd al-ᶜAzīz al-Ṭāʾī. ᶜUmar b. ᶜAbd al-ᶜAzīz is from Homs (Abū Tammām, *Dīwān*, p. 2:184). He is the uncle of Abū al-Khaṭṭāb al-Ḥasan b. Muḥammad al-Ṭāʾī, who was linked with al-Buḥturī in 226/840 (Al-Buḥturī, *Dīwān*, p. 1:294).

رِيَمٌ أبَتْ أنْ يَرِيمَ الحُزنُ لى جَلَداً   والعَيْنُ عَينٌ بماءِ الشَوقِ تَبتدِرُ

142 Al-Buḥturī, *Dīwān*, p. 3:1827, 3. Abū Bakr, known as Jarādat al-Kātib. Jarādat al-Katib was the secretary of the minister Ismāʾīl b. Bulbul. After Ismāʾīl was arrested in 278, Jarādat al-Kātib was arrested in 279/892 (Al-Buḥturī, *Dīwān*, p. 1:260).

زائرٌ في المنام يَهجُرُ يَقظا نَ ويَدنُو مع المنام وِصالُه

143 Farrukhī, *Dīvān*, p. 109, 2104 and 2106. Muḥammad b. Maḥmūd b. Sabuktegīn.

بتی که خانه بدو چون بهار بود ونبود   شگفت ازیرا کز بت کنند خانه بهار ...

بتی که چشم من از بس نگار چهرهٔ او   نگار خانه شد ار چه پدید نیست نگار

144 Al-Buḥturī, *Dīwān*, p. 1:417, 14. Abū Saqr Ismāʿīl b. Bulbul. Ismāʿīl was born in 230/844 and claimed descent from Shaybān. Al-Muwaffaq appointed him minister to his brother al-Mu'tamid in 265/878. After al-Muwaffaq arrested Ṣāʿid b. Makhlad in 272/885, he used Ismāʾīl as secretary to the exclusion of others. Neither al-Muwaffaq nor Ismāʿīl had a good relationship with al-Muwaffaq's son, al-Muʿtaḍid. After the death of al-Muwaffaq in 278/891, al-Muʿtaḍid had Ismāʾīl and his companions arrested and their houses plundered. Ismāʾīl was tortured and locked in extremely heavy shackles, in which he remained until he died later that year, and in which he was buried (Al-Buḥturī, 1:115, 'Ismāʿīl b. Bulbul, Abū'l-Saḳr' in Bearman, *EI*, 2008).

أخو العَزْم لم تَصدُرْ صريمةُ عَزْمِهِ   بمُقْتضَبٍ من عاثر الرأيِ مُخْدَجِ

145 ʿUnṣurī, *Dīvān*, p. 55, 685. Dabīrsiyāqī does not list a patron for this poem.

نیکنام است وعجب باشد جوان نیکنام   بردبار است وعجبتر پادشاه بردبار

146 Abū Tammām, *Dīwān*, p. 2:157, 19. Muḥammad b. al-Haytham b. Shubāna Abū Al-Ḥusayn. In other places he is Muḥammad b. al-Haytham b. Shabāba. Muḥammad b. al-Haytham is described as being from Marv (Abū Tammām, 1:282). He is also listed as Khurasani, and described as the person in charge of state communications. A secretary describes him receiving a poem from Abū Tammām at al-Jabal. In response to Abū Tammām's thank you note in the form of a poem, Muḥammad b. al-Haytham gives Abū Tammām all of the robes in his house (Al-Ṣūlī, *Akhbār Abī Tammām*, pp. 188, 190). In a poem by al-Buḥturī dedicated to an Aḥmad b. al-Haytham al-Asdī, al-Ṣīrafī speculates that Aḥmad is Muḥammad b. al-Haytham's brother and notes that the third verse of the poem refers to the tribe of Azd (Al-Buḥturī, *Dīwān*, p. 3:2029).

حليمٌ والحَفيظةُ منه خِيمٌ   وأيُّ النارِ ليسَ لها شرارُ

147 Farrukhī, *Dīvān*, p. 203, 4048–9. Masʿūd b. Maḥmūd b. Sabuktegīn. Masʿūd ruled the Ghaznavid Empire 421/1030–432/1040. Born in 388/998, he was the eldest son of Maḥmūd and gained experience as a provincial governor and general. After Maḥmūd designated his younger and less experienced son Muḥammad heir in 421/1030, Masʿūd took over and sent Muḥammad into captivity, and the caliph confirmed Masʿūd's legitimacy with titles. He had difficulty balancing control of the eastern and western regions of the empire, which ranged from India to Iran. After he was defeated in the west in 431/1040, he attempted to relocate in the east, only to be deposed and killed by his troops ('Masʿūd b. Maḥmūd, Abū Sa'id, Shihāb al-Dawla, Djamāl al-Milla' in Bearman, *EI*, 2008).

آشتی کردم با دوست پس از جنگ دراز   هم بدان شرط که با من نکند دیگر ناز

زانچه کرده ست پشیمان شد وعذر همه خواست   عذر پذیرفتم ودل در کف او دادم باز

148 Al-Buḥturī, *Dīwān*, p. 3:1819, 12. ʿAlāʾ b. Ṣāʿid b. Makhlad Abū ʿĪsā. ʿAlāʾ's father Ṣāʿid b. Makhlad was the minister of al-Muʿtamid and al-Wāthiq, and also played a leading role in the military response to the revolt of the Zanj in Basra and the Saffarids in southern Iran. Al-Muwaffaq, after sending him to lead the fight against the Saffarids in 271/884, arrested him and his brother and two sons, including ʿAlāʾ Abū ʿĪsā, and plundered their homes. Ṣāʿid, who was Christian, had become Muslim when he first became minister and was known for his piety. Abū ʿĪsā was interested in astrology, and when al-Muwaffaq imprisoned him he made a prediction based on the stars that he would be released after thirteen days, and he was, for he died in prison in 272/885 and was turned over to his family for burial (Al-Buḥturī, *Dīwān*, p. 1:53).

تناسَى عَهدَهُ سَكَنٌ خَلِيٌّ   وناءَ بوَدِّهِ خِلٌّ مَلولُ

149 Abū Tammām, *Dīwān*, p. 3:268, 47. Isḥāq b. Ibrāhīm b. Ḥusayn b. Muṣʿab.

فسننتَ بالمعروف مِن أثَر الندَى   سُنَناً شفَتْ مِن دهرنا المذمومِ

150 Al-Buḥturī, *Dīwān*, p. 3:1608, 14. Al-Fatḥ b. Khāqān.

أطَلَّ بنُعماه فمَن ذا يُطاولُهْ   وعمَّ بِجَدْواهُ فَمَن ذا يُساجِلُهْ

151 Al-Buḥturī, *Dīwān*, p. 3:1604, 41–2. Muḥammad b. Yūsuf Abū Saʿīd al-Thaghrī. Abū Saʿīd al-Thaghrī is described as Ṭāʾī from Marv, and is best known as a successful general who put down the Khurramī revolt of Bābak beginning with a victory in 220/835. He worked for al-Muʿtaṣim and died under al-Mutawakkil in 230/844 while he was in charge of Armenia and Azerbayjan, and was succeeded in his military and tax collecting work by his son Yūsuf (Al-Buḥturī, *Dīwān*, p. 1:5).

وفى يَومِ منويلٍ وقد لَمَسَ الهُدى   بأظفارِهِ أو همَّ أن يتناولا

دَفعتَ عنِ الإسلامِ ما لو يُصيبُهُ   لما زالَ شخصاً بعدها مُتضائلا

152 Abū Tammām, *Dīwān*, p. 3:353, 8. Al-Ḥasan b. Wahb. Al-Ḥasan b. Wahb b. Saʿīd b. ʿAmr Abū ʿAlī was born in 186/802. Al-Ḥasan was secretary to Muḥammad b. ʿAbd al-Malik al-Zayyāt and minister for al-Wāthiq. The family was Christian and became affiliated with Banū Ḥārith b. Kaʿb. His career ended when al-Wāthiq imprisoned the secretaries and confiscated their money, including al-Ḥasan (Al-Buḥturī, *Dīwān*, p. 1:158).

تُعيرُكَ مُقْلَةٌ نَطِفَتْ ولكنْ   قُصاراها على قلبٍ برىٍّ

153 ʿUnṣurī, *Dīvān*, p. 27, 320. Maḥmūd b. Sabuktegīn.

رامش افزایی کند وقتی که در مجلس بود   لشکر آرایی کند روزیکه در میدان بود

154 Al-Buḥturī, *Dīwān*, p. 1:197, 10. Al-Fatḥ b. Khāqān.

سأثنى فؤادى عنك أو أتبَعُ الهوى   إليك إنِ استعصَى فؤادىَ أو أبى

155 Al-Buḥturī, *Dīwān*, p. 1:153, 29. Al-Fatḥ b. Khāqān.

سأصبِرُ حتى ألاقِى رِضا   كَ إمّا بعيداً وإمّا قريباً

156 Abū Tammām, *Dīwān*, p. 2:112, 11. Abū al-Mughīth al-Rāfiqī.

سأجهدُ عَزمِى والمطايا فإنّنِى   أرى العَفْوَ لا يُمتاحُ إلاَّ مِن الجَهْدِ

157 Farrukhī, *Dīvān*, p. 139, 2749. Yūsuf b. Sabuktegīn

ای پسرجنگ بنه بوسه بیار   این همه جنگ ودرشتی به چه کار

158 ʿUnṣurī 231, 2239. Naṣr b. Sabuktegīn.

فرو شکن تو مرا پشت وزلف بر مشکن   بزن بتیغ دلم را بتیغ غمزه مزن

159 Abū Tammām, *Dīwān*, p. 2:153, 3. Muḥammad b. Haytham b. Shubāna.

قِفا نُعطِ المنازلَ من عيون   لها فى الشَوقِ أحساءٌ غِزارُ

160 Abū Tammām, *Dīwān*, p. 1:157, 1–2. Abū Saʿīd al-Thaghrī

مِن سَجايا الطُّلولِ ألاَّ تُجيبا   فصَوابٌ مِن مُقلَةٍ أنْ تَصوبا

فاسألَنْها واجعلْ بُكاكَ جواباً   تجِدِ الشوقَ سائلاً ومُجيبا

161 Farrukhī, *Dīvān*, p. 118, 2287. Muḥammad b. Maḥmūd b. Sabuktegīn.

چرا دوات گهر داد شاه شرق بتو   در اين حديث تأمل كن ونكو بنگر

162 Al-Buḥturī, *Dīwān*, p. 2:1241, 41. Al-Fatḥ b. Khāqān.

لك الخَيْرُ إنّى لاحقٌ بك فاتّئدْ   عليَّ وإنِّى قائلٌ لك فاسمَعِ

163 Abū Tammām, *Dīwān*, p. 2:292, 22. ʿAyyāsh. This is ʿAyyāsh b. Lahīʿa al-Ḥadramī, a tax collector, the patron whom Abū Tammām praised early in his career in Egypt and later composed invective on after his death (Abū Tammām, *Dīwān*, p. 4:605; 'Abū Tammām' in Bearman, *EI*, 2008).

كُنْ طويلَ الندَى عريضاً فقد سا   دَ ثَنائى فيكَ الطويلُ العريضُ

164 Abū Tammām, *Dīwān*, p. 1:81, 16. Mālik b. Ṭawq al-Taghlibī.

فأَقِلْ أُسامةَ جُرْمَها واصْفَحْ لها   عنه وهَبْ ما كان للوهّابِ

165 Al-Buḥturī, *Dīwān*, p. 4:2271, 14. Al-Muʿtazz.

سَلْ به تخبَرِ العَجيبَ وإن كا   ن السَّماعُ المأثورُ دونَ العِيانِ

166 Al-Buḥturī, *Dīwān*, p. 3:1791, 36. Muḥammad b. ʿAbd Allāh b. Ṭāhir. Al-Mutawakkil brought him from Khurasan and appointed him over Baghdad. He flourished under al-Muʿtazz and died in 253/867 (Al-Buḥturī, *Dīwān*, p. 2:962).

فلا تكذِبَنْ عن فضلِهِ ووفائه   فما هو في هاتين إلاّ السمَوألُ

167 Al-Buḥturī, *Dīwān*, p. 1:342, 29. Al-Khiḍr b. Aḥmad.

خُذْها إليك وسيلةً من راغبٍ   مُتَقَرِّبٍ مُتوصِّلٍ مُتسبِّبِ

168 Abū Tammām, *Dīwān*, p. 1:258, 56. Muḥammad b. ʿAbd al-Malik al-Zayyāt. Muḥammad b. ʿAbd al-Malik b. Abān b. Ḥamza known as Ibn al-Zayyāt Abū Jaʿfar was minister under al-Muʿtaṣim and al-Wāthiq. He continued under al-Mutawakkil until he killed him in 233/847 (Al-Buḥturī, *Dīwān*, p. 1:632).

خُذْها مُغَرِّبةً فى الأرضِ آنِسةً   بكلِّ فهمٍ غريبٍ حِينَ تَغْترِبُ

169 Farrukhī, *Dīvān*, p. 360, 7264. Abū Bakr Ḥaṣīrī.

خدمت او كن ومخدوم شو وشاد بزى   من از اينگونه مگر ديدم سالى پنجاه

170 ʿUnṣurī, *Dīvān*, p. 123, 1375. Abū al-Ḥasan. Perhaps this is the son of the minister Isfarāʾinī, Abū al-Ḥasan ʿAlī b. Abū al-ʿAbbās Faḍl b. Aḥmad Isfarāʾinī, one patron with this nickname in Dabīrsiyāqī's list of patrons of ʿUnṣurī's contemporary Farrukhī (Farrukhī, p. 43). Isfarāʾinī was the first minister of Maḥmūd b. Sabuktegīn for ten years until he tortured him to death (Bosworth, *Ghaznavids*, pp. 57, 71). Or perhaps it is Abū al-Ḥasan Manṣūr who is probably Manṣūr b. Ḥasan Maymandī, the other patron with this nickname, brother of the minister Aḥmad b. Ḥasan Maymandī (Farrukhī, *Dīvān*, p. 43).

خدمت او گير ار ايدون افتخارت ارزوست   ار نگيرى خدمت او از تو گيرد افتخار

171 Farrukhī, *Dīvān*, p. 120, 2343. Muḥammad b. Maḥmūd b. Sabuktegīn

دلشاد زى وكامروا باش وظفر ياب   بر كام وهواى دل وبر دشمن غدار

172 ʿUnṣurī, *Dīvān*, p. 46, 549. Maḥmūd b. Sabuktegīn

جهان گیر وکینه کش از بدسگالان ملک باش واز نعمت وملک بر خور

173 Farrukhī, *Dīvān*, p. 46, 922. Abū Bakr Ḥaṣīrī

جاودان زی وهمین رسم وهمین عادت دار خانهٔ قرمطیانرا بفکن لاد از لاد

174 ᶜUnṣurī, *Dīvān*, p. 203, 1988. Maḥmūd b. Sabuktegīn

جاوید جهاندار وخداوند جهان باش تو شاد بکام دل واعدات مغمّم

175 ᶜUnṣurī, *Dīvān*, p. 115, 1319. Naṣr b. Sabuktegīn

خداوند بزی شادان برسم وسیرت رادان ابا شادی تو آبادان بمشکین بادهٔ احمر

176 ᶜUnṣurī, *Dīvān*, p. 120, 1353–54. Maḥmūd b. Sabuktegīn.

تا همی گردد فصول عالم از گشت فلک گه تموز وگاه تیر وگه زمستان گه بهار

شاه را سر سبز باد وجان بجای وتن قوی تیغ تیز وامر نافذ بادش ودل شاد خوار

177 Farrukhī, *Dīvān*, p. 357, 7189 and 7191. Aḥmad b. Ḥasan Maymandī Abū al-Qāsim.

همیشه تا چو هوا سرد گشت وباغ دژم کنند گرم ودل افروز خانه وخرگاه ...

به هر مرادی فرمانبر تو باد فلک به هرهوایی یاریگر تو باد اله

178 Farrukhī, *Dīvān*, p. 275, 5454–5456. Muḥammad b. Maḥmūd b. Sabuktegīn.

همیشه تا چو بر دلبران بود مرمر همیشه تا چو لب نیکوان بود مرجان

همیشه تا چو دو رخسار عاشقان باشد بروزگار خزان روی برگهای رزان

بکام خویش زیاد وبآرزو برساد بشکر باد زعمر دراز وبخت جوان

179 ᶜUnṣurī, *Dīvān*, p. 98, 1171–1172. Maḥmūd b. Sabuktegīn.

بقای شاه حهان باد وعزّ ودولت او تنش درست ونگهدارش ایزد دادار

خجسته باد بدو عید وروزه پذرفته خجسته باد بر او سال وماه ولیل ونهار

180 Kevin Crotty emphasizes that Pindar's poetry praises the victorious, but clarifies that the victorious and the defeated are not completely distinct, since the victor may soon face defeat. Crotty points out: 'Although the description of the world as a moral, orderly place is never rejected … it is by no means the only or the ultimate description. It represents one view, to be set off against another, which lays greater stress on the unpredictability and seeming disorder of the world' (Crotty, Kevin, *Song and Action: The Victory Odes of Pindar* (Baltimore, Maryland, 1982), pp. x, 18).

Chapter 5

1 In a study of Abū Tammām, Suzanne Stetkevych explains that elaborate rhetoric is the obverse of interpretation, so that elaborate rhetoric (*badīᶜ*) is a way of encoding meaning and interpretation (*taʾwīl*) is a way of decoding it (Stetkevych, Suzanne Pinckney, *Abu Tammam and the Poetics of the Abbasid Age* (Leiden, 1991), p. 8).

2 In Greek epic, the describer's interpretation of what is described is an integral feature of description (Becker, Andrew Sprague, *The Shield of Achilles and the Poetics of Ekphrasis* (Lanham, Maryland, 1995), p. 28).

3 Michael Roberts observes in a study of Latin prose, 'Late antiquity preferred juxtaposition and contrast to logical interrelationship; contiguity no longer required continuity. The impression of an organic whole, the sense of proportion, is lost, but it is compensated for by the elaboration of the individual episode' (Roberts, Michael, *The Jeweled Style: Poetry and Poetics in Late*

Antiquity (Ithaca, New York, 1989), p. 56). Dick Davis suggested this book to me, and shared an unpublished essay to illustrate the usefulness of its approach in another genre of Persian literature.

4 Charles-Henri de Fouchécour describes the verse as the basic unit of the Persian *qaṣīda*, and explains that the poet works it like a gem (de Fouchécour, *La description de la nature*, p. 5). Abū Tammām uses the elaborate rhetoric of description to 'bring forth ideas, justify and explain them, and confront and compare them with one another' (Al-Ḥāwī, Ilyā, *Fann al-waṣf wa tatawwuruhu fī al-shi^{c}r al-^{c}arabiyya* (Beirut, 1987), p. 152). Discussing late antique mosaics, Michael Roberts proposes that, 'The preference for this technique of organization probably has something to do with the desire to make comparisons.' (M. Roberts, *Jeweled Style*, p. 89).

5 Citing Gian Biagio Conte, Don Fowler observes that many features of elaborate rhetoric refuse to be one way or the other, generating correspondences and contrasts in whose interpretation there is room for disagreement. Disagreement and discussion are an integral part of the life of a text, since 'art and literature do not exist to be appreciated, but to be discussed and argued over, to function as a focus for social dialogue' (Fowler, Don, 'Narrate and describe' in *Roman Constructions: Readings in Postmodern Latin* (Oxford, 2000), pp. 64–85, p. 84).

6 Description is like a fantasy that is a multifaceted mirror of desire rather than a focus on what is described (Beaujour, Michel, 'Some Paradoxes of Description', *Yale French Studies* 61: *Towards a Theory of Description* (1981), pp. 27–59, p. 58).

7 Poetics in Pindar are about the way 'webs of connotation, implication and association branch out in every direction.' These 'multiple patterns of meaning' are a way in which social groups 'find their openness to the future' (Kurke, *Traffic in Praise*, p. 261).

8 Conte, Gian Biagio, *The Rhetoric of Imitation: Genre and Poetic Memory in Virgil and other Latin Poets*, tr. and ed. Charles Segal (Ithaca, New York, 1986), p. 46.

9 de Man, *Allegories of Reading*, p. 124.

10 Al-Nowaihi, Magda, *The Poetry of Ibn Khafājah: A Literary Analysis* (Leiden, 1993), p. 70.

11 Deleuze, Gilles, *Difference and Repetition*, tr. Paul Patton (New York, 1994), p. 270.

12 In descriptive poetry by the medieval Andalusian Arabic poet Ibn Khafāja, the fusion of rhetoric and the ideas that it expresses makes it unclear where one begins and the other ends (Al-Nowaihi, *Ibn Khafājah*, p. 76).

13 Al-Buḥturī, *Dīwān*, p. 2:1017, 11. Muḥammad b. ^{c}Abd Allāh b. Ṭāhir. Muḥammad b. ^{c}Abd Allāh b. Ṭāhir b. al-Ḥusayn b. Mus^{c}ab Abū Al-^{c}Abbās al-Khuzā^{c}ī was a literary type and poet. Al-Mutwakkil brought him from Khurasan to supervise the caliphate in Baghdad, and he was successful under al-Mu^{c}tazz until he died young in 253/867 (Al-Buḥturī, *Dīwān*, p. 2:962).

سِرنا وأنتِ مُقيمةٌ ولَربَّما   كان المُقيمُ علاقةً للسائرِ

14 Abū Tammām, *Dīwān*, p. 3:66, 5. Nūḥ b. ^{c}Amr al-Saksākī.

أَتظنُّنى أَجِدُ السبيلَ إلى العَزا   وَجَدَ الحِمامُ إذاً إليَّ سَبيلا

15 Farrukhī, *Dīvān*, p. 247, 4913. ^{c}Abd Allāh b. Aḥmad b. Lakshan.

چه شوی تنگدل ار بر همی بازم عشق   عشق بازیدن با خوبان رسمیست قدیم

16 Farrukhī, *Dīvān*, p. 247, 4933–4934. ʿAbd Allāh b. Aḥmad b. Lakshan Abū Sahl. ʿAbd Allāh b. Aḥmad b. Lakshan was administrator for Yūsuf b. Sabuktegīn. After Yūsuf was imprisoned by Masʿūd and then died, ʿAbd Allāh b. Aḥmad b. Lakshan's wealth was confiscated, but eventually he was appointed over Bust, his hometown (Yūsufī, *Kāghaz-i Zarr*, p. 147).

مسکن ومستقر خواجه نعیم دگرست   یک دو سالست که من دور بماندم زنعیم

تا درم خوار ودرم بخش بود مرد سخی   تا درم جوی ودرم دوست بود مرد لئیم

17 Al-Buḥturī, *Dīwān*, p. 2:1065, 39. Ibrāhīm b. al-Mudabbir. Ibrāhīm was a secretary and poet, and is known for his love affair with the prominent slave ʿArīb. Al-Mutawakkil favored him, which led ʿUbayd Allāh b. Yaḥyā b. Khāqān to turn al-Mutawakkil against him until he was imprisoned. He was released by Muḥammad b. ʿAbd Allāh b. Ṭāhir. He was a tax collector in Ahwaz when the Zanj revolt occurred, and he and other elites were imprisoned there. He was released in 257/870 with help from the neighbors of the house in which he was imprisoned. He was later minister to al-Muʿtamid and he died in 279/892 while he was in charge of the department of agriculture under al-Muʿtaḍid (Al-Buḥturī, *Dīwān*, p. 1:289).

فإنْ قصَّرَت تلك الوُلاةُ فقد رمى   إلى المجْدِ والى سُؤدَدٍ لم يُقصِّرٌ

18 Farrukhī, *Dīvān*, p. 241, 4796. Aḥmad b. Ḥasan Maymandī.

عطای او بدوام است زایرانش را   گمان مبر که جز او کس عطا دهد بدوام

19 Abū Tammām 3:194, 56. Mālik b. Ṭawq al-Taghlibī.

حِينَ استَوى المُلْكُ واهتَزَّتْ مضارِبُهْ   فى دَولة الأُسْدِ لا فى دولةِ الخَدَمِ

20 ʿUnṣurī, *Dīvān*, p. 44, 514. Maḥmūd b. Sabuktegīn.

در اندر اجلها املها گشاده   اجلها شده با املها برابر

21 ʿUnṣurī, *Dīvān*, p. 28, 323. Maḥmūd b. Sabuktegīn.

خسرو مشرق که یزدانش بهر جا ناصرست   هر که او یزدان پرستد ناصرش یزدان بود

22 ʿUnṣurī, *Dīvān*, p. 34, 382. Maḥmūd b. Sabuktegīn.

سال نو در باغ نو نو دولت وشادی بود   هر دو نو مر دولت نو را همی ارکان شود

23 Abū Tammām, *Dīwān*, p. 3:169, 12. Isḥāq b. Ibrāhīm b. Ḥusayn.

قرَّتْ بقُرَّانَ عَينُ الدين وانشَتَرتْ   بالأَشْتَرَينِ عُيونُ الشِرْكِ فاصطُلِما

24 ʿUnṣurī, *Dīvān*, p. 52, 650. Naṣr b. Sabuktegīn.

بدو بر موافق فزایند خیر   بدو بر مخالف فزایند شر

25 Raymond Scheindlin on the Andalusian Arabic poet al-Muʿtamid b. ʿAbbād (Scheindlin, *Form and Structure*, pp. 41, 35, 60–1).

26 Francette Pacteau has discussed the fragmented description of women in premodern poetry (Pacteau, *Symptom of Beauty*, pp. 27, 66).

27 Al-Buḥturī, *Dīwān*, p. 3:1365, 1. Al-Mutawakkil.

ومهتزَّةِ الأعطافِ نازحةِ العَطْفِ   مُنَعَّمةِ الأطرافِ فاترةِ الطَّرْفِ

28 ʿUnṣurī, *Dīvān*, p. 117, 1327. Maḥmūd b. Sabuktegīn.

ماهتابستش بناگوش وخطش سنبل بود   آفتابستش رخ وبالاش سرو جویبار

29 Abū Tammām, *Dīwān*, p. 2:231, 24. Al-Ḥasan b. Wahb.

للمَجدِ مُستشرِفٌ وللأَدَبِ الـ   مَجْفُوِّ تِرْبٌ وللندَى حِلْسُ

30 Farrukhī, *Dīvān*, p. 237, 4702. Yūsuf b. Sabuktegīn.

هم موفق پادشاهی هم مظفر شهریار   هم مؤید رای میری هم همایون فر همام

31 Farrukhī, *Dīvān*, p. 373, 7553. Muḥammad b. Maḥmūd b. Sabuktegīn.

کریمست وآزاده وتازه رویی   جوانست وآهسته وبا وقاری

32 In one poem by Abū Tammām, 'The homophony is hermeneutic: the poet sees the objects [of conquest] as immanent in the means [of conquest], and the language is made to bear proof of this immanence … In terms of the whole poem, the idea of immanence eliminates chance. (Hamori, Andras, 'Notes on paronomasia in Abū Tammām's style' *Journal of Semitic Studies* 12 (1967), pp. 83–90, p. 86).

33 Ḥusayn al-Wād on Abū Tammām (al-Wād, Ḥusayn, *Al-Lugha wal-shi^{c}r fī dīwān Abī Tammām* (Beirut, 2005/1425), p. 93.

34 ^{c}Unṣurī, *Dīvān*, p. 78, 944. Yūsuf b. Sabuktegīn.

طمع کند که زمعشوق بر خورد عاشق   بدین جهان نبود کار ازین مخالفتر

35 Al-Buḥturī, *Dīwān*, p. 2:906, 1. Ismā^{c}īl b. Bulbul.

أطلُبُ النَّومَ کی یَعودَ غِرارُهُ   بخیالٍ یَحْلو لدَیَّ اغترارُهُ

36 Abū Tammām, *Dīwān*, p. 3:337, 1. ^{c}Alī b. Murr Abū al-Ḥasan. Al-Ṣīrafī did not find any reference to ^{c}Alī b. Murr Abū al-Ḥasan, but suggests that he may be ^{c}Alī b. Yaḥyā al-Armanī Abū al-Ḥasan, who was placed in charge of Egypt between 226–8/840–2, and then appointed to positions under al-Wāthiq and al-Mutawakkil, and who was a general under al-Mutawakkil in invasions of Anatolia in 239/853 and 249/863 and died that year (Al-Buḥturī, *Dīwān*, p. 1:367).

أراكَ أكبَرتَ إدمانی على الدِّمَنِ   وحَمْلی الشَوقَ مِن بادٍ ومُكتَمِنِ

37 Abū Tammām, *Dīwān*, p. 3:261, 1. Isḥāq b. Ibrāhīm.

یا رَبعُ لو رَبَعوا على ابنِ هُمومِ   مُستسلِمٍ لِجَوَى الفِراقِ سَقیمِ

38 Al-Buḥturī, *Dīwān*, p. 2:775, 1. Sa^{c}īd b. ^{c}Abd Allāh b. al-Mughīra al-Ḥalabī.

أَراجعةٌ سُعْدَى علیَّ هُجُودی   ومُبْدِلتی من أنحُس بسعودِ

39 Andras Hamori observes of two sections of praise in poetry by al-Mutanabbī, 'It is worth noting that the poet both parts and connects summary and chronicle' (Hamori, *al-Mutanabbī*, p. 8).

40 ^{c}Unṣurī, *Dīvān*, p. 51, 631. Naṣr b. Sabuktegīn.

نگاهم که دارد ز بیداد او   مگر خدمت خسرو دادگر

41 Abū Tammām, *Dīwān*, p. 3:267, 44. Isḥāq b. Ibrāhīm b. Ḥusayn b. Muṣ^{c}ab.

أَهبتَ لی ریحَ الرجاء فأقدَمَتْ   هِمَمی بها حتى استبَحن هُمومی

42 Abū Tammām, *Dīwān*, p. 3:325, 15. Al-Wāthiq. Abū Ja^{c}far Hārūn b. Al-Mu^{c}taṣim al-Wāthiq became caliph after his father died, and faced a range of rebellions in Palestine, Jordan, Syria, and Arabia. He subscribed to Mu^{c}tazilī theology. Al-Wāthiq died young in 232/847 ('Al-Wāthiḳ Bi'Allāh' in Bearman, *EI*, 2008).

فغَدَوا وقد وَثِقوا برأفةِ واثقٍ   باللهِ طائرُه لهم مَیمون

43 Al-Buḥturī, *Dīwān*, p. 2:867, 14. Al-Khiḍr b. Aḥmad.

یُرجَى مرجِّیه فیُؤتَنَف الغِنَى   ممّا یُنیلُ ویُستجارُ بجارِهِ

44 Al-Buḥturī, *Dīwān*, p. 2:933, 23. Al-Mu^{c}tazz.

عَمِرتَ أمیرَ المؤمنین مسلَّماً   فعُمْرُ النَّدى والجودِ في أنْ تُعمَّرا

45 ^{c}Unṣurī, *Dīvān*, p. 45, 544. Maḥmūd b. Sabuktegīn.

جهان وبزرگی ودولت تو داری   مر این هر سه را بگذران وبمگذر

46 Al-Buḥturī, *Dīwān*, p. 2:1040, 7. Al-Mutawakkil.

قد تمَّ حُسْنُ الجَعفریّ ولم یَکنْ   لِیَتِمَّ إلاَّ بالخلیفةِ جعفرِ

47 Al-Buḥturī, *Dīwān*, p. 2:1006, 24. Al-Muʿtazz.

ففى الشرق إفلاحٌ لموسى ومفلِحٍ   وفى الغرب نَصرٌ يُرتجى لأبِى نَصْرِ

48 Farrukhī, *Dīvān*, p. 112, 2160. Muḥammad b. Maḥmūd b. Sabuktegīn.

شهزاده محمد ملک عالم عادل   بواحمد بن محمود آن علم خريدار

49 Discussing descriptive poetry by Ibn al-Rūmī, Andras Hamori explains that antithetical diction is a common feature of love poetry around the Mediterranean (Hamori, *On the Art*, p. 168).

50 Michael Glünz on Kamāl al-Dīn Iṣfahānī (Glünz, *Panegyrische*, p. 44).

51 Beatrice Gruendler on Ibn al-Rūmī (Gruendler, *Ibn al-Rūmī*, p. 54).

52 ʿUnṣurī, *Dīvān*, p. 61, 756. Naṣr b. Sabuktegīn.

تيرگى مر خط ترا بنده است   روشنايى رخ ترا چاكر

53 Al-Buḥturī, *Dīwān*, p. 2:1070, 7. Al-Mutawakkil.

وتَميلُ من لِينِ الصِّبا فيُقيمُها   قدٌّ يُؤَنَّثُ تارةً ويُذَكَّرُ

54 Abū Tammām, *Dīwān*, p. 3:261, 4. Isḥāq b. Ibrāhīm.

وظِباءُ أُنسِكَ لم تَبَدَّلْ منهم   بظِباءِ وَحشِكَ ظاعناً بمُقيمِ

55 Al-Buḥturī, *Dīwān*, p. 2:1051, 15. Al-Fatḥ b. Khāqān.

هُمُ ثِمادٌ وأنتَ بحرٌ   وهُمْ ظلامٌ وأنتَ فجرُ

56 ʿUnṣurī, *Dīvān*, p. 55, 681. No patron listed.

خواسته زى ما عزيز وخوار باشد خواستن   خواستن زى او عزيز وخواسته گشته ست خوار

57 Farrukhī, *Dīvān*, p. 163, 3278. Abū al-Ḥasan Manṣūr. Dabīrsiyāqī thinks that he is probably the son of Ḥasan Maymandī (Farrukhī, p. 43).

درم بنزد تو خواراست ونزد خلق عزيز   عزيز خلق جهانرا همى چه دارى خوار

58 Al-Buḥturī, *Dīwān*, p. 2:1064, 29. Ibrāhīm b. al-Mudabbir.

مُعَنًّى بإعجالِ البطىءِ إذا احتبى   وصبٌّ بتقديمِ المُرَجَّى المؤَخَّرِ

59 Al-Buḥturī, *Dīwān*, p. 2:1071, 13. Al-Mutawakkil.

عَمَّتْ فواضِلُكَ البريَّةَ فالتقى   فيها المُقِلُّ على الغِنى والمُكثِرُ

60 Al-Buḥturī, *Dīwān*, p. 2:1054, 23. Al-Muʿtazz.

مواهبُ مكّنَّ الفقيرَ من الغِنى   مِراراً وأعدَيْنَ المُقِلَّ على المُثرِى

61 Abū Tammām, *Dīwān*, p. 3:30, 42. Al-Muʿtaṣim.

رجاؤكَ للباغِى الغِنَى عاجِلُ الغِنَى   وأوَّلُ يومٍ من لقائكَ آجِلُهْ

62 ʿUnṣurī, *Dīvān*, p. 20, 234. Naṣr b. Sabuktegīn.

نيست چون مهر او بخلد نسيم   بجهانم چو خشمش آذر نيست

63 Farrukhī, *Dīvān*, p. 164, 3285. Abū al-Ḥasan Manṣūr.

كسيكه خشم تو اورا بژرف چاه افكند   مگر بمهر توگويد مرا زچاه برآر

64 Abū Tammām, *Dīwān*, p. 3:154, 27. Al-Maʾmūn.

لمّا رأيتَ الدينَ يَخْفِقُ قلبُه   والكفرُ فيه تغَطْرُسٌ وعُرامُ

65 Paradox displays the ambivalent quality of objects and emotions in descriptive poetry by the Andalusian Arabic poet Ibn Khafāja (Al-Nowaihi, *Ibn Khafājah*, p. 40).

66 Paradox in mystical lyric by Rūmī 'creates obstacles that the reader has to acknowledge and negotiate. Thus the reader is aware of the urge to participate instead of drifting into dreamy inaction' (Keshavarz, *Rūmī*, p. 31).

67 ʿUnṣurī, *Dīvān*, p. 112, 1289. Naṣr b. Sabuktegīn.

زمن طاعت وزو فرمان همو وصل و همو حرمان   همو درد وهمو درمان همو دزد وهمو داور

68 ʿUnṣurī, *Dīvān*, p. 32, 359, 365. Maḥmūd b. Sabuktegīn.

دردم آن روی است ودرمانم هم از دیدار او   دیده ای دردی که دروی بنگری درمان شود...

هجر او زامید وصل او بود شیرین چو وصل   وصل او از بیم هجرش تلخ چون هجران شود

69 Al-Buḥturī, *Dīwān*, p. 1:14, 9-10. Abū Saᶜīd al-Thaghrī.

أضحَكَ البَينُ يومَ ذاكَ وأبكَى   كلَّ ذى صَبْوةٍ وسَرَّ وساءَ

فجعلنا الوَداعَ فيه سلاماً   وجعلنا الفراقَ فيه لِقاءَ

70 Abū Tammām, *Dīwān*, p. 1:213, 39. Abū Dulaf al-ᶜIjlī. Abū Dulaf al-Qāsim b. ᶜĪsā b. Idrīs al-ᶜIjlī was a wealthy Arab tribal elite whose family settled in northern Iran, and a well-known military commander and literary type. He led part of an unsuccessful campaign against the Tāhirids under al-Ma°mūn, who disliked him because of his Shi'ite sentiment. He served as governor of Damascus under al-Muᶜtaṣim and led Arab troops against Bābak, so that his efforts caused the Iranian general Afshīn to compete with him. He died in Baghdad around 226/841 ('Al-Ḳāsim b. ᶜĪsā b. Idrīs, Abū Dulaf' in Bearman, *EI*, 2008).

فأنتَ لدَيه حاضِرٌ غيرُ حاضِر   جَميعاً وعنهُ غائبٌ غَيرُ غائبِ

71 Abū Tammām, *Dīwān*, p. 2:232, 32. Al-Ḥasan b. Wahb.

القُرْبُ منهم بُعْدٌ من الروح والـ   وَحْشة مِن مِثْلِهم هى الأُنسُ

72 Farrukhī, *Dīvān*, p. 270, 5357, 5360. Muḥammad b. Maḥmūd b. Sabuktegīn.

تو بقیاس آهنی ودشمن کوهست   کوه فراوان فکنده اند به آهن...

دشمن گویم همی به شعر ولیکن   من بجهان در ترا ندانم دشمن

73 ᶜUnṣurī, *Dīvān*, p. 19, 220–1. Naṣr b. Sabuktegīn.

مردمی چیست مردمی عرض است   جز دل پاک اوش جوهر نیست

ذات آزادگی است صورت او   گر چه آزادگی مصوّر نیست

74 Al-Buḥturī, *Dīwān*, p. 1:138, 45–6. Ibn Bisṭām.

يَسُرُّ افتنانِى مَعْشَراً ويسوءُهم   ويَخلُدُ ما أفتنُّ فيهم وأُسهِبُ

ولم يُبقِ كرُّ الدهر غَيرَ علائقٍ   من القَولِ تُرضِى سامعين وتغضِبُ

75 Conte, *Rhetoric of Imitation*, pp. 23–4.

76 Akiko Sumi on a group of Arabic poems (Sumi, Akiko Motoyoshi, *Description in Classical Arabic Poetry: Waṣf, Ekphrasis, and Interarts Theory* (Leiden, 2004), p. 17).

77 Julie Meisami on Khāqānī (Meisami, *Structure and Meaning*, 342).

78 Gruendler, Beatrice, 'Fantastic aesthetics and practical criticism in ninth-century Baghdad', in Marle Hammond and Geert J. Van Gelder (eds), *Takhyīl: Source Texts and Studies* (Warminster, UK, 2007), pp. 196–220.

79 Farrukhī, *Dīvān*, p. 23, 475. Aḥmad b. Ḥasan Maymandī.

ای وعدهٔ تو چون سر زلفین تو نه راست   آن وعده های خوش که همی کرده ای کجاست

80 Farrukhī, *Dīvān*, p. 148, 2944. Masᶜūd b. Maḥmūd b. Sabuktegīn.

چو روشن ستاره همی ره سپارد   سنان تو اندر سپهر مدور

81 Farrukhī, *Dīvān*, p. 157, 3140–2. Aḥmad b. Ḥasan Maymandī.

هر چند که ویرانست امروز خراسان   هر چند نمانده ست درو مردم بسیار

سال دگر از دولت واز نعمت خواجه   چون باغ پر از گل شود اندر مه آذار

رای ونظر خواجه چو باران وبهارست   این هر دو چو پیوست بخندد گل گلزار

82 Farrukhī, *Dīvān*, p. 148, 2937. Masᶜūd b. Maḥmūd b. Sabuktegīn.

همه مردی آموختی وشجاعت   جهان گشتن وتاختن چون سکندر

83 Morris, Wesley, 'Of wisdom and competence' in Michael Clark (ed), *The Revenge of the Aesthetic: The Place of Literature in Theory Today* (Berkeley, California, 2000), pp. 136–56, p. 149.

84 Al-Wād, *Abū Tammām*, pp. 80–1, 75.

85 ^{c}Unṣurī, *Dīvān*, p. 54, 666. No patron listed.

نافه دارد زیر زلف اندر گشاده بی شمار   لاله دارد زیر نافه در شکسته صد هزار

86 Al-Buḥturī, *Dīwān*, p. 1:186, 24. Yūsuf b. Muḥammad. Yūsuf b. Muḥammad was the son of the general Abū Sa^{c}īd al-Thaghrī and he was appointed to the frontier defense and tax collection of Armenia and Azerbayjan after the death of his father in 236/850. A member of the Armenian patriarchate sought to overthrow him, and Yūsuf captured him and sent him in chains to the caliph, causing a widescale uprising against him in which he was killed in 237/851 (Al-Buḥturī, *Dīwān*, p. 1:27).

حتى تقنَّصَ فى أظافِرِ ضَيغمٍ   ملأَتْ هماهِمُهُ القلوبَ وَجيبا

87 Wolfhart Heinrichs on third-/ninth-century Arabic poetry ('Paired metaphors in *muḥdath* poetry', *Occasional Papers of the School of Abbasid Studies* 1 (1986), pp. 1–22, pp. 1–3, 14).

88 Farrukhī, *Dīvān*, p. 146, 2904. Mas^{c}ūd b. Maḥmūd b. Sabuktegīn.

زبس پیچ وچین تاب وخم زلف دلبر   گهی همچو چوگان شود گاه چنبر

89 Al-Buḥturī, *Dīwān*, p. 1:249, 28. Isḥāq b. Ismā^{c}īl b. Nawbakht.

كالبدْرِ أفرَطَ فى العُلُوِّ وضَوءُهُ   للعُصْبَةِ السَّارين جدٌّ قريبِ

90 Farrukhī, *Dīvān*, p. 147, 2905. Mas^{c}ūd b. Maḥmūd b. Sabuktegīn.

گهی لاله را سایه سازد ز سنبل   گهی ماه را درع پوشد زعنبر

91 ^{c}Unṣurī, *Dīvān*, p. 158, 1664. Abū Ja^{c}far Muḥammad b. Abī al-Faḍl.

زدور شد چو عقیق اشکم از عقیق لبش   حدیث او شنو وکن بر آن عقیق گذر

92 Abū Tammām, *Dīwān*, p. 2:456, 1. Abū Sa^{c}īd al-Thaghrī.

قِرَى دارِهم منِّى الدموعُ السوافِك   وإنْ عاد صُبْحِى بعدَهم وهو حالِكُ

93 Farrukhī, *Dīvān*, p. 147, 2912. Mas^{c}ūd b. Maḥmūd b. Sabuktegīn.

همی گشت زان فخر وزان شادمانی   صنوبر بلند وستاره منور

94 Farrukhī, *Dīvān*, p. 148, 2928. Mas^{c}ūd b. Maḥmūd b. Sabuktegīn.

به نیزه گذارندهٔ کوه آهن   به حمله ربایندهٔ باد صرصر

95 Abū Tammām, *Dīwān*, p. 2:380, 15. Abū Sa^{c}īd al-Thaghrī.

كانوا بُرودَ زمانِهم فتصَدَّعوا   فكانَّما لَبِسَ الزمانُ الصُّوفا

96 Abū Tammām, *Dīwān*, p. 2:433, 15. Abū Sa^{c}īd al-Thaghrī.

يَتساقَون فى الوغَى كأسَ مَوتٍ   وهى مَوصولةٌ بكأسِ رَحيقِ

97 Al-Nowaihi, *Ibn Khafājah*, pp. 32–3.

98 Al-Buḥturī, *Dīwān*, p. 1:231, 7. Ṣā^{c}id b. Makhlad.

هى الشَّمسُ إلاَّ أنَّ شمساً تكشَّفتْ   لمبصرِها وأنَّها فى ثيابِها

99 Al-Buḥturī, *Dīwān*, p. 1:229, 35. Muḥammad b. Badr.

درٌّ مِنَ الشِّعْرِ لا يَظْلِمُهُ ناظمُهُ   ولم يَزُغْ مُخْطِئَ التوسيط ثاقبُهُ

100 Farrukhī, *Dīvān*, p. 147, 2913–24. Mas^{c}ūd b. Maḥmūd b. Sabuktegīn.

برمز این مرا گفت آن شکرین لب   که ای شاعر اندر سخن ژرف بنگر

مرا با صنوبر همانند کردی   بقد وبرخ با ستاره برابر

چه ماند برخسار خوبم ستاره   چه ماند بقد بلندم صنوبر

ستاره کجا دارد از سنبل آذین   صنوبر کجا دارد از لاله افسر
مرازین سپس چون صفت کرد خواهی   بچیزی صفت کن که از من نکوتر
بگفت این وبگذشت واندر گذشتن   همی گفت نرمک بزیر لب اندر
ستاره چو من گل فشانده ست بر رخ   صنوبر چو من مه نهاده ست بر سر
من از گفتهٔ خویشتن خیره گشتم   طلب کردم از بهر او نام دیگر
پری خواندم اورا وزانروی خواندم   که روی پری داشت آن پرنیان بر
دگر باره با من بجنگ اندر آمد   که بس خوارداری مرا ای ستمگر
مرا با پری راست کردی بخوبی   پری مرمرا پیشکارست وچاکر
پری کی بود رودساز وغزلخوان   کمند افکن واسب تاز وکمان ور

101 ᶜUnṣurī, *Dīvān*, p. 202, 1980. Maḥmūd b. Sabuktegīn.

در آهن وسیم است قضا وقدر ایرا   کز آهن وسیمست ترا خنجر وخاتم

102 ᶜUnṣurī, *Dīvān*, p. 158, 1669. Abū Jaᶜfar Muḥammad b. Abī al-Faḍl.

سپه کشی که فلک را زبیم حملهٔ او ستاره غیبهٔ جوشن شد آفتاب سپر

103 ᶜUnṣurī, *Dīvān*, p. 160, 1683. Abū Jaᶜfar Muḥammad b. Abī al-Faḍl.

اگر بطالع سالی بود ستارهٔ او   بر آید آن سال اندر جهان همه اختر

104 Abū Tammām, *Dīwān*, p. 2:385–6, 39–41. Abū Saᶜīd al-Thaghrī.

هذا إلى قِدَمِ الذمامِ بكَ الذى   لو أنَّه وَلَدٌ لكانَ وصيفا
وَحَشاً تُحرِّقُه النصيحةُ والهوى   لو أنَّه وَقتٌ لكانَ مَصيفا
ومَقيلُ صَدْرٍ فيك باقِ رَوعُهُ   لو أنّه ثَغرٌ لكانَ مَخوفا

105 ᶜUnṣurī, *Dīvān*, p. 157, 1656–7. Abū Jaᶜfar Muḥammad b. Abī al-Faḍl.

هزار گونه زره بست زلف آن دلبر   زمشک حلقه شده بر شکست یکدیگر
چنانکه باد هر آنگه که بر وزید بروی   گره گشای شد ومشکسای وحلقه شمر

106 ᶜUnṣurī, *Dīvān*, p. 32–4, 358–86. Maḥmūd b. Sabuktegīn.

ماه رخسارش همی در غالیه پنهان شود   زلف مشکینش همی بر لاله شادروان شود
دردم آن روی است ودرمانم هم از دیدار او   دیده ای دردی که دروی بنگری درمان شود ...

107 ᶜUnṣurī, *Dīvān*, p. 158, 1670. Abū Jaᶜfar Muḥammad b. Abī al-Faḍl.

شنیدن سخن شاه ودیدن سیرش   نگار خانه کند سمع وگنج خانه بصر

108 ᶜUnṣurī, *Dīvān*, p. 201, 1968. Maḥmūd b. Sabuktegīn.

ای مایهٔ هر نیکی واندازهٔ شادی   نیکی بتو نیکو شد وشادی بتو خرّم

109 ᶜUnṣurī, *Dīvān*, p. 202, 1977. Maḥmūd b. Sabuktegīn.

عدل از تو مشهر شد وفضل از تو منوّر   ملک از تو مهنا شد ودین از تو مقدم

110 Farrukhī, *Dīvān*, p. 169, 3403. Abū Bakr Quhistānī. Abū Bakr ᶜAlī b. Ḥasan Quhistānī started out as a drinking companion of Maḥmūd (standing) and worked his way up to a drinking companion (sitting). When Maḥmūd sent Masᶜūd with the help of Abū Sahl Zawzanī to rule from Herat, he sent Muḥammad with the help of Abū Bakr Quhistānī to rule from Guzgan, where he supervised the administration and the army (Yūsufī, *Kāghaz-i Zarr*, pp. 125–6). He later worked for the Seljuk dynasty and died in 431/1039 (Farrukhī, *Dīvān*, p. 43).

باژگونه دشمنانش را زبیم کلک او   موی گردد باژگونه بر بدن دندان مار

111 ᶜUnṣurī, *Dīvān*, p. 201, 1966. Maḥmūd b. Sabuktegīn.

دشمن که سخن گوید او آن تیغ جهانسوز   گردد بزمان اندر هر دولبش اعلم

112 Farrukhī, *Dīvān*, p. 169, 3406. Abū Bakr Quhistānī.

ابر نوروزی بگرید وز سرشک چشم او   گل وگلبن باز خندد در چمن معشوقوار

113 On medieval French poetry (Kay, Sarah, *Subjectivity in Troubadour Poetry* (Cambridge, 1990), p. 26).

114 ^{c}Unṣurī, *Dīvān*, p. 203, 1979. Maḥmūd b. Sabuktegīn.

در امن تو ضیغم نکشد دست بر آهو   با امر تو آهو بکند ناخن ضیغم

115 Al-Buḥturī 1:235, 36. Ṣā^{c}id b. Makhlad on his son.

وفى جودِهِ بالبحرِ والبحرُ لو رَمى   إلى ساعةٍ من جودِهِ ما وفى بها

116 ^{c}Unṣurī, *Dīvān*, p. 201, 1972. Maḥmūd b. Sabuktegīn.

پاکیزه تر از نوری وسوزنده تر از نار   بخشنده تر از ابری وبایسته تر از نم

117 Abū Tammām, *Dīwān*, p. 2:437, 34. Abū Sa^{c}īd al-Thaghrī.

كم أسيرٍ مِن سِرِّهم وقَتيلٍ   رادِع الثَوب من دَمٍ كالخَلوق

118 Abū Tammām, *Dīwān*, p. 2:443, 62–3. Abū Sa^{c}īd al-Thaghrī.

إنَّ أيامَكَ الحِسانَ مِنَ الرُّو   م لَحُمْرُ الصَبوحِ حُمْرُ الغَبوقِ

مُعْلَماتٌ كأنها بالدمِ المُهـ   راقِ أيامُ النَحْر والتشْريقِ

119 Al-Nowaihi, *Ibn Khafājah*, p. 40.

120 Al-Buḥturī, *Dīwān*, p. 1:184, 3. Yūsuf b. Muḥammad Abū Sa^{c}īd al-Thaghrī.

وإنْ اتَّخذْتِ الهَجْرَ دارَ إقامةٍ   وأَخَذَت من مَحْضِ الصُّدودِ نَصيبا

121 ^{c}Unṣurī, *Dīvān*, p. 160, 1688. Abū Ja^{c}far Muḥammad b. Abī al-Faḍl.

رسیده بینی جاهش بهر کجا برسد   چنانکه گوئی حاضر شدست شاه ایدر

122 ^{c}Unṣurī, *Dīvān*, p. 157, 1660. Abū Ja^{c}far Muḥammad b. Abī al- Faḍl.

گل شگفته همی مشک ساید این عجبست   عجبتر آنکه همی جادویی کند عبهر

123 One view of this kind of image is that genitive images can have the effect of alienation (Schippers, A., 'The genitive-metaphor in the poetry of Abu Tammam', in Rudolph Peters (ed), *Proceedings of the Ninth Congress of the Union Européenne des Arabisants et Islamisants* (Leiden, 1981), pp. 248–60, pp. 252, 255).

124 Abū Tammām, *Dīwān*, p. 2:394, 4. Muḥammad b. ^{c}Abd al-Malik al-Zayyāt.

أخَذَ البلَى آياتِها فرمَى بها   بيدِ البوارحِ فى وجوه الصفصفِ

125 Abū Tammām, *Dīwān*, p. 2:426, 13. Al-Ḥasan b. Wahb.

نَصَبٌ على التقارُبِ والتدانى   ويَسقِينا بكاسِ الشَوْقِ ساقِ

126 Abū Tammām, *Dīwān*, p. 2:379, 14. Abū Sa^{c}īd al-Thaghrī.

آرامُ حَىٍّ أنزفتْهم نيةٌ   تركتْكَ من خمر الفراق نزيفا

127 Abū Tammām, *Dīwān*, p. 2:466, 29. Abū Sa^{c}īd al-Thaghrī.

أهَبَّ لكم ريحَ الصفاءِ جنائباً   رُخاءً وكانت وهى نُكْبٌ سواهكُ

128 Al-Buḥturī, *Dīwān*, p. 1:227, 19. Muḥammad b. Badr.

ولن ترى مِثْلَ كَنْزِ المجْد مكتسَباً   يرعاهُ صَوناً من الإنفاقِ كاسبُهُ

129 Abū Tammām, *Dīwān*, p. 2:435, 23. Abū Sa^{c}īd al-Thaghrī.

فحَوَى سوقَها وغادَرَ فيها   سوقَ مَوتٍ طَمَتْ على كلِّ سوقِ

130 Abū Tammām, *Dīwān*, p. 2:378, 9. Abū Sa^{c}īd al-Thaghrī.

وإذا رَمَتْكَ الحادِثاتُ بلحْظَةٍ   رَدَّتْ ظباؤكَ طَرفَها مطروفا

131 Abū Tammām, *Dīwān*, p. 2:440, 47. Abū Sa^cīd al-Thaghrī.

جَأَرَ الدينُ واستغاثَ بكَ الإسـ لامُ للنصْرِ مستغاثَ الغَريق

Chapter 6

1 Beatrice Gruendler discusses this in the context of speech act theory in panegyric poetry (Gruendler, *Ibn al-Rūmī*).
2 The way in which an object is presented gives information about that object itself and about the focalizor' (Bal, Mieke, *Narratology: Introduction to the Theory of Narrative*, second edition (Toronto, 1997), p. 152).
3 'Ways of seeing are not merely indicative of social roles, but actively define them …' Morales extends Teresa de Lauretis' idea of the gaze as a 'technology of gender' to conclude that the gaze is a technology of social position (Morales, *Vision and Narrative*, p. 23).
4 On medieval English literature (Collette, Carolyn P., *Species, Phantasms, and Images: Vision and Medieval Psychology in The Canterbury Tales* (Ann Arbor, Michigan, 2000), pp. 14, 20).
5 Sabra, A. I., 'Sensation and inference in Alhazen's theory of visual perception' in Peter K. Machamer and Robert G. Turnbull (eds), *Studies in Perception: Interrelations in the History of Philosophy and Science* (Columbus: Ohio, 1978), pp. 160–85, p. 171.
6 Zeitlin, Froma, 'The artful eye: vision, ekphrasis and spectacle in Euripidean theatre', in Simon Goldhill and Robin Osborne (eds), *Art and Text in Ancient Greek Culture* (Cambridge, 1994), pp. 138–96, p. 141.
7 Abū Tammām, *Dīwān*, p. 1:138, 3. Al-Ḥasan b. Sahl.

ومُعْتَرَكٍ للشَوقِ أهدَى به الهوَى إلى ذى الهوى نُجْلَ العُيون رَبائبا

8 Abū Tammām, *Dīwān*, p. 1:118, 8. Sulaymān b. Wahb.

بِسقيمِ الجُفونِ غيرِ سقيمٍ ومُريبِ الألحاظِ غيرِ مُريبِ

9 Al-Buḥturī, *Dīwān*, p. 2:913, 7. Ismā^cīl b. Bulbul.

أُليحُ من الغوانِى أنْ ترَى لِى ذوائبَ لائحاً فيها القتيرُ

10 Abū Tammām, *Dīwān*, p. 1:78, 7. Mālik b. Ṭawq al-Taghlibī.

أو ما رأتْ بُردَىَّ من نسج الصِّبى ورأتْ خِضابَ الله وهو خضابى

11 Abū Tammām, *Dīwān*, p. 2:294, 2. Dīnār b. ^cAbd Allāh. This poem is also described as a poem for Dīnār b. Yazīd (Al-Ṣūlī, *Akhbār Abī Tammām*, p. 114).

رَعَتْ طَرَفَها فى هامةٍ قد تنَكَّرَتْ وصوَّحَ منها نَبْتُها وهو بارِضُ

12 Abū Tammām, *Dīwān*, p. 1:109, 1. Al-Ḥasan b. Sahl.

أَبدَتْ أسًى أنْ رأتْنى مُخْلِسَ القُصَبِ وآلَ ما كانَ مِن عُجْبٍ إلى عَجَبِ

13 Abū Tammām, *Dīwān*, p. 1:159, 8. Abū Sa^cīd al-Thaghrī.

خَضَبَتْ خدَّها إلى لُؤلؤِ العِقْـ دِ دماً أنْ رأتْ شَواتِى خَضيبا

14 Abū Tammām, *Dīwān*, p. 1:241, 7. Muḥammad b. ^cAbd al-Malik al-Zayyāt.

أدنَتْ نِقاباً على الخدَّينِ وانتسَبَتْ للناظِرينَ بقدٍّ ليسَ يَنتسِبُ

15 ^cUnṣurī, *Dīvān*, p. 155, 1642. Mas^cūd b. Maḥmūd b. Sabuktegīn.

از دیدن وبسودن رخسار وزلف یار در دست مشک دارم ودر دیده لاله زار

16 Farrukhī, *Dīvān*, p. 213, 4257. Maḥmūd b. Sabuktegīn.

بینی آن زلف سیاه از بر آن روی چو ماه که بهر دیدنی از مهرش وجد آرم وحال

17 Al-Buḥturī, *Dīwān*, p. 2:906, 4. Ismāᶜīl b. Bulbul.

صِبْغُ خدٍّ يكادُ يَدمَى احمِراراً وَردُهُ في العيونِ أو جُلَّنارُهْ

18 Abū Tammām, *Dīwān*, p. 2:309, 4–5. Ibn Abī Duᵓād.

نَظَرتْ فالتفَتُّ منها إلى أحْـ لى سَوادٍ رأيتُه فى بياضِ

يومَ ولّتْ مريضةَ اللحظِ والجفْـ نِ وليستْ دموعُها بِمِراض

19 ᶜUnṣurī, *Dīvān*, p. 158, 1670. Abū Jaᶜfar Muḥammad b. Abī al-Faḍl.

شنیدن سخن شاه ودیدن سیرش نگار خانه کند سمع وگنج خانه بصر

20 ᶜUnṣurī, *Dīvān*, p. 201, 1967. Maḥmūd b. Sabuktegīn.

از رسم جوانمردی وز فخر مدیحش گوینده وبیننده شود اکمه وابکم

21 Al-Buḥturī, *Dīwān*, p. 2:933, 20. Al-Muᶜtazz.

أقام مَنارَ الحقِّ حتى اهتَدَى به وأَبْصرَه مَن لم يَكُنْ قَطُّ أبصرا

22 Abū Tammām, *Dīwān*, p. 2:333, 46. Abū Saᶜīd al-Thaghrī.

رأيتُ رَجائى فيكَ وَحْدَكَ هِمَّةً ولكنَّهُ فى سائرِ الناسِ مَطمَعُ

23 Abū Tammām, *Dīwān*, p. 2:189, 21. ᶜUmar b. ᶜAbd al-ᶜAzīz al-Ṭāᵓī of Homs.

أَنَّى تُرَى عاطِلاً مِن حَلْىِ مُكْرَمَةٍ وكلَّ يومٍ تُرَى فى مالِكَ الغِيَرُ

24 Abū Tammām, *Dīwān*, p. 1:126, 38. Sulaymān b. Wahb. Sulaymān b. Wahb was a secretary for al-Maᵓmūn as a boy, and then for two Turkish military elites. He became minister under al-Muhtadī in 255/869 and under al-Muᶜtamid in 263/876, and was disgraced under al-Wāthiq in 269/882 (Al-Buḥturī, *Dīwān*, p. 1:169). Al-Muwaffaq imposed Sulaymān as a minister on al-Muᶜtamid, and Sulaymān, like al-Muwaffaq, was allied with the Turkish military elite (Kennedy, Hugh, *The Prophet and the Age of the Caliphates: The Islamic Near East from the Sixth to the Eleventh Century* (London, 1986), p. 176).

لو رأَينا التوكيدَ خُطَّةَ عَجزٍ ما شَفعْنا الآذانَ بالتثْويبِ

25 Al-Buḥturī, *Dīwān*, p. 2:947, 17. Isḥāq b. Nuṣayr.

ما رأينا الحُسينَ أَلغَى صَواباً مُذْ شَرَكْتَ الحُسينَ فى التَّدبيرِ

26 Abū Tammām, *Dīwān*, p. 1:276, 42. Muḥammad b. ᶜAbd al-Malik b. Sāliḥ al-Hāshimī. Muḥammad b. ᶜAbd al-Malik b. Sāliḥ b. ᶜAlī b. ᶜAbd Allāh b. al-ᶜAbbās b. ᶜAbd al-Muṭṭalib Abū Al-Ḥasan was from an elite of his tribe, who had groups in northern Syria. His grandfather was the ruler of Aleppo (Al-Buḥturī, *Dīwān*, p. 2:1134).

أما تَرَى الشُّكْرَ مِن ربائطِه جاءَ وسَرْحُ المَديح مِن جَلَبِه

27 Abū Tammām, *Dīwān*, p. 1:144, 23. Al-Ḥasan b. Sahl.

تُحَسَّنُ فى عَينيهِ إن كنتَ زائرًا وتزدادُ حُسْناً كُلَّما جئْتَ طالِبا

28 Abū Tammām, *Dīwān*, p. 2:211, 10. Naṣr b. Manṣūr b. Sayyār.

ماذا تَرَى فيمَنْ رآكَ لِمدحِه أهلاً وصارتْ فى يدَيكَ مَصايَرُه

29 Abū Tammām, *Dīwān*, p. 1:35, 22. Muḥammad b. Hassān al-Ḍabbī.

لمّا رأيتُكَ قد غذَوتَ مَوَدَّتى بالبِشْرِ واستَحسَنتَ وَجْهَ ثنائى

30 Farrukhī, *Dīvān*, p. 204, 4085-86. Maḥmūd b. Sabuktegīn.

رخ روشن را زیر خود مپوش که رخ روشن تو زیر زره گیرد زنگ

زره خود به رخ بر چه نهی خیره که هست رخ گلگون تو زیر زره غالیه رنگ

31 Abū Tammām, *Dīwān*, p. 1:158, 5. Abū Saᶜīd al-Thaghrī.

وكِعاباً كأنَّما ألبَستْها   غفَلاتُ الشبابِ بُرْداً قشيبا

32 Abū Tammām, *Dīwān*, p. 1:95, 8. ʿUmar b. Ṭawq b. Mālik b. Ṭawq al-Taghlibī.

فنَعِمتُ مِن شمسٍ إذا حُجبتْ بدَتْ   مِن نورِها فكأنَّها لم تُحْجَبِ

33 Abū Tammām, *Dīwān*, p. 2:320, 4–5. Abū Saʿīd al-Thaghrī.

فرُدَّتْ علينا الشمسُ والليلُ راغِمٌ   بشمسٍ لهم مِن جانِبِ الخِدْرِ تَطلُعُ

نضا ضوءُها صِبغَ الدُّجنَّةِ فانطوَى   لبَهجتِها ثَوبُ السماءِ المُجزَّعُ

34 Abū Tammām, *Dīwān*, p. 1:241, 8. Muḥammad b. ʿAbd al-Malik al-Zayyāt.

ولو تَبَسَّمُ عُجْنا الطَّرفَ فى بَرَدٍ   وفى أقاحٍ سَقتْها الحَمْرُ والضَّرَبُ

35 Al-Buḥturī, *Dīwān*, p. 2:932, 12. Al-Muʿtazz.

وقد كان محبوباً إلىَّ لو انَّه   أَضاءَ غزالاً عند بِطْياسَ أَحْوَرا

36 Abū Tammām, *Dīwān*, p. 2:186, 8. ʿUmar b. ʿAbd al-ʿAzīz al-Ṭāʾī.

قالوا أَتبكى على رَسْمٍ فقُلتُ لهم   مَن فاتَه العَينُ هَدَّى شَوقَهُ الأثَرُ

37 Abū Tammām, *Dīwān*, p. 2:256, 6. ʿAyyāsh b. Lahīʿa al-Ḥadramī.

إذْ لا نُعَطِّلُ مِنها مَنظَراً أنِقاً   ومَربَعاً بمَها اللذاتِ مأْنوسا

38 Farrukhī, *Dīvān*, p. 209, 4166. Muḥammad b. Maḥmūd b. Sabuktegīn.

هزار یک زان کاندر سرشت او هنرست   نگار ونقش همانا که نیست در ارتنگ

39 ʿUnṣurī, *Dīvān*, p. 166, 1758. Naṣr b. Sabuktegīn.

ردای دولتش را حق میان پود و تار اندر   پراکنده است فضل او ببلدان ودیار اندر

40 Abū Tammām, *Dīwān*, p. 1:156, 32. ʿAyyāsh b. Lahīʿa al-Ḥadramī.

وهاتا ثِيابُ المدحِ فاجْرُرْ ذُيولها عليكَ وهذا مَركَبُ الحَمدِ فاركَبِ

41 Al-Buḥturī, *Dīwān*, p. 2:911, 30. Abū Saqr Ismāʿīl b. Bulbul.

فمتى غابَ فى مِراسِ الأَعادِى   فسَواءٌ مَغيبُهُ وحُضورُهْ

42 ʿUnṣurī, *Dīvān*, p. 201, 1967. Maḥmūd b. Sabuktegīn.

از رسم جوانمردی وز فخر مدیحش   گوینده وبیننده شود اکمه وابکم

43 Farrukhī, *Dīvān*, p. 199, 3988. Yūsuf b. Sabuktegīn.

آز را دیدهٔ بینا دل من بود مدام   کور کردی به عطاهای گران دیدهٔ آز

44 Farrukhī, *Dīvān*, p. 215, 4287. Maḥmūd b. Sabuktegīn.

چشم بیدل به سوی دیدن دلبر نکند   میل زانسان که کنی گوش به آواز سؤال

45 Farrukhī, *Dīvān*, p. 243, 4839. Abū Sahl ʿIrāqī.

لا جرم روی بزرگان همه سوی در اوست   حاجبند ایشان گویی ودر خواجه حرم

46 Abū Tammām, *Dīwān*, p. 1:251–2, 36–8. Muḥammad b. ʿAbd al-Malik al-Zayyāt.

إن تمتنعْ منه فى الأُوقات رؤيتُهُ   فكلّ ليثٍ هَصورٍ غِيلُهُ أَشِبُ

أو تُلْقَ مِن دونِه حَجْبٌ مُكرَّمةٌ   يَوماً فقد أُلقِيتْ مِن دونِكَ الحُجُبُ

والصبحُ تَخلُفُ نورَ الشمس غُرَّته   وقَرْنُها مِن وَراءِ الأُفْقِ مُحتجِبُ

47 Abū Tammām, *Dīwān*, p. 1:80, 12. Mālik b. Ṭawq al-Taghlibī.

لم تَرْمِ ذا رَحِمٍ ببائقة ولا   كلَّمتَ قَومَكَ مِن وراءِ حِجابِ

48 Abū Tammām, *Dīwān*, p. 2:232, 29. Al-Ḥasan b. Wahb.

ردِّى لِطَرْفى عن وَجْهِهِ زَمَنٌ   وساعَتى مِن فِراقِهِ حَرْس

49 Abū Tammām, *Dīwān*, p. 2:168, 10. Abū Saʿīd al-Thaghrī.

لَولا جِلادُ أبى سعيدٍ لم يَزَلْ   للثغْرِ صَدْرٌ ما عليه صِدارُ

50 Abū Tammām, *Dīwān*, p. 2:172, 26–7. Abū Sa^{c}īd al-Thaghrī.

إلاَّ تَفِرَّ فقد أَقَمتَ وقد رأتْ عيناكَ قِدْرَ الحربِ كيفَ تُفارُ

فى حَيث تستمِعُ الهَريرَ إذا عَلا وتَرى عَجاجَ المَوتِ حِينَ يُثارُ

51 Lefebvre, Henri, *The Production of Space*, tr. Donald Nicholson-Smith (Oxford, 1991), p. 10.

52 Abū Tammām, *Dīwān*, p. 2:245, 10. Aḥmad b. al-Mu^{c}taṣim. One index indicates that this person is actually al-Mu^{c}taṣim himself (Abū Tammām, 286).

لا تَنْسَيَنْ تلكَ العُهودَ فإنما سُمِّيتَ إنساناً لأنك ناسى

53 Abū Tammām, *Dīwān*, p. 2:212, 13. Naṣr b. Manṣūr b. Sayyār.

لا تَنْسَ مَن لم يَنْسَ مدحَك والمُنى تَحتَ الُدجَى يَزعُمنَ أنَّكَ ذاكِرُه

54 ^{c}Unṣurī 162, 1695-96. Muḥammad b. Ibrāhīm al-Ṭā°ī.

نه خفته ست آن سيه چشم ونه بيدار نه مستست آن سيه زلف ونه هشيار

يكى بيدار طبع وخفته صورت يكى هشيار طبع ومست كردار

55 Al-Buḥturī, *Dīwān*, p. 2:906, 2. Ismā^{c}īl b. Bulbul.

كم تَلاقٍ أراكَهُ من قريبٍ صِلة الطَيفِ طارقاً وازديارُهْ

56 Al-Buḥturī, *Dīwān*, p. 2:931, 3. Al-Mu^{c}tazz.

وما قَرُبَت بالطَّيفِ إلاَّ لتنتوِى ولا وصلتْ فى النومِ إلاَّ لِتَهجُرا

57 Al-Buḥturī, *Dīwān*, p. 2:909, 6. Ismā^{c}īl b. Bulbul.

زائرٌ فى المَنامِ أَسأَلُ هلْ أَطْـ رُقُهُ فى منامِهِ أو أزورُهْ

58 Farrukhī, *Dīvān*, p. 246, 4911. Abū Sahl ^{c}Abd Allāh b. Aḥmad b. Lakshan.

از همه ابجد بر ميم و الف شيفته ام كه ببالا ودهان تو الف ماند وميم

59 Abū Tammām, *Dīwān*, p. 1:138, 2. Al-Ḥasan b. Sahl.

سنُغْرِبُ تجديداً لعهدِكِ فى البُكا فما كُنتِ فى الأيامِ إلاَّ غرائبا

60 Abū Tammām, *Dīwān*, p. 1:162, 17–8. Abū Sa^{c}īd al-Thaghrī. I think that it may be أقربين.

غَرَّبَتْهُ العُلى على كثرةِ النا سِ فأضحَى فى الأُقربَينَ جَنينا

فلَيَطُلْ عُمْرُهُ فلَوماتَ فى مَرْ وَ مُقيماً بها لماتَ غريبا

61 Abū Tammām, *Dīwān*, p. 1:213, 40. Abū Dulaf al-^{c}Ijlī.

إلَيك أَرَحْنا عازِبَ الشِّعْر بَعدَما تمهَّلَ فى رَوضِ المعانى العَجائبِ

62 Abū Tammām, *Dīwān*, p. 1:107, 43. ^{c}Umar b. Ṭawq b. Mālik b. Ṭawq al-Taghlibī.

غَرُبَتْ خلائقُهُ وأغرَب شاعرٌ فيه فأحْسَنَ مُغرِبٌ فى مُغرِبِ

63 Farrukhī, *Dīvān*, p. 215, 4293–4. Yūsuf b. Sabuktegīn.

هميشه گفتمى اندر جهان به حسن وجمال چو يار من نبود وين حديث بود محال

من آنچه دعوى كردم محال بود ونبود از آنكه چشم من اورا نديده بود همال

64 Abū Tammām, *Dīwān*, p. 3:152, 14. Al-Ma°mūn.

اللهُ أكبرُ جاءَ أكبرُ مَن جرَتْ فتحيَّرَتْ فى كنهِهِ الأوهامُ

65 Farrukhī, *Dīvān*, p. 244, 4862. Abū Aḥmad Tamīmī.

هنر وفضل ترا بر نتوانند شمرد آن بزرگان كه بدانند شمار تقويم

66 Farrukhī, *Dīvān*, p. 237, 4708. Yūsuf b. Sabuktegīn.

از فراوان طوف سايل گرد قصرت روز و شب قصر تو نشناسد اى خسرو كس از بيت الحرام

67 Abū Tammām, *Dīwān*, p. 2:189, 23. ^{c}Umar b. ^{c}Abd al-^{c}Azīz al-Ṭā°ī.

تُتلى وصايا المَعالى بَينَ أظهُرِهم   حتَّى لقد ظَنَّ قَومٌ أنَّها سُوَرُ

68 Farrukhī, *Dīvān*, p. 237, 4719. Yūsuf b. Sabuktegīn.

شکر تو بر من فراوان واجبست ای شهریار   از فراوانی ندانم گفت شکرت را کدام

69 On the topic of secrecy in medieval Arabic literature, see Khan, Ruqayya Yasmine, *Self and Secrecy in Early Islam* (Columbia, South Carolina, 2008).

70 Farrukhī, *Dīvān*, p. 199, 3974. Yūsuf b. Sabuktegīn.

گه بصحبت بر من با بر او بستی عهد   گه ببوسه لب من با لب او گفتی راز

71 Al-Buḥturī, *Dīwān*, p. 2:914, 19. Ismāᶜīl b. Bulbul.

بعيدُ السِّرِّ لم يَقْرُبْ بِبَحْثِ الـ   منقِّبِ ما كمى عنه الضَّميرُ

72 Farrukhī, *Dīvān*, p. 203, 4064. Masᶜūd b. Maḥmūd b. Sabuktegīn.

دولتش بر دل بدخواهان صاحب خبرست   بشنود هر چه بگويند وبرون آرد راز

73 Al-Buḥturī, *Dīwān*, p. 2:913, 8. Ismāᶜīl b. Bulbul.

وجَهْلٌ بَيِّنٌ فى ذى مَشيبٍ   غَدا يَغتَرُّهُ الرَّشَأُ الغريرُ

74 Al-Buḥturī, *Dīwān*, p. 2:913, 3. Ismāᶜīl b. Bulbul.

غُروراً كانَ ما وعدَتْكَ سعدى   وأحلَى الوعْدِ من سُعدى الغُرورُ

75 Al-Buḥturī, *Dīwān*, p. 2:914, 12. Ismāᶜīl b. Bulbul.

لقد نَطَقَ البَشيرُ بما ابتهجنا   له لو كان يَصدُقُنا البَشيرُ

76 Abū Tammām, *Dīwān*, p. 1:143, 21. Al-Ḥasan b. Sahl.

هو الغَيثُ لو أَفرَطْتُ فى الوَصفِ عامِداً   لأُكذِبَ فى مَدحِيهِ ما كنتُ كاذِبا

77 Farrukhī, *Dīvān*, p. 209, 4181–2. Muḥammad b. Maḥmūd b. Sabuktegīn.

موفقيست كه تدبير او تباه كند   هزار زرق وفسون وهزار حيلت ورنگ

بهيچگونه بر او جادوان حيلت ساز   بكار برد ندانند حيلت ونيرنگ

78 Abū Tammām, *Dīwān*, p. 1:163–4, 25-26. Abū Saᶜīd al-Thaghrī.

سَكَّنَ الكَيدَ فيهم إنَّ من أعْ   ظَمِ إربٍ ألاَّ يُسَمَّى أَريبا

مَكْرُهم عِندَهُ فَصيحٌ وإنْ هم   خاطبوا مَكْرَهُ رأوْهُ جَليبا

79 Abū Tammām, *Dīwān*, p. 2:166, 1. Abū Saᶜīd al-Thaghrī.

لا أنتِ أنتِ ولا الديارُ ديارُ   خَفَّ الهوى وتولَّتِ الأوطارُ

80 Abū Tammām, *Dīwān*, p. 1:219, 5. Abū al-ᶜAbbās ᶜAbd Allāh b. Ṭāhir.

ألم تعلمى أنّ الزِّماعَ على السُّرى   أخو النجح عند النائباتِ وصاحبُهْ

81 Abū Tammām, *Dīwān*, p. 1:256, 49. Muḥammad b. ᶜAbd al-Malik al-Zayyāt.

وما ضَميرىَ فى ذِكراكَ مُشتَرَكٌ   ولا طريقى إلى جَدْواكَ مُنشَعِبُ

82 Farrukhī, *Dīvān*, p. 236, 4695. Yūsuf b. Sabuktegīn.

جز زشاه شرق سلطان فضل او برهر شهى   همچنان دانم كه فضل نور باشد بر ظلام

83 Abū Tammām, *Dīwān*, p. 1:274, 31. Muḥammad b. ᶜAbd al-Malik b. Ṣāliḥ al-Hāshimī.

هَيهاتَ أبدَى اليقينُ صَفْحتَه   وبانَ نَبْعُ الفَخارِ من غَرَبِه

84 Abū Tammām, *Dīwān*, p. 1:84, 22. Mālik b. Ṭawq al-Taghlibī.

فإِّذا كَشَفتَهُمُ وجدْتَ لَدَيهِمُ   كَرَمَ النُّفوسِ وقلَّةَ الآدابِ

85 Farrukhī, *Dīvān*, p. 231, 4624. Yūsuf b. Sabuktegīn.

حديث مبهم ومشكل بدو گشاده شود   اگر ندانى رو پرس مشكل ومبهم

86 Abū Tammām, *Dīwān*, p. 1:251, 35. Muḥammad b. ᶜAbd al-Malik al-Zayyāt.

يَعْشُو إليكَ وضَوءُ الرأى قائدُهُ   خليفةٌ إنما آراؤُهُ شُهُبُ

87 Al-Buḥturī, *Dīwān*, p. 2:912, 36. Ismāᶜīl b. Bulbul.

ليس يَعدُو من الإصابةِ والتَّوْ فيقِ فى الرأيِ والحُسينُ وزيرُهْ

88 Farrukhī, *Dīvān*, p. 247, 4917. Abū Sahl ᶜAbd Allāh b. Aḥmad b. Lakshan.

به همه کاری تعلیم ازو خواهد میر ار چه اورا زکسی خواست نباید تعلیم

89 ᶜUnṣurī, *Dīvān*, p. 163, 1728. Muḥammad b. Ibrāhīm al-Ṭāᵓī.

بدو چون دولت ورایش به پیوست که عدل وفضل او دارد با قرار

90 Abū Tammām, *Dīwān*, p. 2:188, 15. ᶜUmar b. ᶜAbd al-ᶜAzīz al-Ṭāᵓī.

مُجَرِّدٌ سَيفَ رأيٍ مِن عزيمتِه للدَّهرِ صَيقَلُه الإطراقُ والفِكَر

عضْباً إذا سلّه فى وجهِ نائبةٍ جاءتْ إليه بناتُ الدهر تعتذِر

91 ᶜUnṣurī, *Dīvān*, p. 166, 1757. Naṣr b. Sabuktegīn.

وقار آرد وقار او بطبع بیوقار اندر قرار آرد قرار او به رای بیقرار اندر

92 ᶜUnṣurī, *Dīvān*, p. 201, 1966. Maḥmūd b. Sabuktegīn.

دشمن که سخن گوید از آن تیغ جهانسوز گردد بزمان اندر هر دو لبش اعلم

Chapter 7

1 Laird, Andrew, *Powers of Expression, Expressions of Power: Speech Presentation and Latin Literature* (Oxford, 1999), p. 4.
2 Laird, *Powers of Expression*, p. 255.
3 Gruendler, *Ibn al-Rūmī*, p. 40.
4 Miller, J. Hillis, *Speech Acts in Literature* (Stanford, California, 2001), p. 3.
5 Al-Buḥturī, *Dīwān*, p. 1:54, 3. Ṣāᶜid b. Makhlad and his son Abū ᶜĪsā.

حَلفتُ لها أنِّى صحيحُ سِوى الذى تعلَّقَهُ قلبٌ مريضٌ بها يَدوى

6 Al-Buḥturī, *Dīwān*, p. 1:103, 39. Abū Al-Muᶜammar al-Haytham b. ᶜAbd Allāh. Al-Haytham b. ᶜAbd Allāh b. al-Muᶜammar al-Taghlibī was put in charge of Mosul in 261/874 and took over the land of Rabi'a after the death of Isḥāq b. Ayyūb in 287/900 and attacked Mosul but was repelled by its inhabitants (Al-Buḥturī, *Dīwān*, p. 1:98).

أهيثمُ يا بنِ عبد اللهِ دعوى مُشيدٍ بالنصيحةِ او مُهيب

7 Abū Tammām, *Dīwān*, p. 2:303–4, 10–11. Ibn Abī Duᵓād.

يا أحمدَ ابنَ أبى دُوادٍ دَعوةً ذلَّتْ بِشُكْرِكَ لى وكانت رَيضا

لمّا انتضيتُكَ للخطوبِ كُفِيتُها والسيفُ لا يَكفِيكَ حتَّى يُنتضَى

8 Farrukhī, *Dīvān*, p. 93, 1771. Muḥammad b. Maḥmūd b. Sabuktegīn.

آنکه زدعوی فزون نماید معنی وانکه زگفتار بیش دارد کردار

9 ᶜUnṣurī, *Dīvān*, p. 29, 332. Maḥmūd b. Sabuktegīn.

پادشاهیها همه دعویست برهان تیغ او آن نکوتر باشد از دعوی که با برهان بود

10 Al-Buḥturī, *Dīwān*, p. 1:56, 22. Ṣāᶜid b. Makhlad and his son Abū ᶜĪsā.

بَلَى لأبى عيسى شواهدُ بارِعٍ من الفَضْلِ ما كانَ انتحالاً ولا دعْوَى

11 Farrukhī, *Dīvān*, p. 100, 1920. Muḥammad b. Maḥmūd b. Sabuktegīn.

شاه روز افزون خوانند ترا باز امسال زآنکه هرروز فزایی چو شکوفه به بهار

12 Farrukhī, *Dīvān*, p. 107, 2056. Muḥammad b. Maḥmūd b. Sabuktegīn.

ایدرست آنکه همی خوانند اورا طوبی ایدرست آنکه همی خوانند اورا کوثر

13 ᶜUnṣurī, *Dīvān*, p. 20, 225. Naṣr b. Sabuktegīn.

هر کجا کفّ او گشاده نشد دعوت جودرا پیمبر نیست

14 Al-Buḥturī, *Dīwān*, p. 1:103, 40. Abū Al-Muʿammar al-Haytham b. ʿAbd Allāh.

وما يُدعَى لِما تُدعَى إليه   سواكَ ابنَ النجيبةِ والنجيبِ

15 Farrukhī, *Dīvān*, p. 66, 1257. Maḥmūd b. Sabuktegīn.

خدای داند کاین پیش تو همی گویم   تنم زشرم همی گردد ای امیر نزار

16 Al-Buḥturī, *Dīwān*, p. 1:57, 40. Ṣāʿid b. Makhlad and his son Abū ʿĪsā.

وما شَطَطٌ أنْ أُتْبعَ الرُّغْبَ أهلَهُ   وأن أطلُبَ الجَدْوى إلى واهبِ الجدْوَى

17 Abū Tammām, *Dīwān*, p. 3:127, 48. Muḥammad b. ʿAbd al-Malik al-Zayyāt.

وما راغِبٌ أَسرى إليكَ براغِبٍ   ولا سائلٌ أمَّ الخَليفةَ سائلُ

18 Abū Tammām, *Dīwān*, p. 3:30, 40. Al-Muʿtaṣim.

لُهىً تَستثيرُ القَلبَ لولا اتّصالُها   بحُسْنِ دِفاعِ الله وُسْوِسَ سائلُه

19 Farrukhī, *Dīvān*, p. 100, 1925. Muḥammad b. Maḥmūd b. Sabuktegīn.

سائلان را زتو سیم آید وزائر را زر   دوستان را زتو تخت آید ودشمن را دار

20 Al-Buḥturī, *Dīwān*, p. 1:14, 10. Abū Saʿīd al-Thaghrī.

فجَعلنا الوَداعَ فيه سلاماً   وجَعلنا الفِراقَ فيه لِقاءَ

21 Abū Tammām, *Dīwān*, p. 3:150, 1. Al-Maʾmūn.

دِمَنٌ ألمَّ بها فقالَ سلامُ   كم حَلَّ عُقْدَةَ صبْرِه الإلمامُ

22 Al-Buḥturī, *Dīwān*, p. 1:59, 6. Khumārawayh b. Aḥmad. Khumārawayh b. Aḥmad b. Ṭūlūn was born in Samarra and took over Egypt, Syria, and the Syrian frontier after his father's death in 270/883. Al-Muwaffaq sent troops against him in Syria and they defeated him in 271/884, and he returned to Egypt. He reconquered Syria in 273/886. He was defeated again by central troops in 274/887. After the death of al-Muwaffaq and al-Muʿtamid, al-Muʿtaḍid became caliph and married Khumārawayh's daughter. Khumārawayh was killed by a servant in Syria and buried in Egypt in 282/895 (Al-Buḥturī, *Dīwān*, p. 1:58).

سَرَى الطيفُ من ظَمْياءَ وَهْناً فمرحَباً   وأهلاً بمسْرَى طَيفِ ظَمياءَ مِن مَسرى

23 Al-Buḥturī, *Dīwān*, p. 1:23, 3. Abū Nūḥ ʿĪsā b. Ibrāhīm. Abū Nūḥ ʿĪsā b. Ibrāhīm b. Nūḥ was a Christian secretary of al-Fatḥ b. Khāqān. He was arrested at the end of al-Muʿtazz's reign in 255/869 in a demand for money to pay the Turkish military, and subsequently whipped to death at the beginning of al-Muhtadī's reign (Al-Buḥturī, *Dīwān*, p. 1:23).

يُهدِى السلامَ وفى اهتَداءِ خيالِهِ   من بُعدِهِ عَجَبٌ وفى اهدائه

24 Al-Buḥturī, *Dīwān*, p. 1:562, 16–17. Abū Muslim al-Kajjī.

أبا مسلمٍ إلقَ السلامَ مُضاعَفاً   ورُحْ سالمَ القُطْرَيْنِ إنِّىَ غادِ

سأشكُرُ نُعماكَ المُرَفْرِفَ ظِلُّها   علىَّ وهل أنسى ربيعَ بِلادِى

25 Abū Tammām, *Dīwān*, p. 3:128, 52. Muḥammad b. ʿAbd al-Malik al-Zayyāt.

ولِى هِمّةٌ تَمضى العُصورُ وإنَّما   كعَهدِك مِن أيَّامِ وعْدِكَ حامِلُ

26 Abū Tammām, *Dīwān*, p. 3:10, 17. Al-Muʿtaṣim.

لو كان فى عاجِلٍ مِن آجِلٍ بَدَلٌ   لكانَ فى وَعْدِه مِن رفْدِه بَدَلُ

27 Al-Buḥturī, *Dīwān*, p. 1:47, 23. Abū Bakr Muḥammad b. al-Faḍl b. al-ʿAbbās.

ولم يَكُ واعداً وَعْداً كَذوباً   ولا قُوَلٌ يقولُ بلا وَفاءِ

28 Abū Tammām, *Dīwān*, p. 3:17, 38. Al-Muʿtaṣim.

قومٌ إذا وعدوا أو أوعدوا غمروا   صَدْقاً ذَوائبَ ما قالوا بما فَعلوا

29 Al-Buḥturī, *Dīwān*, p. 1:98, 3. Abū Al-Muʿammar al-Haytham b. ʿAbd Allāh.

يُكاذِبُنى وأصْدُقهُ وِداداً   ومن كَلَفٍ مُصادَقَةُ الكَذوبِ

30 Farrukhī, *Dīvān*, p. 89, 1669. Maḥmūd b. Sabuktegīn.

گفتار نبوده ست میان من وتو هیچ   ور بوده بیکبار ببستی در گفتار

31 Al-Buḥturī, *Dīwān*, p. 1:19, 55. Abū Saʿīd al-Thaghrī.

فإذا ما رياحُ جُودِك هبَّتْ   صار قَولُ العُذّال فيها هَباءَ

32 Abū Tammām, *Dīwān*, p. 3:38, 23. al-Ḥasan b. Wahb.

أُذُنٌ صَفوحٌ ليس يَفتَحُ سَمَّها   لِدَنِيَّةٍ وأناملٌ لم تُقفَلِ

33 Abū Tammām, *Dīwān*, p. 3:62-63, 7–13. Possibly al-Ḥasan b. Wahb.

فاجْلُ القَذى عن مُقْلَتَىَّ بأَسطُرٍ   يكشِفنَ مِن كُرُباتِ بالِ بالى

سُودٌ يُبيِّضْنَ الوُجوهَ بِمصطَفَى   تلكَ النوادِرِ منكَ والأمثالِ

واحتُثْ أنامِلَكَ السوابغَ بينَها   حتَّى تجولَ هناكَ كلَّ مَجالِ

ما زِلْنَ أظآرَ البلاغةِ كلِّها   وحَواضِنَ الإحسانِ والإجمالِ

فى بَطْنِ قِرطاسٍ رَخيصٍ ضُمِّنَتْ   أحْشاؤُه دُرَرَ الكلامِ الغالى

إنّى أَعُدُّكَ مَعْقِلاً ما مِثلُهُ   كَهفٌ ولا جَبَلٌ مِنَ الأجبالِ

وأَرى كِتابَكَ بالسلامةِ مُغْنياً   عن كُتْبِ غَيرِكَ باللُّهى والمال

34 Farrukhī, *Dīvān*, p. 118, 2285–88, 2298–300. Muḥammad b. Maḥmūd b. Sabuktegīn.

يكان يكان هم از اكنون همی پديد آيد   بر اين حديث گواهی دهد دوات گهر

ايا بمرتبت وقدر وجاه افريدون   ايا بمنزلت ونام نيک اسکندر

چرا دوات گهر دهد شاه شرق بتو   در اين حديث تأمل کن ونکو بنگر

دوات را غرض آن بود کاندرو قلمست   قلم برابر تيغست بلکه فاضل تر...

دوات را غرضی بود وهمچنين غرضست   در آن طويلۀ گوهر که يافتی زپدر

ترا گهر نه زبهر توانگری داده ست   خدايگان را رازيست اندر آن مضمر

عزيز ترزگهر در جهان چه چيز بود   گهر بر تو فرستاد با دوات بزر

35 Abū Tammām, *Dīwān*, p. 3:123–4, 35–7. Muḥammad b. ʿAbd al-Malik al-Zayyāt.

إذا ما امتطَى الخمس اللطاف وأُفرِغَتْ   عليه شِعابُ الفِكْرِ وهى حوافِلُ

أطاعتْه أطرافٌ لها وتقوَّضتْ   لِنَجْواه تَقويضَ الخِيامِ الجحافِلُ

إذا استغزَرَ الذِّهْنَ الذَّكِىَّ وأَقبلتْ   أعاليه فى القِرطاسِ وهى أسافِلُ

36 Farrukhī, *Dīvān*, p. 118, 2294. Muḥammad b. Maḥmūd b. Sabuktegīn.

ملوک را قلم و تيغ برترين سپهيست   بترسد از قلم وتيغ شير شرزۀ نر

بنای ملک به تيغ وقلم کنند قوی   بدين دو چيز بود ملک را شکوه وخطر

37 Farrukhī, *Dīvān*, p. 65, 1241. Maḥmūd b. Sabuktegīn.

همه حديث زمحمود نامه خواند وبس   همانکه قصۀ شهنامه خواندی هموار

38 Farrukhī, *Dīvān*, p. 61, 1166. Maḥmūd b. Sabuktegīn.

حديث جنگ تو با دشمنان وقصۀ تو   محدثان را بفروخت ای ملک بازار

39 Farrukhī, *Dīvān*, p. 106, 2053. Muḥammad b. Maḥmūd b. Sabuktegīn.

او هنر دارد بايسته چو بايسته روان   او سخن راند پيوسته چو پيوسته درر

40 ʿUnṣurī, *Dīvān*, p. 16, 183. Dabīrsiyāqī does not list a patron for this poem.

لفظ او بشنو اگر گوهر همی جویی از آنک   زیر هر حرفی زلفظ او کناری گوهر است

41 Farrukhī, *Dīvān*, p. 124, 2416. Muḥammad b. Maḥmūd b. Sabuktegīn.

گفتگوی تو بر زبان دارند   پیش بینان زیرک وهشیار

42 Abū Tammām, *Dīwān*, p. 3:123, 31. Muḥammad b. ʿAbd al-Malik al-Zayyāt.

له خَلواتُ اللاءِ لولا نجيُّها   لما احتفلتْ للمُلْكِ تِلكَ المحافِلُ

43 Farrukhī, *Dīvān*, p. 114, 2220. Muḥammad b. Maḥmūd b. Sabuktegīn.

خدایگان جهان را درین سخن غرضست   تو این سخن را زنهار تا نداری خوار

44 Farrukhī, *Dīvān*, p. 117, 2280. Muḥammad b. Maḥmūd b. Sabuktegīn.

چو علم خواهد گفتن سپند باید سوخت   که بیم چشم بدان دور باد ازان مهتر

45 Al-Buḥturī, *Dīwān*, p. 1:75, 34. Isḥāq b. Ibrāhīm.

أوفَى فظنُّوا أنَّه القَدَرُ الذى   سَمِعوا به فمُصدِّقٌ ومُكَذِّبُ

46 ʿUnṣurī, *Dīvān*, p. 48–9, 585–6. Naṣr b. Sabuktegīn.

زکلک شاه وصفی کرد خواهم   دو شاخش را بدو معنی مفسّر

یکی مر جهل را ضرّی است بی نفع   یکی مر علم را نفعی است بی ضر

47 Abū Tammām, *Dīwān*, p. 3:123, 32. Muḥammad b. ʿAbd al-Malik al-Zayyāt.

لُعابُ الأفاعى القاتلاتِ لُعابُه   وأرْىُ الجَنى اشتارَتْهُ أَيْدٍ عواسلُ

48 Robert McKinney summarizes research by Jamal al-Din Bencheikh and Geert Van Gelder on the metapoetic description of the poem by Ibn al-Rūmī, Abū Tammām, and al-Buḥturī (McKinney, *Ibn al-Rūmī*, pp. 321–2). Beatrice Gruendler discusses this topic as a way for the poet to advocate the ethics of patronage (Gruendler, *Ibn al-Rūmī*).

49 Al-Buḥturī, *Dīwān*, p. 1: 54, 4. Ṣāʿid b. Makhlad and his son Abū ʿĪsā.

وأُكثرتُ من شكوَى هواها وإنّما   أَمارةُ بَرْحِ الحُبِّ أن نَكثُرَ الشكْوَى

50 Abū Tammām, *Dīwān*, p. 3:131, 58. Muḥammad b. ʿAbd al-Malik al-Zayyāt.

تَرُدُّ قوافيها إذا هى أُرسِلتْ   هوامِلَ مَجْدِ القومِ وهى هواملُ

51 Farrukhī, *Dīvān*, p. 111, 2159. Muḥammad b. Maḥmūd b. Sabuktegīn.

حال دل خود گویم نی نی که نه نکوست   در مدح امیر انده دل گفتن بسیار

52 Farrukhī, *Dīvān*, p. 106, 2035. Muḥammad b. Maḥmūd b. Sabuktegīn.

تو چگویی که من بیدل چون تانم گفت   مدحت خسرو عادل به چنین حال اندر

53 ʿUnṣurī, *Dīvān*, p. 9, 123. Naṣr b. Sabuktegīn.

گفتم از مدح او نیاسایم   گفت چونین کنند اولو الاباب

54 Abū Tammām, *Dīwān*, p. 3:25, 15. Al-Muʿtaṣim.

إلى قُطُبِ الدنيا الذى لو بفَضْلِه   مَدَحْتُ بنى الدُنيا كَفَتْهم فضائلُه

55 Al-Buḥturī, *Dīwān*, p. 1:57, 41–2. Ṣāʿid b. Makhlad and his son Abū ʿĪsā.

دنانيرُ تُجْزَى بالقوافى كأنّما   مُمَيِّزُها بالقَسْمِ عَدَّل أو سَوَّى

إذا ما رَحَلْنا يَسَّرتْ زادَ سَفْرِنا   وإمّا أقمنا وطَّتِ الرحْلَ والمأوَى

56 Al-Buḥturī, *Dīwān*, p. 1:48, 39. Abū Bakr Muḥammad b. al-Faḍl al-ʿAbbās.

وَجودُكَ كلُّه حَسَنٌ ولكن   أجلُّ الجودِ حُسنُ الابتداءِ

57 ʿUnṣurī, *Dīvān*, p. 16, 185. Dabīrsiyāqī does not list a patron for this poem.

تا زجودش پر نشد هر چند آز وطمع بود   پر نگشت از مدح او هر چند درج ودفتر است

58 Abū Tammām, *Dīwān*, p. 3:43, 37. al-Ḥasan b. Wahb.

فمتى أُرَوِّى من لقائكَ هِمَّتى   ويُفيقُ قولى مِن سِواكَ ومِقْوَلى

59 Becker, *Shield of Achilles*, p. 30.

60 Farrukhī, *Dīvān*, p. 61, 1167. Maḥmūd b. Sabuktegīn.

كجا تواند گفتن كس آنچه تو كردى   كجا رسد بر كردارهاى تو گفتار

61 Al-Buḥturī, *Dīwān*, p. 1:15, 14. Abū Sa^{c}īd al-Thaghrī.

كيف نُثنِي على ابنِ يوسف لا كيـ   ـف سَرَى مَجْدُهُ ففاتَ الثناءَ

62 Farrukhī, *Dīvān*, p. 115, 2232. Muḥammad b. Maḥmūd b. Sabuktegīn.

چه چيز دانم كرد وچه شكر دانم گفت   زمين چگونه كند شكر ابر باران بار

63 ^{c}Unṣurī, *Dīvān*, p. 20, 227. Naṣr b. Sabuktegīn.

مر كفش را دو وصف كن كه جز او   بخل فرسا وجود پرور نيست

64 Abū Tammām, *Dīwān*, p. 3:42, 33. al-Ḥasan b. Wahb.

والحَمْدُ شُهْدٌ لا ترى مُشتارَه   يَجْنيه إلا مِن نقيع الحنظل

65 Abū Tammām, *Dīwān*, p. 2:116, 32–3. Abū al-Mughīth al-Rāfiqī.

أألبِسُ هُجْرَ القَولِ مَن لو هجَوتهُ   إذاً لهجانى عنه مَعروفُهُ عندى

كريمٌ متى أمدَحْهُ أمدَحْهُ والوَرَى   معى ومتى ما لُمْته لمتُهُ وحدِى

66 Al-Buḥturī, *Dīwān*, p. 1:47, 32–3. Abū Bakr Muḥammad b. al-Faḍl b. al-^{c}Abbās.

تَعودُ وُجوهُهم سُوداً إذا ما   نَزلتُ بهم لمَدْحٍ أوجَداءِ

فِدْواؤُك منهمُ مَن ليس يدرى   ويعلم كيف مَدْحى من هجائى

67 Al-Buḥturī, *Dīwān*, p. 1:15, 20. Abū Sa^{c}īd al-Thaghrī.

جلَّ عن مَذهبِ المَديح فقد كا   دَ يكونُ المديحُ فيه هجاءَ

68 Farrukhī, *Dīvān*, p. 111, 2141–3. Muḥammad b. Maḥmūd b. Sabuktegīn.

دروغ گفتم ليكن نه ناتوانى بود   كه در نمايش فضلش نداشتم ديدار

چنانكه هست ندانستمش تمام ستود   جز اين نبود مرا در دروغ دستگزار

دروغ گويد هر كس كه گويد اندر فضل   چو شاه شرق وچنو خلق باشد از ديار

69 Al-Buḥturī, *Dīwān*, p. 1:86, 34. Ismā^{c}īl b. Shihāb. Ismā^{c}īl b. Shihāb Abū al-Qāsim was a secretary for Ibn Abī Du$^{\circ}$ād (Al-Buḥturī, *Dīwān*, p. 1:83).

خُذْ لسانى إليكَ فالمِلْكُ للأحْـ   ـسن فى الحُكْمِ عِدْلُ مِلْكِ الرِّقابِ

70 While ethical context and relationships are particularly important in embedded exchange, supplication in literature is not just moral, but is also bound up with material need (Crotty, Kevin, *The Poetics of Supplication: Homer's Iliad and Odyssey* (Ithaca, New York, 1994), p. 134).

71 In medieval Muslim culture, 'The miser is bad because he refuses to participate in the exchanges that bind society together' (Beaumont, Daniel, '*Min Jumlat al-Jamādāt*: The inanimate in fictional and *Adab* narrative' in Philip F. Kennedy (ed), *On Fiction and* Adab *in Medieval Arabic Literature* (Wiesbaden, 2005), pp. 55–69).

72 ^{c}Unṣurī, *Dīvān*, p. 96, 1153. Maḥmūd b. Sabuktegīn.

مده بعشق عنان اى دل ار نخواهى رنج   كه هر كه عاشق شد رنجه دل زيد هموار

73 Al-Buḥturī, *Dīwān*, p. 3:1351, 3. Aḥmad b. Muḥammad al-Ṭā$^{\circ}$ī. Aḥmad b. Muḥammad al-Ṭā$^{\circ}$ī Abū Ja^{c}far was placed in charge of Kufa and environs in 269/882, and al-Mu^{c}tamid put him in charge of Medina and the road to Mecca in 271/884. He also fought the rebel Fāris al-^{c}Abdī in 275/888, but al-Muwaffaq had him bound and imprisoned in the same year. He died in Kufa in 281/894 (Al-Buḥturī, *Dīwān*, p. 1:93).

فكم مَوعدٍ أَتوَيته ولَوَيتَهُ   فأوَّلُهُ مَطْلٌ وآخِرُهُ خُلْفُ

74 Abū Tammām, *Dīwān*, p. 2:111, 6–9. Abū al-Mughīth al-Rāfiqī.

ومن جيدِ غَيداءِ التَثنّى كأنما أتتْكَ بِلَيتَيها مِن الرشأِ الفَرْدِ

كأن عليه كلَّ عِقْدٍ ملاحةً وحُسناً وإنْ أمْسَتْ وأضحَتْ بلا عِقْد

ومن نظرةٍ بين السُجوفِ عليلةٍ ومُحتَضَنٍ شَخْتٍ ومبتَسمٍ بَرِدِ

ومِن فاحِمٍ جَعْدٍ ومن كَفَلٍ نَهْدِ ومن قَمَرٍ سَعدٍ ومِن نائلٍ ثَمْدِ

75 Farrukhī, *Dīvān*, p. 143–4, 2835–6, 2838–41. Mas^cūd b. Maḥmūd b. Sabuktegīn.

كنون خوشتر كه با او بوده ام دی كه بودم بی رخش افكار بسيار

كنون خوشتر كه باوی خفته ام دوش كه بودم در غمش بسيار بيدار . . .

شب دوشين شبی بوده ست بس خوش بجان بودم من آن شب را خريدار

نگار خويش را در بر گرفتم خزينهٔ بوسهٔ او كردم آوار

دو زلفش را بماليدم بدو دست سرای از بوی او شد طبل عطار

گهی شب روز كردم زان دو عارض گهی گل توده كردم زان دورخسار

76 [c]Unṣurī, *Dīvān*, p. 123, 1375. Abū al-Ḥasan.

خدمت او گير ار ايدون افتخارت آرزوست ار نگيری خدمت او از تو گيرد افتخار

77 Farrukhī, *Dīvān*, p. 138, 2729. Yūsuf b. Sabuktegīn.

همه از دولت او جويد نام همه در خدمت او دارد سر

78 Farrukhī, *Dīvān*, p. 142, 2797–9. Mas[c]ūd b. Maḥmūd b. Sabuktegīn.

پادشاهان همه بر خدمت او شيفته اند چون غلامان زپی خدمت او بسته كمر

از پی آنكه همه امن سلامت طلبند نيست شاهانرا جز خدمت او اندر سر

79 Al-Buḥturī, *Dīwān*, p. 3:1360, 14. Ibrāhīm b. al-Ḥasan b. Sahl. The son of the minister under Al-Ma[c]mūn, Ibrāhīm may have worked in reception for al-Mutawakkil, and his sister was married to Al-Ma[c]mūn (Al-Buḥturī, 1:576).

سَبَبٌ بيننا من الأدبِ المَحْـ ـضِ قويُّ الأسبابِ غيرُ ضعيفِ

80 Farrukhī, *Dīvān*, p. 163, 3276. Abū al-Ḥasan Manṣūr.

ايا عزيز ترين كس بنزد تو مهمان چنانكه دوست ترين كس بنزد تو زوار

81 Abū Tammām 2:72, 13. Abū al-Ḥusayn Muḥammad b. al-Haytham b. Shubāna.

أغَرُّ يداهُ فُرْصتا كلِّ طالِبٍ وجَدْواهُ وَقْفٌ فى سبيلِ المَحامِدِ

82 Al-Buḥturī, *Dīwān*, p. 3:1401, 23. Wāṣif.

فلئنْ ثنَيتَ بها فلَيس بمُنكَرٍ أنْ تُتبعَ المعروفَ بالمعروفِ

83 [c]Unṣurī, *Dīvān*, p. 53, 665. Naṣr b. Sabuktegīn.

بشادی بباش وبنيكی بزی برادی ببخش وبشادی بخور

84 Farrukhī, *Dīvān*, p. 144, 2854. Mas[c]ūd b. Maḥmūd b. Sabuktegīn.

بلندی يافته زو نام شاهی قوی گشته بدو اميد احرار

85 Al-Buḥturī, *Dīwān*, p. 3:1389, 25. Isḥāq b. Ya[c]qūb al-Barīdī.

جَمَعْتُ به شَمْلَ الرجاءِ ولم أمِلْ إلى بَدَدٍ مُرْفَضَّةٍ وطوائفِ

86 Abū Tammām, *Dīwān*, p. 2:129, 17. Abū al-Mughīth al-Rāfiqī.

ما لامْرِئٍ أسَرَ القَضاءُ رجاءَهُ إلا رجاؤُكَ أو عَطاؤُكَ فادى

87 Al-Buḥturī, *Dīwān*, p. 3:1400,9. Wāṣif al-Kabīr. Wāṣif was a Turkish slave soldier and leader under Al-Mu[c]taṣim and several other caliphs, although a minister undermined his relationship with al-Muntaṣir. The army rose up

against him and killed him in 253/867 under al-Muᶜtazz (Al-Buḥturī, *Dīwān*, p. 1:139).

فلْتعْزِفَنَّ عن البطالةِ هِمَّتى   ولْيَقْصُرُنَّ على الديارِ وقوفى

88 Abū Tammām, *Dīwān*, p. 2:131, 35. Abū al-Mughīth al-Rāfiqī.

ومِن العجائبِ شاعرٌ قَعَدتْ به   هِمَّاتُه أو ضاعَ عِندَ جَوادِ

89 Abū Tammām, *Dīwān*, p. 2:144, 20. Muḥammad b. Mustahill.

حيَّيْتُ غُرَّتَه بِحُسنِ مدائحٍ   غُرٍّ فحيًّا غرَّتى بالجودِ

90 Al-Buḥturī, *Dīwān*, p. 3:1389, 26–8. Isḥāq b. Yaᶜqūb al-Barīdī. Al-Ṣīrafī has not found this person, but speculates that the two manuscripts in which al-Barīdī is added to his name could be wrong and he could be from the Nawbakht family (Al-Buḥturī, *Dīwān*, p. 3:1386).

وأوقعْتُ حِلْفاً بين شِعرِى وجودِهِ   إذا لم تُناسِبْ فى الثَّراءِ فحالِفِ

طرائفَ من حر القريضِ يَرُدُّها   مقابلةً من رِفْدِهِ بالطرائفِ

إذا ما طِرازُ الشعْرِ وافاه جاءَنا   غريبُ طِرازِ السُوسِ سَبْطَ الرفارِفِ

91 Abū Tammām, *Dīwān*, p. 2:125, 38 and 40. Abū ᶜAbd Allāh Ḥafṣ b. ᶜUmar al-Azdī.

وما كنت ذا فَقْرٍ إلى صُلْبِ مالِه   وما كان حَفْص بالفقير إلى حَمْدى ...

فما فاتنى ما عنده من حِبائه   ولا فاته من فاخر الشعر ما عندى

92 ᶜUnṣurī, *Dīvān*, p. 120, 1349. Maḥmūd b. Sabuktegīn.

گر مرا صد سال باشد عمر وگويم شكر او   هم نگويم شكر كردارش يكى از صد هزار

93 Al-Buḥturī, *Dīwān*, p. 3:1398, 34. Abū Nahshal.

وكم لك عندى من يدٍ صامتيَّةٍ   يَقِلُّ لها شُكْرى ويَعيا بها وَصفى

94 Al-Buḥturī, *Dīwān*, p. 3:1400, 10. Wāṣif.

ولأشكرَنَّ أبا علىٍّ إنَّ مِن   جَدوى يديهِ تالدِى وطريفِى

95 ᶜUnṣurī, *Dīvān*, p. 62, 790. Naṣr b. Sabuktegīn.

خواسته از قياس چون مشكست   جود او آتش وكفش مجمر

96 Farrukhī, *Dīvān*, p. 163, 3278. Abū al-Ḥasan Manṣūr.

درم بنزد تو خوارست ونزد خلق عزيز   عزيز خلق جهانرا همى چه دارى خوار

97 Al-Buḥturī, *Dīwān*, p. 3:1358, 18, 21 and 24–5. Abū Ghālib b. Aḥmad b. Muḥammad b. al-Mudabbir. Abū Ghālib escaped with his uncle, Ibrāhīm b. Muḥammad b. al-Mudabbir, when they were imprisoned in Ahwaz during the Zanj revolt, see note on Ibrāhīm.

كم رَفعتْ حالِى إلى حالِهِ   يدٌ متى تَخلُفْ غِنىً تُتْلِفِ ...

هلُمَّ نجمعْ طرفَى حالنا   إلى سواءٍ بيننا منصِفِ

وما تكافا الحالُ إنْ لم يَقَعْ   رَدٌّ من الأقوى على الأضعَفِ

98 Al-Buḥturī, *Dīwān*, p. 3:1366, 15. Al-Mutawakkil.

وما أَلْفُ أَلفٍ من جداكَ كثيرةٌ   فكيفَ أَخافُ الفَوتَ عندَكَ فى أَلْفِ

99 Al-Buḥturī, *Dīwān*, p. 3:1398, 31–2. Abū Nahshal Muḥammad b. Ḥumayd al-Ṭūsī.

وإنِّى لأستبقِى وِدادَكَ للتى   تُلِمُّ وأرضى منكَ دونَ الذى يَكفى

وأسألُكَ النِّصف احتجازاً وربَّما   أَبَيتُ فلمْ أسمحْ لغَيرِك بالنصْفِ

100 Al-Buḥturī, *Dīwān*, p. 3:1375, 401. Banū Makhlad and Ibn Laythawayh. Al-Ṣīrafī has determined that his nickname was Abū al-Faḍl, based on the poem,

but is not certain whether he is Aḥmad b. Laythawayh, who is referred to as fighting the Zanj rebellion in 262/875, or ᶜAbd Allāh b. Laythawayh, who is referred to as rebelling and then seeking pardon (Al-Buḥturī, *Dīwān*, p. 3:1371). See note 148 on p. 268 on Ṣāᶜid b. Makhlad and his son.

ما مَشى فى هنىءٍ طَولِكَ تَطْويـ ـل ولا دبٌّ فى عِداتِكَ خُلْفُ

غَيرَ أُكرومةٍ سَبَقْتَ إليها صَحَّ نِصْفٌ منها وأَخْدِجَ نِصفُ

أَلِوهمٍ أم كلٌّ ألفين ما لم يُؤخذا عند مبتدا الوعد الف

101 Al-Buḥturī, *Dīwān*, p. 3:1374, 30, 32–5, 38. Banū Makhlad and the secretary Ibn Laythawayh.

يا أبا الفضلِ حَمَّلتْكَ المعالى عِبْئَها والبخيلُ منه مُخِفٌّ ...

شَهِدَ الخَرْجُ إذ توليّتَهُ أَنَّـ ـكَ فى جَمْعِهِ الأمينُ الأَعَفُّ

حَيثُ لا عندَ مُجتَبىً منه إلطا طٌ ولا فى سياقِ جابيه عُنْفُ

سِيرةُ القَصْدِ لا الخُشونةُ عنْفٌ يَتعدَّى المَدى ولا اللِّينُ ضَعْفُ

وكِلا حالتَيكَ يستصلِحُ النا سَ إباءٌ مِن جانبَيكَ وعَطْفٌ ...

فقديماً تداولَ العُسْرُ واليُسْـ ـرُ وكلٌّ قَذىً على الرِّيحِ يَطْفُو

102 ᶜUnṣurī, *Dīvān*, p. 63, 792. Naṣr b. Sabuktegīn.

نرسد هيچ بيمروّت را دست بر شاخ آن خجسته شجر

103 Farrukhī, *Dīvān*, p. 170, 3427. Abū Bakr Ḥaṣīrī.

با مذهب پاكيزه وبا نعمت نيكو نا يافته زو هيچ مسلمان به دل آزار

104 Abū Tammām, *Dīwān*, p. 2:120, 12. Ḥafṣ b. ᶜUmar al-Azdī.

فأصبَحْتُ لا ذُلُّ السؤالِ أصابنى ولا قَدَحتْ فى خاطِرى رَوعةُ الرَّدِّ

105 Al-Buḥturī, *Dīwān*, p. 3:1397, 27. Abū Nahshal.

كَرُمتَ فما كَدَّرتَ نَيلَك عندنا بِمَنٍّ ولا خلَّفتَ وَعْدَكَ في الخُلْفِ

106 Abū Tammām, *Dīwān*, p. 2:106, 26. Aḥmad b. ᶜAbd al-Karīm al-Ṭāʾī al-Ḥimsī.

أنَّى يَفوتُكَ ما طَلَبتَ وإنما وطَراكَ أن تُعْطِى الجَزيلَ وتُحمَدا

107 Abū Tammām, *Dīwān*, p. 2:150, 18. Dāwud b. Muḥammad.

فالجودُ حيٌّ ما حَيِيتَ وإنْ تَمُتْ غاضتْ مناهِلُه ومات الجودُ

108 Abū Tammām, p. 2:65, 14. Nasr b. Manṣūr b. Bassām.

غَنِيت به عمَّن سِواهُ وحُوِّلتْ عِجافُ رِكابى عَن سُعَيدٍ إلى سَعْد

109 Farrukhī, *Dīvān*, p. 129, 2525. Yūsuf b. Sabuktegīn.

كه تا بخدمت او اندرم همى نرسم زشغل تهنيت او بشغلهاى دگر

110 Al-Buḥturī, *Dīwān*, p. 3:1399, 4–5. Wāṣif.

من كلّ مرهفةٍ يُجيلُ وُشاحَها عطفا قضيبٍ فى القوام قضيف

تهتزُّ فى هيَفٍ وما بَعَثَ الهوى منهنَّ مِثلُ المُرهَفاتِ الهِيفِ

111 Farrukhī, *Dīvān*, p. 139, 2747. Yūsuf b. Sabuktegīn.

اى پسر جنگ بنه بوسه بيار اين همه جنگ ودرشتى به چه كار

112 Al-Buḥturī, *Dīwān*, p. 3:1421, 24. al-Fatḥ b. Khāqān.

نِعَمٌ إذا ابتلَّ الحَسودُ بسَيبِها أحيَتْهُ بالإفضالِ وهى حُتوفُهُ

113 Abū Tammām, *Dīwān*, p. 2:130, 25. Abū al-Mughīth al-Rāfiqī.

أحْيَيتَ ثَغرَ الجودِ منكَ بنائلٍ قد مات منه ثغرُ كل فسادِ

114 Farrukhī, *Dīvān*, p. 130, 2545. Yūsuf b. Sabuktegīn.

بروز بزم حدیثی زتو وصد بدره   به روز رزم غلامی زتو و صد لشکر

115 ^{c}Unṣurī, *Dīvān*, p. 115, 1314. Naṣr b. Sabuktegīn.

بیادافراه وپاداش نبشته دو خط روشن   بتیغش بر که لا تأمن بگنجش بر که لا تحذر

116 Abū Tammām, *Dīwān*, p. 2:130, 26. Abū al-Mughīth al-Rāfiqī.

جاهَدتَ فيه المالَ عن حَوبائِه   والمالُ ليسَ جهادُه كجهادِ

117 Al-Buḥturī, *Dīwān*, p. 3:1395, 6. Abū Nahshal.

وجُنَّ الهوى فيها عشيَّةَ أعرَضَتْ   بناظرتی ريمٍ وسالفتَیْ خِشْفِ

118 ^{c}Unṣurī, *Dīvān*, p. 62, 791. Naṣr b. Sabuktegīn.

آفرین کفش یکی شجرست   که گلش نعمتست وجاه ثمر

119 Abū Tammām, *Dīwān*, p. 2:120, 14. Abū ^{c}Abd Allāh Ḥafṣ b. ^{c}Umar al-Azdī.

فلو كان ما يُعطيه غَيثاً لأمطَرتْ   سحائبُه من غير برقٍ ولا رعد

120 Abū Tammām, *Dīwān*, p. 2:90, 27. Muḥammad b. al-Haytham b. Shubāna.

بأوفاهُمُ بَرْقاً إذا أخلَفَ السَّنا   وأصدَقِهم رَعْداً إذا كَذَبَ الرَّعْدُ

121 Al-Buḥturī, *Dīwān*, p. 3:1355, 28. Aḥmad b. Muḥammad al-Ṭā$^{\circ}$ī.

خلائقُ إنْ أَكْدى الحَيا فی غَمامِهِ   تتابَعَ عُرْفاً مِن كرائمِها العُرْفُ

122 Al-Buḥturī, *Dīwān*, p. 3:1411, 6. Yūsuf b. Muḥammad b. Yūsuf al-Ṣāmitī al-Thaghrī.

دمنٌ جنيتُ بها الهوى من غصنه   وسحبتُ فيها اللهوَ سَحْبَ المُطرَفِ

123 Farrukhī, *Dīvān*, p. 128, 2513–15. Yūsuf b. Sabuktegīn.

سه ماه بودم دور از در سرای امیر   مرا درین سه مه اندر نه خواب بود ونه خور

کنون که باز رسیدم بدین مظفر شاه   کنون که چشم فکندم بدین مبارک در

قوی شدم به امید وغنی شدم به نشاط   دلم گرفت قرار وغمم رسید بسر

124 Farrukhī, *Dīvān*, p. 170, 3419. Abū Bakr Ḥaṣīrī.

کس نیست دراین دولت وکس نیست دراین عصر   نابرده بدو حاجت ونایافته زو بار

125 Abū Tammām, *Dīwān*, p. 2:130, 27. Abū al-Mughīth al-Rāfiqī.

ما للخطوبِ طَغَتْ عليَّ كأنَّها   جَهِلتْ بأنَّ نداكَ بالمِرْصادِ

126 Al-Buḥturī, *Dīwān*, p. 3:1360, 15. Ibrāhīm b. al-Ḥasan b. Sahl.

وحليفی على الزمانِ سَماحٌ   من كريمٍ للمَكرُماتِ حليفِ

127 ^{c}Unṣurī, *Dīvān*, p. 78, 943. Yūsuf b. Sabuktegīn.

جگونه بر خورم از وصل آن بت دلبر   که سوخت آتش هجرش دل مرا در بر

128 Abū Tammām, *Dīwān*, p. 2:131, 34. Abū al-Mughīth al-Rāfiqī.

ومفاوِزُ الآمالِ يبعدُ شأْوُها   إنْ لم تكنْ جَدْواكَ فيها زادی

129 Al-Buḥturī, *Dīwān*, p. 3:1421, 33. al-Fatḥ b. Khāqān.

وهو الخليفةُ إنْ أَسِرْ وعَطاؤُهُ   خَلفِی فإنَّ نقيصةً تَخْليفُهُ

130 Abū Tammām, *Dīwān*, p. 2:90, 24. Muḥammad b. al-Haytham b. Shubāna.

ودانی الجَدا تأتی عطاياهُ من عَلٍ   ومَنصِبُهُ وَعْرٌ مطالعُهُ جُرْدُ

131 Farrukhī, *Dīvān*, p. 142, 2799. Mas^{c}ūd b. Maḥmūd b. Sabuktegīn.

ایستادن ملکانرا بدر خانهٔ او   به ز آسایش وآرامش بر تخت بزر

132 Al-Buḥturī, *Dīwān*, p. 3:1420, 17. al-Fatḥ b. Khāqān.

فتفتّحتْ بالإذن لی أبوابُه   وترفّعتْ عنّی إليه سُجوفُهُ

133 Al-Buḥturī, *Dīwān*, p. 3:1374, 28. Banū Makhlad and the secretary Ibn Laythawayh.

شِيمةٌ حُرّةٌ وظاهرُ بِشْرٍ   راحَ من خَلْفِهِ السماحُ يَشِفُّ

134 Abū Tammām, *Dīwān*, p. 2:113, 16. Abū al-Mughīth al-Rāfiqī.

إلى مُشْرِقِ الأخلاقِ للجودِ ما حَوَى   ويَحْوِى وما يُخْفِى مِن الأمْرِ أو يُبدِى

Chapter 8

1 Burton, Joan B., *Theocritus's Urban Mimes: Mobility, Gender, and Patronage* (Berkeley, California, 1995), pp. 34, 23.
2 Mottahedeh, *Loyalty and Leadership*, p. 5.
3 Tetley, *Turks*, p. 91.
4 Sām Mīrzā, *Tuḥfa*, p. 45; ᶜAlīshīr, *Majālis*, pp. 23, 35, 36, 42, 45, 46.
5 Jean-Claude Vadet explains this dynamic in refinement in medieval Arab culture (Vadet, Jean-Claude, *L'Esprit courtois en orient dans les cinq premiers siècles de l'Hégire* (Paris, 1968), pp. 327, 336).
6 Arendt, *On Violence*, p. 42.
7 Michael Cooperson explains this function of medieval Arabic biographical dictionaries (Cooperson, *Arabic Biography*, p. 13).
8 Van Gelder, G. J. 'Mawālī and Arabic poetry: some observations', in Monique Bernards and John Nawas (eds), *Patronate and Patronage in Early and Classical Islam* (Leiden, 2005), pp. 349–69, p. 365.
9 Sourdel, Dominique, *Le Vizirat 'Abbaside de 749 à 936 (132 à 324 de l'Hégire)*, 2 vols. (Damascus, 1959), p. 577.
10 Jawārī, Aḥmad ᶜAbd al-Sattār, *Al-Shiᶜr fī Baghdād ḥattā nihāyat al-qarn al-thālith al-Hijrī* (Beirut, 2006), pp. 141, 148.
11 Drory, Rina, 'The Abbasid construction of the Jāhiliyya: cultural authority in the making', *Studia Islamica* 83 (1996), pp. 33–49, p. 35.
12 Toorawa, Shawkat M., *Ibn Abī Ṭāhir Ṭayfūr and Arabic Writerly Culture: A Ninth-century Bookman in Baghdad* (London, 2005), p. 11.
13 ᶜUtba, ᶜAbd al-Raḥmān, *Al-Ṣanawbarī: shāᶜir al-ṭabīᶜa*, (Libya and Tunisia, 1981), p. 65.
14 On Persian: Vafāyī, ᶜAbbās ᶜAlī, *Qaṣīda-hā-yi maṣnūᶜ: dar ᶜilm-i badīᶜ va bayān va ᶜarūḍ va qāfiya* (Tehran, 1382/2004), p. 8.
15 George Makdisi on Arabic, 'Speech is the mark of man, and the degrees of clarity and eloquence in his speech determine his position on the scale of excellence in this most essential of human attributes' (Makdisi, George, *The Rise of Humanism in Classical Islam and the Christian West* (Edinburgh, 1990), p. 143).
16 On Arabic: Heinrichs, Wolfhart, 'An evaluation of Sariqa', *Quaderni di studi arabi* 5–6 (1987–8), pp. 357–68, p. 367.
17 On Persian: Losensky, Paul E., *Welcoming Fighānī: Imitation and Poetic Individuality in the Safavid-Mughal Ghazal* (Costa Mesa, California, 1998).
18 On Arabic: Ali, Samer M., 'The rise of the Abbasid public sphere: The case of al-Mutanabbī and three middle ranking patrons', *Al-Qantara* 29:2 July–December (2008), pp. 467–94.
19 Arabic: Sourdel, *Le Vizirat 'Abbaside*, p. 571.
20 Arabic: Ouyang, *Literary Criticism*, p. 64; Gruendler, 'Fantastic Aesthetics'.
21 Persian: Losensky, *Fighānī*, p. 139.
22 Green, *Poets and Princepleasers*, p. 134.

23 Stewart, Devin J., 'Professional literary mendicancy in the letters and *maqāmāt* of Badīʿ al-Zamān al-Hamadhānī' in Gruendler and Marlow (eds), *Writers and Rulers*, pp. 39–48, p. 46. For a detailed study of the genre, see Hämeen-Anttila, Jaako, *Maqama: A History of a Genre* (Wiesbaden, 2002).
24 Al-Tawḥīdī, *Baṣāʾir*, p. 2:127.
25 Al-Jāḥiẓ, *Bayān*, p. 3:206.
26 Al-Tawḥīdī, *Baṣāʾir*, p. 1:147.
27 Ibn al-Jawzī, *Adhkiyāʾ*, p. 145.
28 Niẓāmī ʿArūẓī, *Chahār Maqāla*, p. 22.
29 Al-Māwardī, *Adab al-dunyā*, p. 226.
30 Al-ʿAskarī, Abū Hilāl, *Dīwān al-maʿānī* (Beirut, 1980), p. 7.
31 Al-Marzubān, Muḥammad b. Khalaf Abū Bakr, *al-Murūʾa wa-ma jāʾa fī dhalik ʿan al-nabī wa-ʿan al-sahāba wa-al-ṭābiʿīn*, ed. Muḥammad Khayr Ramadān Yūsuf (Beirut, 1420/1999), p. 87.
32 Al-Tawḥīdī, *Baṣāʾir*, p. 1:147.
33 Ibn Rashīq, *ʿUmda*, p. 1:205.
34 Kaykāvūs b. Iskandar, *Qābūsnāma*, p. 192.
35 ʿAlīshīr, *Majālis*, p. 40; Sām Mīrzā, *Tuḥfa*, pp. 69, 288, 302.
36 ʿAlīshīr, *Majālis*, pp. 44, 63.
37 ʿAlīshīr, *Majālis*, 42. Elegance turns up in a range of contexts in this work: where one might expect it, as in elegant people gathering at one poet's copy shop; and elsewhere, as in the elegance of a poet who was also a judge, a poet in service to patrons, and a poor poet (ʿAlīshīr, *Majālis*, pp. 26, 37, 46, 47).
38 ʿAlīshīr, *Majālis*, pp. 64, 466.
39 ʿAlīshīr, *Majālis*, pp. 37, 48.
40 ʿAlīshīr, *Majālis*, pp. 58, 65 and 60, 63.
41 ʿAlīshīr, *Majālis*, pp. 28–30.
42 Sām Mīrzā, *Tuḥfa*, pp. 4–25, 28–9.
43 ʿAlīshīr, Majālis, p. 52.
44 Sām Mīrzā, *Tuḥfa*, p. 281.
45 Losensky, Paul, 'Linguistic and rhetorical aspects of the signature verse (*takhalluṣ*) in the Persian ghazal', *Edebiyat* 8:2 (1998), pp. 239–71.
46 See 'Convention as cognition: On the cultivation of emotion' in Van Gelder and Hammond (eds), *Takhyīl*.
47 ʿAlīshīr, *Majālis*, p. 18.
48 ʿAlīshīr, *Majālis*, p. 65.
49 Lūdī, *Mirʾāt*, p. 26.
50 ʿAbbās, Iḥsān, *Tārīkh al-naqd al-adabī ʿinda l-ʿArab* (Beirut, 1971/1391), p. 78.
51 Ouyang, *Literary Criticism*, p. 64.
52 Ibn al-Muqaffaʿ, *Āthār*, p. 324.
53 Al-Ṣūlī, *Akhbār Abī Tammām*, p. 177.
54 Ibn Qutayba, *Shiʿr*, pp. 1:62, 63.
55 Al-Jumaḥī, *Ṭabaqāt*, p. 1:5.
56 Al-Jumaḥī, *Ṭabaqāt*, p. 1:7.
57 Al-Marzūqī, *Sharḥ al-ḥamāsa*, p. 9.
58 Qudāma b. Jaʿfar, *Naqd al-Shiʿr*, p. 26.
59 Al-Khafājī, *Sirr al-faṣāḥa*, pp. 416–17.
60 al-Āmidī, Abū al-Qāsim al-Ḥasan b. Bishr, *Al-Muwāzana bayna shiʿr Abī Tammām wal-Buḥturī*, ed. Aḥmad Saqr, 2 vols. (Cairo, 1961–5), pp. 1:5–6.
61 Al-Ṣūlī, *Akhbār Abī Tammām*, p. 118.

62 Al-Khafājī, *Sirr al-faṣāḥa*, p. 418.
63 Ibn Ṭabāṭabā, *ᶜIyār al-shiᶜr*, pp. 43–4. Shams-i Qays, *Muᶜjam*, p. 447.
64 Al-Marzūqī, *Sharḥ al-ḥamāsa*, p. 14.
65 Al-Ḥātimī, Muḥammad b. al-Ḥasan Abū ᶜAlī al-Kātib, *al-Risāla al-muḍīḥa fī dhikr sariqāt abī al-ṭayyib al-mutanabbī wa-sāqiṭ shiᶜrih*, ed. Muḥammad Yūsuf Najm, (Beirut, 1385/1965), p. 2.
66 Al-Ḥātimī, *Risāla*, p. 7.
67 Al-Jumaḥī, *Ṭabaqāt*, p. 52.
68 Al-Marzūqī, *Sharḥ al-ḥamāsa*, p. 11.
69 Al-Tawḥīdī, *Baṣāʾir*, p. 3:63.
70 *Kitāb al-tāj*, p. 37.
71 Ibn ᶜAbd Rabbihi, *ᶜIqd*, p. 1:307.
72 Al-Tawḥīdī, *Baṣāʾir*, p. 9:110.
73 Al-Thaᶜālibī, *Yatīma*, p. 3:35.
74 Al-Ḥuṣrī, *Jamᶜ al-jawāhir*, pp. 100, 102. Al-Bayhaqī, *Maḥāsin*, p. 436.
75 Ibn al-Muᶜtazz, *Ṭabaqāt*, p. 57.
76 ᶜAwfī, *Lubāb*, pp. 373, 385, 389, 456. On comedy and invective, see Van Gelder, *The Bad and the Ugly*.
77 ᶜAlīshīr, *Majālis*, pp. 23, 38, 62, 16, Sām Mīrzā, *Tuḥfa*, p. 311.
78 Ibn al-Athīr, *Mathal*, pp. 1:57–8, 159. Al-Khafājī, *Sirr al-faṣāḥa*, pp. 416–17.
79 Kaykāvūs b. Iskandar, *Qābūsnāma*, p. 203.
80 Rāvandī, Muḥammad ᶜAlī b. Sulaymān, *Rāḥat al-Ṣudūr va Āyat al-Surūr dar Tārīkh-i Āl-i Saljūq*, ed. Muḥammad Iqbāl (Tehran?, 1385), p. 406.
81 Al-Ṣūlī, *Akhbār Abī Tammām*, p. 154.
82 Ibn Qutayba, *Shiᶜr*, p. 2:729.
83 Ibn al-Athīr, *Mathal*, pp. 1:340–1.
84 Ibn al-Athīr, *Mathal*, pp. 1:161, 202.
85 Ibn al-Muᶜtazz, *Kitāb al-badīᶜ*, ed. Ignatius Kratchovsky (Baghdād, 1399/1979), p. 1.
86 Al-Jāḥiẓ, *Bayān*, pp. 2:55–6.
87 Ibn Qutayba, *Shiᶜr*, p. 1:62.
88 The link between poetry and prose occurred within texts as well as between them, analyzed by Wolfhart Heinrichs in Arabic and Julie Meisami in Persian in a volume on this topic (Harris, Joseph and Karl Reichl (eds), *Prosimetrum: Crosscultural Perspectives on Narrative in Prose and Verse* (Suffolk, UK, 1997).
89 Ibn Qutayba, *Shiᶜr*, p. 2:863.
90 On Khāqānī, see Beealert, *Khāqānī*; on Sanāʾī, see De Bruijn, *Sanāʾī* and Meisami 'The poet and the patrons: two Ghaznavid panegyrists', *Persica* 17 (2001), pp. 91–105; on Amīr Khusraw see Sharma, Sunil, *Amir Khusraw: The Poet of Sufis and Sultans* (Oxford, 2005) and Gabbay, Alyssa, *Islamic Tolerance: Amir Khusraw and Pluralism* (Routledge 2010); on ᶜIrāqī see Feuillebois-Pierunek, Ève, *A la croisée des voies célestes: Faxr al-Din ᶜErāqī, Poésie mystique et expression poétique en Perse médiéval* (Tehran, 2002).
91 Lūdī, *Mirʾāt*, pp. 26–7.
92 Al-Marzūqī, *Sharḥ al-ḥamāsa*, p. 15. Rādūyānī, *Tarjūmān*, p. 7. Vaṭvāṭ, *Ḥadāyiq*, p. 39.
93 Al-Marzūqī, *Sharḥ al-ḥamāsa*, p. 14. Shams-i Qays, *Muᶜjam*, p. 462.
94 Al-Ṣūlī, *Akhbār Abī Tammām*, pp. 10–11.
95 Al-Ṣūlī, *Akhbār Abī Tammām*, p. 72.

96 James E. Montgomery demonstrates that emotion takes place in public gestures (Montgomery, 'Cognition and emotion', p. 161). I disagree that it takes place *only* in public gestures, if only because we cannot know what goes on in people's heads, so should give them the benefit of the doubt that whatever is going on in there is significant for them. Following up on Montgomery's observation, it seems that emotion takes shape through individual subjectivity and public gestures together.

97 Al-Jāḥiẓ, *Bayān*, pp. 1:76–7.

98 Ibn Ṭabāṭabā, *ᶜIyār al-shiᶜr*, pp. 161, 160.

99 Al-Jurjānī, ᶜAbd al-Qāhir, *Kitāb asrār al-balāgha*, ed. Maḥmūd Muḥammad Shākir (Jidda, 1991/1312), p. 122.

100 See Sharma, Sunil, *Persian Poetry at the Indian Frontier: Masᶜūd-i Saᶜd-i Salmān of Lahore* (Delhi, 2000); Sharma, *Amir Khusraw* and Gabbay, *Amir Khusraw*.

101 Lūdī, Mirᵓāt, pp. 224, 115–17, 153.

102 Ibn Ṭabāṭabā, *ᶜIyār al-shiᶜr*, p. 41.

103 Shams-i Qays, *Muᶜjam*, p. 337.

104 Ibn Rashīq, *ᶜUmda*, p. 1:263.

105 ᶜAlīshīr *Majālis*, for example, pp. 14, 16, 21, 31, 32, 34. For a detailed analysis of this practice in Persian ghazal, see Losensky, *Fighānī*.

106 Heinrichs, Wolfhart, Istiᶜāra and Badīᶜ and their terminological relationship in early Arabic literary criticism', *Zeitschrift für Geschichte der Arabisch-Islamischen Wissenschaft* 10 (1984), pp. 180–211, p. 205.

107 Ali, *Literary Salons*.

108 Larkin, *al-Jurjānī*.

109 Stetkevych, *Abū Tammām*.

110 Ibn al-Muᶜtazz, *Badīᶜ*, p. 1; Al-Qāḍī al-Jurjānī, ᶜAlī b. ᶜAbd al-ᶜAzīz, *al-Wasāṭa bayn al-Mutanabbī wa khuṣūmih*, ed. Muḥammad Abū al-Faḍl Ibrāhīm and ᶜAlī Muḥammad al-Bajāwī (Beirut, n.d.), p. 4.

111 Ibn al-Athīr, *Mathal*, p. 2:61.

112 Ibn al-Athīr, *Mathal*, p. 3:262.

113 Shams-i Qays, *Muᶜjam*, p. 329. Qudāma b. Jaᶜfar, *Naqd al-shiᶜr*, p. 263.

114 Al-Jurjānī, *Asrār al-balāgha*, p. 166.

115 Al-Jurjānī, *Asrār al-balāgha*, p. 160.

116 Vaṭvāṭ, *Ḥadāyiq*, p. 38. Ibn al-Muᶜtazz, *Badīᶜ*, p. 58. Qudāma b. Jaᶜfar, *Naqd al-shiᶜr*, p. 382.

117 Vaṭvāṭ, *Ḥadāyiq*, pp. 52, 55, 72. Ibn Wakīᶜ, Abū Muḥammad al-Ḥasan b. ᶜAlī, *Kitāb al-munṣif lil-sāriq wal-masrūq minhu fī iẓhār sariqat Abī al-Ṭayyib al-Mutanabbī*, ed. Muḥammad Yūsuf Najm, 2 vols. (Beirut, 1412/1992), p. 1:40; Shams-i Qays, *Muᶜjam*, p. 381; Qudāma b. Jaᶜfar, *Naqd al-shiᶜr*, pp. 373, 380.

118 Al-Jurjānī, *Asrār al-balāgha*, p. 228. Qudāma b. Jaᶜfar, *Naqd al-shiᶜr*, pp. 133, 322.

119 Vaṭvāṭ, *Ḥadāyiq*, pp. 5, 50; Rādūyānī, *Tarjūmān*, p. 10; Qudāma b. Jaᶜfar, *Naqd al-shiᶜr*, p. 358; Shams-i Qays, *Muᶜjam*, p. 378.

120 Al-Jurjānī, *Asrār al-balāgha*, p. 78; Qudāma b. Jaᶜfar, *Naqd al-shiᶜr*, pp. 19, 23; Al-Jurjānī, *Asrār al-balāgha*, pp. 68, 251; Qudāma b. Jaᶜfar, *Naqd al-shiᶜr*, p. 289.

121 Al-Jurjānī, *Asrār al-balāgha*, pp. 43, 136.

122 Al-Jurjānī, *Asrār al-balāgha*, pp. 90, 122, 131.

123 Al-Jurjānī, *Asrār al-balāgha*, p. 145.

124 Ibn Ṭabāṭabā, *ᶜIyār al-shiᶜr*, p. 53.
125 Ibn al-Athīr, *Mathal*, pp. 2:39–40.
126 Al-Qāḍī Al-Jurjānī, *Wasāṭa*, p. 232; Al-ᶜAskarī, *Maᶜānī*; Ibn Abī ᶜAwn, *Kitāb al-tashbīhāt*, ed. Muḥammad ᶜAbd Muᶜīd Khān (Cambridge, 1369/1950); al-Kattānī al-Ṭabīb, al-Shaykh Abū ᶜAbd Allāh Muḥammad, *Kitāb al-tashbīhāt*, ed. Iḥsān ᶜAbbās (Beirut, 1966); al-Khālidiyyān, Abū Bakr Muḥammad and Abū ᶜUthmān Saᶜīd, *Kitāb al-ashbāh wal-naẓā'ir min ashᶜār al-mutaqaddimīn wal-jahiliyya wal-mukhadramīn*, ed. al-Sayyid Muḥammad Yūsuf (Cairo, 1958–65); al-Sarī b. Aḥmad al-Raffāᵓ, *al-Muḥibb wal-maḥbūb wal-mashmūm wal-mashrūb*, 4 vols., vols. 1–3 ed. Miṣbaḥ Ghulawanjī, vol. 4 ed. Majīd Ḥasan al-Dhahabī (Damascus, 1986–7); Al-Buḥturī, *Kitāb al-ḥamāsa*, ed. Muḥammad Nabīl Ṭarīfī, 2 vols. (Beirut, 1423/2002); Al-Marzūqī, *Sharḥ*.
127 Gruendler, 'Motif vs. genre', p. 83.
128 Cooperson, *Arabic Biography*, p. 192.

Chapter 9

1 Bauer, *Liebesdichtung*, p. 98.
2 Ḥasanī, Ḥabīb Ḥusayn, *Al-Sarī al-Raffāᵓ: ḥayātuhu wa-shiᶜruhu* (Baghdad, 1976), pp. 33–41.
3 Losensky, *Fighānī*, p. 136.
4 Al-Marzubānī, *Muᶜjam*, p. 152.
5 Al-Ṣūlī, Abū Bakr Muḥammad b. Yaḥyā, *Ashᶜār awlād al-khulafāᵓ*, ed. J. Heyworth Dunne (Beirut, 1982/1401); Sām Mīrzā, *Tuḥfa*.
6 Haravī, Fakhrī, *Rawḍat al-salāṭīn*, ed. ᶜAbd al-Rasūl Khayyāmpūr, (Tabriz, 1345/1966).
7 Al-Ṣūlī, *Akhbār al-Buḥturī*, p. 124.
8 Abū Hiffān, *Akhbār Abī Nuwās*, p. 19.
9 Inalçık, Halil, *Şair ve Patron: Patrimonyal Devlet ve Sanat Üzerinde Sosyolojik Bir Inceleme* (Ankara, 2003), p. 15.
10 Poetry and prose became increasingly permeable in Arabic in Ibn al-Rūmī's time (McKinney, *Ibn al-Rūmī*, p. 300).
11 ᶜAbbās, *Tārīkh al-naqd*, p. 137.
12 Orsatti, 'Anvari's qasides', p. 97.
13 Al-Ṣūlī, *Akhbār al-Buḥturī*, p. 99.
14 Ibn al-Jarrāḥ, *Waraqa*, pp. 66, 126, 131.
15 Al-Ṣūlī, *Akhbār Abī Tammām*, p. 15.
16 Al-Jāḥiẓ, *Bayān*, p. 2:56.
17 Al-Marzubānī, *Muᶜjam*, pp. 182–3.
18 Ibn al-Muᶜtazz, *Ṭabaqāt*, p. 69.
19 ᶜAwfī, *Lubāb*, pp. 62, 143.
20 ᶜAwfī, *Lubāb*, p. 145.
21 Inalçık, *Şair ve Patron*, p. 52.
22 ᶜAlīshīr, *Majālis*, pp. 42, 54.
23 Sām Mīrzā, *Tuḥfa*, p. 294; ᶜAlīshīr, *Majālis*, pp. 45–6.
24 ᶜAlīshīr, *Majālis*, pp. 33, 34; Sām Mīrzā, *Tuḥfa*, pp. 266, 279.
25 ᶜAlīshīr, *Majālis*, p. 44; Sām Mīrzā, *Tuḥfa*, p. 316.
26 Sām Mīrzā, *Tuḥfa*, p. 283; ᶜAlīshīr, *Majālis*, p. 62.
27 Ibn al-Muᶜtazz, *Ṭabaqāt*, p. 87. Literally, 'you who have no mother.'

28   Ibn al-Mu‘tazz, *Ṭabaqāt*, p. 99.
29   Al-Jāḥiẓ, *Bayān*, p. 1:93.
30   Al-Thaʿālibī, *Yatīma*, p. 2:428.
31   Al-Tawḥīdī, *Baṣāʾir*, p. 1:25.
32   ʿAwfī, *Lubāb*, p. 84. Rāzī, Amīn Aḥmad, *Tadhkira-yi haft iqlīm*, ed. Sayyid Muḥammad Riḍā Ṭahari "Ḥasrat", 3 vols. (Tehran, 1378/1999), p. 1:89.
33   Al-Iṣfahānī, *Aghānī*, p. 8:333.
34   Sām Mīrzā, *Tuḥfa*, pp. 59, 59, 72; ʿAlīshīr, *Majālis*, pp. 44, 47.
35   Al-Thaʿālibī, *Yatīma*, p. 2:137.
36   Al-Tanūkhī, *Mustajād*, p. 85.
37   Al-Iṣfahānī, *Aghānī*, p. 4:3.
38   Al-Iṣfahānī, *Aghānī*, p. 4:51.
39   ʿAlīshīr, *Majālis*, pp. 39, 40, 13.
40   Sām Mīrzā, *Tuḥfa*, pp. 366, 369.
41   Sām Mīrzā, *Tuḥfa*, p. 365.
42   Sām Mīrzā, *Tuḥfa*, pp. 254, 298.
43   ʿAlīshīr, *Majālis*, p. 43.
44   Ibn al-Mu‘tazz, *Ṭabaqāt*, p. 92.
45   Niẓāmī ʿArūẓī, *Chahār Maqāla*, p. 71.
46   Rāzī, *Haft Iqlīm*, p. 1:307.
47   Dawlatshāh, *Tadhkira*, p. 58. Compare a Sufi anecdote about the court poet ʿAlī b. Jahm that styles him as a country bumpkin in Ali, *Literary Salons*, chapter 3.
48   Ibn al-Jarrāḥ, *Waraqa*, p. 56.
49   Ibn al-Mu‘tazz, *Ṭabaqāt*, p. 329.
50   Ibn al-Mu‘tazz, *Ṭabaqāt*, p. 316.
51   Ibn al-Jarrāḥ, *Waraqa*, p. 3.
52   Ibn Qutayba, *Shiʿr*, p. 2:755. Al-Jāḥiẓ, *Bayān*, p. 1:95. This kind of outfit did not work for Abū Tammām.
53   On the contradictory role of the figure of the Bedouin in literary culture, see Sadan, Joseph, 'An admirable and ridiculous hero: some notes on the Bedouin in medieval Arabic belles lettres, on a chapter of Adab by al-Rāghib al-Isfahani, and on a literary model in which admiration and mockery coexist', *Poetics Today* 10:3 Autumn (1989), pp. 471–92; Binay, Sara, *Die Figur des Beduinen in der arabischen Literatur 9.-12. Jahrhundert* (Wiesbaden, 2006), pp. 127–86.
54   Al-Bayhaqī, *Maḥāsin*, pp. 197–202.
55   Al-Jāḥiẓ, *Bukhalāʾ*, p. 181.
56   Dawlatshāh, *Tadhkira*, p. 84.
57   Al-Thaʿālibī, *Yatīma*, p. 2:244.
58   Ibn Rashīq, *ʿUmda*, p. 54.
59   Shams-i Qays, *Muʿjam*, p. 451.
60   Qudāma b. Jaʿfar, *Naqd al-shiʿr*, p. 87.
61   Shams-i Qays, *Muʿjam*, p. 370.
62   Al-Jāḥiẓ, *Bayān*, p. 1:144; Ibn Rashīq, *ʿUmda*, p. 140.
63   Al-Jāḥiẓ, *Bayān*, pp. 1:145–6.
64   Ibn al-Mu‘tazz, *Badīʿ*, p. 1.
65   Al-Khafājī, *Sirr al-faṣāḥa*, p. 63.
66   Al-Jāḥiẓ, *Bayān*, pp. 1:89–90.
67   Khulayyif, Yūsuf, *Tārīkh al-shiʿr fī al-ʿaṣr al-ʿAbbāsī* (Cairo, 1981), pp. 118–19.

68 Sanā'ī, *Ḥadīqat al-ḥaqīqa*, pp. 647–8, 650–1.
69 Ibn Rashīq, *ᶜUmda*, pp. 219, 222.
70 Al-Jurjānī, *Asrār al-balāgha*, p. 94.
71 Al-Jurjānī, *Asrār al-balāgha*, p. 141.
72 Al-Khafājī, *Sirr al-faṣāḥa*, pp. 90–6.
73 Ibn Rashīq, *ᶜUmda*, p. 97.
74 Ibn Qutayba, *Shiᶜr*, p. 1:250.
75 Al-Tawḥīdī, *Baṣā'ir*, p. 1:77.
76 Al-Ṣūlī, Abū Bakr Muḥammad b. Yaḥyā, *Akhbār al-shuᶜarā' al-muḥdathīn min kitāb al-awrāq*, ed. J. Heyworth Dunne (Beirut, 1982/1401), pp. 143–4.
77 Al-Iṣfahānī, *Aghānī*, p. 10:281.
78 Al-Ḥuṣrī, *Jamᶜ al-jawāhir*, pp. 100, 102; Ibn al-Jawzī, *Adhkiyā'*, p. 164; Al-Iṣfahānī, *Aghānī*, pp. 10:285, 10:299, 10:303.
79 Ibn al-Muᶜtazz, *Ṭabaqāt*, pp. 42, 46.
80 Ibn Abī al-Dunyā, *Makārim*, p. 225.
81 Ibn al-Jawzī, *Adhkiyā'*, p. 164.
82 Al-Iṣfahānī, *Aghānī*, pp. 1:319–20
83 Al-Iṣfahānī, *Aghānī*, pp. 1:325, 6:132.
84 Al-Iṣfahānī, *Aghānī*, p. 1:337.
85 Al-Washshā', Muḥammad b. Aḥmad b. Isḥāq Abū al-Ṭayyib, *Kitāb al-fāḍil fī ṣifat al-adab al-kāmil*, ed. Yaḥyā Wahib al-Jabbūrī (Beirut, 1411/1991).
86 Ibn Abī Ṭāhir Ṭayfūr, *Balāghāt al-nisā'*, ed. ᶜAbd al-Ḥamīd Hindawī (Cairo, 1998).
87 Al-Ṣūlī, *Adab al-kuttāb*, p. 85; Ibn ᶜAbd Rabbihi, *ᶜIqd*, p. 6:404; Al-ᶜAskarī, *Maᶜānī*, p. 2:75; Al-Washshā', Muḥammad b. Aḥmad b. Isḥāq Abū al-Ṭayyib *al-Ẓarf wal-Ẓurafā'*, ed. Fahmī Saᶜd (Beirut, 1407/1986), p. 314.
88 Szombathy, Zoltan, 'Freedom of expression and censorship in medieval Arabic literature', *Journal of Arabic and Islamic Studies* 7 (2007), pp. 1–24, pp. 18, 20.
89 Bernards, Monique, 'The contribution of Mawālī and the Arabic linguistic tradition', in Monique Bernards and John Nawas (eds), *Patronate and Patronage in Early and Classical Islam* (Leiden, 2005), pp. 426–53, p. 450.
90 Sourdel, *Le Vizirat 'Abbaside*, p. 574.
91 Ibn ᶜAbd al-Barr, *Bahjat al-majālis*, p. 1:313; Ibn Qutayba, *ᶜUyūn*, p. 2:3:185.
92 ᶜAbbās, *Tārīkh al-naqd*, p. 50.
93 Ibn Qutayba, *Shiᶜr*, p. 2:581.
94 Al-Jumaḥī, *Ṭabaqāt*, p. 110.
95 Al-Iṣfahānī, *Aghānī*, p. 7:121.
96 Al-Marzubānī, *Muᶜjam*, pp. 158 and 193.
97 Ibn al-Muᶜtazz, *Ṭabaqāt*, pp. 228, 248, 334, 333.
98 Al-Ṣūlī, *Akhbār Abī Tammām*, pp. 173, 174.
99 Ibn al-Muᶜtazz, *Ṭabaqāt*, p. 69.
100 Al-Marzubānī, *Muᶜjam*, p. 136.
101 Al-Ṣūlī, *Awrāq*, p. 36.
102 Al-Thaᶜālibī, *Yatīma*, p. 2:287.
103 Abū Hiffān, *Akhbār Abī Nuwās*, p. 123.
104 *Kitāb al-tāj*, p. 135; Ibn Rashīq, *ᶜUmda*, p. 83.
105 Dawlatshāh, *Tadhkira*, p. 58.
106 ᶜAwfī, *Lubāb*, p. 270
107 Ibn Qutayba, *Shiᶜr*, p. 1:79.

108 Ibn al-Muᶜtazz, *Ṭabaqāt*, p. 320.
109 Al-Iṣfahānī, *Aghānī*, pp. 7:276, 9:19.
110 Al-Iṣfahānī, *Aghānī*, pp. 7:250–62.
111 Szombathy, 'Freedom of expression', p. 20.
112 Ibn al-Muᶜtazz, *Ṭabaqāt*, p. 21.
113 Ibn al-Muᶜtazz, *Ṭabaqāt*, p. 33.
114 Ibn al-Muᶜtazz, *Ṭabaqāt*, p. 100.
115 Ibn Qutayba, *Shiᶜr*, p. 1:154; Al-Jumaḥī, *Ṭabaqāt*, p. 99.
116 ᶜAwfī, *Lubāb*, p. 518.
117 Rāzī, *Haft Iqlīm*, p. 1:87.
118 Ibn al-Muᶜtazz, *Ṭabaqāt*, pp. 42, 44, 46.
119 Al-Bayhaqī, *Maḥāsin*, p. 161.
120 Al-Ṣūlī, *Akhbār al-Buḥturī*, p. 123.
121 Al-Iṣfahānī, *Aghānī*, pp. 4:33, 4:38.
122 ᶜAwfī, *Lubāb*, p. 163.
123 Haravī, *Tadhkira*, p. 23.
124 Ibn al-Muᶜtazz, *Ṭabaqāt*, pp. 88–92.
125 Ibn al-Muᶜtazz, *Ṭabaqāt*, p. 92.
126 Al-Ḥuṣrī, *Zahr*, p. 2:650.
127 Ibn al-Muᶜtazz, *Ṭabaqāt*, p. 21.
128 Al-Iṣfahānī, *Aghānī*, p. 3:291.
129 Al-Tanūkhī, *Mustajād*, p. 181.
130 Saᶜdī, *Gulistān*, p. 127.
131 Jawārī, *Al-Shiᶜr fī Baghdād*, p. 48.
132 See Tetley, *Turks*, pp. 17–42.
133 Sharma, *Amīr Khusraw*.
134 Schippers, 'Genitive metaphors', p. 252; Abū Zayd, ᶜAlī Ibrāhīm, *Fanniyyat al-taṣwīr fī shiᶜr al-Ṣanawbarī* (Cairo, 2000), pp. 307–9.
135 Khulayyif, *Tārīkh al-shiᶜr*, p. 112; Manūchehrī, *Dīvān*.
136 ᶜAbbās, *Tārīkh al-naqd*, p. 65.
137 See Anooshahr, Ali, *The Ghazi Sultans and the Frontiers of Islam: A Comparative Study of the Late Medieval and Early Modern Periods* (London, 2009). On Persian poets and writers making sense of a complex experience of India in the Safavid-Mughal period, see Sharma, Sunil, 'The land of darkness: images of India in the works of some Safavid poets', *Studies on Persianate Societies* 1 (2003), pp. 97–108 and Alam, Muzaffar and Sanjay Subrahmanyam, 'When hell is other people: a Safavid view of seventeenth-century Mughal India' in Judith Pfeiffer and Sholeh A. Quinn (eds), *History and Historiography of Post-Mongol Central Asia and the Middle East: Studies in Honor of John E. Woods* (Wiesbaden, 2006).
138 Al-Jumaḥī, *Ṭabaqāt*, p. 127.
139 Ibn Qutayba, *Shiᶜr*, p. 1:115.
140 Ibn Rashīq, *ᶜUmda*, p. 85.
141 Al-Jumaḥī, *Ṭabaqāt*, p. 10.
142 Al-Jāḥiẓ, *Bayān*, pp. 1:69, 74.
143 Al-Jāḥiẓ, *Bayān*, p. 1:34.
144 Al-Jāḥiẓ, *Bayān*, p. 1:161.
145 Al-Jāḥiẓ, *Bayān*, p. 1:19.
146 Al-Jāḥiẓ, *Bayān*, p. 1:65.
147 Al-Jāḥiẓ, *Bayān*, p. 1:141.
148 Al-Jāḥiẓ, *Bayān*, pp. 1:88, 92.

149 Al-Khafājī, *Sirr al-faṣāḥa*, pp. 36, 53–6, 63.
150 Al-Khafājī, *Sirr al-faṣāḥa*, pp. 56–60.
151 Al-Washshāʾ, *Fāḍil*.
152 Ibn Qutayba, *Shiʿr*, p. 1:63; Ibn al-Athīr, *Mathal*, p. 2:8.
153 Ibn Qutayba, *Faḍl al-ʿArab*, p. 184.
154 Ibn Qutayba, *Faḍl al-ʿArab*, pp. 62, 55.
155 Ibn al-Rashīq, *ʿUmda*, p. 83.
156 Vadet, Jean-Claude, *Les idées morales dans l'islam* (Paris, 1995), p. 18.
157 Jawārī, *Al-Shiʿr fī Baghdād*, pp. 141, 145, 147.
158 Al-Jahshiyārī, *Wuzarāʾ*, p. 59.
159 Al-Iṣfahānī, *Aghānī*, p. 3:167. Al-Thaʿālibī, *Tuḥfat al-wuzarāʾ*, p. 160.
160 Al-Iṣfahānī, *Aghānī*, p. 4:404.
161 Al-Iṣfahānī, *Aghānī*, pp. 3:127, 10:52, 7:117; Ibn al-Jarrāḥ, *Waraqa*, pp. 15, 69. Ibn al-Jawzī, *Adhkiyāʾ*, p. 164; Al-Iṣfahānī, *Aghānī*, p. 7:117.
162 Ibn Qutayba, *Shiʿr*, pp. 1:250, 2:789. Al-Jāḥiẓ, *Bayān*, p. 1:49.
163 Ibn Qutayba, *Shiʿr*, pp. 2:577, 2:630, 2:853.
164 Al-Marzubānī, *Muʿjam*, p. 141.
165 Ibn al-Jawzī *Adhkiyāʾ*, p. 166.
166 Ibn Qutayba, *Shiʿr*, p. 2:766.
167 See Kilpatrick, Hilary, 'Mawālī and music' in Monique Bernards and John Nawas (eds), *Patronate and Patronage in Early Islamic and Classical Islam* (Leiden, 2005). Descriptions of musicians are related to descriptions of poets, since musicians set poetry to music, a few people work in both poetry and music during their careers, and the largest single source of information on both musicians and poets – al-Iṣfahānī's 27-volume *Book of Songs* – includes both types of work. Ibn Muhriz, of Persian descent, learns lyrics from Persians, takes their songs to Syria and learns tunes from the Greeks, and removes all that is not liked of the two groups and mixes them together to make the songs that he composes using Arabic poetry, bringing forth music the like of which has not been heard before (Al-Iṣfahānī, *Aghānī*, p. 1:363). Ibn Misjaḥ does something similar, picking up songs from Persian construction workers in Arab-ruled regions, and acquiring tunes from the Greeks of Syria, Eastern Anatolians, an island south of France and western Arabia (Al-Iṣfahānī, *Aghānī*, p. 3:273). Al-Gharīd is a client of Berber descent, and al-Gharīd the Jew is listed with his Jewish paternal lineage (Al-Iṣfahānī, *Aghānī*, pp. 2:353, 3:111). As in poetry, musicians may be identified as holding other jobs, such as Yūnus the Persian secretary. As with poets, musicians may be identified with a particular kind of piety, such as Dahmān (Al-Iṣfahānī, *Aghānī*, pp. 4:390, 6:28).
168 Al-Ṣūlī, *Akhbār Abī Tammām*, p. 161.
169 Ibn al-Athīr, *Mathal*, p. 1:344.
170 Ibn al-Muqaffaʿ, *Āthār*, p. 333.
171 Al-Kīk, Viktor, *Taʾthīr-i farhang-i ʿArab dar ashʿār-i Manūchihrī Dāmghānī* (Beirut, 1971), pp. 39, 42.
172 He does not appear in the anthologies of ancient poetry *al-Mufaḍḍaliyyāt* or *al-Aṣmaʿiyyāt*, in the dictionaries of poets that include ancient poets by al-Jumaḥī or Ibn Qutayba, or under his last name in the book of last names by al-Samʿānī.
173 Lūdī, *Mirāt*, pp. 5–7.
174 ʿAwfī, *Lubāb*, p. 20. Dawlatshāh, *Tadhkira*, p. 11. Haravī, *Tadhkira*, p. 5.

175 Gabbay, Alyssa, 'Love gone wrong, then right again: Male/female dynamics in the Bahrām Gūr slave girl story', *Iranian Studies* 42:5 (2009).
176 ᶜAwfī, *Lubāb*, pp. 18, 20–2.
177 Dawlatshāh, *Tadhkira*, pp. 34-36.
178 Imāmī, Naṣrallah, *Ustād-i Shāᶜirān-i Rūdakī* (Tehran, 1378), pp. 48–51.
179 ᶜAwfī, *Lubāb*. Dawlatshāh, *Tadhkira*. Haravī, *Tadhkira*.
180 Sām Mīrzā, *Tadhkira*, pp. 334, 339.
181 Lewis, Franklin, *Rumi Past and Present, East and West: The Life, Teachings and Poetry of Jalāl al-Din Rumi* (Oxford, 2000), p. 316.
182 Sām Mīrzā, *Tadhkira*, pp. 21, 24, 28, 366.
183 ᶜAlīshīr, *Majālis*, pp. kaf–vav.
184 Al-Shūshtarī, *Majālis al-Muᵓminīn*, 2 vols. (Tehran, 1365/1986).
185 ᶜAwfī, *Lubāb*, pp. 235, 423. Rāzī, *Haft Iqlīm*.
186 Inalçık, *Şair ve Patron*, p. 21.
187 Vaṭvāṭ, *Ḥadāyiq*, pp. 2, 5, 39.
188 Vaṭvāṭ, *Ḥadāyiq*, pp. 63, 69.
189 Shams-i Qays, *Muᶜjam*, p. 24.
190 Shams-i Qays, *Muᶜjam*, pp. 329, 335.
191 Shams-i Qays, *Muᶜjam*, pp. 336–7.
192 Rādūyānī, *Tarjūmān*, p. 7.
193 Rādūyānī, *Tarjūmān*, p. 121.
194 Saᶜdī, *Gulistān*; Kaykāvūs b. Iskandar, *Qābūsnāma*, p. 203.
195 Niẓām al-Mulk, *Siyar al-mulūk*, p. 136.
196 Niẓāmī Ganjavī, *Khamsa*.
197 Elinson, Alexander E., 'Tears shed over the poetic past: the prosification of Rithāᵓ al-Mudun in al-Saraquṣṭī's maqāma qayrawāniyya', *Journal of Arabic Literature* 36 (2005), pp. 1–27, p. 6. See Hämeen-Anttila, *Maqāma*.
198 Al-Thaᶜālibī, *Yatīma*, pp. 1:139, 1:293.
199 Al-Ṣūlī, *Akhbār Abī Tammām*, p. 241.
200 Khāqānī Shirvānī, Hakīm-i Afḍal al-Dīn, *Masnavī-yi tuḥfat al-ᶜIrāqayn*, ed. Yaḥyā Qarīb (Tehran, 1333/1954). See Beealert, *Khāqānī*.
201 Asadī Ṭūsī, Abū Naṣr ᶜAlī b. Aḥmad, *Garshasbnāma*, ed. Ḥabīb Nuᶜmānī (Tehran, 1354/1975).
202 Losensky, Paul, 'Shahīdī Qumī: Poet laureate of the Āqquyūnlū court' in Judith Pfeiffer and Sholeh A. Quinn (eds), *History and Historiography of Post-Mongol Central Asia and the Middle East: Studies in Honor of John E. Woods* (Wiesbaden, 2006), pp. 282–300, pp. 283–4.

Conclusion

1 On these poets, see Malḥas, Thurayya ᶜAbd al-Fattāḥ, *Abū al-Fatḥ Kashājim al-Baghdādī fī āthārihi wa-āthār al-dārisīn* (Amman, 2003/1424); Abū Zayd, *Al-Ṣanawbarī*; Al-Ḥasanī, *Al-Sarī al-Raffāᵓ*.
2 The term is from a lecture by Dick Davis in November 2008 at UC Davis. On these poets, see De Bruijn, *Sanāᵓī*; Feuillebois-Pierunek, *ᶜIrāqī*; Lewisohn, L. and Shackle, C. (eds), *ᶜAṭṭār and the Persian Sufi Tradition: The Art of Spiritual Flight* (London, 2006).
3 Monroe, James and Mark Pettigrew, 'The decline of courtly patronage and the appearance of new genres of Arabic literature: the case of the zajal, the

maqāma and the shadow play,' *Journal of Arabic Literature* 34:1–2 (2003), pp. 138–77.

4 Van Gelder, G. J. 'Pointed and well-rounded: Arabic encomiastic and elegiac epigrams', *Orientalia Lovaniensia Periodica* 26 (1995), pp. 101–40.

BIBLIOGRAPHY

Part One: Primary sources

Ibn ᶜAbd al-Barr al-Qurṭubī, Abū ᶜUmar Yūsuf ibn ᶜAbd Allāh, *Bahjat al-majālis wa-uns al-mujālis wa-shaḥdh al-dhāhin wal-hājis*, ed. Muḥammad Mursī al-Khūlī, 3 vols. (Beirut, 1982).

Ibn ᶜAbd Rabbihi, Aḥmad ibn Muḥammad Abī ᶜUmar al-Andalusī, *Kitāb al-ᶜiqd al-farīd*, ed. Muḥammad al-Tūnjī, 7 vols. (Beirut, 2001).

al-Ābī, Abū Saᶜd Manṣūr b. al-Ḥusayn, *Nathr al-Durr*, ed. Muḥammad ᶜAlī Qurna, 9 vols. (Cairo, 1980).

ᶜAlīshīr Navāᶜī, *Tadhkirah-yi Majālis al-Nafāʾis* (ninth century), tr. from Chagatay Turkish to Persian, first version tr. Muḥammad Fakhrī Hirātī, second version tr. Muḥammad Qazvīnī (both tenth century) collated with three Turkish versions by the editor, ed. ᶜAlī Aṣghar Hikmat (Tehran, 1363/1984).

al-Āmidī, Abū al-Qāsim al-Ḥasan b. Bishr, *Al-Muwāzana bayna shiᶜr Abī Tammām wal-Buḥturī*, ed. Aḥmad Saqr, 2 vols. (Cairo, 1961–5).

Asadī Ṭūsī, Abū Naṣr ᶜAlī b. Aḥmad, *Garshasbnāma*, ed. Ḥabīb Nuᶜmānī (Tehran, 1354/1975).

al-ᶜAskarī, Abū Hilāl, *Dīwān al-maᶜānī* (Beirut, 1980).

Ibn al-Athīr, Ḍiyāʾ al-Dīn, *al-Mathal al-sāʾir fī adab al-kātib wal-shāᶜir*, ed. Aḥmad al-Ḥawfī and Badawī Ṭabāna, 3 vols. (Riyāḍ, 1404/1984).

ᶜAṭṭār, Farīd al-Dīn Nishaburī, *Ilāhīnāma*, ed. Fuʾād Rūḥānī (Tehran, 1339/1961).

—— *Manṭiq al-ṭayr*, ed. Muḥammad Rawshan (Tehran, 1374/1995).

ᶜAwfī , Muḥammad, *Lubāb al-albāb*, ed. Saᶜīd Nafīsī (Tehran, 1363/1984).

—— *Guzīda-yi javāmiᶜ al-ḥikāyāt va lavāmiᶜ al-rivāyāt*, ed. Jaᶜfar Shiᶜār (Tehran, 1363/1984).

Ibn Abī ᶜAwn, *Kitāb al-tashbīhāt*, ed. Muḥammad ᶜAbd Muᶜīd Khān (Cambridge, 1369/1950).

al-Baghdādī, al-Khaṭīb Abū Bakr Aḥmad b. ᶜAlī, *Tārīkh Baghdād aw Madīnat al-Salām*, ed. Muṣṭafā ᶜAbd al-Qādir ᶜAṭā, 23 vols. (Beirut 1417/1997).

—— *al-Taṭfīl wa-hikāyat al-ṭufayliyyīn wa-akhbārihim wa-nawādir kalāmihim wa-ashᶜārihim*, ed. Bassām ᶜAbd al-Wahhāb al-Jābī (Beirut, 1999).

—— *Kitāb al-bukhalāʾ*, ed. Bassām ᶜAbd al-Wahhāb al-Jābī (Beirut, 1461/2000).

al-Bayhaqī, al-Shaykh Ibrāhīm b. Muḥammad, *al-Maḥāsin wal-masāwī*, ed. ᶜAdnān ᶜAlī (Beirut, 1420/1999).

al-Buḥturī, *Dīwān al-Buḥturī*, ed. Ḥasan Kāmil al-Ṣīrafī, 5 vols. (Cairo, 1963–72).

—— *Kitāb al-ḥamāsa*, ed. Muḥammad Nabīl Ṭarīfī, 2 vols. (Beirut, 1423/2002).

Dawlatshāh-i Samarqandī, *Tadhkīra-yi Dawlatshāh-i Samarqandī*, ed. Muḥammad ᶜAbbāsī (Tehran, 1337/1958).

Ibn Abī al-Dunyā, ᶜAbd Allāh b. Muḥammad Abū Bakr al-Qurashī al-Baghdādī, *Kitāb makārim al-akhlāq*, ed. James A. Bellamy (Wiesbaden, 1393/1973).

Farrukhī, *Divān-i Hakīm-i Farrukhī Sīstānī*, ed. Muḥammad Dabīrsiyāqī (Tehran, 1349/1970).

Firdawsī, *Shāhnāma-yi Firdawsī*, ed. Saᶜīd Ḥamīdiyān, 9 vols. in 4 (Tehran, 1374/1996).

al-Ghuzūlī, ᶜAlāᵓ al-Dīn ᶜAlī b. ᶜAbd Allāh Al-Bahāᵓī, *Matāliᶜ al-budūr fī manāzil al-surūr* (Cairo, 1419/2000).

Haravī, Fakhrī, *Rawḍat al-salāṭīn*, ed. ᶜAbd al-Rasūl Khayyāmpūr (Tabriz, 1345/1966).

al-Ḥātimī, Muḥammad b. al-Ḥasan Abū ᶜAlī al-Kātib, *al-Risāla al-muḍīḥa fī dhikr sariqāt abī al-ṭayyib al-mutanabbī wa-sāqiṭ shiᶜrih*, ed. Muḥammad Yūsuf Najm (Beirut, 1385/1965).

—— *Ḥilyat al-muḥādara*, ed. Hilāl Nājī (Beirut, 1978).

Abū Hiffān, ᶜAbd Allāh b. Aḥmad b. Ḥarb al-Mihzamī, *Akhbār Abī Nuwās*, ed. ᶜAbd al-Sattār Aḥmad Farrāj (Cairo, 1953).

al-Ḥuṣrī, Abū Isḥāq Ibrāhīm b. ᶜAlī al-Qayrawānī, *Zahr al-ādāb wa-thamr al-albāb*, ed. ᶜAlī Muḥammad al-Bajāwī, 2 vols. (Cairo, 1953).

—— *Jamᶜ al-jawāhir fil-mulaḥ wal-nawādir*, ed. ᶜAlī Muḥammad al-Bajāwī (Cairo, 1953/1372).

al-Iṣfahānī , Abū al-Faraj, *Kitāb al-aghānī*, ed. ᶜAbd A. ᶜAlī Muḥannā, 27 vols. (Beirut, 2002/1422).

al-Jāḥiẓ, Abū ᶜUthmān ᶜAmr b. Baḥr, *al-Bayān wal-tabyīn*, ed. ᶜAbd al-Salām Hārūn, 4 vols. (Beirut, n.d.).

—— *Rasā'il al-Jāḥiẓ*, ed. ᶜAbd al-Salām Hārūn, 4 vols. in 2 (Beirut, 1991/1411).

—— *Al-Bukhalāᵓ lil-Jāḥiẓ*, ed. Ṭahā al-Hajirī (Cairo, 1981).

al-Jahshiyārī, Abū ᶜAbd Allāh Muḥammad b. ᶜAbdūs, *Kitāb al-wuzarāᵓ wal-kuttāb* (Cairo, n.d.).

Ibn al-Jarrāḥ, Muḥammad b. Dāwud Abū ᶜAbd Allāh, *al-Waraqa*, ed. ᶜAbd al-Wahhāb ᶜAzzām and ᶜAbd al-Sattār Aḥmad Farrāj (Cairo, 1967).

Ibn al-Jawzī , Abū al-Faraj, *Akhbār al-adhkiyāᵓ*, ed. Muḥammad Mursī al-Khūlī (Cairo, 1970).

—— *Akhbār al-ḥamqā wal-mughaffalīn min al-fuqahāᵓ wal-mufassirīn wal-ruwāt wal-muhaddithīn wal-shuᶜarāᵓ wal-mutaᵓaddabīn wal-kuttāb wal-muᶜallimīn wal-tujjār wal-mutasabbibīn wa-ṭawāᵓif tattaṣil lil ghafla bi-sabab matīn* (Beirut, 1997/1418).

al-Jumaḥī, Muḥammad b. Salām, *Ṭabaqāt fuhūl al-shuᶜarāᵓ*, ed. Maḥmūd Muḥammad Shākir, 2 vols. (Jidda, 1974).

al-Jurjānī, ᶜAbd al-Qāhir, *Kitāb asrār al-balāgha*, ed. Maḥmūd Muḥammad Shākir (Jidda, 1991/1312).

al-Kattānī, al-Ṭabīb al-Shaykh Abū ᶜAbd Allāh Muḥammad, *Kitāb al-tashbīhāt*, ed. Iḥsān ᶜAbbās (Beirut, 1966).

Kaykāvus b. Iskandar b. Qābūs b. Vashmgīr, *Qābūsnāma*, ed. Ghulāmḥusayn Yūsufī (Tehran, 1345/1967).

Al-Khafājī, Ibn Sinān, *Sirr al-faṣāḥa*, ed. al-Nabawī ᶜAbd al-Wahīd Shaᶜlān (Cairo, 2003).
al-Khālidiyyān, Abū Bakr Muḥammad and Abū ᶜUthmān Saᶜīd, *Kitāb al-ashbāh wal-naẓā'ir min ashᶜār al-mutaqaddimīn wal-jahiliyya wal-mukhadramīn*, ed. al-Sayyid Muḥammad Yūsuf (Cairo, 1958–65).
Khāqānī Shirvānī, Hakīm-i Afḍal al-Dīn, *Masnavī-yi tuḥfat al-ᶜIrāqayn*, ed. Yaḥyā Qarīb (Tehran, 1333/1954).
al-Khwārazmī, Abū al-Wafāᵓ Rayḥān b. ᶜAbd al-Wahīd, *Kitāb al-manāqib wal-mathālib* (Damascus, 1999).
—— *Kitāb al-Tāj fī akhlāq al-mulūk*, ed. Fawzī ᶜAtawī (Beirut, 1970).
Lūdī, Shīr ᶜAlī Khān, *Tadhkirah-yi Mirāt al-Khayāl*, ed. Ḥamīd Ḥasanī (Tehran, 1377/1998).
Manūchehrī, *Dīvān-i Manūchehrī Dāmghānī* ed. Muḥammad Dabīrsiyāqī (Tehran, 1375/1996).
al-Marzubān, Muḥammad b. Khalaf Abū Bakr, *al-Murūᵓa wa-mā jāᵓa fī dhālik ᶜan al-nabī wa-ᶜan al-sahāba wa-al-tābiᶜīn*, ed. Muḥammad Khayr Ramadān Yūsuf (Beirut, 1420/1999).
al-Marzubānī, Abū ᶜUbayd Allāh Muḥammad b. ᶜImrān b. Mūsā, *Muᶜjam al-shuᶜarāᵓ*, ed. ᶜAbd al-Sattār Aḥmad Farrāj (Cairo, 1960).
al-Marzūqī, Abū ᶜAlī Aḥmad b. Muḥammad b. al-Ḥasan, *Sharḥ dīwān al-ḥamāsa*, ed. Aḥmad Amīn and ᶜAbd al-Salām Hārūn, 2 vols. (Beirut, 1411/1991).
al-Māwardī, ᶜAlī b. Muḥammad b. Ḥabīb Abū al-Ḥasan al-Baṣrī, *Adab al-dunyā wal-dīn*, ed. Muṣṭafā al-Saqā (Cairo, 1393/1973).
—— *Adab al-wazīr al-maᶜrūf bi-qawānīn al-wizāra wa-siyāsat al-mulk*, ed. Ḥasan al-Hadī Ḥusayn (Cairo, 1348/1929).
—— *Nasīḥat al-mulūk*, ed. Fuᵓād ᶜAbd al-Munᶜim Aḥmad (Alexandria, 1988).
Ibn al-Muqaffaᵓ, *Āthār Ibn al-Muqaffaᵓ* (Beirut, 1986).
Ibn al-Muᶜtazz, *Ṭabaqāt al-shuᶜarāᵓ*, ed. ᶜAbd al-Sattār Aḥmad Farrāj (Cairo, 1968).
—— *Kitāb al-badīᶜ*, ed. Ignatius Kratchovsky (Baghdād, 1399/1979).
Naṣīr al-Dīn Ṭūsī, *Akhlāq-i Nāṣirī*, ed. Mujtabā Mīnuvī and ᶜAlīriḍā Ḥaydarī (Tehran, 1352/1973).
Niẓām al-Mulk, Abū ᶜAlī Ḥasan Ṭūṣī, *Siyar al-mulūk*, ed. Hubert Dark (Tehran, 1378/2000).
Niẓāmī ᶜArūẓī, Aḥmad b. ᶜAmr b. ᶜAlī Samarqandī, *Chahār Maqāla*, ed. Muḥammad Muᶜīn (Tehran, 1334/1955).
Niẓāmī Ganjavī, *Kuliyyāt-i Khamsa-yi Niẓāmī*, ed. Vahīd Dastgardī, 2 vols. (Tehran, 1374/1995).
al-Qāḍī al-Jurjānī, ᶜAlī b. ᶜAbd al-ᶜAzīz, *al-Wasāṭa bayn al-Mutanabbī wa khuṣūmih*, ed. Muḥammad Abū al-Faḍl Ibrāhīm and ᶜAlī Muḥammad al-Bajāwī (Beirut, n.d.).
Qudāma b. Jaᶜfar, Abū al-Faraj, ed. Kamāl Muṣṭafā, *Naqd al-shiᶜr* (Cairo, 1963, 1979).
Ibn Qutayba, Abū Muḥammad ᶜAbd Allāh b. Muslim, *al-Shiᶜr wal-shuᶜarāᵓ*, ed. Aḥmad Muḥammad Shākir, 2 vols. (Cairo, 1421/2001).
—— *Faḍl al-ᶜArab wa-al-Tanbīh ᶜalā ᶜUlūmihā*, ed. Walīd Maḥmūd Khāliṣ (Abu Dhabi, 1998).
—— *ᶜUyūn al-akhbār*, ed. Yūsuf ᶜAlī Ṭawīl, 2 vols. (Beirut 1986, 1988).

Rādūyānī, Muḥammad b. ᶜUmar, *Tarjūmān al-balāgha*, ed. Aḥmad Atash (Tehran, n.d.).
al-Rāghib al-Iṣbahānī, Abū al-Qāsim Ḥusayn b. Muḥammad, *Muḥādarāt al-udabāʾ wa-muḥāwarāt al-shuᶜarāʾ wal-bulaghāʾ*, 2 vols. (Beirut, 1961, 1980).
Ibn Rashīq, Abū ᶜAlī al-Ḥasan al-Qayrawānī, ed. Muḥammad ᶜAbd al-Qādir Aḥmad ᶜAtā, *al-ᶜUmda fī maḥāsin al-shiᶜr wa-ādābih*, 2 vols. in 1 (Beirut, 1422/2001).
Rāvandī, Muḥammad ᶜAlī b. Sulaymān, *Rāḥat al-Ṣudūr va Āyat al-Surūr dar Tārīkh-i Āl-i Saljūq*, ed. Muḥammad Iqbāl (Tehran, 1385/2006).
Rāzī, Amīn Aḥmad, *Tadhkīra-yi haft iqlīm*, ed. Sayyid Muḥammad Riḍā Ṭaharī "Ḥasrat", 3 vols. (Tehran, 1378/1999).
Rūmī, *Masnavī-yi Maᶜnavī*, ed. Reynold Nicholson (n.p., 1374/1995).
al-Ṣābiʾ, Ghars al-Niᶜma Abū al-Ḥasan Muḥammad b. Hilāl, *al-Hafawāt al-nādira*, ed. Ṣāliḥ al-Ashtar (Beirut, 1967).
Saᶜdī, *Gulistān-i Saᶜdī*, ed. Khalīl Khaṭīb Rahbar (Tehran, 1969).
Sām Mīrzā Ṣafavī, *Tadhkirah-yi Tuḥfah-yi Sāmī*, ed. Rukn al-Dīn Humāyūn Farrukh (Tehran, 1384/2005).
Sanāʾī, *Kitāb ḥadīqat al-ḥaqīqa wa-sharīᶜat al-ṭarīqa*, ed. Mudarris Raḍavī (Tehran, 1940).
—— *Masnavīhā-yi hakīm-i Sanāʾi*, ed. Muḥammad Taqī Mudarris Raḍavī (Tehran, 1348/1969).
al-Sarī b. Aḥmad al-Raffāʾ, *al-Muḥibb wal-maḥbūb wal-mashmūm wal-mashrūb*, 4 vols., vols. 1–3 ed. Miṣbaḥ Ghulawanjī, vol. 4 ed. Majīd Ḥasan al-Dhahabī (Damascus, 1986–7).
Shams-i Qays al-Rāzī, *al-Muᶜjam fī maᶜāyīr ashᶜār al-ᶜAjam*, ed. Muḥammad b. ᶜAbd al-Wahhāb Qazvīnī and Mudarris Raḍavī (Tehran, 1959).
Al-Shūshtarī, *Majālis al-Muʾminīn*, 2 vols. (Tehran, 1365/1986).
al-Ṣūlī, Abū Bakr Muḥammad b. Yaḥyā, *Akhbār Abī Tammām*, ed. Khalīl Maḥmūd, Muḥammad ᶜAbduh ᶜAzzām, and Nazir al-Islām al-Hindī (Cairo, 1356/1937).
—— *Akhbār al-Buḥturī*, ed. Ṣāliḥ al-Ashtar (Damascus, 1964/1384).
—— *Adab al-kuttāb*, ed. Aḥmad Ḥasan Basaj (Beirut, 1415/1994).
—— *Ashᶜār awlād al-khulafāʾ*, ed. J. Heyworth Dunne (Beirut, 1982/1401).
—— *Akhbār al-shuᶜarāʾ al-muḥdathīn min kitāb al-awrāq,* ed. J. Heyworth Dunne (Beirut, 1982/1401).
Ibn Ṭabāṭabā, Muḥammad b. Aḥmad Al-ᶜAlawī, *ᶜIyār al-shiᶜr*, ed. Muḥammad Zaghlūl Salām (Alexandria, 1980).
Ibn Abī Ṭāhir Ṭayfūr, *Balāghāt al-nisāʾ,* ed. ᶜAbd al-Ḥamīd Hindawī (Cairo, 1998).
Abū Tammām, *Dīwān Abī Tammām bi-sharḥ al-Khaṭīb al-Ṭibrīzī*, ed. Muḥammad ᶜAbduh ᶜAzzām, 4 vols. (Cairo, 1964).
al-Tanūkhī, al-Qāḍī Abū ᶜAlī al-Muḥsin b. ᶜAlī, *Kitāb al-faraj baᶜd al-shidda*, ed. ᶜAbbūd al-Shāljī, 5 vols. (Beirut, 1978/1398).
—— *al-Mustajād min faᶜalāt al-ajwād,* ed. Yūsuf al-Bustānī (Cairo, 1985).
al-Tawḥīdī, Abū Ḥayyān ᶜAlī b. Muḥammad, *Akhlāq al-wazīrayn: mathālib al-wazīrayn al-Ṣāḥib b. ᶜAbbād wa Ibn al-ᶜAmīd*, ed. Muḥammad b. Tāwīt al-Tunjī (Beirut, 1412/1992).

—— *al-Baṣā'ir wal-dhakhā'ir*, ed. Wadād al-Qāḍī, 10 vols. (Beirut, 1406/1988).
—— *al-Ṣadāqa wa al-Ṣadīq*, ed. Ibrāhīm al-Kīlānī (Beirut, 1998/1419).
al-Thaᶜālibī, *Adab al-mulūk*, ed. Jalīl ᶜAṭiyya (Beirut, 1990).
—— *Al-Laṭā'if wal-ẓarā'if* (Beirut, 1990).
—— *Taḥsīn al-qabīḥ wa-taqbīḥ al-ḥasan*, ed. Shākir al-ᶜAshūr (Baghdād, 1981/1401).
—— *Tuḥfat Al-Wuzarā'*, ed. Ḥabīb ᶜAlī al-Rāwī and Ibtisām Marhun al-Saffār (Baghdād, 1977).
—— *Yatīmat al-dahr fī maḥāsin ahl al-ᶜaṣr*, ed. Mufīd Muḥammad Qamīḥa, 6 vols. (Beirut, 1420/2000).
al-Tibrīzī, *Sharḥ Dīwān Abī Tammām*, ed. Rājī Al-Asmar, 2 vols. (Beirut, 1414/1994).
ᶜUnṣurī, *Dīvān-i ustād-i ᶜUnṣurī Balkhī*, ed. Muḥammad Dabīrsiyāqī (Tehran, 1984).
Vaṭvāṭ, Rashīd al-Dīn Muḥammad, *Ḥadāyiq al-sihr fi daqāyiq al-shiᶜr*, ed. ᶜAbbās Iqbāl, (n.p., 1362/1984).
Ibn Wakīᶜ, Abū Muḥammad al-Ḥasan b. ᶜAlī, *Kitāb al-munṣif lil-sāriq wal-masrūq minhu fī iẓhār sariqat Abī al-Ṭayyib al-Mutanabbī*, ed. Muḥammad Yūsuf Najm, 2 vols. (Beirut, 1412/1992).
al-Washshā', Muḥammad b. Aḥmad b. Isḥāq Abū al-Ṭayyib, *Kitāb al-fāḍil fī ṣifat al-adab al-kāmil*, ed. Yaḥyā Wahib al-Jabbūrī (Beirut, 1411/1991).
—— *al-Ẓarf wal-Ẓurafā'*, ed. Fahmī Saᶜd (Beirut, 1407/1986).

Part Two: Secondary sources

ᶜAbbās, Iḥsān, *Tārīkh al-naqd al-adabī ᶜinda l-ᶜArab* (Beirut, 1971/1391).
Abū Zayd, ᶜAlī Ibrāhīm, *Fanniyyat al-taṣwīr fī shiᶜr al-Ṣanawbarī* (Cairo, 2000).
Adorno, Theodor W., 'Lyric poetry and society', *Telos* 20 Summer (1974), pp. 56–71.
Alam, Muzaffar and Sanjay Subrahmanyam, 'When hell is other people: a Safavid view of seventeenth-century Mughal India' in Judith Pfeiffer and Sholeh A. Quinn (eds), *History and Historiography of Post-Mongol Central Asia and the Middle East: Studies in Honor of John E. Woods* (Wiesbaden, 2006).
Algazi, Gadi and Rina Drory, 'L'amour à la cour des Abbasides: un code de compétence sociale', *Annales* 35:6 (2000), pp. 1255–82.
Ali, Samer Mahdy, 'Praise for murder? Two odes by al-Buḥturī surrounding an Abbasid patricide' in Beatrice Gruendler and Louise Marlow (eds), *Writers and Rulers* (Wiesbaden, 2004), pp. 1–38.
—— 'The rise of the Abbasid public sphere: the case of al-Mutanabbī and three middle ranking patrons', *Al-Qantara* 29:2 July–December (2008), pp. 467–94.
—— *Arabic Literary Salons in the Islamic Middle Ages,* Manuscript downloaded with the author's permission (December 7, 2009).
Althusser, Louis, 'Ideology and ideological state apparatuses (notes toward an investigation)' in *Lenin and Philosophy and Other Essays*, tr. Ben Brewster (London, 1971), pp. 121–73.

Amer, Sahar, *Crossing Borders: Love Between Women in Medieval French and Arabic Literatures* (Philadelphia, 2008).

Anooshahr, Ali, *The Ghazi Sultans and the Frontiers of Islam: A Comparative Study of the Late Medieval and Early Modern Periods* (London, 2009).

Andrews, Walter G., *Poetry's Voice, Society's Song: Ottoman Lyric Poetry* (Seattle, 1985).

Andrews, Walter G. and Mehmet Kalpakli, *The Age of Beloveds: Love and the Beloved in Early-Modern Ottoman and European Culture and Society* (Durham, North Carolina, 2005).

Arendt, Hannah, *On Violence* (New York, 1969).

ᶜAṭwān, Ḥusayn, *Muqaddimat al-qaṣīda fī al-ᶜaṣr al-ᶜAbbāsī al-awwal* (Cairo, 1974).

Bakkār, Yūsuf Ḥusayn, *Bināʾ al-qaṣīda al-ᶜArabiyya* (Cairo, 1979).

Bal, Mieke, *Narratology: Introduction to the Theory of Narrative*, second edition (Toronto, 1997).

Barchiesi, Alessandro, *The Poet and the Prince: Ovid and Augustan Discourse* (Berkeley, California, 1997).

Barthes, Roland, *A Lover's Discourse: Fragments*, tr. Richard Howard (New York, 1978).

Bauer, Thomas, *Liebe und Liebesdichtung in der arabischen Welt des 9. und 10. Jahrhunderts: eine literatur- und mentalitätsgeschichtliche Studie des arabischen Gazal* (Wiesbaden, 1998).

Bearman, P., Th. Bianquis, C. E. Bosworth, E. van Donzel, and W. P. Heinrichs, *Encyclopedia of Islam*, second edition (Brill Online, 2009).

Beaujour, Michel, 'Some paradoxes of description', *Yale French Studies* 61: *Towards a Theory of Description* (1981), pp. 27–59.

Beaumont, Daniel, '*Min Jumlat al-Jamādāt*: The inanimate in fictional and *Adab* narrative' in Philip F. Kennedy (ed), *On Fiction and* Adab *in Medieval Arabic Literature* (Wiesbaden, 2005), pp. 55–69.

Becker, Andrew Sprague, *The Shield of Achilles and the Poetics of Ekphrasis* (Lanham, Maryland, 1995).

Beelaert, Anna Livia Fermina Alexandra, *A Cure for the Grieving: Studies on the Poetry of the 12th Century Persian Court Poet Khāqānī Širwānī*, Proefschrift (Leiden, 2000).

Benveniste, Emile, *Problems in General Linguistics*, tr. Mary Elizabeth Meek (Coral Gables, Florida, 1966).

Bernards, Monique, 'The contribution of Mawālī and the Arabic linguistic tradition', in Monique Bernards and John Nawas (eds), *Patronate and Patronage in Early and Classical Islam* (Leiden, 2005), pp. 426–53.

Bettini, Maurizio, *The Portrait of the Lover*, tr. Laura Gibbs (Berkeley, California, 1999).

Binay, Sara, *Die Figur des Beduinen in der arabischen Literatur 9.–12. Jahrhundert* (Wiesbaden, 2006).

Borg, Gabrielle van den, 'The Nasībs in the dīvān of Farrukhī Sīstānī: poetical speech versus the reflection of reality', *Edebiyat* 9 (1998), pp. 17–34.

Bosworth, Clifford Edmund, *The Ghaznavids: Their Empire in Afghanistan and Eastern Iran 994–1040* (Edinburgh, 1963).

Bowditch, Phebe Lowell, *Horace and the Gift Economy of Patronage* (Berkeley, California, 2001).

Browne, Edward Granville, *A Literary History of Persia,* 4 vols. (London, 1964–9).

Brummett, Barry, *The World and How We Describe It: Rhetorics of Reality, Representation, Simulation* (Westport, Connecticut, 2003).

Bulman, Patricia, *Phthonos in Pindar* (Berkeley, California, 1992).

Burton, Joan B., *Theocritus's Urban Mimes: Mobility, Gender, and Patronage* (Berkeley, California, 1995).

Butler, Judith, *Bodies that Matter: On the Discursive Limits of 'Sex'* (New York, 1993).

Carruthers, Mary J., *The Book of Memory: A Study of Memory in Medieval Culture* (Cambridge, 1990).

Cheikh-Moussa, Abdallah 'Mouvance narrative et polysémie dans la littérature d'adab: le cas d'Abū Ḥayya al-Numayrī/Abū al-Aġarr al-Nahšalī' in Frédéric Bauden, Aboubakr Chraïbi and Antonella Ghersetti (eds), *Le répertoire narrative Arabe médiéval: transmission et ouverture* (Liège, 2008), pp. 47–61.

Clinton, Jerome, *The Dīvān of Manuchihrī Dāmghānī: A Critical Study* (Minneapolis, Minnesota, 1972).

Collette, Carolyn P., *Species, Phantasms, and Images: Vision and Medieval Psychology in The Canterbury Tales* (Ann Arbor, Michigan, 2000).

Conte, Gian Biagio, *The Rhetoric of Imitation: Genre and Poetic Memory in Virgil and other Latin Poets*, tr. and ed. Charles Segal (Ithaca, New York, 1986).

Cooperson, Michael, *Classical Arabic Biography: The Heirs of the Prophets in the Age of al-Ma'mun* (Cambridge, 2000).

Cooperson, Michael and Shawkat M. Toorawa, *Arabic Literary Culture, 500–925* (Detroit, 2005).

Crotty, Kevin, *Song and Action: The Victory Odes of Pindar* (Baltimore, Maryland, 1982).

—— *The Poetics of Supplication: Homer's Iliad and Odyssey* (Ithaca, New York, 1994).

Dallenbach, Lucien, *The Mirror in the Text*, tr. Jeremy Whiteley with Emma Hughes (Chicago, 1989).

de Blois, Francois, *Persian Literature: A Bio-bibliographical Survey, vol. 5: Poetry of the pre-Mongol Period* (London, 1970).

De Bruijn, J. T. P., *Of Piety and Poetry: The Interaction of Religion and Literature in the Life and Works of Ḥakīm Sanāʾī of Ghazna* (Leiden, 1983).

de Fouchécour, Charles-Henri, *La description de la nature dans la poésie lyrique persane du xi siècle: inventaire et analyse des thèmes* (Paris, 1969).

—— *Moralia: Les notions morales dans la littérature Persane du 3/9 au 7/13 siècle* (Paris, 1986).

de Lauretis, Teresa, *Technologies of Gender: Essays on Theory, Film, and Fiction* (Bloomington, Indiana, 1987).

de Man, Paul, *Allegories of Reading: Figural Language in Rousseau, Nietzsche, Rilke, and Proust* (New Haven, Connecticut, 1979).

Davis, Dick, *Epic and Sedition: The Case of Ferdowsi's Shahnameh* (Fayetteville, Arkansas, 1992).

Ḍayf, Shawqī, *al-ᶜAṣr al-ᶜAbbāsī al-thānī* (Cairo, 1973).

Deleuze, Gilles, *Difference and Repetition*, tr. Paul Patton (New York, 1994).

Derrida, Jacques, *Acts of Literature*, ed. Derek Attridge (New York, 1992).

Douglas, Mary, *Purity and Danger: An Analysis of Concepts of Pollution and Taboo* (New York, 1966).

Drory, Rina, 'The Abbasid construction of the Jāhiliyya: cultural authority in the making', *Studia Islamica* 83 (1996), pp. 33–49.

Eagleton, Terry, *Criticism and Ideology: A Study in Marxist Literary Theory*, new edition (London, 2006).

Elias, Norbert, *The Court Society*, tr. Edmund Jephcott (Oxford, 1983).

Elinson, Alexander E., 'Tears shed over the poetic past: the prosification of Rithāᵓ al-Mudun in al-Saraqusṭī's Maqāma Qayrawāniyya', *Journal of Arabic Literature* 36 (2005), pp. 1–27.

Felson, Nancy, 'The poetic effects of deixis in Pindar's *Ninth Pythian Ode*', *Arethusa* 37 (2004), pp. 365–9.

Feuillebois-Pierunek, Ève, *A la croisée des voies célestes: Faxr al-Din ᶜErāqī, Poésie mystique et expression poétique en Perse médiéval* (Tehran, 2002).

Foucault, Michel, *The History of Sexuality: Volume I An Introduction*, tr. Robert Hurley (New York, 1990).

Foulon, Brigitte, 'Les représentations paysagères dans la poésie descriptive d'Ibn Khafağa: Analyse de la structure hypsométrique du paysage et de l'action desmétéores', *Arabica* 52 (2005), pp. 66–108.

Fowler, Don, 'Narrate and describe' in *Roman Constructions: Readings in Postmodern Latin* (Oxford, 2000), pp. 64–85.

Freud, Sigmund, 'Beyond the Pleasure Principle' in *The Standard Edition of the Complete Psychological Works of Sigmund Freud*, tr. James Strachey with Anna Freud, Alix Strachey, and Alan Tyson, vol. 18 (1920–2), *Beyond the Pleasure Principle, Group Psychology, and Other Works* (London, 1955), pp. 3–64.

Gabbay, Alyssa, 'Love gone wrong, then right again: male/female dynamics in the Bahrām Gūr slave girl story', *Iranian Studies* 42:5 (2009).

—— *Islamic Tolerance: Amir Khusraw and Pluralism* (London, 2010).

Geries, Ibrahim 'L'*adab* et le genre narratif fictif' in Stefan Leder (ed), *Storytelling in the framework of non-fictional Arabic literature* (Wiesbaden, 1998), pp. 168–95.

Glünz, Michael, *Die panegyrische Qaṣīda bei Kamāl ud-Din Ismāᶜīl aus Isfahan* (Beirut, 1993).

Goldhill, Simon, *The Poet's Voice: Essays on Poetics and Greek Literature* (Cambridge, 1991).

Green, Richard Firth, *Poets and Princepleasers: Literature and the English Court in the Late Middle Ages* (Toronto, 1980).

Gruendler, Beatrice, *Medieval Arabic Praise Poetry: Ibn al-Rūmī and the Patron's Redemption* (London, 2003).

—— 'Motif vs. genre: Reflections on the *Dīwān al-Maᶜānī* of Abū Hilāl al-ᶜAskarī' in Thomas Bauer and Angelika Neuwirth (eds), *Ghazal as World Literature I: Transformations of a Literary Genre* (Beirut, 2005), pp. 57–86.

—— 'Verse and taxes: the function of poetry in selected literary *Akhbār* of the third/ninth century' in Philip F. Kennedy (ed), *On Fiction and Adab in Medieval Arabic Literature* (Wiesbaden, 2005), pp. 85–123.

—— 'Meeting the patron: an *Akhbār* type and its implications for *Muḥdath* poetry', in S. Günther (ed), *Ideas, Images, Methods of Portrayal: Insights into Arabic Literature and Islam* (Wiesbaden, 2005), pp. 59–88.

—— 'Fantastic aesthetics and practical criticism in ninth-century Baghdad', in Marle Hammond and Geert J. Van Gelder (eds), *Takhyīl: Source Texts and Studies* (Warminster, UK, 2007), pp. 196–220.

—— '*Qaṣīda*: its reconstruction in performance' in Michael Cooperson (ed), *Classical Arabic Humanities in Their Own Terms: Festschrift for Wolfhart Heinrichs on his 65th Birthday* (Boston, 2008).

Hämeen-Anttila, Jaako, *Maqāma: A History of a Genre* (Wiesbaden, 2002).

Hamori, Andras, *On the Art of Medieval Arabic Literature* (Princeton, New Jersey, 1974).

—— 'Form and logic in some medieval Arabic poems', *Edebiyat* 1 (1976), pp. 163–72.

—— *The Composition of Mutanabbi's Panegyrics to Sayf al-Dawla* (Leiden, 1992).

—— 'Going down in style: the Pseudo-Ibn Qutayba's story of the fall of the Barmakis', *Princeton Papers in Near Eastern Studies* 3 (1994), pp. 89–125.

—— 'Exemplum, anecdote, and the gentle heart in a text by al-Jahshiyārī', *Asiatische Studien*, 50:2 (1996), pp. 363–70.

—— 'Prudence, virtue, and self-respect in Ibn al-Muqaffaᶜ' in Angelika Neuwirth and Andreas Christian Islebe (eds), *Reflections on Reflections: Near Eastern Writers Reading Literature* (Wiesbaden, 2006).

—— 'Notes on paronomasia in Abū Tammām's style', *Journal of Semitic Studies* 12 (1967), pp. 83–90.

Harris, Joseph and Karl Reichl (eds), *Prosimetrum: Crosscultural Perspectives on Narrative in Prose and Verse* (Suffolk, UK, 1997).

Ḥasanī, Ḥabīb Ḥusayn, *Al-Sarī al-Raffāʾ: ḥayātuhu wa-shiᶜruhu* (Baghdad, 1976).

Al-Ḥāwī, Ilyā, *Fann al-waṣf wa tatawwuruhu fī al-shiᶜr al-ᶜarabiyya* (Beirut, 1987).

Heinrichs, Wolfhart, 'Istiᶜāra and Badīᶜ and their terminological relationship in early Arabic literary criticism', *Zeitschrift für Geschichte der Arabisch-Islamischen Wissenschaft* 10 (1984), pp. 180–211.

—— 'Paired metaphors in *muḥdath* poetry', *Occasional Papers of the School of Abbasid Studies* 1 (1986), pp. 1–22.

—— 'An evaluation of Sariqa', *Quaderni di studi arabi* 5–6 (1987–8), pp. 357–68.

Ḥinnawī, al-Muḥammadi ᶜAbd al-ᶜAzīz, *Shiᶜr al-Sarī al-Raffāʾ fī ḍawʾ al-maqāyīs al-balāghiyya wal-naqdiyya* (Cairo, 1405/1984).

Imāmī, Naṣrallah, *Ustād-i Shāᶜirān-i Rūdakī* (Tehran, 1378).

Inalçık, Halil, *Şair ve Patron: Patrimonyal Devlet ve Sanat Üzerinde Sosyolojik Bir Inceleme* (Ankara, 2003).

Irigaray, Luce, *To Be Two,* tr. Monique M. Rhodes and Marco F. Cocito-Monoc (New York, 2000).

Iser, Wolfgang, *The Fictive and the Imaginary: Charting Literary Anthropology* (Baltimore, Maryland, 1993).
—— 'What is literary anthropology? The difference between explanatory and exploratory fictions', in Michael Clark (ed), *The Revenge of the Aesthetic: The Place of Literature in Theory Today* (Berkeley, California 2000), pp. 157–79.
Jawārī, Aḥmad ᶜAbd al-Sattār, *Al-Shiᶜr fī Baghdād hattā nihayat al-qarn al-thālith al-Hijrī* (Beirut, 2006).
Kay, Sarah, *Subjectivity in Troubadour Poetry* (Cambridge, 1990).
Kennedy, Hugh, *The Prophet and the Age of the Caliphates: The Islamic Near East from the Sixth to the Eleventh Century* (London, 1986).
Kennedy, Philip F., *The Wine Song in Classical Arabic Poetry: Abu Nuwas and the Literary Tradition* (Oxford, 1997).
Keshavarz, Fatemeh, *Reading Mystical Lyric: The Case of Jalal al-Din Rumi* (Columbia, South Carolina, 1998).
Khan, Ruqayya Yasmine, *Self and Secrecy in Early Islam* (Columbia, South Carolina, 2008).
Khulayyif, Yūsuf, *Tārīkh al-shiᶜr fi al-ᶜaṣr al-ᶜAbbāsī* (Cairo, 1981).
al-Kīk, Viktor, *Taʾthīr-i farhang-i ᶜArab dar ashᶜār-i Manūchihrī Dāmghānī* (Beirut, 1971).
Kilpatrick, Hilary, *Making the Great Book of Songs: Compilation and the Author's Craft in Abu l-Faraj al-Iṣbahānī's Kitāb al-aghānī* (London, 2003).
—— 'Mawālī and music' in Monique Bernards and John Nawas (eds), *Patronate and Patronage in Early Islamic and Classical Islam* (Leiden, 2005).
Kristeva, Julia, *Powers of Horror: An Essay on Abjection*, tr. Leon S. Roudiez (New York, 1982).
Kurke, Leslie, *The Traffic in Praise: Pindar and the Poetics of Social Economy* (Ithaca, New York, 1991).
Lacan, Jacques, *The Four Fundamental Concepts of Psycho-analysis*, ed. Jacques-Alain Millers, tr. Alan Sheridan (New York, 1981).
Laclau, Ernesto and Chantal Mouffe, *Hegemony and Socialist Strategy: Towards a Radical Democratic Politics*, second edition (London, 2001).
Laird, Andrew, *Powers of Expression, Expressions of Power: Speech Presentation and Latin Literature* (Oxford, 1999).
Larkin, Margaret, *The Theology of Meaning: ᶜAbd al-Qāhir al-Jurjānī's Theory of Discourse* (New Haven, Connecticut, 1995).
Lefebvre, Henri, *The Production of Space*, tr. Donald Nicholson-Smith (Oxford, 1991).
Lewis, Franklin, *Rumi Past and Present, East and West: The Life, Teachings and Poetry of Jalāl al-Din Rumi* (Oxford, 2000).
—— 'Sincerely flattering panegyric: the shrinking Ghaznavid Qaṣīda' in Franklin Lewis and Sunil Sharma (eds), *The Necklace of the Pleiades: Studies in Persian Literature Presented to Heshmat Moayyad on his 80th Birthday* (Amsterdam, 2007).
Lewisohn, L. and Shackle, C. (eds), *ᶜAṭṭār and the Persian Sufi Tradition: The Art of Spiritual Flight* (London, 2006).
Losensky, Paul E., *Welcoming Fighānī: Imitation and Poetic Individuality in the Safavid-Mughal* Ghazal (Costa Mesa, California, 1998).

—— 'Linguistic and rhetorical aspects of the signature verse (takhalluṣ) in the Persian ghazal', *Edebiyat* 8:2 (1998), pp. 239–71.

—— 'The equal of heaven's vault' in Beatrice Gruendler and Louise Marlow (eds), *Writers and Rulers: Perspectives on their Relationship from Abbasid to Safavid Times* (Wiesbaden, 2004), pp. 195–216.

—— 'Shahīdī Qumī: poet laureate of the Āqquyūnlū court' in Judith Pfeiffer and Sholeh A. Quinn (eds), *History and Historiography of Post-Mongol Central Asia and the Middle East: Studies in Honor of John E. Woods* (Wiesbaden, 2006), pp. 282–300.

—— 'Words and deeds: message and structure in ᶜAṭṭār's *Tadhkirat al-awliyāᵓ*' in Lewis Lewisohn and Christopher Shackle (eds), *ᶜAṭṭār and the Persian Sufi Tradition: The Art of Spiritual Flight* (London, 2006).

Macherey, Pierre, *A Theory of Literary Production*, tr. Geoffrey Wall (London, 1978).

Makdisi, George, *The Rise of Humanism in Classical Islam and the Christian West* (Edinburgh, 1990).

Malḥas, Thurayya ᶜAbd al-Fattāḥ, *Abū al-Fatḥ Kashājim al-Baghdādī fī āthārihi wa-āthār al-dārisīn* (Amman, 2003/1424).

Mannāᶜ, Hāshim Ṣāliḥ, *Abū Tammām al-Ṭāᵓī, 188–231 H: hayātuhu wa-shiᶜruhu* (Beirut, 1994).

—— *al-Buḥturī: hayātuhu wa-shiᶜruhu* (Beirut, 2002).

Marlow, Louise, 'The way of viziers and the lamp of commanders (*Minhāj al-wuzarāᵓ wa-sirāj al-umarāᵓ*) of Aḥmad al-Isfahbādhī and the literary and political culture of early fourteenth-century Iran' in Beatrice Gruendler and Louise Marlow (eds), *Writers and Rulers: Perspectives on their Relationship from Abbasid to Safavid Times* (Wiesbaden, 2004), pp. 169–94.

Mauss, Marcel, *The Gift: The Form and Reason for Exchange in Archaic Societies*, tr. W. D. Halls (London, 1990).

McKinney, Robert C., *The Case of Rhyme Versus Reason: Ibn al-Rūmī and his Poetics in Context* (Leiden, 2004).

Meisami, Julie Scott, 'The body as garden: nature and sexuality in Persian Poetry', *Edebiyat* 6 (1996), pp. 245–74.

—— 'Ghaznavid panegyrics: some political implications', *Iran* 28 (1990), pp. 31–44.

—— 'The poet and the patrons: two Ghaznavid panegyrists', *Persica* 17 (2001), pp. 91–105.

—— *Structure and Meaning in Medieval Arabic and Persian Poetry: Orient Pearls* (London, 2003).

Miller, J. Hillis, *Speech Acts in Literature* (Stanford, California, 2001).

Monroe, James and Mark Pettigrew, 'The decline of courtly patronage and the appearance of new genres of Arabic literature: the case of the zajal, the maqāma, and the shadow play', *Journal of Arabic Literature* 34:1–2 (2003), pp. 138–77.

Montgomery, James, 'Dichotomy in Jāhilī poetry', *Journal of Arabic Literature* 17 (1986), pp. 1–20.

—— 'Convention as cognition: on the cultivation of emotion' in Van Gelder and Hammond (eds), *Takhyīl*.

Morales, Helen, *Vision and Narrative in Achilles Tatius' Leucippe and Clitophon* (Cambridge, 2004).

Morris, Wesley, 'Of wisdom and competence' in Michael Clark (ed), *The Revenge of the Aesthetic: The Place of Literature in Theory Today* (Berkeley, California, 2000), pp. 136–56.

Mottahedeh, Roy P., *Loyalty and Leadership in an Early Islamic Society* (Princeton, New Jersey, 1980).

Nāfiᶜ, ᶜAbd al-Fattāḥ Ṣāliḥ, *Lughat al-ḥubb fī shiᶜr al-Mutanabbī* (Amman, 1983/1403).

Al-Nowaihi, Magda, *The Poetry of Ibn Khafājah: A Literary Analysis* (Leiden, 1993).

Orsatti, P., 'Anvarī's qasides as letters and the problem of identifying the addressee' in Daniela Meneghini (ed), *Studies on the Poetry of Anvarī* (Venice, 2006).

Ortner, Sherry B., 'Is female to male as nature is to culture?' in Michelle Zimbalist Rosaldo and Louise Lamphere (eds), *Woman, Culture, and Society* (Stanford, California, 1974), pp. 67–88.

Ouyang, Wen-Chin, *Literary Criticism in Medieval Arabic-Islamic Culture: The Making of a Tradition* (Edinburgh, 1997).

Pacteau, Francette, *The Symptom of Beauty* (Cambridge, Massachusetts, 1994).

Qutbuddin, Tahera, *Al-Muʾayyad al-Shīrāzī and Fatimid Daᶜwa Poetry: A Case of Commitment in Classical Arabic Literature* (Leiden, 2005).

Roberts, Jeanne Addison, *The Shakespearean Wild: Geography, Genus, and Gender* (Lincoln, Nebraska, 1991).

Roberts, Michael, *The Jeweled Style: Poetry and Poetics in Late Antiquity* (Ithaca, New York, 1989).

Sabra, A. I., 'Sensation and inference in Alhazen's theory of visual perception' in Peter K. Machamer and Robert G. Turnbull (eds), *Studies in Perception: Interrelations in the History of Philosophy and Science* (Columbus: Ohio, 1978), pp. 160–85.

Sadan, Joseph, 'The "nomad versus sedentary" framework in Arabic literature', *Fabula* 15 (1974), pp. 59–86.

—— 'An admirable and ridiculous hero: some notes on the Bedouin in medieval Arabic belles lettres, on a chapter of Adab by al-Raghib al-Isfahani, and on a literary model in which admiration and mockery coexist', *Poetics Today* 10:3 Autumn (1989), pp. 471–92.

Scheindlin, Raymond P., *Form and Structure in the Poetry of Al-Muᶜtamid ibn ᶜAbbād* (Leiden, 1974).

Schippers, A., 'The genitive-metaphor in the poetry of Abū Tammām', in Rudolph Peters (ed), *Proceedings of the Ninth Congress of the Union Européenne des Arabisants et Islamisants* (Leiden, 1981), pp. 248–60.

Sells, Michael A., 'Along the edge of mirage: The mufaḍḍaliyyah of al-Mukhabbal as-Saᶜdī, an interpretation', in Mustansir Mir (ed), *Literary Heritage of Classical Islam: Arabic and Islamic Studies in Honor of James A. Bellamy* (Princeton, New Jersey, 1993), pp. 119–38.

Shamīsā, Sīrūs, *Sayr-i ghazal dar shiᶜr-i Fārsī* (Tehran, 1362/1984).

—— *Anvāᶜ-i adabī* (Tehran, 1370/1993).

Sharlet, Jocelyn, 'Inside and outside the pleasure scene in descriptive poetry about locations by al-Sarī al-Raffāʾ al-Mawṣilī', *Journal of Arabic Literature* 40/2 (2009), pp. 133–69.

Sharma, Sunil, *Persian Poetry at the Indian Frontier: Masʿūd-i Saʿd-i Salmān of Lahore* (Delhi, 2000).

—— 'The land of darkness: images of India in the works of some Safavid poets', *Studies on Persianate Societies* vol. 1 (2003), pp. 97–108.

—— *Amir Khusraw: The Poet of Sufis and Sultans* (Oxford, 2005).

Shershow, Scott Cutler, *The Work and the Gift* (Chicago, 2005).

Silay, Kemal, *Nedim and the Poetics of the Ottoman Court: Medieval Inheritance and the Need for Change* (Bloomington, Indiana, 1994).

Sourdel, Dominique, *Le Vizirat 'Abbaside de 749 à 936 (132 à 324 de l'Hegire)*, 2 vols. (Damascus, 1959).

Sperl, Stefan, 'Islamic kingship and Arabic panegyric poetry in the early 9th century', *Journal of Arabic Literature* 8 (1977), pp. 20–35.

Sperl, Stefan and Christopher Shackle (eds), *Qasida Poetry in Islamic Asia and Africa* (Leiden, 1996).

Stetkevych, Jaroslav, 'The Arabic qaṣīdah: from form and content to mood and meaning', *Harvard Ukrainian Studies* 3–4 (1979–80).

—— *The Zephyrs of Najd* (Chicago, 1993).

Stetkevych, Suzanne Pinckney, *Abū Tammām and the Poetics of the Abbasid Age* (Leiden, 1991).

—— *The Poetics of Islamic Legitimacy: Myth, Gender, and Ceremony in the Classical Arabic Ode* (Bloomington, Indiana, 2002).

Stewart, Devin J., 'Professional literary mendicancy in the letters and *maqāmāt* of Badīʿ al-Zamān al-Hamadhānī' in Gruendler and Marlow (eds), *Writers and Rulers*, pp. 39–48.

Sumi, Akiko Motoyoshi, *Description in Classical Arabic Poetry: Waṣf, Ekphrasis, and Interarts Theory* (Leiden, 2004).

Szombathy, Zoltan, 'Freedom of expression and censorship in medieval Arabic literature', *Journal of Arabic and Islamic Studies* 7 (2007), pp. 1–24.

Tetley, G. E., *The Ghaznavid and Seljuq Turks: Poetry as a Source for Iranian History* (London, 2009).

Toorawa, Shawkat M., *Ibn Abī Ṭāhir Ṭayfūr and Arabic Writerly Culture: A Ninth-century Bookman in Baghdad* (London, 2005).

ʿUtba, ʿAbd al-Raḥmān, *Al-Ṣanawbarī: shāʿir al-ṭabīʿa* (Libya and Tunisia, 1981).

Vadet, Jean-Claude, *L'Esprit courtois en orient dans les cinq premiers siècles de l'Hejire* (Paris, 1968).

—— *Les idées morales dans l'islam* (Paris, 1995).

Vafāyī, ʿAbbās ʿAlī, *Qaṣīda-hā-yi maṣnūʿ: dar ʿilm-i badīʿ va bayān va ʿarūḍ va qāfiya* (Tehran, 1382/2004).

Van Gelder, Geert, *Beyond the Line: Classical Arabic Literary Critics on the Coherence and Unity of the Poem* (Leiden, 1982).

—— 'The bad and the ugly: attitudes toward invective poetry (hijāʾ)' in *Classical Arabic Literature* (Leiden, 1988).

—— 'Pointed and well-rounded: Arabic encomiastic and elegiac epigrams', *Orientalia Lovaniensia Periodica* 26 (1995), pp. 101–40.

Van Gelder, Geert, 'The apposite request: a small chapter in Persian and Arabic rhetoric', *Edebiyat* 12 (2001), pp. 1–13.
—— 'Beautifying the ugly and uglifying the beautiful: the paradox in classical Arabic literature', *Journal of Semitic Studies* 48:2 (2003), 321–51.
—— 'Mawālī and Arabic poetry: some observations', in Monique Bernards and John Nawas (eds), *Patronate and Patronage in Early and Classical Islam* (Leiden, 2005), pp. 349–69.
Vazīnpūr, Nādir, *Madḥ, dāgh-i nang bar sīmā-yi adab-i fārsī: bar-rasi-yi intiqādī va taḥlīlī az ᶜilal-i madīḥa-sarā-yi shāᶜirān-i īrānī* (Tehran, 1374/1995).
al-Wād, Ḥusayn, *Al-Lugha wal-shiᶜr fī dīwān Abī Tammām* (Beirut, 2005/1425).
White, Peter, *Promised Verse: Poets in the Society of Augustan Rome* (Cambridge, Massachusetts, 1993).
Yamamoto, Dorothy, *The Boundaries of the Human in Medieval English Literature* (Oxford, 2000).
Yūsufī, Ghulām Ḥusayn, *Kāghaz-i Zarr: Yāddashthā-yi dar Adab va Tārīkh* (Tehran, 1363/1984).
—— *Farrukhī Sīstānī: baḥthī dar sharḥ-i aḥvāl va rūzgār va shiᶜr-i u* (Tehran, 1989).
Zeitlin, Froma, 'The artful eye: vision, ecphrasis and spectacle in Euripidean theatre', in Simon Goldhill and Robin Osborne (eds), *Art and Text in Ancient Greek Culture* (Cambridge, 1994), pp. 138–96.

INDEX

Abān b. ᶜAbd al-Ḥamīd 19, 33, 41, 218, 219, 221
al-ᶜAbbās b. ᶜAbd al-Muṭṭalib 223
ᶜAbbās, Iḥsān 294, 297
ᶜAbd al-ᶜAzīz 215
ᶜAbd al-Fattāḥ al-Nāfiᶜ 254
ᶜAbd al-Ḥamīd 190
ᶜAbd al-Malik 9, 15, 16, 195, 214, 215, 222
ᶜAbd al-Raḥmān b. al-Ḥakam 10
ᶜAbd al-Raḥmān b. Nahīk 262
ᶜAbd al-Wasīᶜ 211
ᶜAbd Allāh b. Aḥmad b. Ḥarb al-Mihzamī 245
ᶜAbd Allāh b. Aḥmad b. Lakhsan 55, 271, 272, 282, 284
ᶜAbd Allāh b. Muḥammad Abū Bakr al-Qurashī al-Baghdādī 242
Abel 35
al-Ābī 36, 243, 249, 250
Abraham 8
Abū ᶜAbd Allāh Ḥafṣ b. ᶜUmar al-Azdī 290, 292
Abū Aḥmad Muḥammad b. Maḥmūd Ghaznavī Niẓām al-Dīn Jalāl al-Dawla 259
Abū Aḥmad Tamīmī 282
Abū al-ᶜAbbās ᶜAbd Allāh b. Ṭāhir 283
Abū al-ᶜAbbās Naṣr b. Manṣūr b. Bassām 264
Abū al-Aswad al-Duᵓlī 196
Abū al-ᶜAtāhiya 32, 208, 222
Abū al-ᶜAynāᵓ 32
Abū al-Faraj 244
Abū al-Ḥasan 269, 289
Abū al-Ḥasan ᶜAlī b. Faḍl b. Aḥmad (Ḥajjāj) 261
Abū al-Ḥasan Manṣūr 269, 274, 289, 290
Abū al-Ḥusayn Muḥammad b. al-Haytham b. Shubāna 289
Abū al-Ḥusayn Muḥammad b. Ṣafwān al-ᶜUqaylī 266
Abū al-Khaṭṭāb al-Ḥasan b. Muḥammad al-Ṭāᵓī 266
Abū al-Mughīth b. Ibrāhīm al-Rāfiqī 47, 48, 265, 268, 288, 289, 290, 291, 292, 293
Abū al-Muᶜammar al-Haytham b. ᶜAbd Allāh 284, 285, 286
Abū al-Muẓaffar Fakhr al-Dawla Aḥmad b. Muḥammad 55
Abū al-Muẓaffar Naṣr b. Sabuktegīn 53, 258
Abū al-Qāsim Ḥusayn b. Muḥammad 242
Abū Bakr (Jarādat al-Kātib) 9, 221, 267
Abū Bakr Ḥaṣīrī 55, 261, 265, 269, 270, 291, 292
Abū Bakr Muḥammad b. al-Faḍl b. al-ᶜAbbās 285, 287, 288
Abū Bakr Muḥammad b. Yaḥyā 243, 244, 245, 297, 299
Abū Bakr Quhistānī 277, 278
Abū Dulaf al-ᶜIjlī 40, 48, 49, 251, 258, 275, 282
Abū Dulāma 19, 32, 39, 196, 214
Abū Firās 38, 187, 205
Abū Firᶜawn al-Sāsī 210
Abū Ghālib b. Aḥmad b. Muḥammad b. al-Mudabbir 290
Abū Hiffān 205, 219, 245, 248, 251, 297, 299
Abu Hilal al-‘Askari’ 254
Abū ᶜĪsā 268
Abū Jaᶜfar Muḥammad b. Abī al-Faḍl 277, 278, 280
Abū Muslim al-Kajjī 265, 285

Abū Nahshal Muḥammad b. Ḥumayd al-Ṭūsī 264, 290, 291, 292
Abū Nūḥ ᶜĪsā b. Ibrāhīm 51, 285
Abū Nuwās: and Abū Tammām 218; as envied 44; imprisonment 37, 219; and invective 19; mentor 207; on patronage 205; and payment 41; Persian pride 229; and resistance 31, 32; themes 9
Abū Sahl ᶜIrāqī 281
Abū Sahl Zawzanī 277
Abū Saᶜīd al-Thaghrī: 50; references in notes 255, 263, 269, 275, 277, 278, 279, 280, 281, 283, 285, 286, 288
Abū Ṣalt 210
Abū Saqr Ismāᶜīl b. Bulbul 267, 281
Abū Tammām 46–9; adaptation of poem 17; and al-Buḥturī 50; and ambiguity 19; Christianity 49; and culture 225; ethnic identity 230; literary criticism 193, 194, 198, 206; 'modern' Arabic poetry 45, 48; patronage 51; poetry as elitist 213; on poetry and ethics 8; poetry and intercession 38; and recycling poetry 14; references in notes 248, 258, 259, 261, 270, 271, 273, 275; and religion 218; travel 235
Abū ᶜUbayda 197
Abū Zayd, ᶜAlī Ibrāhīm 300, 302
ᶜĀd 226
Adam 35, 231
Adorno, Theodor 59, 254
Afshīn 48, 275
Aḥmad b. ᶜAbd al-Karīm al-Ṭāʾī al-Ḥimsī 291
Aḥmad b. al-Haytham al-Asdī 267
Aḥmad b. al-Muᶜtaṣim 282
Aḥmad b. Ḥanbal 48, 259
Aḥmad b. Ḥasan Maymandī 27, 54, 55, 219, 255, 257, 259, 265, 269, 270, 272, 275
Aḥmad b. Ḥasan Maymandī Abū al-Qāsim 270
Aḥmad b. Muḥammad al-Ṭāʾī 51
Aḥmad b. Naṣr 48, 259, 260
Aḥmad b. Ayyūb 263
Aḥmad b. Muḥammad al-Ṭāʾī 288, 292
Aḥnaf al-Qays 34
al-Akhfash 197
al-Akhtal 15, 19, 218, 219
ᶜAlāʾ Abū ᶜĪsā 268
Alam, Muzaffar and Subrahmanyam, Sanjay 300
Alexander 18
Algazi, Gadi and Drory, Rina 255
ᶜAlī 26, 221
ᶜAlī Aṣghar Hikmat 243
ᶜAlī b. Jabla 40
ᶜAlī b. Jahm 39, 220, 221
ᶜAlī b. Khalīl al-Kūfī 218
ᶜAlī b. Muḥammad b. Ḥabīb Abū al-Ḥasan al-Baṣrī 242, 243
ᶜAlī b. Murr Abū al-Ḥasan 273
ᶜAlī b. Yaḥyā al-Armanī Abū al-Ḥasan 273
Ali, Samer M. 239, 240, 241, 246, 251, 293, 296, 298
ᶜAlīshīr 13, 192, 200, 208, 233, 243, 293, 294, 295, 296, 297, 302
Althusser, Louis 3, 23, 241, 246
ᶜAlwa 49
Amer, Sahar 239
al-Āmidī 194, 294
al-Amīn 32, 37, 44, 259
Amīr Khusraw 197
ᶜAmr b. ᶜAbd al-Raḥmān 41
Andrews, Walter G. 241
Andrews, Walter and Mehmet Kalpakli 254
Anoorshahr, Ali 300
ᶜAntar (ᶜAntara) 201, 214
Anvarī 192
Ardashīr 25
Arendt, Hannah 23, 70, 188, 246, 261, 293
Aristotle 18
Asadī 235, 302
al-Aᶜshā 31, 33, 195, 211, 226
Ashᶜar 231
Ashjaʾ 33
al-Ashtar, Ṣāliḥ (ed) 244
al-ᶜAshūr, Shākir (ed) 245
ᶜAsjadī 54
al-ᶜAskarī 191
al-Aṣmaᶜī 194, 197, 217, 226
ᶜAtawī, Fawzī (ed) 247
al-ᶜAttābī 197
ᶜAṭṭār 237, 249
ᶜAṭiyya b. Samura 217
ᶜAṭwān, Ḥusayn 253
Austin, J. L. 151
ᶜAwfī: on coercion 34; on comedy 196; on conflict 35; on Persian poetry 231, 232, 233; on poetry for payment 11; on prose writers 206; references in notes 243, 248, 249, 250, 295, 297, 298, 299, 300, 301, 302; on religious conversion of poets 221, 222; on ᶜUnṣurī 52; on working men as poets 211
Ayāz 27, 38, 52, 54, 219
ᶜAyyāsh b. Lahīᶜa al-Ḥadramī 47, 269, 281
Azraqī 38

Bābak 275
al-Babbaghā' 235
Badi' al-Zamān 29
al-Baghdādī 245, 265, 266
Bahrām Gūr 24, 25, 195, 231, 234
Bakkār, Yūsuf Ḥusayn 253
Bal, Mieke 279
Banū 'Abd al-Karīm al-Ṭa'iyyīn 256, 261
Banū Ḥārith b. Ka'b 268
Banū Makhlad 290, 291, 292
Barchiesi, Alessandro 241, 253
Barthes, Roland 60, 255
Bashshār: ethnic background 188, 229; failure of poetry 15; invective 42; narratives on 42, 43; and payment 33; and religion 220, 221
Bauden, Frédéric, Chraïbi Aboubakr and Ghersetii Antonella (eds) 246
Bauer, Thomas 255, 297
al-Bayhaqī 10, 11, 25, 210, 222; references in notes 242, 243, 244, 247, 250, 295, 298, 300
Bearman, P. 251, 252, 257, 258, 259, 260, 264, 267, 269
Beaujour, Michel 271
Beaumont, Daniel 288
Becker, Andrew Sprague 270, 287
Beelaert, Anna Livia Fermina Alexandra 240, 295
Benveniste, Emile 74, 80, 262, 264
Bettini, Maurizio 254
Bidpai 30, 37
Binay, Sara 298
Borg, Gabrielle van den 255
Bosworth, Clifford Edmund 252, 258, 264
Bowditch, Phebe Lowell 242
Browne, Edward Granville 252
Brummett, Barry 248
Bū Tammām 42
al-Buḥturī 49-52; accusation of heresy 50; advised to simplify poetry 15; and ambiguity 19; criticised as disloyal 12; failure of poetry 16; and improvisation 30; literary criticism 194, 198; 'modern' Arabic poetry 45; patronage 205; and patron's crimes 43; and reception 27; and recycling poetry 14; references in notes 251, 258, 259, 260, 263, 280, 297; on religion 222; and resistance 32
Bulman, Patricia 253
Burton, Joan B. 293
Butler, Judith 3, 241
Buzurjmihr 38, 39

Cain 35, 231
Carruthers, Mary J. 252
Chakravorty-Spivak, Gayatri 4
Cheikh-Moussa, Abdallah 246
Clinton, Jerome 252
Collette, Carolyn P. 279
Conte, Gian Biagio 271, 275
Cooperson, Michael 240, 253, 254, 293, 297
Cooperson, Michael and Toorawa, Shawkat M. 251
Crotty, Kevin 270, 288

Dabīrsiyāqī 262, 267, 269, 274, 286, 287
Dallenbrach, Lucy 255
Davis, Dick 240, 241, 271, 302
Dawlatshāh 219, 232, 233, 249, 250, 252, 298, 299, 302
Dāwūd al-Mutrān 227
Dāwud b. Muḥammad 291
Ḍayf, Shawqī 240
de Blois, François 252
De Bruijn, J. T. P. 241, 295, 302
de Fouchécour, Charles-Henri 246, 256, 271
de Lauretis, Teresa 4, 241, 279
de Man, Paul 72, 95, 261, 271
Deleuze, Gilles 96, 271
Derrida, Jacques 23, 246
Dhū Rumma 13
Dīnār b. 'Abd Allāh 279
Djamāl al-Milla' 252
Douglas, Mary 35, 249
Drory, Rina 255, 293

Eagleton, Terry 3, 241
Elias, Norbert 249, 264
Elinson, Alexander E. 302

al-Faḍl b. Rabī' 40, 206
al-Faḍl b. Sahl 206, 264
al-Fārābī 67
al-Farazdaq 15, 33, 40, 218, 222
Fāris al-'Abdī 288
Farrukhī 27, 45, 54–6, 209, 239, 256, 259, 277
al-Fatḥ b. Khāqān 15, 32, 50, 51, 206, 251, 256, 260, 263, 268, 269, 274, 285, 291, 292
Felson, Nancy 260
Feuillebois-Pierunek, Ève 295
Firdawsī: and Ghaznavid court 53–4, 209; and patronage relationship 24; and reception 27; references in notes 247, 249; and religious identity 219, 220
Foucault, Michel 28, 248

Foulon, Brigitte 256
Fowler, Don 271
Freud, Sigmund 60, 74, 255
Furāt b. Ḥayyān 18

Gabbay, Alyssa 295, 296, 302
Geries, Ibrahim 246
Ghulām-Ḥusayn Yūsufī 247, 252
al-Ghuzūlī 9, 26, 242, 247
Glünz, Michael 253, 257, 274
Goldhill, Simon 247
Green, Richard Firth 240, 249, 293
Gruendler, Beatrice 239, 245, 247, 253, 254, 274, 275, 279, 284, 293, 297

al-Hādī 14
Ḥafṣ b. ᶜUmar al-Azdī 291
al-Ḥajjāj 9, 15
Ḥamdawayh 219
Hämeen-Anttila, Jaako 294, 302
Ḥammād 30, 39
Ḥammād ᶜAjrad 206, 218
Hammond, Marle and Van der Gelder, G. 275
Hamori, Andras 246, 248, 249, 253, 263, 273, 274
Haravī 22, 205, 233, 297, 300, 301
al-Ḥarīrī 190
Hārūn al-Rashīd 259, 264
Ḥasan Kāmil al-Ṣīrafī 251
al-Ḥasan b. Rajāᵓ 37
al-Ḥasan b. Sahl 48, 251, 264, 279, 280, 282, 283
al-Ḥasan b. Wahb 47, 48, 49; references in notes 261, 268, 272, 275, 278, 281, 286, 288
al-Ḥasanī 302
Ḥasanī, Ḥabīb Ḥusayn 297
Ḥātīm al-Ṭāᵓī 19
al-Ḥātimī 194, 295
al-Ḥāwī, Ilyā 271
al-Hazen 126
Heinrichs, Wolfhart 275, 293, 295, 296
Ḥimyar 226
Hindavi 225
Ḥinnawī, al-Muḥammadi ᶜAbd al-ᶜAzīz 253
Hishām b. ᶜAbd al-Malik 9, 12, 21, 31
al-Ḥuṣrī 25, 243, 247, 248, 250, 295, 299, 300
al-Ḥuṣrī, Abū Isḥāq Ibrāhīm b. ᶜAlī al-Qayrawānī 243, 248

Ibn ᶜAbd al-Barr 36, 217, 249, 250, 299
Ibn ᶜAbd Rabbihi 25, 37, 244, 245, 247, 248, 250, 295, 299
Ibn Abī ᶜAwn 297
Ibn Abī al-Dunyā 8, 214, 242, 247, 250, 299
Ibn Abī Duᵓād 17, 47, 48, 251, 258, 259, 260, 261, 280, 284, 288
Ibn Abī Ṭāhir Ṭayfūr 12, 215, 299
Ibn al-ᶜAmīd 191
Ibn al-Athīr 196, 197, 201, 202, 228, 230; references in notes 244, 245, 295, 296, 297, 301
Ibn al-Athīr, Ḍiyāᵓ al-Dīn 244
Ibn al-Fayyāḍ 261
Ibn al-Ḥajjāj 195
Ibn al-Jarrāḥ 206, 209, 210, 245, 250, 297, 298, 301
Ibn al-Jawzī 17, 190, 214, 244, 245, 294, 299, 301
Ibn al-Khaṣīb 12, 43, 50, 51
Ibn al-Mudabbir 10
Ibn al-Munajjim 50
Ibn al-Muqaffaᶜ 30, 35, 37, 193, 230, 248, 249, 250, 294, 301
Ibn al-Muᶜtazz: background 187; and Bashshār 220, 221; on Bedouin culture 212; on bohemians 207; references in notes 243, 244, 245, 249, 250, 295, 296, 297, 298, 299, 300; on religion 218, 222, 223; on slaves 214; social mobility of poets 209, 210; works 197
Ibn al-Rūmī 18, 40, 229, 297
Ibn al-Zayyāt 48
Ibn Bisṭām 51, 263, 275
Ibn Harma 223
Ibn Isḥāq 193
Ibn Khafāja 271, 274
Ibn Lankak 208
Ibn Laythawayh 290, 292
Ibn Mawlā 223, 224
Ibn Mayyāda 12
Ibn Qutayba 242, 244, 248; on Bedouin 210; on ethnicity 228, 229, 230; on literary criticism 193, 197; and nature images 35; on Persia 226; references in notes 244, 248, 249, 250, 294, 295, 298, 299, 300, 301; and religion 217, 220, 221; on slaves 214
Ibn Rashīq: on innovation 200; on manners of poets 191; on patronage 36; on the Persians 226; poetry to avert crises 38; pragmatism 43; references in notes 243, 244, 245, 246, 249, 250, 251, 294, 296, 298, 299, 300, 301; on status in patronage 23; on working men as poets 211, 212, 213
Ibn Sinān 245

Ibn Sīrīn 9
Ibn Ṭabāṭabā 24, 194, 199, 202, 206, 246, 262, 266, 295, 296, 297
Ibn ᶜUyayna 194
Ibn Wakīᶜ 202, 213, 296
Ibn Zayyāt 48, 50, 51
Ibrāhīm al-Mawṣilī 44
Ibrāhīm b. al-Ḥasan b. Sahl 289, 292
Ibrāhīm b. al-Mahdī 40, 260
Ibrāhīm b. al-Mudabbir 272, 274
Ibrāhīm b. Hāniᵓ 207
Ibrāhīm b. Muḥammad b. al-Mudabbir 290
Imāmī, Naṣrallah 302
Imruᵓ al-Qays 9, 195
Inalçık, Halil 297, 302
ᶜIrāqī 197, 225, 234, 237
Irigaray, Luce 241
al-Iṣfahānī 42, 208, 214, 217, 220; references in notes 244, 248, 249, 250, 251, 298, 299, 300, 301
Isfandyār 34
Isfarāᵓinī 261, 269
Isḥāq b. Ayyūb 284
Isḥāq b. Ibrāhīm 259, 274, 287
Isḥāq b. Ibrāhīm b. Muṣᶜab 48
Isḥāq b. Ibrāhīm b. Ḥusayn b. Muṣᶜab 268, 273
Isḥāq b. Ismāᶜīl b. Nawbakht 276
Isḥāq b. Kundāj 51, 261, 266
Isḥāq b. Nuṣayr 263, 280
Isḥāq b. Sulaymān 11
Isḥāq b. Yaᶜqūb al-Barīdī 289, 290
al-Iskāfī 190
Ismāᶜīl b. Bulbul 51, 267, 273, 279, 280, 282, 283
Ismāᶜīl b. Shihāb 288
Ismāᶜīl b. Yasār 229
ᶜIzz al-Dawla 205

Jaᶜfar b. Yaḥyā al-Barmakī 33
al-Jāḥiẓ: accused of exaggeration 17; on Arabic language 226, 227; attitude to truth 11; on Bedouin 210, 211, 212, 213; on merchants 28; on poetry as art 197, 198, 202; on poets' avarice 13; on prose 206; on reception 26; references in notes 243, 245, 246, 247, 294, 295, 296, 297, 298, 300, 301; on status in patronage 12, 23, 190
al-Jāḥiẓ, Abū ᶜUthmān ᶜAmr b. Baḥr 243, 247
al-Jahshiyārī 25, 27, 42, 243, 247, 250, 301
Jaḥẓa 208
Jamal al-Din Bencheikh and Van Gelder, G. 287
Jarīr 16, 40, 218, 219
Jawārī, Aḥmad ᶜAbd al-Sattār 293, 300, 301
Joseph 39
al-Jumaḥī 9, 193, 195, 217, 221, 226, 242; references in notes 242, 245, 249, 250, 294, 295, 299, 300
al-Jurjānī 72, 126, 199, 201, 202, 213, 296, 299

Kaᶜb b. Zuhayr 37, 221
al-Kattānī al-Ṭabīb, al-Shaykh Abū ᶜAbd Allāh Muḥammad 297
Kay, Sarah 278
Kaykāvūs b. Iskandar 24, 30, 35, 191, 196, 234, 247, 248, 249, 294, 295, 302
Keshavarz, Fatemeh 253
al-Khabbāz al-Baladī 211
al-Khafājī 18, 194, 196, 212, 213, 227–8; references in notes 245, 294, 295, 299, 301
Khalaf al-Aḥmar 193, 230
Khalaf-i Bānū 54
Khālid b. ᶜAbd Allāh al-Qaṣrī 12
Khālid b. Barmak 229
Khālid b. Ṣafwān 31
Khālid b. Yazīd al-Shaybānī 262
al-Khālidiyyān, Abu Bakr Muḥammad and Abū ᶜUthmān Saᶜīd 197, 297
Khalīl b. Aḥmad 10
Khan, Ruqayya Yasmine 283
al-Khansāᵓ 15
Khāqānī 33, 206, 235, 302
al-Khiḍr b. Aḥmad 257, 262, 263, 269, 273
al-Khubzᵓaruzī 207
Khulayyif, Yūsuf 300
Khumārawayh 50, 51, 263, 266, 285
al-Khwārazmī 244
al-Kīk, Viktor 301
Kilpatrick, Hilary 253, 301
al-Kindī 37
Kisāᵓī 220
al-Kumayt 39, 217, 220
Kurke, Leslie 242, 271
Kushājim 187
Kuthayyir ᶜAzza 208, 220

Labīd b. Aswad al-Bāhilī 231
Labīd b. Rabīᶜa 217, 231
Lacan, Jacques 60, 255
Laclau, Ernesto 4
Laclau, Ernesto and Mouffe, Chantal 241

Laird, Andrew 284
Larkin, Margaret 261, 296
Lefebvre, Henri 139, 282
Lewis, Franklin 242, 245, 302
Losensky, Paul 240, 246, 293, 294, 297, 302
Lūdī 199, 252, 294, 295, 296, 301

al-Mahdī: on bohemians 207; invective 196; jealousy 9, 15; risk in patronage 209; significance of poetry 40; violence 42, 43, 220, 222
Maḥmūd 27, 34, 38, 52, 53, 55, 241, 259, 267, 277
Makdisi, George 293
Malḥas, Thurayya ᶜAbd al-Fattāḥ 302
al-Mālik al-Murādī 11
Mālik b. Ṭawq 47, 50
Mālik b. Ṭawq al-Taghlibī 262, 269, 272, 279, 281, 283
al-Maᵓmūn 40, 47, 48, 49, 275; references in notes 251, 258, 259, 260, 261, 262, 264, 274, 280, 282, 285, 289
Maᶜn b. Zāᵓida 15
Mānī 219
Mannāᶜ, Hāshim Ṣāliḥ 251
al-Manṣūr 11, 39, 266
Manṣūr al-Namarī 29, 223
Manṣūr b. Ḥasan Maymandī 269
Manūchehrī 225, 300
Marlow, Louise 248
Marwān b. Abī Ḥafṣa 13, 14, 214, 222
al-Marzubān, Muḥammad b. Khalaf Abū Bakr 294
al-Marzubānī 191, 205, 206, 217, 245, 250, 264, 297, 299, 301
al-Marzūqī 13, 193, 195, 198, 243, 294, 295
Maslama 31
Masᶜūd b. Maḥmūd b. Sabuktegīn 52, 53, 252, 257, 258, 259, 263, 265, 267, 272, 275, 277, 279, 283, 289, 292
Masᶜūd-i Saᶜd-i Salmān 33, 233, 234, 239
Mauss, Marcel 7, 242
al-Māwardī: and patronage 23; and payment for praise 18; references in notes 242, 243, 245, 246, 247, 249, 294; and social order 25, 191; on truth 10, 11; on uncertainty 35
Maymandī 27, 54, 219
McKinney, Robert C. 245, 287, 297
Meisami, Julie 240, 241, 254, 275, 295
Miller, J. Hillis 151, 284
Monroe, James and Perrigrew, Mark 302
Montgomery, James 254, 296
Morales, Helen 241, 254, 255, 279
Morris, Wesley 275
Mottahedeh, Roy P. 239, 293
Mouffe, Chantal 4
Mouffe, Chantal and Laclau, Ernesto 241
al-Muᶜāwiya 10, 14, 26, 34
al-Mubarrad 29
al-Muhallabī 205
Muḥammad ᶜAbd al-Qādir Aḥmad ᶜAtā 243
Muḥammad b. ᶜAbd al-Malik al-Zayyāt (Ibn al-Zayyāt Abū Jaᶜfar) 268, 269, 278, 279, 281, 283, 285, 286, 287
Muḥammad b. ᶜAbd al-Malik b. Sāliḥ al-Hāshimī 280
Muḥammad b. ᶜAbd Allāh b. Ṭāhir 259, 269, 271
Muḥammad b. al-ᶜAbbās al-Kilābī 264
Muḥammad b. al-Dawraqī 33
Muḥammad b. al-Haytham b. Shubāna 267, 292
Muḥammad b. Ḥumayd al-Ṭūsī Abū Nahshal 264
Muḥammad b. Badr 266, 275, 278
Muḥammad b. Hassān al-Ḍabbī 280
Muḥammad b. Haytham b. Shubāna 262, 269, 292
Muḥammad b. Ibrāhīm al-Ṭāᵓī 282, 284
Muḥammad b. Jahm al-Barmakī 17
Muḥammad b. Maḥmūd b. Sabuktegīn 255, 256, 261, 262, 264, 266, 267, 269, 270, 274, 275, 281, 283, 284, 285, 286, 287, 288
Muḥammad b. Mustahill 290
Muḥammad b. Yūsuf Abū Saᶜīd al-Thaghrī 268
Muḥammad Mursī al-Khūlī 244, 249
Muḥammad Nabīl Ṭarīfī 297
al-Muhtadī 51, 280, 285
Muᶜizzī 27, 187
al-Muktafī 205, 260
Mundhir 226
al-Muntaṣir 12, 50, 258, 289
Murād II 205
Muslim 218
al-Mustaᶜīn 43, 50, 51, 258, 260, 266
al-Mutalammis 41
al-Muᶜtamid 263, 266, 268, 272, 280, 285, 288
al-Mutanabbī 16, 17, 31, 194, 195, 227, 233, 254
al-Muᶜtaṣim 17, 47, 258, 274, 285; references in notes 259, 260, 268, 275, 287, 289
al-Mutawakkil 29, 32, 43, 48, 50, 51; references in notes 258, 259, 260, 262, 263, 264, 268, 269, 272, 273, 274, 289, 290

al-Mu^c^tazz 50, 51, 222, 252; references in notes 255, 258, 259, 260, 261, 262, 266, 269, 273, 274, 280, 281, 290
Muṭīᶜ b. Iyās 207, 218
al-Muwaffaq 51, 263, 267, 268, 280, 285
al-Muᵓayyad al-Shīrāzī 240

al-Nabawī ᶜAbd al-Wahīd Shaᶜlān (ed) 245
al-Nabigha 217, 225
Nafīsī, Saᶜīd (ed) 243
Najm, Muḥammad Yūsuf (ed) 296
Naṣīr al-Dīn Ṭūsī 9, 242
Nasr b. Manṣūr b. Bassām 291
Naṣr b. Manṣūr b. Sayyār 280, 282
Naṣr b. Sabuktegīn 255, 260, 261, 262, 268, 270, 272, 273, 274, 275, 281, 284, 287, 288, 289, 291, 292
Niẓām al-Mulk 24, 234, 247, 302
Niẓāmī ᶜArūẓī 190, 191, 209, 247, 249, 250, 252, 294, 298
Niẓāmī Ganjavī 24, 54, 234, 247, 302
Nizār 230
al-Nowaihi, Magda 271, 274, 278
Nūḥ b. ᶜAmr 264, 271
Nuṣayb 31, 214
Nūshirvān 25, 38, 39, 226, 228, 232

Orsatti, P. 254, 297
Ortner, Sherry 255
Ouyang, Wen-Chin 242, 293, 294

Pacteau, Francette 255
Prophet Muḥammad: and ambiguity 18; and conversion by poets 221; criticism of praise poetry 12; forgiveness 37; and patronage power 65–6, 79; on praise poetry 8, 9, 10; relatives 25

al-Qāḍī al-Jurjānī 200, 203, 296, 297
al-Qāsim b. ᶜUbayd Allāh 51
Qubād 226
Qudāma b. Jaᶜfar 67, 193, 201, 202, 211, 244, 248, 253, 294, 296, 298

Rabīᶜ 230
al-Rāḍī 205
Rādūyānī 198, 234, 295, 296, 302
Rādūyānī, Muḥammad b. ʻUmar 244
al-Rāghib al-Iṣbahānī 8, 9, 10, 18, 19; references in notes 242, 243, 244, 245, 249, 250, 251, 298
al-Rashīd: and Bedouin 210; and beggars 14; and poetic resistance 32; and quotation 40; and invective 19; and religion 218, 219, 223; and violence 43, 44
Rashīd al-Dīn Muḥammad 244
Rāvandī 196, 295
al-Rāwī, Ḥabīb ᶜAlī and al-Saffār, Ibtisām Marhun (eds) 247
Rawshan, Muḥammad (ed) 249
Rāzī 208, 209, 222, 233, 300
Rāzī, Amīn Aḥmad 298
Rosaldo, Michelle Z. and Lamphere, Louise (eds) 255
Rūdakī 232, 233
Rukn al-Dīn Humāyūn Farrukh 243
Rūmī 28, 36, 233, 247, 250, 274

al-Ṣābiᵓ 11, 36, 197, 205, 219, 221, 244
al-Ṣābiᵓ, Ghars al-Niᶜma Abū al-Ḥasan Muḥammad b. Hilāl 244
Sabra, A. I. 279
Sadan, Joseph 246, 298
Saᶜdī 11, 36, 224, 234, 243, 249, 250, 300, 302
al-Saffāḥ 32, 35, 39, 42
al-Ṣāḥib b. ᶜAbbād 29, 205, 248
Sahl b. Hārūn 39, 212
Saᶜīd b. ᶜAbd Allāh b. al-Mughīra al-Ḥalabī 273
Ṣāᶜid b. Makhlad 267, 268, 275, 284, 285, 287; son Abū ᶜĪsā 284, 285, 287
Salām, Muḥammad Zaghlūl (ed) 246
Ṣāliḥ b. ᶜAbd al-Qudūs 222, 223
Salm al-Khāsir 207
Sām Mīrzā 243; on begging 14; on bohemians 207; on ethics of poetry 13, 192; on prose 206; references in notes 293, 294, 295, 297, 298, 302; rulers as poets 205; on Turkish poets 233; on working men as poets 208, 209
Sanāᵓī 12, 19, 25, 197, 213, 237, 243, 245, 247, 299
al-Ṣanawbarī 187, 189, 197, 225, 237
al-Sarī al-Raffāᵓ 197, 205, 208, 237, 297
Sayf al-Dawla 15, 30, 38, 195, 205
al-Sayyid al-Ḥimyarī 220, 221, 223
Sayyid Muḥammad Riḍā Ṭahari "Ḥasrat" 298
Scheindlin, Raymond P. 253, 272
Schippers, A. 278, 300
Sells, Michael 256
al-Shāh b. Mīkāl 256, 260
Shahīdī Qumī 235
Shamīsā 255
Shamīsā, Sīrūs 241
Shams-i Qays: on excessive praise 17; on literary criticism 194, 198; on Persian

rhetoric 234; poetry to avert crises 38; references in notes 244, 246, 250, 296, 298, 302; on rhetoric 200, 201, 202; on status in patronage 23, 24; on status amongst poets 211
Sharaf al-Mulk 16
Sharlet, Jocelyn 241
Sharma, Sunil 239, 295, 296, 300
al-Shaykh Ibrāhīm b. Muḥammad 242
al-Shayzamī 15
Shershow, Scott Cutler 7, 242
Shihāb al-Dawla 252
Shīrawayh 217
al-Shūshtarī 233, 302
Silay, Kemal 254
al-Ṣīrafī 261, 267, 273, 290
Siyāvash 34
Sourdel, Dominique 293, 299
Sperl, Stefan 240
Stetkevych, Jaroslav 254, 256
Stetkevych, Suzanne 239, 240, 270, 296
Sudayf 42
Sulaymān b. Wahb 48, 279, 280
al-Ṣūlī: on ethnic identity 230; on excessive praise 17; literary criticism 193, 198; professional skill 196, 205; on promises 25; on prose 206; on reception 27; references in notes 243, 244, 245, 247, 248, 249, 250, 251, 261, 265, 267, 294, 295, 297, 299, 300, 301, 302; on slavery 214; on travel 235
Sumi, Akiko Motoyoshi 275
Sūzānī 196
Szombathy, Zoltan 99, 300

Ṭahā al-Hajirī 243
al-Tanūkhī 208, 247, 250, 298, 300
Ṭarafa 41
al-Tawhidi 242, 243; on comedy 195; on ethics of poetry 10; on inappropriate praise 17; on material gain 13, 37; on patronage relationships 190, 191; on praise poetry 8; references in notes 242, 243, 244, 245, 247, 248, 250, 294, 295, 299; on slaves 214; on status of poetry 13; on working men as poets 208
Tetley, G.E. 239, 252, 293, 300
al-Thaᶜālibī: on comedy 195; on patronage 24; on reception 26; references in notes 244, 245, 247, 248, 249, 250, 254, 295, 298, 299, 302; on rhetoric 18; on travel 235; on working men as poets 207, 208, 211
Thādhūs 46
Thamūd 226
al-Tibrīzī 47
Ṭirmāḥ 217
Toorawa, Shawkat M. 293
Ṭurayḥ 39

Ubayd Allāh b. Yaḥyā b. Khāqān 263, 272
al-ᶜUmānī 210
ᶜUmar 9, 26, 221
ᶜUmar b. ᶜAbd al-ᶜAzīz al-Ṭāʾī 266, 280, 281, 282, 284
ᶜUmar b. Ṭawq b. Mālik b. Ṭawq al-Taghlibī 281, 282
ᶜUmar Ibn Abī Rabīᶜa 31
ᶜUmāra b. ᶜAqīl 210
ᶜUnṣurī 27, 38, 45, 52–4, 198, 209, 258
Utamish 43
ᶜUtba, ᶜAbd al-Raḥmān 293
ᶜUtba b. Abī ᶜUṣaym 261
al-ᶜUtbī 17
ᶜUthmān 221, 222, 225

Vadet, Jean-Claude 293, 301
Vafāyī, ᶜAbbās ᶜAlī 293
Van Gelder, G. J. 242, 253, 260, 293, 295, 303
Vazīnpūr, Nādir 253
Vaṭvāṭ 197, 201, 234, 244, 295, 296, 302

al-Wād, Ḥusayn 273, 275
Wāliba 207
al-Walīd 12, 30, 34, 39, 41, 42
Wāṣif 52, 289, 291
al-Washshāʾ 215, 228, 299, 301
al-Wāthiq 47, 48, 50, 259, 262, 268, 273, 280
White, Peter 246, 254

Yaḥyā b. Khālid al-Barmakī 33
Yamamoto, Dorothy 255
Yaᶜqūb b. Layth 232
Yazīd b. ᶜAbd al-Malik 25
Yazīd b. al-Muhallabī 33, 43
Yūsuf b. Muḥammad 275
Yūsuf b. Muḥammad Abū Saᶜīd al-Thaghrī 278, 292
Yūsuf b. Sabuktegīn 53, 55; references in notes 262, 264, 268, 272, 273, 281, 282, 283, 289, 291, 292
Yūsufī 252,259, 265

Zeitlin, Froma 279
Ziyād b. Abīhi 10
Zuhayr 195
Zuhrī 9